Yale Historical Publications, Miscellany, 104

FROM RADICALISM TO SOCIALISM

Men and Ideas in the Formation of Fabian Socialist Doctrines,
1881–1889

Willard Wolfe

New Haven and London: Yale University Press

1975

Published with assistance from the Louis Stern Memorial Fund.

Library of Congress catalog card number: 74–14371
International standard book number: 0–300–01303–5

Designed by John O. C. McCrillis
and set in Baskerville type.
Printed in the United States of America by
The Murray Printing Co., Forge Village, Mass.

Published in Great Britain, Europe, and Africa by
Yale University Press, Ltd., London.
Distributed in Latin America by Kaiman & Polon,
Inc., New York City; in Australasia and Southeast
Asia by John Wiley & Sons Australasia Pty. Ltd.,
Sydney; in India by UBS Publishers' Distributors Pvt.,
Ltd., Delhi; in Japan by John Weatherhill, Inc., Tokyo.

2-26-79

To the memory of Bradley Thompson and Henry Lilly,
who in different ways set me on the road to this book.

Contents

Abbreviations Used in Footnotes

Libraries and Collections

BLPES	British Library of Political and Economic Science (London)
BM	British Museum Additional Manuscripts (London)
IISH	International Institute of Social History (Amsterdam)
M–TC	Mill–Taylor Collection (BLPES)
NYPL	New York Public Library
Nuffield	Nuffield College Library (Oxford)
PP	Passfield Papers (BLPES)
WP	Wallas Papers (BLPES)
WSHS	Wisconsin State Historical Society (Madison)
Yale	Yale University Library, Historical Manuscripts Division

Journals

Chr. Soc.	Christian Socialist
Con. Rev.	Contemporary Review
Edin. Rev.	Edinburgh Review
Fort. Rev.	Fortnightly Review
JBS	Journal of British Studies
JEH	Journal of Economic History
JHI	Journal of the History of Ideas
N. Amer. Rev.	North American Review
Nin. Cen.	Nineteenth Century
Prac. Soc.	Practical Socialist
QJE	Quarterly Journal of Economics
Vic. Stud.	Victorian Studies
West. Rev.	Westminster Review

1

Introduction: The Radical and Socialist Traditions

A Labour M.P. campaigning in the 1930s was once upbraided with the charge: "Call yourself a Socialist! Why you drink, and go to church; you're nothing but a Tory!" It was a refreshing point of view, as the candidate noted, "and one for which, historically considered, there is much to be said." [1] In fact, it aptly summarizes an aspect of the relationship between Victorian Radicalism and Socialism that has characterized the British Labour Party from its inception. For the chief Radical strongholds of Victorian England became strongholds of the Labour Party in the twentieth century and their Radical faith acquired a Socialist label.[2] Thus the Socialism of the Labour Party remained essentially old Radicalism writ large: a new way of stating the prejudices, animosities, ambitions, and group identifications that had sustained the older movement, and the anecdote quoted above highlights several of the key attitudes that underlay that Radical creed. These included, above all, a rankling hatred of the Establishment—the established church, its privileges, and the whole system of class privilege and social discrimination of which it formed the spiritual embodi-

1. Ivor Bulmer Thomas, *The Party System in Great Britain* (London, 1953), p. vi, n.
    Note on capitalization: Capitalization will be employed throughout this book to distinguish specific movements and organizations (e.g., Radicalism and the Radical Party) from the commoner, adjectival forms of the same words (e.g., radical, in the general sense of thoroughgoing and extreme). Thus liberalism as an ideology will be distinguished from the organized movement and from the Liberal Party; philosophical Idealism from idealism in the conventional sense, and so on.
    2. See, e.g., the voting records of five major Radical strongholds, S. Wales, Central Scotland, the W. Riding of Yorks., the E. Midlands, and Durham-Tyneside, where the transition from Liberal–Radicalism to the Labour Party was most clear cut, in H. Pelling, *Social Geography of British Elections, 1885–1910* (London, 1967). Elsewhere, as in London and S. Lancs., the process was more roundabout and may best be explained by the arguments of D. Butler and D. Stokes in their *Political Change in Britain* (London, 1969), chap. 11, although they fail to make essential geographical distinctions and are also dubious on other grounds. The terms Radical and Socialist are defined beginning on p. 4.

ment [3]—together with such moralistic crotchets as temperance, retrenchment, "purity," and a "career open to talents."

Although the vitality of these slogans has declined drastically since the Second World War, they were once widely felt to embody the essence of Socialist politics—at least within traditionally Radical regions of Great Britain, where the Establishment was the hereditary enemy and social equality, with its promise of fuller human dignity, remained the chief political objective. On a more sophisticated level, similar views have continued to characterize a large segment of the leadership of the Labour Party—especially the spokesmen for its Socialist right wing, who have typically steered the party's course in Parliament.[4] Their aims are epitomized by Anthony Crosland's claim that the primary objective of "modern Socialism" is not to possess the nation's industry but to "capture the commanding heights of private privilege and social separatism in English life." For the latter are still the foundations of the Establishment (in the extended sense) and of its social and economic power. More specifically, the "values which . . . constitute the essence of Western Socialism" are said to include "a more equitable distribution of educational resources, personal freedom, equality of incomes, the rights of the consumer, and the greatest possible diffusion of power." [5] Above all, however, this school of thought, whose classical exponents were the early Fabians, has insisted that "Socialism is about equality." [6] And—insofar as its beliefs may be reduced to any single formula—British Radicalism was also "about equality."

3. "Establishment" has been used in reference to the Church of England since at least 1667 (*OED* [Oxford, 1933], 3:298c). Victorian Radicals helped to extend that usage by treating the Church as the foundation of the system of social privilege that they deplored. Now, by further extension, both that system and its characteristic institutions, all closely associated with the Church, have come to be included in the twentieth-century Establishment.

4. E.g., "The basis of democratic Socialism is that every human being has a right to equal status, without distinction of class, color, or creed" (Hugh Gaitskell, *Recent Developments in British Socialist Thinking* [London, n.d.], p. 42; also pp. 38 ff.).

5. C. A. R. Crosland, *The Conservative Enemy* (London, 1963), p. 142.

6. See esp. W. Arthur Lewis, *Problems of Economic Planning* (London, 1949), p. 10. Also, R. H. Tawney, *Equality* (London, 1931); Douglas Jay, *The Socialist Case* (London, 1937) and *Socialism and the New Society* (London, 1962); and Crosland, *Conservative Enemy* and *The Future of Socialism* (London, 1957) —all Fabian-inspired books.

Such views, which are typical of the Socialism that has taken firmest root in British politics, also suggest an important, if little explored, line of historical inquiry: how and why did the attitudes of Victorian Radicalism become transmuted into the rhetoric of twentieth-century Socialism? By what process was its "individualist" ethos transformed into a "collectivist" one? What was changed, what was added, and what remained, in the transition from Radical to Socialist ideology? More concretely, why were so many young Radical intellectuals of the 1880s and their successors [7] moved to identify with Socialism in the face of growing popular hostility to the word? What was the relevance of Socialism for their lives?

None of these questions has been answered (or even seriously posed) in the existing histories of English Socialism, least of all with regard to the Fabian Society; nor have such histories yet made systematic use of the rich manuscript collections in this field.[8] These, therefore, are the starting points of the present study. But such questions also require a type of study that has thus far been rare in English history: a study of the ways in which established attitudes and intellectual traditions shape the development of new ideas and impose their content on them. In order to avoid the "woolliness" to which this kind of intellectual history is sometimes prone, such a study must rely heavily on intellectual biography, which alone can show concretely how new ideas are assimilated to existing ones and how older intellectual traditions are transformed. It must also limit its focus to a group of persons and a time span that are small enough to be explored in depth.[9] For these reasons, the present work is focused chiefly on the

---

7. The "young men and women of the universities," who, in C. F. G. Masterman's phrase, "would have called themselves Radicals . . . a generation ago and now call themselves Socialists" (*The Condition of England*, 6th ed. [London, 1911], p. 127).

8. An impressive exception to this pattern is S. Pierson, *Marxism and the Origins of British Socialism* (Ithaca, 1973), which, unhappily, was published too recently to be of use to the present study. See the Bibliographical Note for other studies of Fabianism and British Socialism as well as relevant MS collections—many of which are used systematically for the first time in the present work.

9. For further discussion of this methodology, see Franklin L. Baumer, "Intellectual History and Its Problems," *Journal of Modern History* 21 (1945): esp. 195, and the Introduction to Melvin Richter, *The Politics of Conscience* (Cambridge, Mass., 1964), a book that splendidly exemplifies this methodology.

decade of the English Socialist "revival," which culminated in the *Fabian Essays* of 1889, and on the intellectuals who worked out its leading doctrines. The latter were, of course, the early leaders of the Fabian Society, and their theory, which was disseminated to an astonishingly wide audience through the *Fabian Essays,* became the dominant theory of the Labour Party—and thus the main line of British Socialist thought—in subsequent decades.[10] Accordingly, their speeches, letters, and early writings have formed the basis of the present study, which will analyze the formation of their mature Socialist theory by closely examining the chief intellectual roads along which such Fabians of the 1880s moved from Radicalism to the type of Radical-Socialism[11] that formed their major contribution to British political and intellectual history.[12]

Such a study, however, requires at least a preliminary account of the British Radical and Socialist traditions. Unfortunately, neither one can be defined for historical purposes in merely conceptual terms. They can only be described as they appeared on the historical landscape of Victorian England: broad and variegated popular movements with more or less coherent ideological bases, whose origins lay in the late eighteenth and early nineteenth centuries. Indeed, Radicalism, the older and more amorphous movement, lacked even a distinctive social theory of its own, unless

10. This point has been so widely accepted that it may now be regarded as "given." See, e.g., Carl Brand, *The British Labour Party: A Short History* (Stanford, Calif., 1964) , pp. 56–57, 299; G. D. H. Cole, *The Second International, Part I* (London, 1956), pp. 104–248; Henry Pelling, *America and the British Left* (London, 1956) , p. 61; Alan McBriar, *Fabian Socialism and English Politics, 1884–1918* (Cambridge, Eng., 1962) , pp. 291 ff., 341 ff.; and Eric Hobsbawm, *Labour's Turning Point* (London, 1948) , p. xxiv.

11. Social-Democratic is now a more conventional label for this type of theory, but nineteenth-century usage (which characteristically applied that label to Marxist groups) was often the opposite of its present-day usage. Radical-Socialist, in contrast, involves no such ambiguity.

12. Such assumptions, however, are by no means universally accepted. Eric Hobsbawm. "The Fabians Reconsidered," in *Labouring Men* (New York, 1967), pp. 295–320 (paper ed.) , e.g., asserts that the early Fabians were "not in any sense Liberals" and formed no part of the English Radical tradition. This argument, which leans for support on B. Semmel, *Imperialism and Social Reform* (London, 1960) , and finds some confirmation in S. Letwin, *The Pursuit of Certainty* (Cambridge, Eng., 1965) , pp. 365 ff., will be shown to be false through the evidence in subsequent chapters.

hostility to social privilege and the privileged classes can constitute a kind of theory. In practice, to be sure, most Radicals accepted classical liberal theories[13] and did so more thoroughly—more radically—than ordinary liberals did, because they sought to apply them to all men (or almost all) without regard to class distinctions. But the distinctive features of the movement were not intellectual but political: a parliamentary party—often shadowy and usually disorganized, but always recognizable as the extreme left wing of English national politics—and a vast but still more incoherent protest movement that spread deep into the subelectoral levels of the population.[14]

The origins of the Radical Party lay in the "Wilkite" agitation of the 1760s and the subsequent Association movement (including the Constitutional and Corresponding Societies that were its offshoots), which first mobilized massive extraparliamentary support for the reform of Parliament. From such origins it inherited the methods of agitation, the democratic bias, and the quasi-egalitarian philosophy that characterized it throughout the nineteenth century.[15] The other side of Radical politics, its concern with social amelioration, was a product of the distressful years following Waterloo, when the movement took firm root among

13. Classical liberalism will refer to the type of social theory emanating from the Enlightenment (and ultimately from Locke), whose foundations were a faith in individual autonomy and self-determination and a belief that the fullest development of the moral and intellectual capacities of every person could be achieved only within an atmosphere of freedom from external coercion or restraint (except as the latter might be necessary to guarantee the same liberty to others). "Mere liberals" were usually satisfied to apply such principles only to the propertied classes; Radicals tended, at least in principle, to give them an egalitarian interpretation. The economic corollary of that belief (also derived from Locke) was that every individual should have as his property the fruits of his own labor—a doctrine that was crucial both to English Radicalism and its Socialist offshoots. (See n. 28.)

14. On the distinction between Liberal and Radical traditions in British politics, see S. H. Beer, *British Politics in the Collectivist Age* (New York, 1965), pp. 33–68, and John Vincent, *The Formation of the British Liberal Party* (New York, 1967). The Radical Party long antedated the formation of the Liberal Party in the 1860s, after which it functioned chiefly as the left wing of the resulting Gladstonian coalition.

15. For the basis of this interpretation, see esp. E. C. Black, *The Association* (Cambridge, Mass., 1963), pp. 60 ff, 175 ff; I. Christie, *Wilkes, Wyvil, and Reform* (London, 1962); and G. Rudé, *Wilkes and Liberty* (London, 1962). S. Maccoby, "Radical," in *Chamber's Encyclopedia* (London, 1955), 9:459–61, is a useful brief statement. For other works on Radicalism, see the Bibliographical Note.

the people of the newly industrialized north. But for all the symptoms of distress and dislocation of those years, the Radical spokesmen, steeped in traditions of parliamentary reform, knew only
one all-purpose panacea: the "radical reform" of parliamentary
representation—reform in "root and branch," without regard for
the privileges of rank and property that Whig reformers cherished
as the essence of the constitution.

Yet such reform was never sought by Radical politicians as a
mere "metaphysical whim," however much it may have seemed
so in the abstract arguments that were their intellectual stock-in-
trade. Instead, the hope of "radical reform" was always that it
might "do us some good," by removing the causes of popular
distress and providing means of social amelioration.[16] That point
of view, which was common to all schools of Radicals during
the early stages of the movement, was summed up with special
clarity by Richard Carlile, the early nineteenth-century ultra-
Radical, who asked in his *Political Catechism,* "How can reform
in representation alone relieve us?" and answered,

> By restoring to the People their constitutional share in gov-
> ernment; when they will be enabled by their representatives
> to prevent all unnecessary wars and to abolish all useless places;
> to reduce the whole expenditure of government; and to make
> such laws only as will promote . . . the happiness and welfare
> of the People.[17]

Peace, economy, retrenchment, and reform, combined with faith
in the wisdom of the common people: as a summary of basic Radical demands throughout the nineteenth century this list will
probably suffice, for it embodies all that most English Radicals
thought necessary to perfect their world. (That it was also, in
Marxist terms, invincibly "bourgeois" further helps to explain the
politically moderate character of even working-class Radicalism in
the subsequent mid-Victorian era.)

But traditional Radical arguments were also typically com-

16. *Cobbett's Political Register* (1833), quoted in Asa Briggs, *The Age of Improvement* (London, 1959), p. 245.
17. Richard Carlile, *A Political Catechism* (London, 1817), pp. 14–15.

pounded of at least four disparate elements: a theory of rights (usually derived from Locke, but often colored with historical allusions to the laws of imaginary Saxon forebears) ; utilitarianism; a protest against distress; and dreams—seldom mutually consistent —of "a different system of society once the Reform Bill is disposed of." [18] The protean character of nineteenth-century Radicalism stemmed, in large measure, from the diversity of that list. Moreover, though the dreams of working-class Chartists, at one end of the Radical spectrum, were often Socialist or even millenarian in character, none managed to survive the breakup of the Chartist movement and the onset of prosperity in the 1850s. What survived instead was chiefly a commercial type of Radicalism— originally middle class, though it spread downward to the "aristocracy of labor" in the 1850s—that was wholly liberal and individualist in outlook. Thereafter, though they still flaunted the rhetoric of Paine and Carlile, Victorian Radicals protested no longer against distress as such, but against the invidious position of the privileged classes, on whom they blamed all evidence of popular distress. These Radicals also had "dreams" of a new world to come, but they were conceived entirely in individualist terms. Free trade, an end to foreign wars, and curtailment of aristocratic spending were the elements of the mid-Victorian Radical millennium; and if more panaceas were needed to alleviate distress, they might be found in birth control (the hope of classical economics) , temperance, thrift, and other similar Radical crotchets.[19]

The essence of the Radical tradition, however, will not be found in crotchets, theories, or programs of reform (which were often little more than rationalizations) , but at a deeper psychological level in the hostilities, frustrations, ambitions, and group identifications that were the movement's real lifeblood. These, for the most part, may be traced to nonconformity in religion and to a sense of alienation from the sources of social and political power. Thus it was middle-class Dissenters, together with skilled artisans and "members of the less socially regarded professional classes,"

18. Briggs, *Age of Improvement,* p. 245.
19. There is a nice summary of the principles of Victorian Radicalism in H. N. Brailsford, "Radical Democracy in the Victorian Era," in *Ideas and Beliefs of the Victorians* (New York, 1966) , pp. 298 ff. (paper ed.) .

who chiefly sustained the movement and supplied its drive and organizing zeal. Even its leadership, after about 1785, came chiefly from "outside the old political circles," resting with self-made intellectuals such as Thelwall and Tom Paine, backed up by "artisans, shopkeepers, dissenting ministers and school masters"— in short, by all the disinherited or "disqualified classes" of the new urban-industrial world. Their grievances gave the movement its characteristic tone, which was perhaps most perfectly exemplified in the second part of Tom Paine's *Rights of Man*.[20]

The emotional core of Radicalism, however, lay in the kind of vigorous morality that Matthew Arnold called "Hebraic," whose chief sources were traditional Dissent and the newer vogue of Evangelical preaching. Its favorite text was the scriptural injunction that "if any man would not work, neither should he eat" (2 Thess. 3:10)—a slogan that served to inspire so many Radical harangues that it became virtually the movement's first article of faith. Radical enthusiasts unstintingly applied it to the landed and aristocratic classes, asserting that the latter were social parasites and "idle drones," and that their government was solely directed to enabling them to live from taxes on the necessities of the poor and levies on the industry of honest men.[21] All the iniquities of class rule and social discrimination were traced to that one source, along with the evils of foreign war and domestic oppression. But most frequently and emphatically, Radical orators asserted that the existence of privileged and propertied classes—"idle" and "wasteful" from their very nature—was a moral evil, and one that, in the words of John Stuart Mill, was "worth any struggle to get rid of":

20. Christie, *Wilkes, Wyvil, and Reform*, p. 34; J. Steven Watson, *The Reign of George III, 1760–1815* (London, 1960), p. 357; Charles Cestre, *John Thelwall* (London, 1906), p. 159; and John Stuart Mill, "The Reorganization of the Reform Party," in Gertrude Himmelfarb, ed., *Essays on Politics and Culture* (New York, 1962), p. 271. The latter defined Radicals as "all those who feel oppressed or unjustly dealt with by any of the institutions of the country." Regarding Paine's influence, see E. P. Thompson, *The Making of the English Working Class* (London, 1963), pp. 90 ff.

21. Such were the claims of the Anti-Corn Law League. The taxes referred to were the "bread tax" (or Corn Law), the "taxes on knowledge" (stamp duties), and all other forms of excise then in use.

First, because it made the conduct of government an example of gross public immorality, through the predominance of private over public interests in the state, and the abuse of the powers of legislation for the advantage of classes. Secondly, in a still greater degree, . . . because [of] the respect of the multitude always attaching itself to the chief passport to power, . . . riches, and the signs of riches, were almost the only things really respected.[22]

Even the behavior of the privileged classes was an offense to zealous Radicals because it seemed to undermine the virtues that formed the basis of industrial prosperity—diligence, thrift, honesty, and independence—and in their place encouraged idleness, snobbishness, and extravagance. The results of a government conducted on such principles were inevitably "jobbery," corruption, waste, and incompetence—the "sewers," it was said, into which taxation flowed. But of such evils the Radicals found jobbery, the system of presenting public contracts and "places" to political favorites, the most offensive. It epitomized the system of rewards for idleness (again, the cloven hoof) and formed, in the words of John Bright, the greatest Victorian Radical orator, "a gigantic system of out-relief for the aristocracy." High taxes and incompetence necessarily flowed from such a system, justifying in large measure the Radical belief that government—"Old Corruption" —spoiled everything it touched. And therein lay the basis of the Radicals' hostility to government, the symbol and citadel of Privilege, that helped to keep most of them within the liberal–individualist camp throughout the nineteenth century.

The same complex of moral attitudes, hostilities, and values, however, also underlay most forms of English Socialism in the nineteenth century. It is very clear, for example, in J. S. Mill's Socialist credo in his *Autobiography*, where the thrust of the argument is almost entirely anti-aristocratic and egalitarian.[23]

22. John Stuart Mill, *Autobiography*, ed. J. J. Coss (New York, 1924) , p. 120. Unless otherwise noted, all further reference will be to this edition.

23. Mill, *Autobiography*, p. 162, esp. the declaration that, as a Socialist he "looked forward to a time when society will no longer be divided into the idle and the in-

The Socialist revival of the 1880s once again brought such arguments to prominence in the writings of the Social–Democratic Federation and the Christian Socialists, as well as in those of the Fabian Society.[24] And in the twentieth century they have continued to dominate the writings of such Radical Socialists as Tawney, Jay, and Crosland, whose arguments against capitalism are essentially the ones that nineteenth-century Radicals used against the landed interest and its privileges. If nineteenth-century landlords and aristocrats lived idly on the labor of industrious men, they argue, no less do present-day capitalists and rentiers, and the moral consequences are the same. Likewise, if unrepresentative parliaments in earlier centuries levied taxes in the interest of supporting a privileged and incompetent ruling class, no less do the twentieth-century owners of land and industry levy private "taxes" on the laborer and consumer in the interest of maintaining an unproductive leisure class.[25] Even the Marxian analysis of "monopoly capital" was often made to fit that pattern, as it tapped traditional Radical hostility to the "political monopoly" of the ruling class and showed the idle robbing the industrious of surplus value.

In all these respects, new Socialism was indeed old Radicalism "writ large," with its animus extended to all forms of "exploitative" property and to all forms of social power and status that were not based on strict moral desert. So true has this seemed, in fact, that eminent historians have offered as a universal generalization the conclusion that, "at the deepest level," Socialism is always an extreme manifestation of Radical tendencies: "The hidden origin of Socialist thought everywhere in the West is to be found

---

dustrious; when the rule that they who do not work shall not eat, will be applied not to paupers only, but impartially to all; when the division of the produce of labour, instead of depending, as in so great a degree it now does, on the accident of birth, will be made by concert on an acknowledged principle of justice."

24. Shaw, Webb, and Annie Besant provide the best examples, but see esp. Sydney Olivier, "The Basis of Socialism: Moral," in G. B. Shaw, ed., *Fabian Essays in Socialism* (London, 1889), and chap. 7 below. Regarding Christian Socialism, see Peter d'A. Jones, *The Christian Socialist Revival, 1877–1914* (Princeton, N.J., 1968).

25. Such practices, according to R. H. Tawney, "involve the establishment of Privilege as a national institution, as much as the most arbitrary exactions of a feudal *seigneur*" (*The Acquisitive Society* [London, 1961], p. 69 [paper ed.]).

in [reaction against] the feudal ethos. . . . In MacDonald's England hardly less than in Kautsky's Germany, Socialism was inspired considerably by the class spirit that hung over, not from capitalism, but from the feudal system itself." Thus all characteristic Socialist demands might be reduced to one demand for freedom and equality, "made loud and insistent through frustration" and pushed to maximum intensity by the insistence upon "real" freedom and "real" equality, applicable to all men, without exception. "Its emphasis upon the 'collective' was simply the insistence that *all* men have the right to become complete human beings." [26]

Such arguments have the great merit of emphasizing the continuity of liberal attitudes and values within the Socialist tradition —its powerful individualist and egalitarian tendencies and its persistent affirmations of distributive justice—which were fundamental to all phases of nineteenth-century Socialism, though they have nearly disappeared from twentieth-century histories of the subject. In their most extreme forms, to be sure, such tendencies have usually been identified with Anarchism (which was always regarded as a form of Socialism in the nineteenth century),[27] but more moderate versions of the same beliefs were found throughout the whole spectrum of nineteenth-century Socialist thought, and in England they most typically took the form of an insistence upon the workman's right to the "whole produce" of his labor.[28] This was the chief theoretical foundation of traditional English Socialism, and its indebtedness to liberal individualism is obvious. The doctrine of surplus value (which, in its most popular English version, derived from the liberal "Ricardian Socialists") was merely an extension of that theory, showing more explicitly how under capitalism workingmen were "robbed" of the economic

26. Louis Hartz, *The Liberal Tradition in America* (New York, 1955), pp. 6, 234; and Martin Malia, *Alexander Herzen and the Birth of Russian Socialism* (Cambridge, Mass., 1961), pp. 112–13 (italics in original).

27. On the significance of Anarchists as Socialists, see, eg, G. D. H. Cole, *Marxism and Anarchism, 1850–1890* (London, 1954), pp. 337–41, and chap. 4 below. Many Socialists of the 1880s, most notably, Bernard Shaw, came to Socialism by way of Anarchism.

28. See Anton Menger, *The Right to the Whole Produce of Labour*, trans. M. E. Tanner (London, 1899). That doctrine was accepted by virtually all Socialists prior to Marx (who repudiated it in, e.g., *Critique of the Gotha Programme*). For its theoretical basis, see n. 13.

value they produced in order to sustain a leisure class that had no claim of right or justice to the wealth that it consumed. That leisure class—a class of capitalist rentiers that flourished most conspicuously in the depression years of the late nineteenth century and in the subsequent Edwardian era[29]—provided the most powerful *negative* inspiration for the late-Victorian Socialist movement, replacing the landed classes and the church as the chief object of hostility for Radicals who turned to Socialism. It was also the key to the prevailing Socialist theory of poverty in the 1880s, which held that the misery of the slums was a direct consequence of the affluence of the leisure class, expanding as that class expanded, and could only be abolished by abolishing that class (see chapter 3). For only then could workingmen obtain the "full produce" of their labor, thus satisfying the liberal–individualist criterion of justice that was the foundation of both Radical and Socialist rhetoric.

If such tendencies had formed the whole of the British Socialist tradition the transition from Radicalism to Socialism would be easily explained and the theory cited above would be sufficient for the task. But there were other aspects of that tradition—its emphasis on the collective, its concept of an organic society, and its most distinctive social and moral values—which the theory either fails to notice or quite inadequately explains. These tendencies moved directly against the mainstream of the Radical tradition and had closest affinities with romantic–conservative theories of early nineteenth-century Europe. Their classical English exponents were men such as Coleridge, Southey, and Robert Owen, who repudiated Radical politics entirely, while the most authentic late-Victorian successor of those men was probably William Morris, with his intensely conservative, neo-romantic emphasis upon community and his insistence that "fellowship is life and lack of fellowship is death," which formed the most powerful *positive* inspiration for British Socialism in the last quarter of the nineteenth century. Such positive social idealism was largely missing from the British Radical tradition, but it formed a distinctive

29. See E. Hobsbawm, *Industry and Empire* (New York, 1968), pp. 96–97, 106, and chap. 3 below.

and essential element in the making of British Socialist theory.[30]

The most historically important contrast between the Radical and Socialist traditions, however, was probably the fact that the latter, through its claim to transform the moral character of mankind, constituted a fully fledged substitute faith—a "complete Weltanschauung"[31]—whereas Radicalism did not. British Radicalism rested chiefly on social-religious foundations provided by Nonconformity and the closely allied Evangelical theology, but it never attained the status of a faith in its own right, nor, owing to its primarily negative thrust, could it form more than a truncated ideology. For Radicals who continued to believe in Christianity and to derive spiritual comfort from the old creeds, such considerations probably made little difference. But for those whose faith was undermined by the strong currents of nineteenth-century skepticism, the old Radical creed might, thereafter, seem inadequate either to make up the loss or to function independently. And that was precisely why dissatisfied Radical intellectuals in need of a secular faith turned increasingly to Socialism to fill that need in the decades following the Darwinian revolution. For Socialism, by uniting religious and social reconstruction within a single system of belief, and by promising a new, regenerated "moral world" on earth to compensate for the loss of heaven, was peculiarly well suited to the needs of nineteenth-century skeptics.[32]

It was also no accident that so many of the Socialist converts of the late nineteenth century—almost certainly a majority—were trained as Evangelicals and, despite rejecting formal Christianity, retained their Evangelical consciences under a variety of secular disguises. The familiar Evangelical fixation on righteousness and the demand for its public implementation were consequently carried over into their Socialist careers by many of those converts,

30. W. Morris, "The Dream of John Ball," in *The Collected Works of William Morris,* 24 vols. (London, 1910–15), 16:230. (Hereafter cited as Morris, *Collected Works.*) The uneasy coexistence between this essentially conservative social idealism and the radical–individualist approach to Socialism will be discussed in subsequent chapters.

31. Graham Wallas, *Men and Ideas* (London, 1940), p. 106. For the concept of substitute faith, see Franklin L. Baumer, *Religion and the Rise of Scepticism* (New York, 1960).

32. This was also recognized by contemporaries, e.g., Gustav Le Bon, *The Psychology of Socialism,* Eng. trans. (New York, 1899), pp. ix–x, xii.

forming an important psychological link between late-Victorian Evangelicalism and Socialism. For although Victorian Evangelicals (including the majority of Nonconformist Radicals) typically interpreted the demands of conscience in merely individual terms, whereas Socialists interpreted such demands in terms of society at large, both groups shared an optimistic belief in the efficacy, even the necessity, of applying conscience to politics and of doing so without the kinds of compromises that might undermine its full authority.[33] Such beliefs, therefore, made it easy for late-Victorian Evangelical agnostics to take up the demand for a thorough-going moralization of society that is the basis of the Western Socialist tradition, and thus to accept some form of Socialism as a substitute faith.

For these reasons, nineteenth-century Socialism is best described as a quasi-religious phenomenon: the earliest and most familiar of the socially oriented substitute faiths that arose out of the religious, moral, and economic crises of early nineteenth-century Europe and sought to cope with them by means of a renewed emphasis upon the values of community.[34] Its essential character in England was indicated fairly accurately by the credo of the first English group to use Socialism as a party label: the followers of Robert Owen, who in 1837 proclaimed the grand objectives of their faith to be

> an entire change in the character and condition of mankind
> . . . [to be brought about] peaceably and by reason alone, . . .
> by establishing over the world the principle and practice of
> the religion of charity, . . . combined with a well devised,
> equitable and natural system of united property.[35]

33. David Martin, *A Sociology of English Religion* (London, 1966), esp. pp. 59–60; also the conclusion that the same "logical structure of ideas" is found in Evangelical and "Progressive" (including Socialist) thought, and that the antagonisms expressed in their mutually hostile rhetoric are merely verbal and emotional (ibid., p. 66).

34. See J. F. C. Harrison, *Robert Owen and the Owenites in Britain and America* (London, 1969), pp. 47 ff. Here too the conservative character of Socialist values is very evident.

35. Credo of the (Owenite) Society of All Classes of All Nations, quoted in Frank Podmore, *Robert Owen: A Biography*, 2 vols. (London, 1906), 2:66–67. For earliest use of the term in various countries, see Carl Grünberg, "L'Origine des mots 'Socialisme' et 'Socialiste,'" *Revue d'histoire des doctrines economiques et sociales* 2 (1909).

Soon the new religion was also equipped with formal congregations, meeting in their own "social churches" or "halls of science" under the direction of designated pastors, teachers, and "social missionaries." Appropriate bibles, catechisms, and hymnbooks appeared soon thereafter.[36]

In a more general sense, however, both "social" and "Socialist" had already become key words within the Owenite vocabulary, where they served to designate the benevolent moral tendency that was the opposite of self-interest or selfishness, and the "New Moral World," based on cooperation rather than competition, in which the social principle would form the rule of life. The idea of social communities thus became the heart of Owen's grand design for regenerating humanity. By eliminating the evil influences of competition, reward, and punishment from such societies and replacing them with social practices, he hoped to form a nobler character in every citizen and a harmonious social life for all. Similar usage was adopted by Saint-Simonians and Fourierists in France, and soon spread to like-minded groups elsewhere. In every case the terms "Socialist" and "Socialism" were intended to imply an ideal of comprehensive social reconstruction, whose ultimate aim was to reform the social habits of mankind upon a truly "moral" basis.[37]

"Moral," of course, was another of Owen's key words, for he proposed to bring an end to the old, immoral society, based upon conflict and competition, and to replace it with a cooperative "New Moral World." In this the Owenite faith was closely akin to the "New Christianity" of Saint-Simon and to the "Religion of Humanity" of Auguste Comte.[38] All three saw in moral regeneration the great requirement of the age, and all three understood morality in a similar sense: as charity, benevolence, or altruism.

36. See Podmore, *Owen*, 2:470 ff., and Harrison, *Owen*, pp. 136 ff., for details, including specimens of early Socialist hymns.

37. Arthur Bestor, "The Evolution of the Socialist Vocabulary," *JHI* 9 (1948). All the groups mentioned above are included within the "Socialist tradition." For a recent, psychologically oriented analysis of the work of Saint-Simon, Fourier, and Comte, see Frank Manuel, *The Prophets of Paris* (Cambridge, Mass., 1962).

38. On the question of Comte's relation to Socialism, see his *General View of Positivism*, trans. J.H. Bridges (London, 1865), pp. 167 ff., where Positivism is said to embody the virtues of "communism." Also Frederic Harrison's judgment that "Comte was (philosophically speaking) a Socialist" (*Tennyson, Ruskin, Mill* [New York, 1902], p. 300).

They agreed that such regeneration depended upon the systematic cultivation of social sympathies, which had been too long repressed by the power of competition, egoism, or social anarchy. Each looked to his newly formed faith—a secular version of Christian ethics, supported by appropriate liturgical trappings—to instill essential sympathies in the people, and to prepare them morally for the social order of the future. (In these faiths, therefore, social and moral came to be almost interchangeable terms.)

The devices intended to establish that new social order were variously styled as "cooperation," "association," or simply "moralization" by the several branches of the faith; and from them, in turn, evolved the theories of "united property," which ranged from complete denial of private ownership (or strict communism) to the varied arguments that private property should "no more be suffered" in the basic instruments of production that gave their owners an "unsocial" power over the livelihood of their fellow men. These theories have ever since been identified with Socialism itself; and doubtless there can be no Socialism without some system of united property. But it would be erroneous to conclude from these considerations that systems of property, or economic theories of any kind, formed the essence of the Socialist tradition. Such theories, at most, were corollaries of the Socialist faith, and followed from its insistence that economic arrangements must be subordinated to moral ends and social values.[39]

This distinction between theories and values in the history of Socialism has not been sufficiently recognized, although, as Ignazio Silone has written, "it is fundamental. On a group of theories one can found a school; but on a group of values one can found a culture, a civilization, a new way of living together among men.[40] And the latter was precisely the aim of those who called themselves Socialists in nineteenth-century England. It forms the one contin-

39. For an elaboration of this point of view, see Emile Durkheim, *Socialism*, ed. Alvin Gouldner (New York, 1962), p. 61 (paper ed.), where the function of Socialism is said to consist in "summoning [industrial arrangements] . . . to the light of conscience." Hereafter, this meaning will be designated by the term "traditional" Socialism, a phrase preferable to "utopian," both because of the pejorative meaning attached to the latter and because it refers properly only to blueprints for an ideal society.

40. In R. H. Crossman, ed., *The God That Failed* (London, 1949), p. 114.

uous thread connecting all the members of the English Socialist tradition, both the early Owenites and such middle-class intellectuals—practically the sole bearers of the Socialist tradition from the 1850s to the early 1880s—as John Stuart Mill, F. D. Maurice and his Christian Socialist allies, John Ruskin and his "aesthetic" followers, the second wave of Christian Socialists, and early Socialist converts of the eighties such as William Morris and the Founding Fabians. All affirmed the fundamental Socialist belief, established by the Owenites, "that the condition of competition between man and man is bestial only, and that of Association [or cooperation] is human." [41] The words happen to have been written by Morris, but the sentiment was shared by practically everyone who called himself a Socialist up to and through the early 1880s.

Nevertheless, this is not what Socialism meant to the average educated person in late-Victorian England any more than it does today, and that too poses an historical problem. So far as popular usage is concerned, the "traditional" meaning of the word died out in the third quarter of the nineteenth century, following the demise of organized Utopian Socialism, and was replaced by a new meaning that was virtually a foreign import, lacking any organic connection with the English Socialist tradition. Unhappily, the avowed Socialists and those sympathetic to the movement continued to use the term in its traditional sense, without regard to changing fashions in vocabulary, so that confusion and misunderstanding were inevitable. Even as late as 1892, the first English history of Socialism that took a favorable view of the movement insisted that the "best usage" had always connected Socialism with the Owenite vision of a cooperative commonwealth and its appropriate social values. Then, noting "the growing tendency to regard as Socialist any interference with property . . . in behalf of

41. William Morris, "Art Under Plutocracy," *To-day* 2 N.S. (Feb. 1884), in *Collected Works*, 23: 172. Among others, John Burns, the working-class stalwart of the (Marxist) SDF, made similar proclamations in 1888. (See Joseph Clayton, *The Rise and Decline of Socialism in Great Britain, 1884–1924* [London, 1926], p. 217) Clayton also insisted that such emphasis on moral and social regeneration in the Socialist movement of the 1880s was precisely what made it Socialist, in contrast to the mere social reformism that increasingly supplanted it in the early twentieth century. That is the contention of the present study.

the poor," the writer denounced that usage as "neither precise nor accurate, [although] it seems to be the tendency of use and wont." [42] The Socialist revival of the eighties only compounded this confusion by adding Marxist and broadly humanitarian meanings of the term to those that were already in use, with the result that it became (and remains) impossible to find any universally accepted definition. Hence it is necessary to ascertain the particular meaning or meanings of Socialism intended by each individual Socialist before his ideas can be fitted into any broader intellectual patterns. [43]

The latter problem was especially acute during the decade of the English Socialist revival, because at least four different meanings of the term were in the air, and Socialist converts tended to shift or evolve imperceptibly from one to another (the most notable example being the Fabian evolution from semi-utopian to collectivist ideas). Nevertheless, the most striking feature of that revival was the extent to which the traditional idea of Socialism persisted. Most of the new recruits to Socialism entered the movement through that door, and it continued to color their views of Socialism even after they had learned to conceive of the movement in different terms. If, in contrast, the Socialist revival had involved no more than an outburst of legislative collectivism among disgruntled Radicals it would require little explanation, for the development of collectivism through successive waves of Radical legislation had become an established pattern of British history by the 1880s, despite the apparent incongruity between

42. Thomas Kirkup, *A History of Socialism* (London, 1892), pp. 1–5, a work much praised by Fabians, which treated Socialism as virtually synonymous with altruism. Also compare the following, characteristic definition: "Individualism and Socialism correspond with opposite views of humanity. . . . The method of Socialism is co-operation; the method of Individualism is competition" (B. F. Westcott [Bishop of Durham], *Socialism, A Paper Read to the Church Congress* [London, 1890], pp. 3–4).

43. A paradoxical result of this situation was that the usage of Socialists themselves came gradually to conform to popular usage, so that in the course of the 1880s the center of gravity in Socialist theory moved from a frequently reiterated primary concern for fellowship and moral regeneration to an emphasis on legislative collectivism—although the former concerns generally remained latent and unspoken beneath the later Socialist formulas.

collectivism and the Radical tradition.[44] But such collectivism never constituted more than a subordinate aspect of the new English Socialism and was called forth more by the exigencies of Radical politics than by any inner logic of the Socialist faith. Indeed, it was probably "called forth" primarily by a lack of workable alternatives to legislation as a means of achieving at least preliminary Socialist goals. And this was recognized even by Anarchists, who were sometimes driven to accept legislative remedies as provisional measures when there seemed no other hope for change. It was only in the later eighties, however, that English Socialists began to identify Socialism in general with Radical collectivism, and then they did so chiefly as a means of winning Radical support (see chapter 8).

On the other hand, the new Socialist movement would have been far less successful if it had not been able to tap the moral and political resources of the Radical tradition and to present its demands in a manner that appealed to dissatisfied Radical voters. Socialist groups that ignored the necessity of appealing to Radical sensibilities, as the English Marxists often did (despite an early tendency to reinterpret Marx in Radical terms), were unable to generate a massive following (see chapter 3). Instead, it was the fusion of traditional Socialist values with Radical political attitudes and programs that produced the tradition of Radical Socialism, whose importance to the Labor Party has been seen. The chief makers of that tradition, and of its basic theory, were the

44. Regarding the growth of Radical collectivism, see D. C. Somervell, *English Thought in the Nineteenth Century* (London, 1929), pp. 195 ff., and J. B. Brebner, "Laissez-Faire and State Intervention in Nineteenth-Century Britain," *JEH*, supp. 8 (1948). In the present study, collectivism will be defined as "state interference" in industry, with complete public ownership and operation of the means of production as its ultimate extension. Unlike Socialism, this was not the name of an historic movement in nineteenth-century Britain, so it may be defined according to the best contemporary usage. Indeed, one of its features is the ad hoc character of most nineteenth-century collectivism. Until the eighties, there was no coherent collectivist theory with "resources available for immediate use . . . for any particular game a Collectivist 'eleven' had to be formed from the mob which had turned out to play for the Individualists" (W. L. Burn, review of O. MacDonagh, *A Pattern of Government Growth*, in *Historical Journal* 6 [1963]: 140). In the 1880s, collectivism was most commonly used in its established French sense, as the opposite of anarchism.

early members of the Fabian Society, although they built upon foundations laid by earlier Socialist and Radical groups. And the most important of those foundations—the necessary starting point for any study of Radical Socialism in England—was John Stuart Mill's pioneering attempt to fuse Radical and Socialist values in his own work. That work, ended only by his death in 1873, prepared the ground both for the Socialist revival that occurred a decade later and for the Socialist theory of the early Fabian Society.

Part I
The Precursors

2

John Stuart Mill and the English Socialist Tradition

John Stuart Mill and the early Fabians are the key figures in the transition from Radicalism to Socialism on the British intellectual Left. In their work the attempt to fuse Radical and Socialist values so as to create a new form of Socialist faith may be seen most clearly, and their accomplishments were chiefly responsible for the development of Radical Socialism within the British Labour Party.

Probably few students of British Socialism would question that conclusion as regards the Fabians; for, whatever assessment may be made of their success as politicians, it is at least clear that when theory was required, either by the Independent Labour Party in its early days, or by the British Labour Party, the Fabians were the ones who could provide it.[1] But the role of John Stuart Mill has been less well understood. There are, to be sure, some authorities who hold that he was the crucial influence in the formation of Fabian thought. Sir Ernest Barker, for example, has written that Mill "serves, in the years between 1848 and 1880, as the bridge from *laissez-faire* to the idea of social readjustment by the State, and from political Radicalism to economic Socialism." And he identifies Mill's economic theory as the chief inspiration for subsequent Fabian ideas.[2] The trouble with this argument, and with

1. See Cole, *Second International, Pt. I,* pp. 104–248; A. McBriar, *Fabian Socialism,* pp. 290 ff., 341 ff.; H. M. Pelling, *Origins of the Labour Party,* chap. 8; and S. Pierson, *Marxism and British Socialism,* pp. 161 ff., 198 ff.

2. Sir Ernest Barker, *Political Thought in England, 1848 to 1914,* 2d ed. (London, 1959), p. 190; also p. 182, where a "trend to something like State Socialism" is attributed to Mill's writings. For a more recent example of such claims, see G. Lichtheim, *The Origins of Socialism* (London, 1969), pp. 139, 141; for a more extreme example, see J. B. Brebner, "Laissez-Faire and State Intervention in Nineteenth-Century Britain," *JEH,* supp. 8 (1948); for an early Fabian example, see *The Progress of Socialism,* Fabian Tract No. 15 (London, 1890), p. 11—one of Sidney Webb's many efforts to co-opt Mill for Fabian Socialism.

others advanced by Fabians themselves, is that they are true in their main contention, but false in their details. Mill did not, at least consciously, build a bridge to *"economic* Socialism," and his economic theories were never very favorable to socialistic schemes. In fact, he approached Socialism not on economic but on moral grounds, and it was, therefore, through his moral teaching that he prepared subsequent generations of Radical intellectuals to view Socialism in a more favorable light.[3]

But the Socialist implications of that teaching were not widely recognized. Indeed, Mill was not generally known in the nineteenth century to have been a Socialist at all. Even as recently as the 1950s some of his biographers found the idea so improbable as to conclude that Socialist beliefs could only have been forced upon him by an imperious wife-to-be. Happily, that argument has since been exploded.[4] But Mill's attachment to Socialist ideals was, in any case, both too profound and too long-standing to have been alien to his own world view. It has been well said that "temperamentally [he] was always prepared to go to hell with those whom he regarded as intellectuals rather than to heaven with . . . [the] philistines." [5] And Socialism was just the sort of cause that brought that distinction into high relief.

1. The Nature of Mill's Socialism

The Socialist beliefs that Mill affirmed were those of Owen, Saint-Simon, and Fourier—the makers of the Socialist tradition. "All supporters of Association [or cooperation], as opposed to competition, call themselves, or are called, Socialists," he wrote; and he

3. Cf. Henry Sidgwick's judgment that it was "the high ideal of human well-being which burns like a flame at the core of his social philosophy . . . that has given [Mill] so large a share in forming the thought of the present generation" (From an obituary notice, May 1873, in M-TC.)

4. For one side of the argument see F. Hayek, *John Stuart Mill and Harriet Taylor* (London, 1951), and following him, Michael Packe, *The Life of John Stuart Mill* (London, 1954), pp. 313–14. The evidence for such claims is based entirely upon letters from Mill to Harriet Taylor in the Mill Collection, Yale. For the other side, see H. O. Pappe, *John Stuart Mill and the Harriet Taylor Myth* (Melbourne, 1960); also Jack Stillinger's Introduction to *The Early Draft of Mill's Autobiography*, ed., Stillinger (Urbana, Ill., 1963), and cf. n. 28 below.

5. Lionel Robbins, *The Theory of Economic Policy in the English Classical Economists* (London, 1952), p. 167.

never understood the term in any other sense. The corollaries of that faith were that "individual ownership . . . in the instruments of production should no more be suffered," and that, instead, all should work for a "common account" and "share the produce on a prearranged principle of justice." His own conclusion to such arguments was that "nothing valid can be said against Socialism in principle; . . . the attempts to assail it, or to defend private property on the grounds of justice, must inevitably fail." Indeed, the "existing distribution of the means of life and enjoyment could only be defended as an imperfection" resulting from economic arrangements that, in other respects, were necessary and desirable. Thus the proven expedience of competition as a stimulus to increased productivity amply justified its use, so long as total wealth remained insufficient to meet the needs of the whole population. But as the final goal of human progress nothing less than Socialism would do, and Mill was stern in his denunciation of the "trampling, crushing, elbowing and treading on each other's heels" that formed the vulgar "ideal" of contemporary capitalism.[6]

Even at his most optimistic, however, Mill was never convinced that any known Socialist scheme would work well in practice. That was the burden of his repeated analyses of Socialism both in the *Political Economy* and in the fragmentary "Chapters on Socialism" of his last years. Thus he defended Socialism only in principle and only on social (or moral) grounds. On the positive side, he believed that Socialism would create social harmony and end the chicanery and fraud that characterized industrial competition; that it would restore the dignity of labor, making work again meaningful to the workman; and that it would end the demoralizing divorce between "master and servant," with its unhealthy disparity

6. [J. S. Mill], "Newman's Political Economy," *West. Rev.* 56 (1851) : 84 ff. (this now appears in *Essays on Economics and Society*, in *Collected Works*, vols. 4–5 [Toronto, 1967], pp. 439–58) , and *Principles of Political Economy*, in *Collected Works*, vols 2–3 (Toronto, 1965) , p. 754. Also cf. the arguments regarding Socialism in ibid, bk. 2, chap. 1 and bk. 4, chap. 7, esp. pp. 201–03 and 794–96, and cf. Mill's nearly contemporary letters to the Christian Socialist, F. J. Furnivall, including the claim that "the principle of property is . . . far inferior to the law of community; & there is not & cannot be any reason against the immediate adoption of some form of this last, unless it be that mankind are not yet prepared for it" (Mill to Furnivall, 19 Nov. 1850, in Burns Collection, BM 46345, no. 1823) .

in remuneration, status, and cultural opportunity. But he could conceive of the practice of Socialism only as a final stage in the moral evolution of mankind. It would be economically appropriate, he believed, only in the ultimate, "stationary" stage of society, when population would be stabilized and economic growth no longer needed. Moral and intellectual perfection would then become the prime concern of the body politic, resting upon an intellectual consensus much like that foreseen by Comte. Such, in its outlines, was the secular salvation that Mill desired for mankind, and his defense of Socialism was very largely a confession of that faith.[7]

Most of the foregoing points were also stated or implied in the Socialist credo in Mill's *Autobiography*, especially in its insistence that the advent of Socialism depended upon an "equivalent change of character" at all levels of the population, making it possible for men to "labour and combine for generous, or at all events, for public and social purposes." And Mill's belief in the infinite modifiability of human nature led him to conclude that "education, habit, and the cultivation of the sentiments," if systematically pursued, could bring about such a change among "the uncultivated herd," and thus prepare them for the cooperative commonwealth.[8] For the time being, however, he advocated only small-scale, voluntary cooperative experiments, embodying the "social" principle in a limited form, as the agencies best suited to prepare men for a future social state.

Mill's economic writings, on the other hand, treated Socialism much less favorably. Even the third edition of his *Political Economy*, the fullest expression of Mill's sympathy for Socialism, merely suspended judgment on the ultimate desirability of a Socialist economy.[9] But this was less inconsistent than it may seem, since in

7. See his evaluation of various Socialistic schemes in *Political Economy*, bk. 2, chap. 1, secs. 3–6, pp. 203–32; also "Chapters on Socialism," *Fort. Rev.* 25 n.s. (1879), republished in *Essays on Economics and Society*, pp. 705–53. For the most recent and authoritative analysis of Mill's Socialist ideas, see John M. Robson, *The Improvement of Mankind* (Toronto, 1968), esp. pp. 168–71. Although this distinguished book appeared too late to be of use in writing the present chapter, I have been pleased to discover that its conclusions agree substantially with my own.

8. Mill, *Autobiography*, p. 163.

9. *Political Economy*, 3d ed., bk. 2., chap. 1, is collated with the first edition of the same in *Collected Works*, 3:975–87. For evaluation, cf. Mill, *Principles of Po-*

the *Autobiography* Mill affirmed belief in Socialism as a private act of faith, not as a "scientific" judgment (for which, in any case, he had no adequate evidence) ; and he affirmed it on the basic moral ground that cooperation and altruism were more ethically desirable, though less efficient, than competition and acquisitiveness. Finally, he affirmed it on the ground that moral considerations should rule economic ones, insofar as these considerations could be extended without impairing the fulfillment of basic material needs.

By 1874, when the *Autobiography* was published, however, such an idea of Socialism had already come to seem archaic, leaving Mill's credo open to widespread misunderstanding. "If to look forward to such a state of things as an ideal to be striven for is Socialism, I at once acknowledge myself a Socialist," Mill's friend and economic ally, J. E. Cairnes, wrote in a critical review:

> But it seems to me that the idea which "socialism" conveys to most minds is not that of any particular form of society to be reached at a future time when human beings and the conditions of human life are widely different from what they now are, but rather certain modes of action, more especially the employment of the powers of the State for the instant accomplishment of ideal schemes.[10]

Mill, of course, would also have repudiated that conception of Socialism—a fact that was made clear in his fragmentary "Chapters on Socialism," published some six years after his death.[11] Thus any attempt to read collectivism into his arguments for Socialism, as some of the early Fabians liked to do, is certainly a misinterpretation.

Nevertheless, Mill was by no means unfavorably disposed to the

---

litical Economy, ed. W. J. Ashley (London, 1909) , Appendix K, and Robbins, *Theory of Economic Policy,* pp. 147–67, esp. 166.

10. J. E. Cairnes, *Some Leading Principles of Political Economy* (London, 1874) , p. 316.

11. See esp. his claim that the "idea of conducting the whole industry of the country . . . from a single centre is so obviously chimerical that nobody ventures to propose [how] . . . it should be done" ("Chapters on Socialism," in *Essays on Economics and Society,* p. 748) .

kinds of partial and fragmentary collectivism that were advocated
by advanced Radical reformers in his own lifetime, although he
never regarded them as Socialism. He approved explicitly of factory acts, health and sanitary regulations, publicly subsidized
artisans' dwellings, graduated and differential income and property
taxes, and death duties. Sometimes he even argued that industries
essential to the public welfare that were "practical monopolies"
should be owned and operated by a public agency.[12] On more than
one occasion, furthermore, he berated the widespread "jealousy
of Government interference," which had become "a blind feeling
preventing or resisting even the most beneficial exertion of legislative authority" in England.[13] And, by way of indicating what
such "beneficial" state interference was, he laid down the following principles in a neglected article from 1862: "As long as any
wrongful authority is exercised by human beings over oneanother,
the State has still the duty of abolishing it. . . . Whenever the de-
pressed classes of society are striving upwards, the constitution of
property will infallibly require modification." [14] In effect, the
only rule that could be established regarding state interference
was that the government must have the authority necessary to
promote all serious national interests but should not meddle "with
anything which it could let alone without touching public welfare
in any vital part. And the line neither is nor can be very definitely
drawn." Indeed, Mill was adamant only in insisting that no industry should be regulated for purely economic ends, or merely
for the sake of regulation—a fear of "Colbertism" that was

12. See the discussion of the latter point in *Public Agency vs. Trading Companies . . . Correspondence Between J. S. Mill, Esq. . . . and the Metropolitan
Sanitary Association on the proper agency for regulating the water-supply for
the Metropolis* (London, 1851), pp. 19–20. It has been partially reprinted and
discussed (wrongly, I believe) in A. L. Harris, "J. S. Mill on Monopoly and Socialism," *Journal of Political Economy* 67 (1959), and more adequately in Pedro
Schwartz, "John Stuart Mill and Laissez-Faire," *Economica* 33 n.s. (Feb. 1966). All
the examples of state interference mentioned above are in *Political Economy*: See
sec. 4, below, for discussion; also the less familiar examples in "Centralisation,"
Edin. Rev. 115 (1862): 335, 345–46.

13. Mill, *Autobiography*, p. 135. Its importance is increased by virtue of the fact
that it forms part of a defense of central against local government. "Centralisation"
was treated as the key question in most Victorian discussions of state power.

14. [J. S. Mill], "Centralisation," *Edin. Rev.* 115 (1862): 332–33. Not reprinted.

scarcely realistic in an economy so largely dominated by free trade. He also insisted that every act of "interference" should be specifically justified by its expedience in promoting social welfare.[15]

In that generalization, however, Mill made the word expedience bear a very heavy weight; for if a genuine public benefit could be proved to flow from the collective action of the state and was not counterbalanced by its probable ill effects, he had no grounds for objecting to it.[16] Thus, so long as compensation was provided (a matter of very great expediency), "society is fully entitled to abrogate or alter any right of property which . . . it judges to stand in the way of public good." Consequently,

> the terrible case which . . . Socialists are able to make out against the present economic order of society demands a full consideration of all means by which [the ownership of property may be] . . . made to work in a manner more beneficial to that large portion of society which at present enjoys the least share of its direct benefits.[17]

Thus there was a sense in which Mill seemed to agree with later advocates of Radical collectivism and might even be taken as a

15. Ibid., pp. 355–56. "Everything depends on the correct balance" between public and private power (p. 330); and Mill conceded that England and America had not yet developed government to the full desirable extent. The article, significantly, was a review of *La Centralisation*, by the French liberal collectivist, Charles Dupont-White, who has been called the "founder of the modern doctrine of State Socialism" (Emile de Laveleye, "Dupont-White et Socialisme," *Revue des deux mondes* [Jan. 1890]). Mill's appraisal was most delicately balanced, agreeing with Dupont-White's general principle that "the State, in all stages of civilisation, has been the main instrument of progress," and then explaining away much of its significance. But Mill did unequivocally advocate extensive state regulation of industry, especially as a countervailing force in large corporate enterprises (which he always mistrusted, p. 339). And he repudiated the "pure doctrine of competition" equally with that of complete centralization.

16. Even arguments for complete communism, Mill insisted, "cannot be met . . . by any arguments but those of expediency—which once let in would open the whole question of the rights of the poor and the obligations of the rich and lead to conclusions very different from" those of abstract individualism (Mill to Thornton, 19 Oct. 1867, in F. E. Mineka and D. M. Linley, eds., *Later Letters of John Stuart Mill* [Toronto, 1972], p. 320).

17. "Chapters on Socialism," *Fort. Rev.* 25 n.s., reprinted in *Essays on Economics and Society*, p. 753.

kind of Fabian before his time.[18] But he never, in his own work, associated such arguments with Socialism, and the conclusions that he drew from them were typically far milder than the principles themselves. As he understood it, the whole problem turned on the questions of what was, in fact, expedient, and of what major values were to be balanced in the equations of expediency. On such issues Mill's verdict typically came down on a moderate (not to say conservative) side, dominated by the traditional Radical fear of "Old Corruption." [19] It was only at certain times of great excitement and great personal involvement in the issues that he allowed his immediate reform proposals to become as radical as the principles upon which they were based. Those occasions arose chiefly at the end of his life and will be examined in greater detail in section 4 below.

Taking all aspects of Mill's work into account, there were three distinct ways in which he contributed to the development of Fabian Socialism: through his advocacy of Socialist values and of the cooperative commonwealth as an ultimate ideal; through his sympathy for Positivism (to be discussed below), which was, in turn, one of the chief sources of Fabian thought;[20] and through his vigorous support in the last years of his life for measures of Radical collectivism, as applied to land, education, and improving the conditions of labor. All three tendencies helped to prepare the ground for the new growth of Socialism in the early eighties, both through the specific reform proposals that they engendered and through the propagation of a genuinely "social" point of view, which separated Mill's work fundamentally from the prevailing tone of liberal individualism. All these considerations were also relevant to the early Fabians, many of whom originally understood Socialism in precisely the cooperative and moralistic sense that

18. A particularly "Fabian" view is implied in Mill's judgment that "the intellectual and moral grounds of Socialism . . . [afford], in many cases, the guiding principles of the improvements necessary to give the present system of society its best chance" (ibid., p. 736) .

19. Thus, while repudiating "the *laisser faire* doctrine, stated without large qualifications," as "unpractical and unscientific," he still thought that it would be appropriately applied "nineteen times out of twenty" (*Auguste Comte and Positivism* [London, 1865], p. 78) .

20. Mill's relation to English Positivism is discussed in sec. 3, below; Fabian use of Positivism as a stepping-stone to Socialism is discussed in chaps. 6 and 8 below.

Mill approved of, were inclined strongly to social Positivism, and were first drawn to Socialism by the movement for land nationalization and the special taxation of unearned income that Mill helped to set in motion. Still more important, his attempt to fuse Radical and Socialist values into a new and more balanced social faith prefigures the early Fabian attempt to do the same and serves as an intellectual bridge between the advanced Radicalism of the 1860s and Fabian Socialism in the 1880s.

2. *Sources of Mill's Socialism*

The taproot of Mill's Socialist faith was his belief in the "improvement" of mankind through the inculcation of social and altruistic sympathies—a belief that was absolutely fundamental to his *Weltanschauung,* and to which he clung tenaciously, despite the fact that it came into continual conflict with the principles of Benthamite Utilitarianism. That Mill declared himself a Socialist in spite of such conflicts is evidence both of the strength of his social feeling and of the fact that "his thought continually followed where his emotions led." [21] Neither fact has been sufficiently recognized by twentieth-century students of Mill, although both were evident to contemporaries who had known him personally.[22] And one of the latter—not otherwise sympathetic to Mill—stated the nature of his emotional and religious bent in a manner that can scarcely be improved:

> By temperament he was essentially religious, [although] . . . as far as positive doctrine went his mind was an absolute blank. We believe that this sharp contrast between theory and feeling . . . drove him into the schemes for the improvement of the world that have been exposed [in the Tory press] to so many objections. . . . Having to love somebody, he struggled to make a religion out of man as he might become [through the effect of progressive social improvements]. [23]

21. J. P. Scanlon, "Mill and the Definition of Social Freedom," *Ethics* (April 1958) : 208; also Robbins, *Theory of Economic Policy,* pp. 143–44.

22. See, e.g., Frederic Harrison's comment that his works were "red hot with passion," and everywhere betrayed "the logic of feeling" (*Tennyson, Ruskin, Mill,* pp. 271, 298) , and Sydney Olivier's similar point in "J. S. Mill and Socialism," *Today* 2 (Nov. 1884) : 496.

23. Obituary notice, *Pall Mall Gazette* (May 1873) . Cf. A. O. J. Cockshut, *The Unbelievers* (New York, 1966) , pp. 20–30.

The latter points, indeed, could almost have been abstracted from Mill's posthumously published *Three Essays on Religion,* wherein the nature and extent of his social faith were revealed with striking clarity. His primary contention in those essays was that "a sense of unity with mankind, and a deep feeling for the general good, may be cultivated into a sentiment and a principle capable of fulfilling every important function of religion." And its chief function should be to train everyone to feel an "absolute obligation towards the universal good. . . . identifying [his] feelings with the entire life of the human race." Such an achievement "implies a certain cultivation," Mill admitted, "but not superior to that which might be, and certainly will be, if human improvement continues, the lot of all." These phrases reveal not only the nature of Mill's substitute faith (which was completely "social" in its orientation), but also the assumptions upon which it rested: his belief in the infinite perfectibility of human nature by means of a systematic moral education appealing to both the intellect and the "social sympathies." (And for those who failed to respond to such education—the "inferior"—he would add the "force of shame," mediated through public opinion.) [24]

Recently, Maurice Cowling's remarkable book, *Mill and Liberalism,* has called attention to the importance of such attitudes as the emotional center of Mill's thought; but the usefulness of Cowling's analysis is largely vitiated by his intense hostility to Mill's whole frame of mind and by his fondness for polemical exaggeration. Thus, while Mill undoubtedly put a high premium on "spontaneous action for the collective interest," and always regarded the essence of morality as the subordination of self-interest to that of the community, this scarcely justifies such epithets as "moral collectivism" and "moral totalitarianism." [25] Instead, Mill's values are more properly described as emanating from the

24. Mill, "The Utility of Religion," in *Three Essays on Religion* (London, 1874), pp. 110, 108, 106. (The essay was written in 1854.)

25. Maurice Cowling, *Mill and Liberalism* (Cambridge, 1964), pp. 46, xii, xvii, and passim; also such recurrent phrases as "sociological self-deception," which are made to bear the brunt of the attack on Mill. For more balanced analyses of the same phenomena, see Robert Carr, "The Religious Thought of John Stuart Mill: A Study in Reluctant Scepticism," *JHI* 23 (1962): esp. 493–95, and Gertrude Himmelfarb, "The Other John Stuart Mill," in *Victorian Minds* (New York, 1968),

"social" point of view that formed the common basis of Owenite Socialism, Positivism, and Christian humanitarianism. But although Mill was attracted to all these movements, he sought to temper each with a strong sense of the value of liberty and individuality as indispensable elements, along with the social sympathies, in the ultimate improvement of mankind. All Mill's writing reveals his continued attempt to strike an appropriate balance between the varied elements that, he believed, must be combined to form the true "ideal of human well being;" and this element of balance and flexibility—the key, in fact, to all Mill's social thought—is precisely what Cowling fails to grasp.[26]

Such balance and the attempt to fuse apparently conflicting tendencies were particularly evident in Mill's writing of the middle fifties—the period of his most varied literary achievement —in which, almost simultaneously, he produced the bulk of his *Autobiography,* with its great Socialist credo, *On Liberty* in its original form, the essays that subsequently formed the *Utilitarianism,* and the essays on religion cited above.[27] It was the high-water mark both of his belief in Socialism and of his concern with personal and, above all, intellectual freedom, and their conjunction in his thought has not been sufficiently noticed.[28] The great unifying aim of his writings at that time was the formation of a social

pp. 113 ff., esp. 120–23. (The latter, however, is more concerned to expose the authoritarian strain in Mill's thought than to understand how it fitted with the other strains.)

26. Such "balance" was simply the corollary of Mill's vaunted "many-sidedness," and follows as a strict application of the idea of utility. Especially in questions of policy, "everything depends on a correct balancing of opposite considerations" ("Centralisation," p. 330).

27. The dates are derived from Mill's letters to Harriet Taylor Mill, Jan.–Feb. 1854, in Hayek, *JSM and Harriet Taylor,* pp. 190–94, 215 ff. Also cf. Helen Taylor's Introductory Note to *Three Essays on Religion;* A. W. Levi, "The Writing of Mill's Autobiography," *Ethics* 61 (1950): 248–96; and Stillinger, ed., *Early Draft of Mill's Autobiography,* pp. 5–10.

28. Gertrude Himmelfarb, in *Victorian Minds,* pp. 115, 139 ff., has also noted that conjunction, but has argued that *both* his Socialism and his libertarianism were imposed on Mill by his wife, contrary to his own inclinations, which sets the problem in a completely different context. However, like Hayek, *JSM and Harriet Taylor,* on which she relies heavily, Himmelfarb has not noted the long history of both beliefs in Mill's earlier writing, most of it quite independent of his wife's influence. Some examples of this writing have been quoted above, but for Mill's earliest libertarian views, cf. B. Wishy, ed., *Prefaces to Liberty* (Boston, 1959).

theory that would effectively combine moral community and personal freedom, so as to be both genuinely "social" and genuinely
libertarian.[29] But both of those tendencies were chiefly valued
by Mill as means to a still higher end—"the highest and most
harmonious development of [human] powers to a complete and
consistent whole" [30]—which was only possible within a social environment in which fully developed social sympathies and an
exalted ideal of truth would, together, form the rule of life. Hence
Mill's *On Liberty* may be seen, in the perspective of his ideas in
the 1850s, as an attempt to define the necessary sphere of individual freedom within a socialized community. It has been frequently noted that the only entirely consistent portions of that
work are the ones defending freedom of thought and expression,
chiefly because those forms of freedom are the only ones that
follow directly from the essay's basic premise regarding the "end
of man"—his "highest and most harmonious development"—and
from its ultimate standard of judgment: "utility in the larger
sense, grounded on the permanent interest of man as a *progressive*
being" (chapter 1). For the sake of continuous intellectual and
moral improvement, which was essential both to human progress
and to individual self-development, Mill believed that intellectual
liberty in the fullest sense was an absolute requirement. (For
knowledge could be advanced only by the perpetual challenge of
new ideas and the perpetual broadening of old perspectives.) But
at the same time such liberty could only be an effective means of
promoting the highest good for man if it were coupled with an
equally exalted sense of community—individuality balanced by
a sense of social interdependence—and of the importance of subordinating (and even "sacrificing") personal wants and interests

29. Thus "we considered the social problem of the future to be, how to unite the
greatest individual liberty of action, with a common ownership in the raw material
of the globe, and an equal participation of all in the benefits of combined labour"
(*Autobiography*, p. 162).

30. Mill, *On Liberty* (Everyman ed., London, 1910), p. 115, quoting Wilhelm
von Humboldt. This is really the central premise of the essay, and it is reinforced
by the other quotation from Humboldt proclaiming the "importance of human
development in its richest diversity," which forms its epigraph. For Mill's debt to
Humboldt and German Idealism, see R. Aris, *German Political Thought, 1789–1815*
(London, 1936), 158–59, and Humboldt, *The Limits of State Action*, ed. J. W.
Burrow (Cambridge, Eng., 1969), Introduction, p. 16; also p. 51 of text.

which lay outside the intellectual sphere to those of the community as a whole.[31]

These social aims, and the attempt to balance them with the just requirements of individuality, were by no means late additions to Mill's thought. Both were integral developments of his early intellectual experiences culminating in his early twenties, and both remained thereafter among the most passionately held commitments of his life. It should be possible, then, to find their origins in the history of Mill's early "mental training." It is well known that his notorious education, conceived according to the strictest principles of Benthamism, so thoroughly conditioned his mind to the mechanics of utilitarian psychology and to the immutable "laws" of human nature derived from it, that even as an adult he was unable to break completely free of its limitations. He was bound for life by the conceptual apparatus of Benthamite hedonism, and by its individualist and rationalist mental set. Consequently, his youthful reading of Bentham's "Treatise on Legislation" in Dumont's French redaction was a profoundly convincing experience. For it revealed to the youth of fifteen his personal mission and purpose in the world: to promote the general happiness and welfare of mankind in a perfectly disinterested manner, by the application of Bentham's legislative principles.[32]

There was, however, another side to Mill's education, not so easily brought into focus but potentially more important: his immersion in classical, especially Greek, moral thought. From that experience he could scarcely have failed to imbibe a strong sense of community and of civic duty—what he called the "Socratic virtues"—while the "lofty moral standard exhibited in the writings of Plato," impressed the young scholar "with great force," throughout his education.[33] The point is worth elaboration, since

31. Self-sacrifice for the sake of public welfare is, in the current state of civilization, "the highest virtue that can be found in man" (*Utilitarianism* [Everyman ed., London, 1910], p. 15, and cf. pp. 30 ff., 48 ff.) . For the fullest recent discussion of such points, see David Spitz, "Freedom and Individuality. Mill's *Liberty* in Retrospect," in C. J. Friedrich, ed., *Liberty,* Nomos Ser., 4. (New York, 1962) , pp. 176–226.

32. *Autobiography,* esp. pp. 45–50. Except as noted the following three pages are based on the same.

33. *Autobiography,* p. 33; cf. Ruth Borchardt, ed., *Three Dialogues of Plato, Translated by John Stuart Mill* (London, 1946) .

elsewhere Mill claimed that "I have felt myself, beyond any modern I know, a pupil of Plato." And at least one distinguished scholar has concurred and cites as evidence of Mill's Platonic training his combination of strict logic with a passion for social regeneration, his intense social morality, his religious aspirations, and, above all, his belief that the state exists, ideally, as an agency of moral education.[34]

Such training, coupled with a sensitive, religious temperament, also suggests why the young Mill failed to become a reproduction of the older Benthamite generation. But his state of mind inevitably made him easy prey to any form of romantic doctrine that could penetrate his logical chain mail and touch the springs of his emotions. In the event, the transformation from a doctrinaire Utilitarian into a kind of romantic philanthropist was facilitated by the well-known emotional crisis of his twentieth year. In effect, this seems to have been a severe postadolescent "identity crisis," [35] but it also had roots in the sheer psychological inadequacy of his Benthamite beliefs, which were proved false by his own inner experience. Thus, as he concluded, "the whole foundation on which my life was constructed fell down," and was only reconstructed through his apprehension of a radically different psychological principle, that of "social sympathy." [36]

Through the good offices of romantic poetry and metaphysics, especially as mediated by new friends who were under the influence of Coleridge, Mill discovered that the Benthamite world view had failed to take any account of the spontaneous social sentiments that made up a spirit of community, or of the other emotional ligaments that bound societies together. From them he learned to value the principle of community as a living, historical unit, through which individuals were enabled to cooperate in pursuing their common material and moral aims, and to regard

34. Paul Shorey, *Platonism, Ancient and Modern* (Berkeley, Calif., 1938), pp. 231–32; Stillinger, *Early Draft of Mill's Autobiography*, pp. 12, 48; and compare Mill's review of "Grote's Plato," *Edin. Rev.* 123 (1866): 297–363.

35. For the concept of identity crisis, see Erik Erikson, "Identity and the Life Cycle," *Psychological Issues* 1 (1959), and *Identity, Youth and Crisis* (New York, 1968). The same author's *Young Man Luther* (New York, 1958) develops the biographical uses of this concept in ways that could also be fruitfully applied to Mill.

36. *Autobiography*, pp. 93–95.

cooperation itself as a noble social ideal, rather than as a fortuitous juxtaposition of social atoms.

Likewise, Mill and his friends were drawn to the Owenite meetings in Red Lion Square, where the new gospel of "Association" was preached as a panacea for all the pains of a disjointed industrial society. But Mill's first encounters with these Socialists were superficially not encouraging, as he was firmly identified with the Philosophic Radical opposition in a series of debates which ranged over such doctrinal issues as the economic value of competition, the Malthusian remedy for poverty, and the Owenite system of society, on all of which he took a strictly "orthodox" line. Yet the suspicion remains that he absorbed far more of Owenite social idealism than he realized at the time, and that those debates planted the seeds of his future fondness for "association" as an ultimate ideal of social reconstruction. The debates, however, took place before his "mental crisis" had opened his mind to the significance of social feeling, so it required the experiences of the subsequent two years to bring the Owenite seeds to germination. It was only after the "influences of . . . continental thought, especially the reaction of the nineteenth century against the eighteenth," came "streaming in" on him, both from the Coleridgians (as mediators of German Idealism) and from the Saint-Simonians, that such seeds received the cultivation necessary to their future growth.[37]

Above all, it was the Saint-Simonians who were responsible for directing Mill's social thought to new conclusions during the late twenties and early thirties. Under their influence he began to believe that the capacity for consciously altruistic behavior (such as the Benthamites practiced, in apparent contradiction to their laws of human nature) had always existed in mankind, but was largely repressed by the habits and attitudes—especially the prevailing "critical Spirit"—of the modern age. Thus he came to believe that a systematic cultivation of social sympathies, leading to al-

37. Ibid., pp. 86–87,107–10, 113; but cf. G. J. Holyoake, *History of Co-operation*, 2 vols. (London, 1875), 1:141, noting Mill's extensive involvement with that movement—much greater than his *Autobiography* suggests—during his early manhood. (Owenites were also the most conspicuous contemporary advocates of women's rights and sexual equality, causes that Mill also adopted early in life.)

truistic habits of feeling, was the mainspring of social progress. What was chiefly required to guarantee such progress, therefore, was an adequate system of "moral education," operating powerfully on public opinion and public sentiment. And to achieve that end, Mill noted, it must also be "well directed." [38]

Thus even before his first encounter with the Saint-Simonians, Mill was sympathetically disposed to their idea of establishing *un pouvoir spirituel*: a moral and intellectual leadership at the head of society, responsible for directing its moral education. "Reason itself," he wrote, in one of his strongest passages, "will teach most men that they must, in the last resort, fall back on the authority of more cultivated minds." And he dilated at length on the "wholesome state of the human mind," wherein "the body of the people, i.e., the uninstructed, shall entertain the same feelings of deference and submission to the authority of the instructed in morals and politics, as . . . now in the physical sciences." Nor did he shrink from assigning such work, in large measure, to the state, insisting that the sphere of government must include "all purposes that are for man's good: and the highest . . . of these is the improvement of man himself as a moral and intelligent being." [39]

Nevertheless, if Mill regarded the emergence of such a spiritual power in society, representing a broad intellectual consensus of the people, as a necessary step toward their ultimate regeneration, he was not satisfied with the devices by which the Saint-Simonians proposed to organize it. "It appears to me that you cannot organise it at all," he wrote to his Saint-Simonian friend, Gustave d'Eichthal. "What is the *pouvoir spirituel* but the insensible influence of mind over mind?" Its appropriate channels were simply the ordinary media of public discussion and instruction. Thus, Mill insisted, the claims of a spiritual elite to leadership could not

38. For Mill's relations with the Saint-Simonians, see R. K. P. Pankhurst, *The Saint Simonians, Mill, and Carlyle* (London, 1951). Even before meeting them, however, Mill had adopted the idea of organizing moral education. See his lecture on "Moral Perfection," in Mill, *Autobiography*, with an Appendix of Hitherto Unpublished Speeches and a Preface by Harold Laski (London, 1924), pp. 292–99.

39. Mill, *The Spirit of the Age* [Essays from the *Examiner*, 1831], ed. F. A. Hayek (Chicago, 1942), p. 33; Mill to d'Eichthal, 7 Nov. 1829, 8 Oct. 1829, in F. E. Mineka, ed., *The Earlier Letters of John Stuart Mill, 1812–1848*, 2 vols. (Toronto, 1963), 1:40, 36.

be established in any way except through open and free discussion, leading to their spontaneous acceptance by the people at large. As early as 1829, his correspondence also revealed the main outlines of his theory of liberty, grounding it firmly within the larger problem of establishing a moral community. Free discussion, then and always, was not an end in itself for Mill, but the only reliable way of promoting human "improvement" and of guaranteeing that it would not stagnate at some point along the way.[40]

It thus became Mill's hope that moral order and consensus would be instilled in society through the medium of free and open discussion. For, indeed, there was no other way. If one sought to appoint a spiritual elite through the usual political channels it would merely turn out to be as vulgar and unprogressive as the existing Establishment. And Mill believed, in the traditional Radical manner, that it was precisely that Establishment, embodying all the "great sinister social interests" surviving from the ancien regime, that was responsible for "demoralising" society and obstructing the emergence of a real *pouvoir spirituel*.[41] Hence the necessity of a "moral and spiritual revolution . . . which shall leave

40. Mill to d'Eichthal, 2 Nov. 1829, 9 Feb. 1830, in Mineka, *Earlier Letters,* 1:40–42, 45–46. Here, as in the *Liberty,* Mill's model is scientific method, and the one thing needful for it is the constant presentation of new alternatives and new insights to supplement the old. "The great instrument of [moral] improvement in men is to supply them with the other half of the truth, one side of which they have" never seen (ibid., p. 42). Against such liberal arguments, however, one must set the authoritarian ones of Mill's letter to John Sterling, 20–22 Oct. 1831, e.g., "that it is good for men to be ruled" and "to submit" to "higher intelligence and virtue" (ibid., p. 84). If consistently maintained, such arguments would surely have destroyed Mill's liberalism. In fact, they were only characteristic of a brief phase in his intellectual career and were not repeated later. In part, they may be attributed to the continuing dialectic of liberal and authoritarian beliefs in Mill's writings; more specifically, they were the result of his current policy of exaggerating the extent of his agreement with all correspondents, even at the risk of distorting his own views (see Mill to Carlyle, 18 May 1833, in ibid., p. 153). For somewhat different treatments of this problem, see Himmelfarb, *Victorian Minds,* pp. 120 ff., and S. R. Letwin, *The Pursuit of Certainty* (Cambridge, Eng., 1965), pp. 249 ff.

41. Mill to d'Eichthal, 7 Nov. 1829, 9 Feb. 1830, in Mineka, *Earlier Letters,* 1:41, 40, 48, especially Mill's insistence that in unreformed England it was necessary first "to alter those parts of our social institutions . . . which at present oppose improvement, degrade and brutalize the intellects and morality of the people, and by giving all ascendency to mere wealth, which possession of political power confers, prevents the growth of a *pouvoir spirituel* capable of commanding the faith of the majority" (p. 48).

no man one fraction of unearned distinction or . . . importance"
and would transfer effective leadership of society to the "more
progressive, intelligent classes," through whom, alone, the work
of regeneration could begin. But Mill never suggested that such
political reformation would, of itself, establish the millennium;
it was merely the necessary first step, completing the work of the
critical era before the organic one could begin.[42]

By the early 1830s Mill had become convinced that the "organic" reconstruction of society would take the form of Socialism,
although he did not profess to know the exact variety. He did not
accept the Saint-Simonian scheme of industrial reorganization,
fearing its centralized, authoritarian character, and thought it
"impracticable, and not desirable if practicable, like that of Mr
Owen." But he did concede in 1831 that the Saint-Simonian "organisation, under some modification or other, . . . is likely to be
the final and permanent condition of the human race." And this,
together with the favorable references to Owen, with whom he
was in personal contact during the thirties, suggests the extent
to which he was becoming committed to Socialist ideals. Characteristically, however, he also added that most of the "attainable good"
in the Saint-Simonian system lay "on the road to it[s achieve-
ment]," so that it would never have to be established in totality—
a view of Socialism that was not unlike the view of many early
Fabians.[43]

If Mill thought such Socialism a long way off in the 1830s—the
product of "several ages" of improvement—he was nevertheless
becoming increasingly impatient with the standard economic
teachings of his age, which, he concluded, were doing nothing to
encourage the moral evolution of society, and, in their more

42. Mill, *Spirit of the Age,* pp. 48–49. I disagree with the interpretation of this
passage in Walter Simon, *European Positivism in the Nineteenth Century* (Ithaca,
1963), p. 179, which holds that Mill used the Saint-Simonian law of the three
stages only for Radical or destructive purposes. On the contrary, Mill treated Radical reform itself as a necessary stage preliminary to the third or "organic stage" of
human development.

43. Mill to d'Eichthal, 9 Feb. 1830, 30 Nov. 1831, in Mineka, *Earlier Letters,*
1:47, 88–89; references to Mill's meetings with Robert Owen are on pp. 47, 73; and
cf. Pankhurst, *Saint Simonians.* Regarding the Fabians, see the quotation from
Sidney Webb, p. 213 below.

"vulgar" forms, were doing a good deal to restrain it. Hence his remarkable letter to Carlyle, agreeing that Harriet Martineau, the chief vulgarizer of classical economics, had reduced

> the *laissez faire* system to an absurdity, so far as the *principle* goes, by merely carrying it out to all its consequences. In the meantime, that principle, like other negative ones, has work to do yet, work, namely, of a destroying kind, & I am glad to think it has strength left to finish that, after which it must soon expire: peace be with its ashes . . . for I doubt much if it will reach the resurrection.[44]

It must expire, of course, because its function was merely critical and destructive and had no place in the new, organic synthesis that was to come. Thus, in his new frame of mind, Mill appealed to the "orthodox" economists "that they . . . not require us to believe" that such "destructive" work is all that is needed now; "nor, by fixing bounds to the possible reach of improvement in human affairs, set limits to that ardour in its pursuit." Finally, there was a real note of exasperation with the older, classical economics in his contemporary "hope" that "the time is coming for more rational modes of distributing the products of nature and art than this expensive and demoralizing plan of individual competition, the results of which have risen to such an enormous height." [45] He wished, in effect, that the destructive work of the existing, critical era would rapidly come to completion, so that the work of reconstruction on a "higher" social basis could begin in earnest.

That, however, was the high-water mark of his Socialist and world-reforming enthusiasm in the 1830s. Thereafter, increasing political disillusionment, brought on in part by the evident impotence of the parliamentary Radicals in the late thirties and, perhaps in greater part, by his reluctant acceptance of Tocqueville's judgment on democracy, induced a mood of all-round "practical

44. Mill to Thomas Carlyle, 11 & 12 Apr. 1833, in Mineka, *Earlier Letters*, 1:152: a good example of Mill's outlook following the Reform Act of 1832.

45. [Mill], review of Harriet Martineau in *Monthly Repository* 8 (1834) ; "The House and Window Tax," in ibid. 7 (1833) : 580; article identified as Mill's in F. E. Mineka, *The Dissidence of Dissent* (Chapel Hill, N.C., 1944) , pp. 277–79.

conservatism."[46] And from that mood he was aroused only by the exhilirating effects of 1848. Like many Radical intellectuals he saw the rising of the Paris masses as a sign of increasing moral consciousness among the people. The plan for national workshops and the various unofficial cooperative experiments that followed it further served to stir his latent belief in the practical possibilities of Socialism. Subsequent years were, therefore, the period of his greatest Socialist enthusiasm, when he looked forward most confidently to the ultimate regeneration of mankind along cooperative and altruistic lines. And that state of mind was reflected, not only in the very large concessions to Socialism in the second and third editions of the *Political Economy* (1849, 1852), but also in the Socialist "credo" in his *Autobiography,* in his correspondence with Christian Socialist F. J. Furnivall, and in his other writings of the early and middle 1850s.[47]

Thereafter, his formal views regarding Socialism changed very little. But his active interest in the cause again abated in the later fifties and was replaced by another mood of social pessimism, stimulated both by the reemergence of authoritarian government in France and by the extreme sensitivity to social pressures that accompanied his long-deferred marriage to Harriet Taylor. Such a combination of public and personal anxieties then helped to create that exaggerated concern with "individuality" that is so evident in the final version of the essay *On Liberty,* and in his increasing unwillingness to tolerate any democratic experiments in England that might repeat the unfortunate outcome of the second French Republic.[48] The same mood of ultrasensitivity to

46. Mill's own phrase. See his comments in *Autobiography* pp. 134, 136 ff., and his table talk from the 1840s in Caroline Fox, *Memories of Old Friends,* ed. H. M. Pym (Philadelphia, 1882), pp. 87, 95–96, 101–02. There are frequent references to the "tyranny of public opinion" and the need for a strong governing class.

47. See *Political Economy* (Toronto, 1965), Appendix A, for relevant changes in second and third editions; also *Autobiography,* pp. 162–63; Mill to F. J. Furnivall, 19 and 27 Nov. 1850, in *Later Letters,* pp. 50–51, 53–54; and "Newman's Political Economy," in *Essays on Econ. and Soc.,* pp. 441–57.

48. There are frequent allusions to Napoleon III in Mill's later letters, but the clearest is in "Centralisation," *Edin. Rev.* 115 (1862). From the spring of 1854 Mill's outlook became increasingly "conservative" [his own word], due to serious illness and expectation of death. This seriously colored his rewriting of *Liberty* and *Representative Government* in the later fifties. (Mill's *Diary,* 25 May 1854, cited in Hayek, *JSM and Harriet Taylor,* p. 204.)

the authoritarian possibilities inherent in current schemes of social reconstruction led him to take an increasingly unfavorable view of nearly all such systems of social doctrine—and especially of one with which he had once been sympathetic, but whose authoritarian implications were becoming too uncomfortably apparent in the late fifties: the Positive philosophy of Auguste Comte.[49]

3. Mill and the English Positivists

Up to this point, our discussion of Mill's social theory has dealt only with the formative influences on his beliefs, for it can scarcely be supposed that Mill himself exercised any comparable influence on the theory of Owenites, Coleridgians, Saint-Simonians, or Christian Socialists. In the case of Positivism, however, it may have been otherwise. The social theory developed by the English Positivists—specifically those who followed the lead of Frederic Harrison[50]—was very close to that of Mill. It was so close, in fact, that the two schools of thought must at least be regarded as parallel developments, each attempting to work out a similar social philosophy by taking leading doctrines from Comte and Saint-Simon (or from the broader Socialist tradition to which both belonged) but developing them along liberal–Radical lines. For that reason a comparison of their theories, with a search for intellectual cross-fertilization, is likely to prove instructive—especially because the doctrines of the Harrisonian Positivists, which were concerned chiefly with social reconstruction, formed one of the major sources of Fabian Socialist theory in the 1880s.

It is probably true, as Professor Simon has noted, that all Mill's judgments on Comte's social and moral system were at least implicit in his earlier judgments on the Saint-Simonians.[51] But Mill's state of mind in the late fifties and early sixties was more charged

49. Regarding Mill and Comte, see Iris W. Mueller, *John Stuart Mill and French Thought* (Urbana, Ill., 1956), pp. 94 ff., and Simon, *European Positivism*, pp. 180–95.

50. For the English Positivist schism between Harrisonians and Congrevians, see Simon, *European Positivism*, pp. 60 ff., and Simon, "Auguste Comte's English Disciples," *Vic. Stud.* 8 (Dec. 1964), which, however, only adds details and does not adequately consider the liberal character of English Positivism. Such liberalism (like that of the later Mill) also formed an important anticipation of the "New Liberalism" of the 1890s.

51. Simon, *European Positivism*, p. 180.

with fear of authoritarianism than it had been in the twenties, and the "despotism" of Comte's "sociocracy" was far more explicit than any comparable despotism among the Saint-Simonians. Thus Mill's later judgments, especially those in his long review of *Auguste Comte and Positivism,* had at least the appearance of greater severity than his earlier ones. In practice, however, Mill differed from Comte chiefly in seeing many of his doctrines as excessively rigoristic. He argued, for example, that the rigor with which Comte demanded that all egoistic propensities should be suppressed and treated as morally culpable left too much room for exercise of coercive power, even if, as Comte intended, that power was to derive solely from public opinion, without legal sanctions. Mill's own position, in contrast, was the more subtle (but not always logically distinct) doctrine that while every unselfish act and every subordination of individual aims to the general good was praiseworthy and should be encouraged by public opinion, not all acts of self-indulgence, but only excessive ones, should be held culpable or be condemned by such opinion. Again, he criticized Comte for insisting that all life should be directed to "some one [exclusive] end;" but Mill, himself, never swerved from his belief that there was, indeed, a highest end of life—the moral and cultural improvement of mankind—and shrank only from Comte's rigor in subordinating everything to that end, and from his apparent denial of the intellectual liberty that Mill regarded as the essential means of achieving it.[52]

Nor should it be supposed, either from his criticisms of Comte or from his arguments in *On Liberty,* that Mill shrank from employing public opinion as the chief instrument of social–moral regeneration. In fact, he demanded its use.[53] He not only looked forward to the achievement of a public consensus modeled on that of the sciences, and thus on the *pouvoir spirituel* of Comte and the Saint-Simonians, but he also argued that public education should have the function of developing that consensus. Even as early as his first intellectual encounter with Comte (then one of the Saint-Simonians), Mill had agreed that "convictions regarding what is

52. Mill, *Auguste Comte and Positivism* (two review articles reprinted from *West. Rev.)* (London, 1865), pp. 120, 139–48, esp. 147–48.
53. Ibid., and *Three Essays in Religion,* p. 108.

right and wrong, useful and pernicious, [should be] deeply engraven on the feelings by early education and by general unanimity of opinion, and so firmly grounded in reason . . . that [they could thereafter endure perpetually]." And in the 1850s Mill still agreed that "the moral and intellectual ascendency once exercised by priests, must pass into the hands of the philosophers, and will naturally do so when they become sufficiently unanimous"—and when public opinion, through the progress of consensus, becomes ready to accept it spontaneously.[54] It was Comte's attempt to "organize" that spiritual power, vesting it formally in a sacerdotal hierarchy headed by the High Priest of Humanity, that Mill found repulsive. Unhappily, Comte's own personality and his later, more detailed schemes for organizing the sociocracy of the future only seemed to make the authoritarian implications of that priesthood clearer.

Oddly enough, however, Mill's notion of a desirable *pouvoir spirituel* was very similar to that of Comte's most notable English disciples—the group headed by Harrison, Bridges, and Beesly, who, because of their literary eminence, came to be identified with English Positivism per se by the Victorian reading public. Like Mill, they construed Comte's doctrines in a thoroughly liberal spirit, seeking to combine the ideas of spiritual power and hierarchy of functions with complete individual freedom. Unlike Mill, however, they did not reject Comte's later and more authoritarian teachings, but instead reinterpreted them—a tendency that must have been second nature to such former devout Anglicans, bred to the niceties of interpretation required by the Thirty-nine Articles.[55] It was in this fashion that they claimed to accept all Comte's teachings without departing from basic liberal standards. The best example of that phenomenon is probably Harrison's reinterpretation of *pouvoir spirituel*, which, by the simple expedient of translation, he turned into "moral force," (a phrase that still had Chartist overtones) . Far from being coercive or authori-

54. *Autobiography*, pp. 116–17, 148; cf. *Comte and Positivism*, p. 120.
55. See, e.g., Bridges's objection to a "literal interpretation" of Comte: Bridges to Congreve, 30 June and 9 July 1868, quoted in Simon, "Comte's English Disciples," *Vic. Studies*, pp. 163–64. Bridges and Beesly had been trained as Evangelicals; Harrison combined Evangelical and Broad Church attitudes.

tarian, Harrison insisted, it could be established only through the inherent, self-authenticating excellence of scientific truth and involved nothing more than "public opinion, moralized and organized, apart from political agitation, laws, parties, or force." Its only organs were the usual media of communication, and the only "organization" that it needed was the intellectual systematization of the doctrine itself, which could only be completed through spontaneous public consensus.[56]

Such a doctrine differed very little from Mill's own, although he thought the Positivist attempt to organize a body of social knowledge premature. But so, in a sense, did the Harrisonian Positivists, who held that Comte had "constituted" sociology only provisionally and in its bare outlines. And this, added to their belief that the attempt to practice the Religion of Humanity was also premature, was the crux of the Harrisonians' quarrel with the rival branch of English Positivism, headed by Richard Congreve. The Congrevians chiefly sought to establish a church with pretensions to spiritual discipline, whereas the Harrisonians chiefly sought to influence social life and thought by molding public opinion. "Public opinion [is] the life of Positivism," Harrison said, and the real business of Positivists was, therefore, to act as an intellectual ginger group—religiously motivated and guided by doctrines which they held to be scientific, but chiefly concerned with reforming the "practical life" of society in accordance with their doctrine, rather than with instilling the doctrine itself.[57] And that was precisely Mill's approach to social reconstruction.

Indeed, it might almost be argued that the Harrisonian Positivists were Millite Radicals at heart and identified themselves

56. Frederic Harrison, "The Radical Programme," *Con. Rev.* 50 (1886): 265–66; cf. Harrison's similar treatment of Positivist princples in *Order and Progress* (London, 1875), esp. pp. 39–43, where he further minimizes the authoritarian character of Comte's teaching and insists that Comte, like Mill, made practical expediency the only binding rule of political policy.

57. Thus Harrison wrote to Congreve that the real business of Positivists was "to work for the spread of Positivist conceptions and Positivist life and leave the formation of a formal church . . . to the spontaneous result of . . . a society finding itself permeated with the same sentiments and faith" (10 March 1872, Congreve Papers, BM 45228). Cf. Bridges to Congreve, in Simon, "Comte's English Disciples," *Vic. Stud.*, pp. 163–64, and Mill to d'Eichthal, 9 Feb. 1830, in Mineka, *Earlier Letters*, 1:47–48.

with Comte's doctrine because they saw it as the most powerful instrument of social and moral "improvement" then available. Thus it is significant that they accepted most fully the aspects of that doctrine with which Mill was also most sympathetic and tended to explain away the parts to which he objected. Such a tendency was particularly clear in Bridges's ingenious attempt (in which Harrison and Beesly concurred) to prove that Mill really agreed with Comte, as *they* interpreted Comte, on all essential points, and was thus, in reality, an "incomplete Positivist." [58] Bridges argued that Mill, by his own admission, accepted the chief intellectual foundations of Positivism (the law of the three stages and the hierarchy of sciences—though the latter with modifications), plus the desirability and validity of the Religion of Humanity, the validity of altruism as the supreme moral ideal and the necessity of strengthening it systematically against the selfish passions, the value of training men in habits of socialization and ascetic self-discipline, the necessity of reorganizing the property system on a moral basis, the elimination of an idle and unproductive rich class (a very radical interpretation of Comte), and the organization of intellectual resources to at least the extent of censuring their waste. Of these eight points, Mill probably disagreed only with the last; and he was really of two minds about it. Therefore, the Positivists seem to have been justified in stressing the closeness of their position to Mill's, and in reducing the differences between them to matters of emphasis and detail: "You value not less highly than ourselves ideal nobleness of life," Bridges wrote to Mill. The testimonial gains added weight from the fact that both understood "nobleness" in the same sense.

> We, too, feel no less strongly than you that individual excellence must be the test of a right social system; that the ideal state is that in which the individual develops his powers in the fullest and most fruitful way; that government without freedom, [and] systematization without original thought and

58. See J. H. Bridges, *The Unity of Comte's Life and Doctrine* (London, 1866). Harrison's "concurrence" is in *Tennyson, Ruskin, Mill,* p. 299. For the distinction between "complete" and "incomplete" Positivists, see Royden Harrison, "Prof. Beesly and the English Working-class Movement," in Briggs and Saville, eds., *Essays in Labour History* (London, 1960), pp. 206–07.

effort . . . are vanity of vanities. . . . But the restoration of
social and individual energy is to be sought [not merely in
libertarian negations, but] . . . in obedience . . . to Law [which
is] the primary condition of freedom.[59]

The chief source of their disagreement with Mill, then, stemmed
from the fact that the Positivists, like most Victorians, identified
him primarily with the essay *On Liberty*. Hence their conclusion
that Mill did not recognize law as the foundation of freedom
(which was scarcely true), and the difficulties of attempts by Positivists to explicate the differences between their views and Mill's.
Thus Harrison wrote that "Mill was (in theory) an Individualist,
whilst Comte was (philosophically speaking) a Socialist. . . . Both
aimed at combining liberty with duty. But Mill would put liberty
first: Comte . . . duty." [60] Bridges concluded his tract on Mill by
noting that "there are two inseparable aspects of the social problem: union of efforts and individuality of efforts. The first is for us,
in the present generation, . . . the more important," and he implied that individuality alone was important to Mill.[61] A more
balanced view of Mill's social philosophy, however, might have
suggested that he was no less a Socialist, "philosophically speaking," than Comte, and that his enthusiasm for the values of association was, in fact, considerably stronger. The crux of the diffi-
culty lay in the fact that Mill saw Comte not merely as valuing
liberty less than himself, but as disregarding it altogether, whereas
the Harrison Positivists read into Comte's writing adequate
guarantees of personal liberty, but imagined that Mill was prepared to jettison all other social values in its name. The curious
result is that the English Positivists' reading of Comte closely approximated the real character of Mill's social faith.

Thus it becomes exceedingly difficult to find the true measure
of the Harrisonian Positivists' agreement with Mill; for it is certain that they agreed with him more closely than they realized,

59. Bridges, *Unity*, pp. 50–52, esp. p. 51. The choice of "essential points" in
Comte's doctrine indicates a clear bias.

60. Harrison, *Tennyson, Ruskin, Mill*, p. 300.

61. Bridges, *Unity*, p. 51; but compare Mill's views in "Centralisation," *Edin.
Rev.* 115, pp. 331–33, stressing the positive role of government in the improvement
of society.

particularly on social and economic issues. Like Mill, they made social utility the sole basis of right; their idea of a "moralized" and ideally just property system closely resembled his notion of the most desirable arrangement for the foreseeable future. Unlike Mill, the Positivists did not accept cooperative production and exchange as the ultimate economic goal, but they did at least accept the idea of Socialism in a "moral and religious" sense. Since they held that joint ownership and administration of productive property were inherently impracticable, they sought to accomplish the aims of Socialism through a "moral equivalent": "moralising" the capitalists through the power of public opinion, and thus gradually superceding competition by social sentiment as the chief inducement to productivity.[62] Such a solution to the problem of industrial organization was close in spirit to Mill's social teaching. and from an "orthodox" point of view, had the added advantage of retaining the system of property to which the laws of classical economics were appropriate.

Indeed, the English Positivists were great admirers of the economic theories of Mill, to whom, as Harrison proclaimed, "England largely owes her true conception of social laws." This lauditory view, however, was complicated by the fact that Positivists were supposed to reject classical economics as a "metaphysical" system that was based on an "abstract" view of man, on competition as the sole basis of human relations, and on the divorce of economic from other social functions. But, Harrison insisted, "Mill is not an economist [in the derogatory sense], but a social philosopher; and his Political Economy is simply a branch of his general system of Society," formed in accordance with his basic moral principles. His ideal system of property "would rest on social and moral changes vaster than those which separate the middle ages from ourselves." It was precisely Mill's emphasis on the transitory nature of existing economic arrangements and on the infinite modifiability of economic "laws"—points that did in

---

62. See Harrison, "Moral and Religious Socialism," in *National and Social Problems* (London, 1908), and for criticism of cooperation, "Industrial Co-operation," in ibid. Comte also held that Positivism adopted the essential moral and social values of Socialism and did so in a manner more compatible with individual liberty than Socialism itself (*General View of Positivism*, pp. 173 ff.) .

fact reflect the Positivist view of relativism and social progress—
that Harrison found most impressive. By popularizing these aspects of Mill's economic thought and emphasizing their implied
demand for social reconstruction, the English Positivists showed
their own affinity for Mill's views and helped to form a climate of
opinion that was more favorable to the idea of social reconstruction.[63]

Of all the Radical intellectuals who were close to Mill in spirit,
the English Positivists best understood and interpreted his desire
for social transformation and the radical, world-reforming implications of his social thought. Like Mill they saw that great changes
in the existing economic system were necessary, and they were
willing to work as agitators in order to bring them about. In this
they differed markedly from the rather timid economists who
were commonly thought to have been Mill's successors—the epi-
gones of the pure classical system, Cairnes, Courtney, and Fawcett.[64] The Harrisonian Positivists, in contrast, were the most vigorous advocates of Radical collectivism before the 1880s and were
practically its only defenders on a systematic basis. Thus Frederic
Harrison, in one of his most striking passages, urged workingmen
to "fear not over-legislation," because the tendency of the times
was to give them too little of it, but rather to "look to the State"
for redress of their grievances as a class.[65]

Finally, the English Positivists acted for more than a decade as
the chief advisers to the trade union movement and took a leading
part in the early agitation for free schools, for public construction of

63. Harrison, "The Limits of Political Economy," *Fort. Rev.* 1 (1865), reprinted
in *National and Social Problems*, pp. 288–89, 279. Cf. his contention that "all reasonable social inquiry now proceeds on the ground that the social state requires
much improvement" (ibid., p. 290).

64. For brief sketches of their positions, see T. W. Hutchison, *A Review of
Economic Doctrines: 1870–1929* (Oxford, 1953), chap. 1. All three were exponents
of rigid individualism, tempered only by a cautious approval of industrial cooperation.

65. Harrison, *Order and Progress*, p. 226. Noel Annan, *Leslie Stephen* (Cambridge, Mass., 1952), p. 204 n., calls this "the one political treatise of the period
(other than the works of the English pre-Marxists) which challenges *laissez-faire*
economics and argues that the duty of the State is to promote a moral society even
if this leads to State interference"—a judgment substantially true, although it
exaggerates the book's uniqueness.

artisans' dwellings, and for more stringent factory acts—all causes that Mill had supported and would support more vigorously at the end of his life. And they pursued all these interests within a context of organized Radical politics.[66]

In summary, then, what can be concluded regarding Mill's influence on English Positivism? Apart from certain economic doctrines there seem to be no clear and direct lines of influence. If the leading English Positivists interpreted Comte in the light of liberal and Radical values that were also characteristic of Mill, this can be safely ascribed only to the fact that such ideas were "in the air" and enjoyed an intellectual vogue during the formative period of the Positivists' intellectual careers. Yet Mill himself was the person most responsible for giving such ideas their vogue, "as high priest or 'rabbi' of the new Victorian [university] intelligentsia"; and none of the English Positivists escaped that influence. As John Morley, himself almost a Positivist, wrote in 1873, "For twenty years no one at all open to serious impressions has left Oxford without undergoing the influence of Mr Mill." The leading English Positivists were Oxford men and ardent Radicals, and perhaps that is all that need be said.[67]

Yet one further connecting link remains between Mill and English Positivists: all were involved deeply with the "New Radicalism" of the seventies. The intellectual leaders of this movement, Dilke and Morley, were deeply influenced by Positivism and worked frequently in tandem with Harrison. Their connections with Mill, which also were very close, will be discussed in the following section. For the present, it will be sufficient to note that Mill's support for advanced social policies, such as those mentioned above that link him most clearly with both the "New Radi-

66. For the social and political work of English Positivists, see Royden Harrison, "Beesly and the Working Class," pp. 205–41, and his *Before the Socialists* (London, 1965), pp. 251 ff.

67. John Vincent, *The Formation of the British Liberal Party* (New York, 1967), p. 151, and John Morley, "The Death of Mr. Mill," *Fort. Rev.* (1873), reprinted in Morley, *Critical Miscellanies*, 4 vols. (London, 1892–94), 3:39. Harrison, in particular, had been an ardent follower of John Bright and had written appreciatively of Mill's work in his younger days: letters from Harrison to Beesly in the 1850s (esp. 15 Nov. 1857, Harrison Papers, BLPES); also Harrison, *Autobiographic Memoirs*, 2 vols. (London, 1911), 1:110 ff.

cals" of the seventies and the English Positivists as social agitators, were chiefly in evidence during the last five or ten years of his life. Before the middle sixties, Mill had taken no part in any popular agitation. But after 1865, when almost unwillingly he was elected to Parliament for Westminster, his practical opinions and his degree of involvement in worldly affairs underwent a rapid trans-formation. As Sir Charles Dilke, one of his closest associates during those years, noted, Mill "passed from Whiggism in youth to an extreme Radicalism . . . which was of a comparatively recent date." And the greatest share of his influence over the young Radicals of the seventies derived precisely from the leftward swing of his opinions during the last years of his life. All the residual "Whig-gishness" that had marked his political thought during the decade before 1866 finally vanished when Mill "found himself face-to-face with the obstructive realities of British politics." His opinions became "semi-Socialist" in the sense of favoring state interference, and he took up active agitation in their behalf.[68]

If true, these statements are of the greatest importance, indicat-ing that in his last years Mill was at the head of the movement from Radicalism to Socialism. Thus it only remains to evaluate them in more detail, and to ask to what extent such opinions and activities enabled Mill to influence the course of Radical politics —especially its tendency to veer toward Radical collectivism— during the subsequent two decades.

4. Land Reform and the New Radicalism

Mill's relation to collectivism has been one of the most con-sistently misunderstood aspects of his thought. At one extreme, scholars have taken his confession of Socialist faith to refer to

68. [Sir Charles Dilke], obituary of J. S. Mill, *Atheneum* (17 May 1873), p. 627. The claim that Mill was "Whiggish" in his youth is certainly an exaggeration, but it seems a more appropriate designation for his political views in the early sixties, as seen in *Considerations on Representative Government* (London, 1861). Also, cf. Dilke, "John Stuart Mill, 1869–1873," *Cosmopolis* 5 (March 1897): 629–31: In his last years, Mill "was very far from being an Individualist, and was abreast of the most modern tendencies in a Socialist direction . . . [and] the change carried him from one camp into another." These claims have not received their due attention in any study of Mill.

collectivism and have tried to show that collectivist tendencies in Benthamism were carried to their logical conclusions by Mill. Similarly they have noted his "ostentatious relegation of economic liberalism to a question of mere expediency" in *On Liberty*.[69] At the other extreme, they have noted that Mill left intact in the last edition of *Political Economy* the section entitled *"Laisser-Faire, the General Rule,"* and, in spite of numerous exceptions, evidently thought it still desirable as a rule of thumb.[70] In fact, all Mill's theoretical discussions of the problem were, at best, indecisive. His own bias was plainly against state interference, except where a strong case for its expediency could be made out—which, of course, left the door wide open. It is more important, therefore, to ask the extent to which his opinions on and activities in support of practical issues during his last years reflected what Sir Charles Dilke described as "semi-Socialist views." Such a change in practical opinions is, after all, the thing of chief significance in cases where the underlying theory is vague enough to support a variety of interpretations.

The commonest nineteenth-century view of Mill, heavily colored by *On Liberty*, pictured him as an incarnation of abstract Individualism, economic as well as intellectual. Prior to 1866, he did little in a public way to rectify that view. Indeed, he was for so long a kind of intellectual recluse, indulging a "fugitive and cloistered virtue" in the elaboration of abstract principles, that he seemed to have lost touch with the social realities of his age. There was a strong streak of innocence—of high ideals unclouded by common experience—in his economic and political judgments of that period: in his vision of a free, competitive economy gradually transforming itself into congeries of producers' cooperatives, and of an intellectuals' parliament, wholly devoted to free expression of opinion, which would resolve all issues through the exercise

69. E.g., Brebner, "Laissez-Faire and State Intervention," *JEH*, supp. 8 (1948): 66–69. The quotation is from Vincent, *Formation*, p. 150 n.

70. *Political Economy*, bk. 5, chap. 2, sec. 7, in *Collected Works*, 3:944 ff. But Mill also made a fundamental distinction between "authoritative" [or coercive] and "non-authoritative" interference by the state, the latter being far more acceptable than the former (ibid., pp. 937–38). For a fuller discussion of this problem and its wider implications, see W. D. Grampp, *Economic Liberalism*, vol. 2, *The Classical View* (New York, 1965), pp. 125–40.

of disinterested reason. Nothing in the decade prior to 1866 served to arouse the latent radicalism in his temperament, or compelled him to measure issues by any other standard than that of sheer intellectual fitness. Such attitudes had bred a generation of disciples who were sheer doctrinaires, arguing economic and political issues in terms of fixed principles, of which the chief was an uncompromising individualism; and they were commonly taken to reflect Mill's own beliefs.[71]

After Mill entered Parliament in February 1866, however, all the fastidious "conservatism" that had characterized his opinions for the previous decade vanished within a year.[72] He adopted steadily more Radical and more democratic views, allied himself with working-class democrats and republicans, achieved some success as a mob orator and devoted the best energies of his last four years to organizing an agitation in favor of radical reform of the property and educational systems. The change was immediately apparent to his contemporaries. "His old friends and colleagues used to shake their heads and declare that he had been ruined by politics and was no longer the same man," Sir Charles Dilke noted, while Leslie Stephen, writing Mill's obituary, concluded that "he [had] swallowed the popular Radical creed wholesale and descended into the arena to fight for it."[73] The Tory papers, predictably, were even less restrained in their evaluations. Although exaggerated, charges such as these from Saturday Review (17 May 1873) did contain a core of truth:

> The most serious blot on Mr. Mill's political reputation is the support he gave to the subversive schemes of socialist agitators. . . . In his eagerness to realize his aspirations he allied himself with the most revolutionary clubs, bent on rapine

71. See Mill, *Representative Government* (1861), and his 1865 election address, in which he insisted that his "only object" in Parliament would be "to promote my special opinions" (Mill to his election committee, March 1865, quoted in Packe, *Life of JSM*, p. 447). cf. Vincent, *Formation*, pp. 152, 154.

72. "Through all my lifetime, . . . in every real pinch Radicals have had to do duty as Conservatives," Mill wrote to Prof. Fawcett, 5 Feb. 1860 (*Later Letters*, p. 62), urging a "conservative" stand in opposition to "American-style democracy."

73. Dilke, "JSM, 1869–73," p. 630; [Leslie Stephen] obituary of Mill, *Nation* (15 May, 1873).

and spoliation. . . . It was in the highest degree encouraging to discover that the austere philosopher could arrive at the same conclusions as [those taught by] the unsophisticated appetites of human nature.

Mill's initiation into the "obstructive realities" of politics was performed chiefly by the great spokesman for the propertied interest in the House of Commons, Robert Lowe,[74] supported by the ranks of Whig and Tory backbenchers, who vividly brought home to Mill the vast, reactionary power still wielded by the landed class. The latter, of course, was scarcely a new discovery for Mill. Even before entering Parliament he had gone out of his way to castigate the "grovelling superstition," still current "among the higher classes, . . . that human society exists for the sake of property in land." [75] But none of his previous experience had quite prepared him for the tactics used by Lowe, a man who professed strict Utilitarian principles but who approached economic and social problems in terms of a theory so rigid and simplistic that it cannot, in fairness, even be labeled Benthamite. In his view, economics formed a wholly "deductive science," admitting of no modifications—"a green oasis in the desert of political controversy"—whose whole teaching was summed up in the rule of laissez-faire. And he used that rule consistently to shore up the "grovelling superstition" of the propertied class, by arguing that "a man is at liberty to do as he likes with his own." [76]

These arguments permeated Lowe's speeches in the House of Commons and roused Mill to a peak of anger. For they represented

74. Subsequently Lord Sherbrooke and Chancellor of the Exchequer in Gladstone's first government. As leader of the "Cave of Adullam" he was the chief intellectual opponent of reform in 1866 and acted as spokesman for all the propertied interests.

75. Mill to Fawcett, 1 Jan. 1866 (*Later Letters*, p. 1130) .

76. Lowe, speech in House of Commons, 12 March 1868, *Hansard's Parliamentary Debates*, 3d series, 191:1493 (hereafter cited as 3 *Hansard*) and Lowe, address in honor of Adam Smith, in *Revised Report of the Proceedings . . . 31 May, 1876* (London, 1876), pp. 7–21, for his view of political economy as an elaboration of laissez-faire. Although this view was rejected by most professional economists it was widely accepted among politicians and in the press. See, e.g., Gladstone's remarks at the same meeting, deploring the "unwise and unnecessary extensions of the functions of government" (p. 41) that characterized current politics.

precisely the kind of crass, selfish vulgarization of social theory that he had always sought to combat in his economic writings. The result was that in 1868 he began a virtual crusade against the *"Laisser-Faire* principle" and the obstructive uses to which it was being put. Even in the previous year he had begun to comment on the need to work for "the emancipation of political economy—its liberation from . . . doctrines of the old school (now taken up by well to do people), which treat what they call economical laws . . . as if they were laws of inanimate matter." [77] Now the sinister quality of that tendency was made manifest. In the eyes of Lowe and his fellow doctrinaires, Mill stormed in rebuttal, "Political Economy seems to exist as a bar even to consideration of anything that is proposed for the benefit of the economic condition of the people in anything but the old ways." Thus their superstitious belief in the "sacredness of private property" probably prevented most gentlemen from even considering any plans for overcoming destitution. Finally, with regard to the supposed law of laissez-faire, Mill concluded that economic science does not contain "a single practical rule that must be applicable to all cases." [78] In fact, the only rule governing the use of property is that it must serve the public welfare; thus, so long as just compensation is awarded, Mill contended, "society is fully entitled to abrogate or alter any particular right of property which . . . it judges to stand in the way of public good." [79]

Although there was nothing novel about such arguments from a theoretical point of view, they were evidently novel to most of Mill's audience in Parliament, and that fact must have given redoubled force to his belief that it was necessary to "emancipate political economy" from its association with laissez-faire. Thus it was scarcely coincidental that within two years his closest economic ally, J. E. Cairnes, in an important and much publicized public lecture, insisted bluntly that "the maxim of *laissez-faire* has no scientific basis whatsoever," and when allowed to obstruct useful reforms became simply a "public nuisance"—especially in the

77. Mill to Thornton, 19 Oct. 1867 (*Later Letters*, p. 1320).

78. Mill, speech in the House of Commons, 12 March 1868, in 3 *Hansard*, 190: 1525, 1526.

79. "Chapters on Socialism," in *Essays on Economics and Society*, p. 753. It was written in 1869, forming a sequel to the arguments cited above.

case of landed property, where "State control of private enterprise
. . . is indispensable, at least at certain stages of social progress."[80]

Nevertheless, it was Mill rather than Cairnes who proved most
willing to put such principles into practice by agitating for essential social reforms. He had already asserted, as a corollary to
his denial of laissez-faire that the state must be free to take "the
initiative in social progress" wherever public welfare demanded
it.[81] And as early as 1866 he had proclaimed in the House that the
"mere repeal of bad laws," which was all that Parliament had
hitherto accomplished, would not be sufficient to avert catastrophe
in the future:

> Are there not all the miseries of an old and crowded society
> waiting to be dealt with—the curse of ignorance, the curse of
> poverty, the curse of pauperism, the curse of disease, and the
> curse of a whole population bred and nurtured in crime? All
> these things we are just [now] beginning to look at. . . . By
> the time two or three more generations are dead and gone
> we may, perhaps, have discovered how to make their lives
> worth living.

And that work, although hitherto ignored by Parliament, was
precisely "the most important part of the function of government." [82] Or, as he stated the matter elsewhere, "We are looking
to [Parliament] for a general revision of our institutions," and for
initiating an effort "against the many remediable evils which
still infest the existing state of society." He was looking particularly
for those evils which applied to the land, education, and the
living conditions of labor.[83]

80. J. E. Cairnes, "Inagural Lecture," delivered at University College, London,
January 1870, reprinted in *Fort. Rev.* 9 n.s. (July 1871): 86; and "Political Economy and Land," *Fort. Rev.* 8 n.s. (Jan. 1870): 42. Early in 1870 Cairnes also moved
to Blackheath so as to keep in closer contact with Mill in their joint endeavors.

81. *Comte and Positivism* (1865), p. 78; but Mill's denial that laissez-faire formed
a binding rule was qualified by the conclusion that it would be nearer the truth
than its opposite "19 out of 20 times."

82. Mill, speech in House of Commons, 13 April 1866, 3 *Hansard* 182:1262; also
his speech calling for "more administration" to deal with such problems, 5 May
1868.

83. Mill to T. Beggs, 27 Sept. 1868 (*Later Letters*, p. 1450); and "An Interview
with John Stuart Mill," *Chicago Tribune* (15 March 1868).

These pronouncements have particular importance for the present study because they virtually laid the foundations for the New Radicalism of the 1870s and 1880s—both its special concern with land reform and education, and its general concern with social amelioration. But Mill's speech in favor of reform also highlighted another aspect of his approach to the problem of social reconstruction that was to have its analogue in subsequent decades: his belief in the possibility of social revolution, and in the necessity of forestalling it by serious measures of social reform. As early as 1866 he had noted that the "notions, right or wrong, which are fomenting in the minds of the working classes . . . go deep down into the foundations of society and government," [84] creating a great uncertainty about "the prospects of society for a generation or two to come." Of such ideas, however, only those relating to the land system might "possibly become dangerous" in the near future.[85] Following his defeat in the General Election of 1868, therefore, he determined to devote a large portion of his time and energy to building up an organization devoted to land reform on lines as radical as the current state of public opinion would allow.

Because Mill's Land Tenure Reform Association has been widely misunderstood as an orthodox liberal body, bent only on securing the middle-class goal of "free trade in land," it will be worthwhile to analyze its development at greater length. For it was Mill's dearest wish to include in that organization the more "intelligent" members of the working class in an alliance with middle-class Radicals, so that by necessary measures of compromise, the best interests of both groups would be served. Thus Mill sought to demonstrate that even the abolition of primogeniture and entails ("free land") would benefit workingmen by making land cheaper and more readily obtainable for their own housing. And it would also be a first step toward more radical and extensive land reforms in the future.[86]

84. Speech, House of Commons, 13 April 1866, 3 *Hansard*, 182:1262.
85. Mill to C. L. Brace, 21 Sept. 1871, and to C. E. Norton, 24 Sept. 1868 (*Later Letters*, pp. 1837, 1442).
86. *Programme of the Land Tenure Reform Association, with an Explanatory Statement by John Stuart Mill, Esq.* (London, 1871) (hereafter cited as *LTRA Programme*), also in *Essays on Economics and Society*, pp. 689–95.

These ambitions necessarily involved a delicate balancing of alternatives—an elaborate web of compromise and accommodation, from which it becomes difficult to extract Mill's personal opinions. From the beginning, however, he conceded to the working-class leaders that land nationalization was justified "on principle," although a number of considerations made it inexpedient at that time.

> I think it will be a generation or two before the progress of public intelligence and morality will permit so great a concern [as the land] to be entrusted to public authorities . . . without a perfectly intolerable amount of jobbing. . . . while if the [LTRA] . . . were to adopt [outright nationalization as its purpose] . . . it could not hope for any support except from a portion of the working classes.[87]

The latter occurrence was scarcely what Mill had in mind. Nevertheless, he sought to retain the support of working-class leaders with proclamations that "the country belongs, . . . in principle, to the whole of its inhabitants," and even that "those countries are fortunate—or would be so if decently governed—in which the land has not become permanent property of individuals and the state is consequently sole landlord." But as things stood, he concluded, "the [public] administration of waste lands is as much . . . as we are presently equal to."[88]

Thereafter, the public appropriation and administration of waste or unused lands became the established toehold of land nationalization in advanced Radical programs. And the "socialistic" implications of that measure were made clearer by Mill's

87. Mill to C. E. Norton, 24 Sept. 1868, to A. Campbell, 28 Feb. 1870, and to A. Reid, 5 Oct. 1869 (*Later Letters*, pp. 1442, 1702, 1644)—letters regarding, not *to*, workingmen. For a recent discussion of Mill's position between the older liberalism of his LTRA stalwarts and the more radical demands of the working-class Land and Labour League, see E. Eldon Barry, *Nationalisation in British Politics* (Stanford, Calif., 1965), pp. 50–52.

88. *LTRA Programme,* and speeches reprinted from the *Examiner,* 11 Jan. 1873, in H.R.F.B., ed., *John Stuart Mill, Notices of his Life and Work* (London, 1873), p. 73. Such statements enabled the LTRA to win the support of virtually all Radical land reformers except the most extreme believers in nationalization. See Barry, *Nationalisation,* p. 51.

insistence that such lands should then be used for cooperative experiments or for the construction of public housing, rather than for individual allotments in the old manner.[89] Indeed, Mill took almost every opportunity short of endorsing outright land nationalization to affirm the public and "social" character of land and to keep as much of it as possible in public or quasi-public hands:

> The appropriation of the land of the country by private individuals and families has gone far enough; [now] . . . a determined resistance should be made to any further extension of it . . . [especially] to any conversion of what is still a kind of public property [including commons, corporate and charitable holdings] into private.[90]

It was not Mill, however, but his new "disciple," Sir Charles Dilke, a fledgling M.P. only recently converted to the validity of public land ownership, who gave such arguments their effective cutting edge. "Free land" was useless, he insisted, unless it was balanced by increased state intervention and "control" of the land. "Of what good is it merely to sell the land . . . [unless it serves to promote] the extension of landholding among the many?" And he outlined a scheme of small holdings under state patronage and control that was very like the nucleus of Joseph Chamberlain's "Unauthorised Programme" in 1885. By the latter date, of course, it no longer seemed a "socialistic" measure, since its aim—creating a new race of "independent yeomanry"—was obviously individualist. But the scheme remained an important link in the chain of Radical collectivism because it called on the power of the state to bring about a major change in the system of property ownership, and because, in the minds of such proponents as Dilke, it was conceived as a great step forward for "state interference" and an affirmation of the public character of land.[91]

89. Dilke, "JSM, 1869-73," *Cosmopolis* 5, p. 635, and Mill to Dilke, 25 Oct. 1871 (Dilke Papers, BM 43987, no. 34, and in *Later Letters*, pp. 1844-45) .

90. Mill, speech, 11 Jan. 1873, in *Notices of His Life and Work*, p. 73; cf. report of speech at Exeter Hall, 18 March 1873, in *Times*, (London), 19 March, 1873. (London *Times* hereafter referred to as the *Times*.)

91. Speech of Sir Charles Dilke, *LTRA Programme*. (These proposals were subsequently incorporated into Dilke's Public Lands Bill, 1871, which called for con-

Mill, on the other hand, was more anxious to stress the role of municipalities than that of the state—an idea that stemmed from the older Radical tradition, with its hostility to "Old Corruption" but frequent willingness to entrust large measures to town councils, whose members were solid, middle-class men.[92] Thus Mill was willing to support quite extensive "municipal trading" on the ground that public activity at the local level more effectively stimulated initiative and responsibility among the people. Wherever utilities and services formed "practical monopolies," he was an advocate of their municipal ownership.[93] And one of his most significant parliamentary acts was the first bill to create a comprehensive local government for London, a "central, federal, municipal administration" with power to manage public utilities, working-class housing, "and the hundred similar arrangements which are now required at the hand of government." [94]

Thus it was only appropriate that Mill directed much of his land reform activity to increasing the scope of municipal land ownership and regulation, including the all-important power to tax the land for public purposes. In support of such demands he made use of the very words and imagery that Henry George would subsequently employ:

> If the Grosvenor, Portman and Portland estates belonged to the municipality of London, the gigantic incomes of those estates would probably suffice for the whole expense of the local government of the capital. But those gigantic incomes

solidation and administration of all public and quasi-public lands under state control.) Mill ultimately endorsed the use of such state power with the plea that "there is nothing a government can do that does not look frightfully difficult until we consider how many more difficult things a government does already" (speech at Essex Hall, quoted in *Times,* 19 March 1873).

92. Regarding the growth of Radical collectivism in town governments, see A. Temple Patterson, *Radical Leicester* (London, 1954); R. A. Church, *Economic and Social Change in a Midland Town: Victorian Nottingham* (London, 1966), chap. 7, esp. p. 205; and Geoffrey Best, *Mid-Victorian Britain* (London, 1971), pp. 42 ff.

93. *Public Agency vs. Trading Companies.* (For full citation and discussion, see n. 11, above.)

94. Speeches, House of Commons, 21 May 1867 and 5 May 1868, in 3 *Hansard,* 187:883 and 191:1859.

are still swelling; by growth of London they may again be doubled. . . . [Why should] this increase of wealth, produced by other peoples' labour and enterprise . . . *fall into their mouths while they sleep,* instead of being applied to the public necessity of those who created it? [95]

In principle, therefore, Mill asserted "the right of taking all rent for public purposes"—a moral claim on behalf of society to the "whole value" of the land. In practice, however, he held such claims to be inexpedient, and limited his actual demands to appropriation of the "unearned increment" of rental value, which represented the amount of its increase after a certain date, solely due to the pressures of population and without any exertion by the owner.[96]

Again, there was nothing fundamentally new in such arguments. They had formed a part of Mill's *Political Economy* since 1848, following logically from his Lockean theory of private property and from the argument that "no man made the land." [97] But they were also ignored by the public at large, along with practically all Mill's "socialistic" proposals, until the Land Tenure Reform Association made them a part of current political controversy and gave them serious newspaper coverage. Then they began to form a part of the new Radical tradition that was taking shape in the early seventies.

Although from a financial point of view Mill's proposals were very moderate—hedged about with careful qualifications to protect the landlord—in principle they were far more radical, treating the land as a public trust that was held by landlords only for reasons of expedience.[98] Indeed, some of his arguments were even

95. Mill, "Advice to Land Reformers," *Examiner,* 4 Jan. 1873 (reprinted in *Dissertations and Discussions,* 5 vols. [New York, 1875], 5:265), emphasis added. The italicized phrase was a favorite of Henry George's.

96. Mill in *Examiner,* 19 July 1873. These arguments formed the basis of Henry George's theories, which are discussed in chap. 3 below.

97. *Political Economy,* bk. 5, chap. 2, sec. 5–6, in *Collected Works,* 3:819–22. Mill held that, properly speaking, the function of property was to guarantee to every man the fruits of his own labor; thus where property served to guarantee income without such labor it was morally unjustifiable. This was, of course, the basis for most Socialist arguments based on the ground of justice.

98. Even by implication, however, Mill did not extend such theories beyond the land, whereas Positivists applied them to capital as well: a fact of much significance for the development of Socialism. (See chap. 6 below.)

based on the premise that property was theft, or had been so in the past, although it was not now expedient to treat it as such.[99] Moreover, the idea of "special taxation" of land values could lead to far more dramatic consequences when employed by reformers of a bolder temperament than Mill. Thus Mill and his association directly prepared the way for Henry George's land campaigns of the eighties, not only by providing the theories upon which they were based but also by starting an organized land agitation under middle-class Radical auspices of which George's, a decade later, was really a continuation. If the flame of that agitation died with Mill himself in 1873, however, the coals continued to burn slowly until they were again fanned to a blaze by the excitement of the early eighties.

Yet land reform was not Mill's only contribution to the growth of Radical collectivism. He also urged the levying of heavy death duties on property, graduated and differentiated income tax, and publicly subsidized workman's housing. These, in turn, became the favorite panaceas of the "New Radicals" in the eighties. Finally, Mill also joined actively in the agitation for a national system of free, compulsory, and secular education, which was the earliest rallying cry of the New Radicals and formed a sharp departure from his earlier, more timid opinions in *On Liberty*.[100]

In a certain sense, Mill had always supported a "national system" of education, but even in the late sixties he had mistrusted "Old Corruption" sufficiently to repudiate compulsory education provided entirely by the government. He thought that parents, when able, should be made to bear at least a part of the cost as individuals.[101] He was partly reconciled to government control, however, by the arrangements for locally elected school boards— another evidence of his preference for collectivism at the municipal level—and he eventually came to accept the idea of completely free and compulsory education, "much to the consternation of his

99. Mill, in *Examiner*, 14 Jan. 1873 (reprinted in *Dissertations and Discussions*, 5:264).

100. Regarding taxation, see *Political Economy*, bk. 5, chap. 2, esp. sec. 3–4, in *Collected Works*, 3:809–19; regarding artisans' housing, cf. *Later Letters*, p. 1155; regarding publicly provided education, see *Political Economy* bk. 5, chap. 2, sec. 8, in *Collected Works*, 3:949.

101. Mill to Fawcett, 24 Oct. 1869, and to Rev. L. J. Bernays, 8 Jan. 1868, (*Later Letters*, pp. 1658, 1347–48; also Mill to Dilke, 28 Feb. 1870, ibid., pp. 1702–03).

old disciples," as an aspect of the larger struggle for a comprehensive and secular system of public schools. The latter was, in fact, the special program of the London Branch of the National Education League, whose president, Sir Charles Dilke, was probably responsible for winning Mill's support for free public education.[102] Such, then, were the issues on which Mill's opinions became "semi-Socialist," and on which, according to Dilke, he broke away from his individualist disciples and led the arguments against them at the Radical Club and the Political Economy Club, until death cut short his mental evolution.[103]

These opinions, and Mill's willingness to propagate them actively, put him at the head of a new body of Radical opinion—that of the younger generation of Radical intellectuals in the seventies, led by Dilke and Morley, in close association with the Harrisonian Positivists and with the Radical politics of the South Midlands, under the leadership of Joseph Chamberlain.[104] The distinctive feature of that New Radicalism was precisely its interest in social, rather than merely political, reform, involving the premise that government had an active responsibility to promote

102. Dilke, "JSM, 1869–73," pp. 632–35, corroborated by Dilke, MS lecture, 16 Nov. 1873, in Dilke Papers, BM 43943, f. 132; and *Speech by J. S. Mill, Esq. at the National Education League Meeting*, St. James's Hall, 25 March 1870 (London, 1870). Dilke also reported that Mill joined the London Branch of the League and gave it full support in its fight against the official Liberal bill that called for subsidizing denominational schools ("JSM, 1869–73," pp. 632–35).

103. Dilke, "JSM, 1869–73," pp. 640–41. Evidence in Political Economy Club, *Minutes, Members, Attendance, Questions, 1821–1882* (London, 1882) is indecisive. Mill debated his favorite proposition regarding "unearned increment" on 2 Feb. 1872. Other propositions of similar character—public land management, public ownership of mineral rights—were debated in his presence. Unfortunately, no quotations are given from the debates.

104. The only adequate studies of this development are biographies: J. L. Garvin, *The Life of Joseph Chamberlain, 1836–1885* (London, 1932); Peter Fraser, *Joseph Chamberlain: Radicalism and Empire, 1868–1914* (New York, 1966); F. W. Hirst, *The Early Life and Letters of John Morley*, 2 vols. (London, 1927). The official *Life* of Dilke, by Gwyn and Tuckwell has been cited, but cf. Roy Jenkins, *Sir Charles Dilke: A Victorian Tragedy* (London, 1958), recently transformed into a Broadway hit, under the title, "The Right Hon. Gentlemen." These three politicians plus Harrison, who, as yet, has no biography, were close friends and collaborators in the late seventies and eighties. For their collaboration with the English Positivists, see R. Harrison, *Before the Socialists*, pp. 299 ff.

social improvement.[105] That Mill was associated with this movement in its early stages on terms of political intimacy with its intellectual leaders, and that he subsequently became its patron saint were, therefore, facts of no small importance. The land, education, and tax reform programs that he sponsored, and, above all, the demand for appropriating "unearned increments" of land value that was his special passion, formed the real cutting edge of the New Radical agitation in the eighties, passing over into subsequent Socialist programs, where they remained enshrined for many years. And though the leading points of the New Radical program—"Free Land, Free Schools, Free Labour, and Free Churches"—were not (except for free schools) subsequently advocated by English Socialists, they too helped to promote the new birth of Socialism in the eighties by creating a climate of opinion that was more favorable to collectivism and to the idea of government initiative. Finally, the New Radicalism helped to stimulate the resurgence of social conscience in the early 1880s that formed the chief seedbed of Socialist convictions in that decade.

105. On the "New Radicalism" of the 1880s, see Garvin, *Chamberlain, 1836–1885,* pp. 147 ff., and Chaps. 3 and 7 below.

3

Origins of the English Socialist Revival: Land Reform and the Social-Democratic Federation

At least for purposes of intellectual history, the English Socialist "revival" of the 1880s may be said to have begun in the January 1881 lead article of *Nineteenth Century*—the most prestigious English liberal review—which informed its startled readers that "the dawn of a revolutionary epoch" was at hand:

> Never, perhaps, has the certainty of approaching trouble been more manifest than it is today. . . . For the questions now being discussed by hundreds of thousands on the Continent go to the very foundation of all social arrangements . . . and move vast masses of men to almost religious exasperation against their fellows. . . . [So] a large portion of the urban population are being . . . indoctrinated with notions that cannot be put into practice save at the expense of those above and around them.[1]

Incredulity and amazement must have been the typical reactions to that claim. For among readers of Victorian reviews, Socialism and proletarian revolt were thought to have vanished with the last Chartist uprising. Nor did any popular unrest appear to darken the domestic skies now that Chamberlain and his fellow Radicals had been safely drawn under the Gladstonian umbrella. So far as any eye could see—Ireland, of course, being excepted—all social currents appeared to flow quietly, and a continued harmony among all classes was the general expectation.

At the same time, the evidence of *economic* difficulties was becoming increasingly ominous. Even the London *Times* noted at

1. H. M. Hyndman, "The Dawn of a Revolutionary Epoch," *Nin. Cen.* 9 (Jan. 1881): 1–2. The last sentence reveals something of the author's ingrained social conservatism. For other discussions of the Socialist revival, see the Bibliographical Note.

the outset of the new decade that 1879 had "combined more circumstances of misfortune and depression than any other [year] within general experience." [2] In fact, it was the bottom of the first "trough" of what contemporaries called the "Great Depression": a phenomenon originating in British agriculture around 1873 which, by the late seventies, had spread to industry and trade, creating widespread (if erratic) unemployment and recurring gluts of unskilled labor. All forms of urban misery were thus intensified, increasing the distress that was already endemic among the urban poor.[3] Nor were such conditions much improved by the brief economic rally of the early eighties, for they lingered on in working-class districts, only to intensify as the depression itself, with its attendant increase in unemployment, revived and grew more virulent following 1884.[4]

But little of this was widely understood among the educated middle class—the real English ruling class—in January 1881. Indeed, so peculiar were the effects of the depression that many middle-class persons benefited from it. Thus the lead article of *Nineteenth Century* had to shock its Liberal and Radical readers into a vivid sense of injustice and social degradation—the

2. *Times*, 1 Jan. 1880, lead article.

3. For a discussion of "the Poor" as a distinct and presumably permanent class in Victorian society, see H. M. Lynd, *England in the Eighteen-Eighties* (New York, 1945), pp. 85 ff.

4. There is still no authoritative analysis of the Great Depression, and even its existence is now a subject of scholarly debate. For recent and comprehensive summaries of that debate, however, see Jones, *Christian Socialist Revival*, pp. 31–40, and S. B. Saul, *The Myth of the Great Depression, 1873–1896* (London, 1969), pp. 30 ff. (Both include extensive bibliographies.) The crux of the problem is that because the last quarter of the nineteenth century was a period of fairly steady economic expansion, with long-term reversals chiefly in agriculture, it cannot be considered a period of depression in the technical sense. Nevertheless, the name Great Depression, which was given to it by contemporaries, remains a conventional and useful way of calling attention to its recurrent social distress. Such distress rose to peaks of intensity at the low points of the trade cycle in 1879, 1886, and 1893—unemployment remaining at or above the unprecedented level of $7\frac{1}{2}$ percent throughout the middle eighties—but also subsided with the partial economic recoveries centering on 1882 and 1889–90. Despite the fact that working-class distress was sporadic and selective, however, it seemed no less real and painful to contemporaries on that account, and it was just such contemporary *consciousness* of distress, formed largely through journalism and heightened by protest demonstrations, that provided the most powerful stimulus to the English Socialist revival.

"crowded room, the dingy street, . . . the pleasureless existence [and] gradual deterioration of . . . [the poor man's] offspring"— and to dramatize the consequences of such conditions, now that the masses were being "educated to understand the disadvantages of their position," to "brood" on them, and "to right them." [5]

Yet the article was by no means a revolutionary tract. It was the work of a financial entrepreneur and free-lance journalist named H. M. Hyndman, a Tory Radical by inclination, sympathetic to Chartism and the continental struggles for national independence, who had just begun to view social crises in a new light as a result of reading Marx.[6] In 1881, however, his ideal was still a "conservatism which has come to be revolutionary," and the main thrust of his article was an appeal to England's ruling class to make concessions to the populace to stave off the threat of violence.[7] His tone throughout was patriotic, upper class, and imperialistic, looking to English traditions of fair play to "satisfy the legitimate claims of the many without trenching upon the rights *or privileges* of the few." Denouncing continental "fanatics of the new Socialist gospel," he urged that "society is not prepared to transcend all previous experience of human motives and rise at one bound to this lofty conception." In short, he favored gradualism and looked to English politicians to "lead the way with safety in the great social reorganization" that would ultimately "secure for all the same happiness and enjoyment of life that now belong to the few." [8]

1. Hyndman and the Socialist Revival

Such was the beginning of the English Socialist revival. From the first its ideology was largely Hyndman's handiwork. In a series of remarkable articles and books published between 1881 and

5. Hyndman, "Dawn of a Revolutionary Epoch," *Nin. Cen.* 9, p. 2.

6. See his autobiography, *The Record of an Adventurous Life* (London, 1917), and Chsushichi Tsuzuki, *H. M. Hyndman and British Socialism* (Oxford, 1961), the most recent and authoritative biography.

7. *The Text-Book of Democracy: England for All* (London, 1881), pp. 192, 31, and "Dawn of a Revolutionary Epoch." Both expound what may be called the "prophylactic theory" of Socialism: Socialism to prevent revolution.

8. "Dawn of a Revolutionary Epoch," pp. 12 (italics added), 4–5, 18, 15.

1884, he laid the foundation for its expansion and stated most of
its characteristic doctrines.[9] In particular he identified Socialism
with the growth of Radical collectivism, preached its gradual,
piecemeal extension by constitutional means, and appealed to the
educated middle class to take the lead in bringing it to fruition.
"If the [revolutionary] theories now gaining ground . . . are to be
met peacefully, and turned to the advantage of all," Hyndman
proclaimed, "the State, as the organized common-sense of public
opinion, must step in . . . to regulate the nominal individual freedom which simply strengthens the domination of the few." [10]
Happily, he noted, such a tendency was already at work in England, so that "whilst we are arguing about Communism . . . and
competition . . . we ourselves are slowing advancing, without perhaps observing it, towards the system [of state management] . . .
which, when proposed in all its bluntness, we denounce as a
chimera under the present circumstances of mankind." Thus, the
historic tendency of Radical legislation was toward Socialism. If
it were only strengthened and pushed forward vigorously under
enlightened leadership, therefore, the whole transition to social-
democracy could be peaceful and gradual—a further extension of
principles that were already accepted by the majority of English
people.[11]

Even in 1881 such arguments were no great novelty. The Radical tendency toward collectivism was widely recognized—though
chiefly by its opponents—and was popularly called Socialism.[12]
Even some spokesmen for the Radical Party used the word in that
sense. In 1881, for example, John Morley, definining Socialism as
"the exertion of the power of that state in its strongest form,

9. In addition to "Dawn of a Revolutionary Epoch," these included "Lights and
Shades of American Politics," *Fort. Rev.* 29 (March 1881) ; *England for All* (June
and Sept. 1881) ; *The Historical Basis of Socialism in England* (London, 1883) ;
and several pamphlets: *The Coming Revolution in England* (1883) , *The Social
Reconstruction of England* (1883) , and *The Revolution of To-day* (1884) .

10. *England for All,* p. 6.

11. "Dawn of a Revolutionary Epoch," pp. 12–13. Every extension of "State
rule" was thus a "stepping-stone to Socialism" (*Historical Basis,* p. 444) .

12. For contrasting treatments of this point, see John Rae, *Contemporary Socialism* (London, 1883) , p. 11, which deplored such usage, and the Rev. William
Cunningham, "The Progress of Socialism in England," *Con. Rev.* 34 (Jan. 1879) ,
which favored it.

definitely limiting in the interest of the labourer the administration of capital," concluded that in England, where "Socialism [had] been least discussed," its policies had been "most extensively applied." [13] Nor did he disapprove of such results, so long as every "socialistic" act served specifically to improve the education, health, or morals of the community in an area where individual initiative could not suffice.

To their detractors, of course, such advanced Radicals appeared to be propagating dangerous views. For example, a partisan "Dialogue on Political Optimism" in 1880 attributed to Morley the belief "that the political systems tend, in all progressive societies, towards socialistic democracy. . . . We feel, too, that nothing we can do can avert or long delay the consummation."[14] But in the context of current usage, the socialistic reforms advocated by the New Radicals implied no very fundamental changes in the social system. Morley and his allies were no more prepared than John Stuart Mill, their mentor, to advocate comprehensive state interference as the basis of economic organization. At most, they were convinced that the balance had tipped too far in the direction of "free administration of capital," creating an unhealthy social situation, and that it needed to be restored by means of additional legislation—factory acts, Irish land acts, artisans' dwellings acts—for the special benefit of labor.

This was also the doctrine of the English Positivists. "Fear not over-legislation," Frederic Harrison advised English workingmen, urging them to place their trust in the power of "the State."[15] But they were to do so precisely because the balance had been too long tipped in the opposite direction. For all his Positivism, Harrison was still a Liberal-Radical at heart, who believed in the power of public opinion to "moralize" and regenerate capitalism without any formal changes in the property system. Nor did Arnold Toynbee, in 1882, imply anything more drastic by his

13. John Morley, *Life of Richard Cobden* (London, 1881), pp. 203–04.
14. H. D. Traill, "A Dialogue on Political Optimism," *Nin. Cen.* 8 (Aug. 1880). Internal evidence indicates that the Radical protagonist, designated "M," is a caricature of Morley. Subsequently, the Tory *Saturday Review* also described Morley as "the principal leader of the revolutionary movement" (quoted in *Pall Mall Gazette*, 27 Oct. 1883).
15. Frederic Harrison, *Order and Progress* (London, 1875), p. 226.

declaration that, in sponsoring the Irish Land Act of 1881, "the Radicals have finally accepted . . . the fundamental principle of Socialism, that between men who are unequal in wealth there can be no freedom of contract." But "we have not abandoned our old belief in . . . self-help," he insisted, characteristically adding that such "interference must not diminish self-reliance. . . . Nothing must be done to weaken those habits of individual self-reliance and voluntary association that have built up the greatness of the English people." [16]

It was precisely in the lack of such qualifications, however, that Hyndman's appeal for social regeneration differed from those of the most advanced Radicals of the early eighties. For although the latter, following Mill and Cairnes, might recognize that laissez-faire no longer provided a reliable guide to economic policy, they were not yet prepared to abandon it in practice or to adopt its opposite.[17] For the time being, therefore, "orthodox" economics conspicuously lacked any "rational and discriminating theory of the proper limits of public authority." [18] But its bias, inherited from early Radical politics, remained opposed to any economic action by the state. Under the influence of Marx and of his recently acquired knowledge of American trusts, however, Hyndman broke free of such restrictive beliefs and, by the end of 1881, had developed a comprehensive argument in favor of collectivism that was based on the moral values of the English Radical tradition.

The latter point is especially important because vulgarized Marxism in England was so typically reformulated in moral terms. Surplus value, its "sole doctrine" (said by some English Marxists to have done for economics what natural selection did for biology),[19] exposed the immorality of capitalism and the exploita-

16. Arnold Toynbee, *Lectures on the Industrial Revolution of the Eighteenth Century* (1882), rev. ed. (London, 1908), pp. 223, 237.

17. Regarding Mill and Cairnes, see pp. 56–57 above. Free competition, of course, remained the ideal basis of their economics, and any interference with such freedom could only be justified as an exceptional policy.

18. Rae, *Contemporary Socialism*, p. 11.

19. John Rae, "Social Philosophy," *Con. Rev.* 45 (1884): 296; W. Graham, *Socialism, New and Old* (London, 1891), p. xxvi; and Edward Aveling, quoted in *Prac. Soc.* (Jan. 1887):11.

tion practiced by capitalists. Accordingly, the primary aim of Socialism, as Hyndman presented it, was to restrain "the selfishness of the capitalists and middle classes . . . in the interest of the people." But such restraint was necessary precisely because the laissez-faire policies characteristic of the Radical tradition were in conflict with its moral values: because "full individual freedom leads, under present economic conditions, to monopoly; that monopoly speedily develops into oppression and tyranny; and then the common sense of society as a whole must step in to correct the mischief" by appropriate legislation. Thus Hyndman reduced the contradictions of capitalism to English Radical terms and used them to undermine popular belief in the slogans of liberal economics:

> Private enterprise has been tried and found wanting: *laissez-faire* has had its day. Slowly the nation is learning that the old hack arguments of "supply and demand," [and] "freedom of contract" . . . are but so many bulwarks of vested interests. . . . [Consequently,] competition is being given up as a principle in favor of organisation for the common benefit.[20]

The crux of Hyndman's method was to state such anticapitalist arguments in the language of Radical polemics, so that capitalism stood indicted as a system of "monopoly" built upon special privilege—an approach well calculated to appeal to the sensibilities of advanced Radicals, from whose ranks the future Socialist converts were to come. In a similar fashion, Hyndman's positive arguments for collectivism followed the lines already laid down by such Radical politicians as Dilke and Morley, in their contention that "Socialism" was already widely practiced in England. As evidence of that tendency, Hyndman listed national postal and telegraph systems, municipal gas and water, public education, housing, paving, and lighting; and in all instances, he concluded, the results had been beneficial. Even the Poor Law and Board Schools were "Communistic in principle," while the free school

20. Hyndman, "Lights and Shades," p. 357; *England for All*, p. 4; "Dawn of a Revolutionary Epoch," p. 12.

lunches demanded by many London Radicals amounted to "Communism, pure and simple." [21]

In retrospect, his arguments appear almost Fabian in character —gradual, constitutional, and "practical;" and that quality extended even to Hyndman's proposed methods of social transformation. If the government adopted an eight-hour day and minimum wages for its employees, he urged, then the advantages of "State employment" would become so great that it might be "advantageously extended" from the post office and armament factories "to the wider fields of Railways, Shipping, the Land, and general production." What was done in the post office might be done equally well in any other business, and soon such an extension of state employment to all major industries would drive profit-squeezing capitalism from the field. [22] Alternatively, appropriate industries and public services might be taken over by local governing bodies, enabling rural councils (such as those proposed by Joseph Chamberlain) to own and manage agricultural land. Such exercise of power and initiative through local self-government would "give the working classes that impetus toward social improvement by their own energy which is so manifestly necessary," and would help to develop the moral and political resources needed to sustain a Socialist state. [23] "State management, which is practical enough within certain limits," would make possible a "peaceful" transition to Socialism, obviating demands for confiscation, with its attendant "anarchy and bloodshed." If the "rich and powerful" could only be induced to lead the way, the whole process would be accomplished smoothly, without strife or social dislocation. [24]

21. *Historical Basis,* p. 464, and "Dawn of a Revolutionary Epoch," pp. 12–13. Hyndman consistently used Communism rather than Socialism to mean "State and Municipal management" of industry.

22. Hyndman, *Historical Basis,* p. 464, and "The Radicals and Socialism," *Nin. Cen.* 18 (Nov. 1885): 837–38. There was also a Tory Radical precursor of those proposals in the program adopted by a joint committee of Tory politicians and working men in 1871, which demanded a great extension of public management of industry on the model of the post office. (See E. J. Feuchtwanger, *Disraelian Democracy and the Tory Party* (Oxford, 1968), pp. 92–93.)

23. Hyndman, *England for All,* pp. 100–01. Such emphasis on the moral benefits of democratic self-government closely parallels the theory developed by J. S. Mill in *Representative Government* (London, 1861).

24. Hyndman, "Dawn of a Revolutionary Epoch," p. 17; and *England for All,* p. 31.

2. *The Formation of the Democratic Federation*

Hyndman's arguments formed a kind of intellectual bridge between the New Radicalism of the seventies and the Radical Socialism developed by the Fabians and the Independent Labour Party in the later eighties and nineties—a bridge that is particularly important to the present study because the transition from individualist to collectivist economic assumptions always formed the most difficult stage in the acceptance of Radical Socialist theories. Yet Hyndman is not usually regarded as a pioneer of Fabian ideas. On the contrary, he is quite properly identified with a form of doctrinaire, revolutionary Marxism that never won a massive following in Britain. In fact, Hyndman moved virtually from one position to the other within two years of his first Socialist pronouncements (although he never entirely abandoned his belief in "constitutional" methods, even in his most "revolutionary" years). The reasons for that change are, doubtless, ultimately concealed in the man's enigmatic personality; but some impression of them may be obtained from an analysis of his efforts to found an English Socialist party between 1881 and 1884, and of the peculiar influence of his Tory Radical beliefs.

His original intention was to work through the Radical workingmen's clubs of London and to found, with their support, a "centre of organisation" for propagating more advanced Radical policies in "times of excitement." By such means he hoped to "permeate" all London Radicalism with socialistic aims—driving further those tendencies that had already been set in motion by the party of Chamberlain, Dilke, and Morley—just as the older Radicals had attempted to "permeate" Liberalism with democratic and egalitarian aims.[25] After several meetings with the leaders of Radical clubs and others interested in ultra-Radical politics, the Democratic Federation was founded, under Hyndman's chairmanship, in June 1881.

From its foundation the character of the Federation was de-

25. Cf. Sir Charles Dilke's claim that Radicals sought to "permeate" the Liberal Party as "a leaven in the liberal lump" (quoted in *Pall Mall Budget,* 12 Jan. 1882). For other details, see Manifesto of the Democratic Federation, in *The Radical,* 11 Feb. 1882.

termined by the fact that its most active support was drawn from the most disaffected and intransigent elements of London Radicalism: persons currently obsessed with the fight against Irish coercion, who necessarily regarded the parliamentary leaders of their party as traitors for accepting it, if not, indeed, for taking office in a "Whiggish" government in the first place. Their political hero was Charles Bradlaugh, the old Republican anticlerical warhorse, currently leading the fight against coercion, whose lonely opposition in the House of Commons symbolized their own feelings of intransigent hostility to the ruling class.[26] Insofar as such feelings were directed against the Liberal government of the early eighties, however, they were also congenial to Hyndman, who despised Gladstonian politics. Accordingly, he joined vigorously in the anticoercion struggle. The more "respectable" middle-class supporters of his organization, on the other hand, drifted away before its actual founding, perhaps recognizing that it would not turn out to be "practical politics." Thereafter, its only restraining element was provided by representatives of the affiliated Radical clubs, and their support was permanently lost by the first political act undertaken by Hyndman and his new friends: a manifesto, in the fall of 1881, denouncing the "hollowness and hypocrisy of capitalist Radicalism," and subjecting the Gladstone government to strong abuse.[27] That act—which revealed Hyndman's profound ignorance of popular Radical attitudes and of the loyalty of Radical workingmen to their traditions and their leaders —was too much for the "federated" clubs, and all save one withdrew in protest, leaving Hyndman only a residual working-class following.[28] Thereafter, Hyndman increasingly treated Radicals and Radicalism as enemies, rather than as potential allies.

Hyndman's lack of rapport with Liberal-Radicalism also cre-

26. Such views were most clearly stated in *The Radical* in 1881, which also gave the Federation its best early publicity. See F. W. Soutter, *Recollections of a Labour Pioneer* (London, 1923).

27. Tsuzuki, *Hyndman*, pp. 39, 47, citing *Justice*, 4 Aug. 1884.

28. Hyndman to Helen Taylor, 2 Oct. 1881, M—TC. For analyses of late Victorian working-class Radical attitudes, see J. B. Baernreither, *English Associations of Working Men*, trans. A. Taylor (London, 1889), chap. 3, esp. pp. 144–47, and H. M. Pelling, *Popular Politics and Society in Late Victorian Britain* (London, 1968). "Revolutionary" rhetoric had been alien to such attitudes since the demise of "physical force" Chartism, soon after 1848.

ated tensions within the Federation. For even after the loss of the Radical clubs an influential block of working-class Republicans remained. Their chief spokesman was Helen Taylor, the very advanced stepdaughter of John Stuart Mill, who, next to Hyndman, was probably the most important personage in the infant Federation. As such, she must also have presented at least an implied threat to Hyndman's leadership, as she was a far more important figure than he in London working-class politics,[29] and her opinions, cast in the old freethinking-Republican-woman's-suffrage mold, made a striking contrast to Hyndman's preference for Radical Toryism laced with Marx. Indeed, Helen Taylor even favored the existing Radical Party to the extent of arguing (against Hyndman) that a government with Chamberlain and Morley for its ministers would be "a little better than any government now existing in the world, although contemptibly behind public opinion." [30]

Hyndman, in contrast, had only recently denounced such attitudes as "disloyal," and he continued to prefer Tory landlords to their Liberal critics.[31] But his "Marxism" was fundamentally congruent with such preferences because they predisposed him to welcome the ideas of class conflict (which Tory Radicals had typically preached in contrast to Liberal insistence on the harmony of interests between capital and labor) and of the inevitable breakdown of liberal capitalism through its internal contradictions.[32] Tory pro-

29. Helen Taylor had close connections with the workingmen who produced *The Radical* and a large following in the Radical borough of Southwark, from which she was twice elected to the London School Board (one of the first women to hold such office). See Soutter, *Recollections*, and "Helen Taylor," in *DNB: 1901–1912*, pp. 483–84. For her Socialist views, see p. 106 below.

30. Helen Taylor to H. M. Hyndman, [Sept. 1881], M-TC. She also believed that "the majority of [English] people were Republicans" at heart but were betrayed by self-seeking politicians, among whom she included Gladstone (*The Radical*, 3 June 1882, quoting Miss Taylor, and Helen Taylor to Henry George, 3 Jan. 1882, George Papers, NYPL.

31. Tsuzuki, *Hyndman*, p. 40; Hyndman to Henry George, 6 April 1883. George Papers, NYPL.

32. Regarding Tory Radicalism, see Cecil Driver, *Tory Radical* (New York, 1946), pp. 30 ff, 111 ff, 424 ff, and Beer, *British Politics in the Collectivist Age*, pp. 91–102 and n. 22 above. Harvey Glickman, "The Toryness of English Conservatism," *JBS* 1 (Nov. 1961), argues somewhat more broadly that Toryism always tended to view individualism as an abberation and therefore found it easy to accept

clivities also predisposed him to dislike captains of industry, whose
way of life he found crude, ugly, and distasteful; while his advocacy of social reform was tinged with paternal attitudes, suggestive
of Disraeli, to whom, in fact, he had first broached his hopes of
social reconstruction. Consequently, though he remained at heart
an advocate of order, his hatred for existing society led him, in the
middle eighties, to welcome the prospect of revolution.[33] And that
attitude was further reinforced by his closest remaining allies in the
Federation, who were now men of a much more militant outlook
than himself: old Chartists and continental exiles of an Anarchist
and insurrectionary persuasion, whose pressure probably pushed
Hyndman much faster along the road to insurrectionism than
he himself had any wish to go. For his basic political objective
remained the creation of a disciplined organization through which
he and other leaders of his stripe could control the revolutionary
forces and impose new order at their consummation.[34]

Throughout 1882, therefore, the Federation followed an uneven
course, combining the Republicanism of Helen Taylor and its
remaining Radical working-class adherents with the kind of Marx-
ist-insurrectionary attitudes that Hyndman was fast adopting.[35]
For at least a short time, however, an attempt was made to combine
these tendencies in a projected "grand alliance" of "Irish Nation-

---

measures of paternalist collectivism. Thus it was appropriate that a high proportion of the earliest English advocates of Marxism, including Hyndman, H. H.
Champion, Hubert Bland, R. P. B. Frost, and Maltman Barry, were Tories. (The
last actually became a paid Tory agent while working closely with Engels.) It has
also been claimed that the SDF appealed most characteristically to Tory workingmen (P. F. Clarke, *Lancashire and the New Liberalism* [Cambridge, Eng., 1971],
p. 41).

33. "As I go through the courts and lanes of this city [and]...watch the capitalist
class grinding hours on hours of unpaid toil out of half-starved women and half-
starved men, I feel that no bloodshed, no anarchy, no horror conceivable could be
worse for the mass of people than the existing state of things" (Hyndman to
Henry George, [Nov. 1882?], George Papers, NYPL).

34. H. W. Lee and E. Archbold, *Social-Democracy in Britain* (London, 1935),
pp. 50, 45; E. P. Thompson, *William Morris: Romantic to Revolutionary* (London,
1955), pp. 331–32; and Andreas Scheu, *Umsturzkeime*, 3 vols. (Vienna, 1923),
3:45 ff.

35. Its official program consisted chiefly of Radical political reforms, drawn from
the People's Charter of 1837, plus land nationalization, but its activities and
proclamations indicated a far more militant point of view. For the former, see
The Radical, 16 July 1881, and Tsuzuki, *Hyndman*, p. 41; for the latter, see
Parliamentary Manifesto of the Democratic Federation, in *The Radical*, 11 Feb 1882.

alists and English Democrats." Hyndman was reported to be willing to give the leadership to Bradlaugh,[36] while he and his followers would presumably seek to instill Socialism from within. Had such an attempt been successful, in the highly charged atmosphere of Radical politics during the spring of 1882, the results might have been politically significant enough to deflect the development of the Federation in a quasi-Fabian direction, bringing its propaganda more into harmony with English Radical attitudes. In the event, however, the "alliance" came to nothing, and the Federation was drawn instead into the wake of Henry George's triumphant tour of Britain in the summer of 1882, with the paradoxical result that it became more Socialist and more intransigent.

The paradox in that situation lay in the fact that Henry George, the American land reformer, was neither Socialist nor intransigent. Nevertheless, by popularizing the idea and the practicability of comprehensive social reconstruction, his lecture tour sparked the great outburst of Socialist feeling that swept over England during 1883. George accomplished this, however, by reviving the agitation for land reform in England, which had lain practically dormant since the death of Mill; and this, in turn, created a mass audience throughout Great Britain that was primed with semi-Socialist ideas and eager to put them into practice.

3. Land Reform

The movement for land reform was probably the only force in England capable of creating a mass audience for Socialism in the early eighties. For English land, to an extent unknown elsewhere, was still the near-monopoly of a privileged class and was kept so by legal barriers to its sale. As such, it was perpetually vulnerable to Liberal and Radical attack—especially as mere ownership, separated from cultivation of the soil, was contrary to traditional liberal theories of property.[37] Thus Radical attacks on private property traditionally began (and, for the most part, also ended) with the land. But in the later nineteenth century such attacks also

36. Report in *Irish World,* quoted in *The Radical,* 25 March 1882.

37. See p. 62 above, and chap. 1, n. 13. Such theories typically rested on the arguments that land was not produced by human labor and was inherently monopolistic, as in Mill, *Principles of Political Economy,* bk. 2, chap. 2, sec. 1, and Henry George, *Progress and Poverty,* bk. 7, chap. 1.

repeatedly began in Ireland, where the anomalies of landlordism
were intensified by absenteeism and rack rents, and from there the
movement was exported back to England.

Thus, in the 1860s and again in 1880 the land question reached
England with campaigns for Irish independence. The Land
League, pledged to rid Ireland of "the curse of landlordism," was
its chief political arm, and its massive success in Ireland in the
General Election of 1880 generated the pressure necessary to pry
the Irish Land Act of 1881 from the ineffectual Gladstone government. Because of its collectivist tincture, that act has been hailed
as the first major break in the pattern of Liberal legislation. Its
new machinery of land courts, empowered to fix "fair rents" and
to regulate tenure, interfered openly with the landlord's cherished
right to "free disposal" of his property. And that produced both
cries of "Socialism" from the guardians of the older Liberal faith,
and rejoicing from such Radicals as Arnold Toynbee, who saw it
as the opening of a new era of social responsibility.[38]

The latter view was surely closer to the mark; but at that time in
England, Irish land agitation was chiefly useful for stimulating
renewed interest in land reform among English Radicals—an
interest that was naturally focused on the problems of unemployment and poverty in the great towns. A Radical tradition of long
standing, going back to Owenite and Chartist roots, supported
their belief that the land, properly parceled out and cultivated, was
capable of supporting the whole English population, and that the
great mass of the urban unemployed consisted of laborers who had
been turned off the land by grasping landlords. The landlord,
therefore, was really the chief instigator of urban distress. "All
reforms were futile whilst the land remained monopolized. . . .
To this basic cause nearly all preventable social evils may be
traced."[39]

Although such agitation had lapsed in the later seventies, it was

38. See Toynbee, *Industrial Revolution*, pp. 233, 237, and, for a more traditional
Liberal view, George Brodrick, "The Progress of Democracy in England," *Nin.
Cen.* 14 (1883): 916, which stigmatized the Irish Land Act as "by far the most
important and disastrous" of the Socialist measures that had resulted from the
unprincipled competition among parties for the democratic vote.

39. A. C. Swinton, secretary of the Land Nationalisation Society, quoted in J. M.
Davidson, *The Annals of Toil* (London, [1889]), p. 414.

revived by the Agricultural Labourers' Union in 1879, and on their motion a resolution demanding reform of the land laws (on the very moderate ground that "ownership of land involved duties as well as rights") was approved by the Trade Union Congress.[40] Soon thereafter, the leadership was taken up by Charles Bradlaugh, an outspoken supporter of "land law reform" during the 1860s, when he had argued that such measures were essential to prevent starvation and rebellion. Similar conditions prompted him to take up that cause again in 1880, with the support and encouragement of leading trade unionists. In February of that year he called a national conference on the land question, and his prestige, coupled with the urgency of the problem, proved sufficient to attract delegates from all levels of working-class life and from all parts of industrial England.[41]

What Bradlaugh proposed to his conference, however, was little more than a rehash of John Stuart Mill's program of ten years earlier. Of its provisions, only Bradlaugh's special panacea, the "compulsory cultivation of cultivable waste lands," was specifically designed to aid the working classes, by resettling the unemployed on waste or unused land.[42] It was a scheme that seemed to answer the persistent longing among workingmen to return to the soil as independent cultivators and ultimately promised to provide every landless laborer with an agricultural alternative to factory wages. Nevertheless, it was regarded by most of the non-Radical press as more "socialistic" than the Irish Land Act. It struck directly at the landlord's right to "free disposal" of his property, and did so at home, where the special circumstances of Ireland could not be held to justify it. But Bradlaugh, in his own eyes, was not a Socialist at all. Indeed, he was soon to emerge as the most bitter anti-Socialist orator in English working-class life and would not countenance even discussion of land nationalization.[43] His special panacea for

40. See the account in "English Land Nationalisation," in *Our History* (1957): 15–18, and in Barry, *Nationalisation*, chap. 2.

41. See reports in *National Reformer*, 8, 15, and 22 Feb. 1880.

42. Landlords who refused to open such lands to new tenants were to be expropriated (with compensation) and the land was to be let by the state for small holdings with secure tenure. For further details see *Our History* (1957): 18 ff.

43. The issue was raised by a group of old Chartists, still echoing the phrases of Bronterre O'Brien, and was speedily put down by Bradlaugh. See *National Reformer*, 15 Feb. 1880.

the land problem—the lineal descendant of schemes proposed by
Owenites and Chartists, Mill, Cobden, and Bright—thus served to
demonstrate just how far advanced Radicals were prepared to go in
attacking the landed interest without feeling that any legitimate
rights of property were compromised thereby. The landlord's
interest was the interest of monopoly, they were fond of repeat-
ing. No man made the land, and by ancient right and custom it
could not be permanently alienated from the nation at large. As
a monopoly, held in trust for the people, therefore, it must be
made to bear its fair obligations to the public weal.[44]

Similar arguments also underlay Bradlaugh's other "socialistic"
demand for a graduated land tax, to be doubled with each additional 5,000 acres of estate. Unlike Socialist taxation, this was not
intended to be confiscatory, but only to encourage the great landed
magnates to break up their estates into small holdings suitable for
"peasant" cultivation. Such a policy was the only way to avert starvation among the present generation of unemployed laborers,
Bradlaugh insisted, and it was the landlord's duty to make the
necessary land available.[45] These had been traditional Radical
arguments for over a generation, in 1881, yet it had never occurred
to Bradlaugh or his fellow Radicals that the same arguments might
be applicable to capital and to other forms of property. Land, in
their view, remained unique and could not become private property in the complete sense, as the latter term applied only to goods
produced by human labor.

Unhappily, Bradlaugh's Land Law Reform League proved to
be short-lived, for the great man virtually abandoned it after a
year, as he became engrossed in the long struggle against parliamentary oaths, and without his leadership it rapidly collapsed.[46]
Yet it did succeed in stimulating latent interest in land nationalization among several older Radicals who had ties with Chartism

44. For such advanced Radical theory, see Davidson, *Annals*, pp. 395 ff.
45. Charles Bradlaugh, *The Land, the People, and the Coming Struggle* (London,
[1870s]) , esp. point 9. John Stuart Mill had also advocated opening the wastelands
to "peasant" cultivators (see p. oo above).
46. Affiliated Radical clubs and trades unions with a total membership of over
400,000 were enrolled by 1881. (*National Reformer*, Dec. 1880, quoted in *Our
History* [1957]: 19) . For Bradlaugh's political career, see Walter Arnstein, *The
Bradlaugh Case* (New York, 1965) .

and the land reform movements of the 1860s. And they, in turn, set up an agitation to add land nationalization to the official program of the Democratic Federation (over Hyndman's initial opposition) and to the program of the Trades Union Congress at its annual meeting in 1882.[47]

At the same time, similar ideas preached by the well-known naturalist Alfred Russel Wallace were gaining support among middle-class intellectuals. In his youthful study of the Malay Archipelago, Wallace had argued that the method of land tenure in England was among the world's most "barbarous."[48] That conclusion had come to the attention of Mill, who had drawn him into the Land Tenure Reform Association. Subsequently, however, Wallace had come to regard its program as too moderate, so that when, in 1880, Irish land agitation and the depression again roused him to action, he argued for complete land nationalization. "Peasant proprietorship," as demanded by Bradlaugh and the Land League, he argued, would bring no permanent advantage to the working class, but would create a new, privileged class of landowners. Soon these would be in debt; the land would be sold; and absentee landlords would reemerge. The only way to keep the land in small holdings and the people on the land, therefore, was to make the state sole landlord—by nationalization.[49]

Although that word alone was enough to shock moderate readers, Wallace's scheme for "nationalising" the land was really very cautious. He would allow up to four generations for transfer, give full compensation, and let the land to small cultivators with the state merely as rent collector.[50] In principle, nevertheless, his scheme constituted the first widely publicized departure from the established pattern of Radical land reform. His demand that land

47. Mira Wilkins, "Non-Socialist Origins of England's First Important Socialist Organization," *International Review of Social History* 4 (1959). (The TUC vote for land nationalization was probably a fluke, as it was not soon repeated.)

48. A. R. Wallace, *The Malay Archipelago* (London, 1868), appendix, cited in A. R. Wallace, *My Life*, 2 vols. (London, 1905), 2:238.

49. Ibid., pp. 175 ff., and A. R. Wallace, "How to Nationalise the Land," *Con. Rev.* (Nov. 1880).

50. Ibid.; the latter was expanded as *Land Nationalisation: Its Necessities and Aims* (London, 1882). He would provide compensation in the form of "terminable annuities" from the state, and use the scheme to give every citizen "free access" to the land as an alternative to work at capitalist wages.

become public property so that it could be regulated in the public interest and his denunciation of "free trade in land" as the "grossest of delusions" emphasized that break. Because of Wallace's intellectual eminence, his ideas received widespread publicity in liberal intellectual circles in 1880 and 1881, and a group of like-minded, middle-class reformers soon joined him in establishing the English Land Nationalisation Society.[51]

Again, the most notable recruit to the new organization was Helen Taylor. Already an ardent supporter of the Land League, she found it easy to shift her allegiance to the more radical solution to landlordism proposed by Wallace—especially as the latter took pains to demonstrate that land nationalization provided the most convenient means of appropriating the "unearned increment" of land value to which her stepfather had given such high priority in his own land reform campaign. Her presence also helped to establish a firm link between the nationalization movement of the eighties and the older movement for land tenure reform. But, most importantly, it was through her efforts that Henry George, who was deeply attached to the social ideas of her stepfather, was brought into active partnership with the two English organizations professing land reform programs similar to his own.[52]

Within a few months George was speaking from their platforms, advocating their programs, and—by virtue of his impassioned oratory—becoming the most powerful advocate of land reform in England. His lectures had extraordinary effects on English audiences, projecting a deep sense of moral earnestness that roused their consciences against the "sins of the landlords" as no other speaker could. Nor did George hesitate to utilize the full resources of religious sentiment to increase the emotional impact of his lectures. He repeatedly identified land nationalization as "His [God's] work," as "succoring the poor, the starving, and the degraded," and as making the laws of England conform to that

51. See the account in Davidson, *Annals*, pp. 413 ff.
52. See Henry George's correspondence with Helen Taylor and John Stuart Mill, esp. George to Mill, 22 Aug. 1869, M-TC, box 1, no. 138; also Charles A. Barker, *Henry George* (New York, 1955), pp. 355–56.

"higher moral law" with which, as an American, he claimed as intimate familiarity.[53]

As an American politician in the late 1880s, George ultimately acquired a very different image as champion of the single tax and an outspoken anti-Socialist. In 1882, however, he scarcely touched the subject of taxation and made no attempt to minimize his Socialist connections. He spoke consistently as an advocate of land nationalization, identifying himself with organizations that preached that doctrine in uncompromising form. Under their auspices, he roused working-class Radicals up and down the land by preaching that "the land question had become the great labour question," and that the only way to restore prosperity to working-men was to "abolish private property in land." To make the land thus "free" was, in turn, the basis of all other freedoms, and a great step toward "equality and true Socialism."[54]

In particular, those were the sentiments expressed in George's last English lecture of 1882—although it was his first in London—given at the Memorial Hall under the auspices of the Land Nationalisation Society. Hitherto he had been ignored by the London press and had, therefore, remained obscure to metropolitan Liberal and Radical intellectuals. But his London lecture changed that overnight. The *Times* reported it at length the next day and soon followed it with reviews of *Progress and Poverty* and *The Irish Land Question*. And though the latter were scarcely favorable to George, they quoted his words so copiously as to make splendid vehicles for spreading the new gospel *in partes infidelium*. Sale of his books increased spectacularly: the cheap, workman's edition of *Progress and Poverty* alone sold nearly 100,000 copies within a year, and by the end of that year scarcely a British journal of opinion had failed to review it.[55] It was read by everyone who

53. See, e.g., Henry George's lectures at Glasgow and Portree, Scotland, 23 Feb. and 22 Dec. 1884, quoted in E. P. Lawrence, *Henry George in the British Isles* (E. Lansing, Mich., 1957), p. 48.

54. Henry George, lecture at Memorial Hall, London, quoted in the *Times* 6 Sept. 1882. The *Times* also identified George as a "Socialist," and his doctrine as "Socialism in disguise."

55. *Times*, 6 and 14 Sept. 1882; Barker, *George*, pp. 373–74; Max Beer, *A History of British Socialism*, 2 vols. (London, 1948), 2:243; and Lawrence, *George in British Isles*, p.

mattered, from the Prime Minister and his Radical allies—who were "electrified" by its effect—to the Radical workingmen who flocked to purchase the sixpenny edition.[56] Thus land nationalization became, unavoidably, a major issue of the day, and Socialism appeared to be a force to reckon with: not through a specially

> formulated program advocated by a special party, as in Germany, but . . . [through a more general] revolution . . . as to interference with private property, relations of labour and capital, and a very great spreading of the doctrine of nationalisation of the land. [As a result,] the old political economy of Ricardo is gone to the wall, and Henry George's book has had a most enormous sale.[57]

4. Henry George and Joseph Chamberlain

It was not so much the intrinsic merits of Georgian theories, however, as their "dramatic opportuneness" in the fall of 1882—their precise suitability to the current crises in British society—that made them a "new gospel" for the Radical movement.[58] Land reform, labor unrest, and newspaper accounts of misery in the urban slums had crowded into public consciousness in the early eighties, and George's work had the good fortune to combine them all, arguing that their origins were the same, and offering for their solution one "simple and sovereign remedy"—nationalization through taxation—that was precisely suited to the English Radical bias.

Nevertheless, it remains paradoxical that so relatively orthodox an economist as George—an ardent believer in competition and free trade—should have been the catalyst needed to produce an

56. Garvin, *Life of Chamberlain*, pp. 385–86. Both Chamberlain and Morley read *Progress and Poverty* late in 1882, and the latter brought it to Gladstone's attention.

57. William Clarke (later a Fabian essayist) to H. D. Lloyd, 23 May 1883, Lloyd Papers, WSHS.

58. J. A. Hobson, "The Influence of Henry George in England," *Fort. Rev.* 62 (1897), and William Morris to C. E. Maurice, 22 June 1883, in J. W. Mackail, *Life of William Morris*, 2 vols. (London, 1899), 2:104. John Rae even went so far as to argue that "Nobody accepts [George's] actual ideas . . . [but] everybody feels that he has laid his hand on a true seat of danger" ("Social Philosophy," p. 295).

English Socialist revival. In fact, his social and economic doctrines were thoroughly ambiguous, caught between the rival claims of economic individualism and Christian charity (which was the source of his deep sympathy for Socialism). In this respect, and in his constant efforts to reconcile those poles of doctrine, George was probably the most authentic late-Victorian successor of John Stuart Mill.[59] But unlike Mill he made the radical implications of his ideas so clear that they were credited with being even more subversive of the existing order than he had intended them to be.

Such tendencies were especially clear in George's treatments of land nationalization and Socialism. The former, of course, was his all-sufficient "remedy" for the ailments of society, summarized in his demand that *"we must make land common property."* Only several chapters later, near the end of his massive work, did he add that a tax absorbing the whole value of rent "amounted to the same thing" and therefore constituted a "simpler and easier" method of nationalization.[60] His sympathy for Socialism, so often expressed in his English lectures, was of a similarly ambiguous type, partly Anarchist and partly collectivist: a synthesis of the "truths perceived by Proudhon and Lassalle"—Anarchist and collectivist truths, respectively—with those of Smith and Ricardo.[61] Accordingly, George would "reduce the work of government" until it approached the "ideal of Jeffersonian democracy," but only so as to clear the way for a vast increase of new public services—public utilities, sanitation facilities, and cultural amenities of all types—to be provided free, subsidized by the land tax, which would constitute a practical realization of the ends of Socialism.[62]

59. His intellectual indebtedness to Mill and personal relations with Helen Taylor have been noted (p. 84 above); more important was his essentially Millite vision of the "great co-operative society, uniting capitalist and laborer in [one] person," that he saw as the ultimate stage of social evolution. *Progress and Poverty*, (London, 1881), pp. 410, 420.

60. *Progress and Poverty*, pp. 295 (italics in original), 363–64. The single tax does not appear until bk. 8, chap. 2, and George did not argue for it in his 1882 tour of Britain.

61. Ibid., p. xi. Lassalle's approach to Socialism by way of state-subsidized self-governing workshops was more acceptable to most individualists than, e.g., Marxist-style collectivism—a point discussed in chap. 4, n. 74, below.

62. Ibid., pp. 409–10. An exhaustive list of such potential public services follows, very similar to the passages by Hyndman (cited p. 74 above) and by Sidney Webb in G. B. Shaw, ed. *Fabian Essays* (London, 1889), pp. 30–61.

Thus far, George's idea of Socialism was deduced chiefly from individualist premises, but after his first English lecture tour he shifted to more forthright arguments for collectivism. As society grew more complex and interdependent, he reasoned, individuals must, of necessity, become more closely integrated with the social organism, and the functions of government must increase proportionately. "This is the truth in socialism which . . . is being forced on us daily by industrial progress and social development" —an argument remarkably reminiscent of the Positivism of Auguste Comte.[63] In George's usage, however, "co-operative" and "socialist" were almost interchangeable terms, suggesting a remarkably *traditional* idea of Socialism, while his rhetoric, with its religious tone and its appeals to love and charity, was almost that of Christian Socialism. His apparent endorsement of collectivism, then, must be interpreted in light of such traditions—especially their tendency to combine sweeping moral imperatives with only moderate positive reforms. What George *really* endorsed was chiefly the idea of the welfare state, grounded in the belief that the entire community was morally responsible for the welfare of its members.[64]

But although such an endorsement linked George firmly with the humanitarianism of the eighties, and with the Fabian doctrines that it spawned, it was probably less effective in sparking a Socialist revival than his more orthodox economic arguments, built around the theory of rent. For the latter, in effect, first broke the spell that laissez-faire had cast for so long over liberal attitudes in England. They did so in two ways: by convincing many readers for the first time that it was feasible to modify the development of society by intelligent use of legislation (which was what land nationalization proposed to do), and by arguing vividly that the economic system itself was at the root of poverty and social crisis. For it was precisely in the most highly developed capitalist economies, George insisted, that "we find deepest poverty, the sharpest struggle for existence,

63. *Social Problems* (London, 1883), 176–77; and cf. the valuable discussion in E. J. Rose, *Henry George* (New York, 1968), pp. 92–94, to which I am heavily indebted. Such views also invite comparison with the slightly later organismic arguments of Sidney Webb (for which, see chap. 8, sec. 4, below).

64. See Rose, *Henry George*, esp. pp. 97, 68–75, and Jones, *Christian Socialist Revival*, pp. 49 ff.

the most enforced idleness." There, most conspicuously, "supply is . . . prevented from satisfying demand, . . . laborers [are prevented] from producing the things laborers want," and cyclical depressions take the greatest tolls in human misery. But most important, George argued, such conditions would not disappear (as economic optimists had taught), but must increase, in an exact proportion to the progress of technology and economic growth, so long as the present economic system lasted.[65]

In George's view, of course, the loose screw in the economic works was private ownership of land and consequent private appropriation of rent. But for many readers his pessimistic view of economic progress overshadowed his more limited attacks on landed property and rent. And that same pessimism—qualified as it was—was crucial to the growth of Socialist belief in England. For George, by virtue of the enormous circulation of his works, probably introduced most of his English readers to serious criticism of the economic system. (And for working-class readers, products of the 1870 Education Act, this was doubly important, as few of them had previously been exposed to economic reasoning of any sort.) Thus, to a greater extent than he could have known or wished, his work led English readers on to anticapitalist conclusions, which were the necessary prelude to adopting Socialist ideas.[66]

At the same time, *Progress and Poverty* contributed in more specific ways to the development of English Socialist theory because it contained equivalents or analogies of several key doctrines of Marxian economics. In the passage from that book quoted above, for instance, the increasing misery of the proletariat is asserted, while the "contradictions of capitalism" are implicit in the Georgian paradox of "poverty spawned by [economic] progress." But the most crucial instance of that tendency was George's law of rent, the mainspring of his economic system, which formed a moral and economic analogue to Marx's law of surplus value. For both were treated, in their respective systems, as the all-inclusive sources of

65. *Progress and Poverty*, pp. 6–9.
66. Hobson, "Influence of Henry George," p. 837; and for a more personal testimony to the same effect, J. Kier Hardie, quoted in "Character Sketches: I," *Review of Reviews* (June 1906): 571.

injustice and distress within industrial society, and both led on to alienation of the working class. In essence, George argued that in all advanced economies, where the "natural" means of production had been privately appropriated, rent inexorably absorbed all increase in the nation's wealth beyond the bare cost of production. It was rent alone, therefore, that drove men's wages to the level of subsistence (as in Lassalle's "iron law") and robbed the working-man of his humanity:

> Producing goods in which he has no share, . . . working with tools he cannot hope to own, . . . compelled to ever closer more continuous labor than the savage, . . . he loses [even] the independence of the savage. . . . Under such circumstances the man loses the essential quality of manhood. . . . He becomes a slave, a machine, a commodity.

All this, George thundered, so that the few who "lived by own-ing," the rent receivers, might have the unearned increments created by the whole society. Thus "labor [is] . . . robbed of its earnings, while greed rolls in wealth"—a charge that even Marx had seldom made so forcefully.[67]

When readers had gone that far with George, it was scarcely surprising that the bolder ones went on to Marx; and this was, in fact, the route taken by the majority of English converts to Marxism in the early eighties.[68] They will be treated in due course. But George's arguments, suffused with vintage Radical hostility toward the landed class, were also tigers' milk for Radical politi-cians seeking new ways to generate enthusiasm in the electorate. Hence the blistering attack that Joseph Chamberlain—now the

67. *Progress and Poverty*, pp. 256–57, 495. The theory of alienation (or, more accurately, of reification) presented here has clear affinities with Marx's, although George probably had no knowledge of Marx, and Marx's major discussion of that theory (in the Economic and Philosophic Manuscripts of 1844) remained unknown in the nineteenth century. Among contemporary English "Marxists," only William Morris showed a similar awareness of the problem of alienation. Cf. ibid., p. 244 for more revolutionary rhetoric.

68. Bernard Shaw claimed that "fully $\frac{5}{6}$" of the Socialist converts in the early eighties were initially followers of George (quoted in A. Henderson, *George Bernard Shaw: Man of the Century*, [New York, 1956], p. 216). Beer, *History of British Socialism*, 2:245, estimated the proportion as $\frac{4}{5}$.

most prominent Radical in Parliament—leveled at Lord Salisbury, the Tory leader, early in 1883, as "spokesman of a class [of land owners] . . . who toil not neither do they spin,"

> whose fortunes . . . originated by grants made in times gone by for the services which courtiers rendered kings, and have since grown and increased while they have slept by levying an increased share of all that other men have done by toil and labour to add to the general wealth and prosperity.[69]

—thus heaping upon that class the guilt for all the nation's poverty and distress.

From a lesser Radical such rhetoric would have attracted little notice, as Chamberlain himself had used it years before without effect.[70] But from a cabinet minister widely proclaimed as Gladstone's probable successor, it was sensational, and his application of the ancient metaphor of idleness to unearned increment was soon reverberating through the land. Unearned increment, of course, was an idea he had learned many years before from John Stuart Mill; but Henry George revived his interest in it and the success of his campaign made it again seem ripe for politics. Thus, though he disapproved of nationalization, Chamberlain was deeply moved by George's analysis of urban misery and agreed with him that legislative remedies were needed to provide relief.[71] Consequently, he followed up his attack on Salisbury with a new campaign for social reform, with unearned increments and democratic franchise as its twin spearheads. Manhood suffrage, made real by equal electoral districts, equally valued votes, and payment of members were its essential preconditions. Once achieved, they would "open the gates and social legislation would march in" on a grand scale.[72]

This was hope held out to the Radical electorate, aroused al-

69. Speech at Birmingham, 5 March 1883, quoted in Garvin, *Life of Chamberlain, 1836–1885,* p. 392. Hyndman characteristically added that following that speech "the whole Conservative press turned around and asked Chamberlain where *his* wealth came from. It was splendid. A little more of this and we shall be in full Socialist cry after *both* robbers" (to Henry George, 5 April 1883, George Papers, NYPL).

70. Speech at Sheffield, 1 Jan. 1874, quoted in Fraser, *Chamberlain,* p. 17.

71. Fraser, *Chamberlain,* pp. 48–49; also Garvin, *Life of Chamberlain,* p. 385.

72. Garvin, *Life of Chamberlain, 1836–1885,* pp. 394, 400.

ready by the rhetoric of Henry George. As a program it differed little from that of the Democratic Federation, early in 1883, except
that it omitted land nationalization. And Chamberlain—now
"Robespierre" to the conservative press—was widely believed to be
reserving that as his next offering to the demos.) In any case, he
was preparing to tax property heavily for the abolition of slums
and to use the resources of taxable rent to provide amenities for
the disadvantaged population. That was "Socialism" enough in the
eyes of respectable people and it was also a large installment of
what Henry George had meant by "nationalization." Now it
seemed possible that such notions would become the policy of the
nation's largest party, under the leadership of Chamberlain and
Dilke. Indeed, it was widely claimed in the conservative press that
the Radical Party had sold out to Socialism as the price of popular
support; and Chamberlain's increasing willingness to use that
word, in 1884 and 1885, did much to stimulate such hopes and
fears.[73]

Thus Chamberlain's agitation, like that of Henry George,
helped to create an atmosphere in which the claims of Socialism
could find a hearing—especially among the working class.[74] For,
despite Chamberlain's conservative intentions,[75] his rhetoric
(again, like that of George) was so much more dazzling than anything his panaceas seemed likely to accomplish that ardent listeners
must have been carried by the emotional thrust of his words to more
thorough Socialist conclusions than he (or George) intended; and
some were carried in that fashion to the theories of Karl Marx.
For, as already noted, there was a logical progression from the idea
of unearned increment to surplus value, rooted in the claim that
capital as well as land formed a monopoly in advanced industrial

73. Ibid., pp. 385–86, 406; also Chamberlain's Introduction to *The Radical
Programme* (London, 1885), pp. v–vi, 13, where he endorsed the idea of "Socialistic" reform, and described Socialism as a "modern tendency" pressing for expression. For further discussion, see chap. 7 below.

74. See the appeal by John Sketchley, popular Socialist writer of the eighties,
to Chamberlain, that "great numbers of the working classes place in you their
strongest hopes because they believe you to be the 'coming man,' . . . the man
destined to lead them on to liberty and the nation to prosperity" (*Commonweal*
1, no. 5 (June 1885).

75. Fraser, *Chamberlain*, esp. pp. 49 ff.: "conservative" in the sense of seeking
to reinforce private property by reforming its chief abuses.

societies, that it too was a bastion of class privilege and levied "tolls" on the work of other men. Thus Marxism, as it was understood in England,[76] completed the analysis begun by Mill and Henry George—an analysis that acquired added potency in the mid-eighties because it alone, by showing labor systematically "robbed," seemed adequate to explain the worsening condition of the urban poor.

5. The Socialism of the Social-Democratic Federation

Such, in any case, was the road to Socialism taken by the most brilliant and influential new recruits to the Democratic Federation in the winter of 1882–83: H. H. Champion, R. P. B. Frost, J. L. Joynes, and William Morris.[77] All were middle-class Radicals (though Champion and Frost, like Hyndman, were Tory Radicals) who, as economic novices, had been converted by the arguments of Henry George, then reinforced their faith by reading Smith, Ricardo, Mill, and ultimately Marx.[78] Nevertheless, their Socialism, in 1883, was still highly eclectic, infused with the aims of Owen, Ruskin, and the earlier Christian Socialists, and marked by an amorphous yearning for the "Higher Life" (or, in Morris's case, for the "fellowship" of olden times). Doctrinally, they gave about equal weight to restoring "the land to the people" and surplus value to the workers. Consequently, all except Morris joined both the Federation and the Land Nationalisation Society and, in the spring of 1883, took part in organizing a more distinctly Georgian body, the Land Reform Union, which aimed to fight the landlords in a more aggressive manner. To promote that aim they also helped to found a journal called the *Christian*

76. The term Anglo-Marxism will serve to distinguish the theories of the (Social) Democratic Federation both from the Marxism of Marx himself and from that of his contemporary German disciples includng Engels. For objections to this term (which I believe to be unwarranted), see Hobsbawm, *Labouring Men,* p. 234; for fuller discussion, see p. 98, below.

77. Biographical sketches of the SDF recruits of winter, 1882–83, will be found in Appendix A. For further biographical details, see Pelling, *Origins of the Labour Party,* pp. 23–24; C. Tsuzuki, *Hyndman,* pp. 48–49; and H. Ellis, *My Life* (London, 1940), pp. 156–57.

78. Such a sequence was actually followed by Champion in 1882 (Pelling, "H. H. Champion," *Cambridge Journal* 6 (Jan. 1953).

Socialist, the first avowedly Socialist periodical in England since the 1850s, whose mixed ideology, ranging from simplified Marxism to quotations from Ruskin and admonitions to love one another, reflected the eclectic thinking of its founders.[79]

Despite such eclecticism, those converts had precisely the qualities needed to revitalize the Federation and make it an influential center of Socialist propaganda. They were highly educated, wealthy, articulate, and enthusiastic. Moreover, they were all talented journalists and were willing to expend both their talents and their money on the cause almost unstintingly.[80] Hence, with the help of such earlier converts from the Freethought movement as Herbert Burrows, Belfort Bax, and J. C. Foulger, plus a later convert, Edward Aveling,[81] they soon turned the federation into an articulate and well-publicized ginger group with several journals under its control (*Justice, To-day,* the *Christian Socialist*). More paradoxically, they were also instrumental in turning it into an avowedly, even militantly Marxist organization, which was renamed the Social-Democratic Federation (SDF) in 1884.

Despite the eclectic and traditional character of their Socialism, the SDF's new recruits were also angry and "rebellious" men who had seen squalor, filth, and hunger at close range in London slums and were determined to *do* something about them. Champion, for example—"in many ways the most able man" among them—was reported to "'care not a twopence about Collectivism or any other Ism, but sees that people in the East End are hungry and wants to force the government to give them a job.'" (Yet he also combined

79. The *Christian Socialist* also reflected the mixture of Christian social conscience and ethical Socialism that Henry George had inspired in England. Joynes was its original editor. The Land Reform Union was founded in June 1883, with Champion and Frost as its officers (*Chr. Soc.* 1 [June 1883]).

80. All had public school backgrounds: Champion, Frost, and Morris at Marlborough; Joynes at Eton. Champion had also graduated from Woolwich (military academy), Joynes from Cambridge, and Morris from Oxford, and Hyndman was also a Cambridge man. As for affluence, Champion's father had given him nearly £ 4,000 to establish and maintain himself in business, and Champion claimed to have spent most of it on propagating Socialism. Morris, who inherited very substantial wealth, made up the weekly deficit of £ 10 on the Federation's paper, *Justice,* and funded other Socialist projects. Joynes and Frost also inherited incomes, and all wrote voluminously for the Socialist press. (For sources, see Appendix A.)

81. For biographical sketches of these Freethought recruits, see Appendix A.

such activism with a deep sense of the "inwardness of Socialism" and its roots in human brotherhood that reflected the persistence of his Christian Socialist beliefs.) With Frost, his schoolmate at Marlborough, who was also "fanatically in earnest," he started a brisk agitation in the East End, and soon, by "sticking together and working," the two of them virtually "boss[ed] the Federation." [82] Burrows was similarly motivated by experiences of working-class distress—especially that of striking miners he had visited in south Staffordshire—and he too advocated "blood and thunder straight off." But Bax, though most militant of all in theory, was too frightened by stories of squalor in the slums to risk going there himself and therefore limited his activism to the symbolic wearing of a silk-and-sealskin imitation of a costermonger's cap.[83] Morris and Joynes, on the other hand, displayed more complex responses to the challenge of current poverty—perhaps more genuinely revolutionary, in the sense of working for a deeper and more permanent transformation in the lives and relationships of their fellow men, but less prone to militant rhetoric, with its allusions to "gunpowder" and barricades, and less inclined to rush into action without careful study. Both were motivated primarily by a deep "hatred of modern civilization," which they found soul-destroying even where it did not produce squalor or starvation. And that hatred formed the basis of their revolutionary hope.[84]

This militancy and hostility, alike, were soon reflected in the official rhetoric of the Federation, which came of age in 1883 through the activities of its new recruits. There were two stages in this process. First, at its annual meeting in June 1883, the Federation formally adopted the program of Radical collectivism that Hyndman had advocated since 1881 as its "stepping stones" to Socialism. Then that program was embedded in a new mani-

82. P. Chubb to T. Davidson, 25 Oct., 17 Nov. 1883; Champion to Davidson, 6 July 1887, Davidson Papers, Yale; Shaw to Scheu, 14 Oct. 1884, Scheu Papers, IISH; and Shaw's lecture, "The New Politics," 1889, BM 50683. Champion's paper, *Common Sense*, reflected that Christian Socialist outlook as late as 1887–88.

83. Ellis, *My Life*, pp. 156–57; Nethercot, *First Five Lives of Annie Besant*, p. 264; and Shaw to Scheu, 14 Oct. 1884, Scheu Papers, IISH. There is a more sympathetic treatment of Bax in J. C. Cowley, "The Life and Writings of E. Belfort Bax" (Ph.D. thesis, London School of Economics, 1965).

84. Morris, "How I Became a Socialist," *Justice* (16 June 1894), and Winsten, *Salt*, pp. 57–58; also H. S. Salt, "J. L. Joynes," *Social Democrat* 1 (1897).

festo entitled "Socialism Made Plain," in which the militant spirit of the Federation's new leaders was first explicitly expressed. Regarding land nationalization, for example, it asserted that

> the handful of marauders who now hold possession have and can have no right save brute force against the tens of millions whom they wrong. But private ownership of Land . . . is only one and not the worst form of monopoly which enables the wealthy classes to use the means of production against the labourers whom they enslave. . . . Above all, the active capitalist class . . . turn every advance in human knowledge . . . into an engine for accumulating wealth out of other men's labour, and for exacting more and yet more surplus value out of the wage slaves whom they employ. So long as the means of production . . . are the monopoly of a class, so long must the labourers . . . sell themselves for a bare subsistence wage.[85]

The use of such militant rhetoric highlights one of the key problems of the early SDF: the unresolved conflict between its theory and its rhetoric. For rhetoric such as that quoted above had, in fact, no necessary connection with the Socialist theory of the SDF and tended to conflict with it. Indeed, when stripped of its surface rhetoric, that theory usually followed quite traditional Radical lines, as in the emphasis on monopoly and class privilege in the passages above, and in the similar tendency to use the Georgian case against land rents as a foundation on which to build an exposition of the law of surplus value. In essence, that theory consisted of the amplifications of three economic "laws": two of them, the labor theory of value and the iron law of wages, taken from simplified versions of early classical economics, and the third, the law of surplus value, conceived as the logical outcome of the former two. Moreover, the early leaders of the SDF repeatedly insisted that such theory was the inevitable outcome of "orthodox" economic principles, once the latter were freed from their traditional capitalist bias; they even propounded their theory

85. Reprinted in H. M. Pelling, ed., *The Challenge of Socialism* (London, 1954), pp. 130–32.

in the characteristic *manner* of such economics, faithfully copying its rigidity, abstractness, and lack of sociological perspective, despite the fact that these had already brought it into widespread disrepute.[86] Thus, despite their militant rhetoric, the early leaders of the SDF took pains to base their theory on familiar—even (as they supposed) "orthodox"—economic arguments, so as to make it more readily acceptable to potential Radical recruits.

The consequence of that tendency was that the early Socialist theories of the SDF resembled the theories of the early nineteenth-century "Ricardian" Socialists (who were themselves British Radicals) more closely than those of Marx.[87] The early SDF theory of surplus value, for example, typically took the form of a claim that capitalists and idle shareholders "filched" at least half of the value created by their workmen every day, followed by a condemnation of that transaction from the point of view of natural law ethics.[88] Probably the greater simplicity and familiarity of such "Ricardian" arguments, as compared with Marx's, formed their strongest recommendation to the leaders of the SDF, who seldom took the trouble to master Marx's economic reasoning for themselves. But it is also probable that they found these Radical arguments more emotionally satisfying than Marx's: first, because "Ricardian" theories were more simply and forthrightly ethical, whereas Marx refused to make any formal ethical claims, and, second, because they utilized such familiar and congenial Radical demands as the workman's right to the "whole produce" of his

86. For evidence of this disrepute, see P. Abrams, *The Origins of British Sociology* (Chicago, 1968), pp. 77 ff. For subsequent analysis of economic arguments I am heavily indebted to G. Lichtheim, *Marxism* (New York, 1965).

87. For the doctrines of the Ricardian Socialists (especially Thompson, Hodgskin, and Bray), see, e.g., J. Schumpeter, *History of Economic Analysis* (New York, 1954), pp. 479–80, and such recent studies as G. Lichtheim, *The Origins of Socialism* (New York, 1968), chap. 8, and J. F. C. Harrison, *Robert Owen and the Owenites in Britain and America* (London, 1968).

88. "The Death of Karl Marx," *Chr. Soc.* 2 (July 1883): 22–23; and "Surplus Value," *Chr. Soc.* 10 (Mar. 1884): 154–55 (articles by Joynes [?] and Champion, respectively); also Hyndman, *Historical Basis*, chap. 4, esp. pp. 105, 116–17, 121–22; and "Surplus Value," *To-day* (Apr. 1889). Marx, of course, had repudiated natural law ethics and had based his own theory of surplus value on the difference between use value and exchange value, rather than on the moral implications of the labor theory of value, as his SDF followers supposed.

labor, which Marx had rejected as unscientific and unsocialistic. In any case, two of the three "laws" on which their Socialist theory rested were not even genuinely Marxian. For Marx himself had rejected the iron law of wages, and the SDF theory of surplus value (as has been seen) differed radically from Marx's, both in its implicit individualism—the workman's right to the whole produce of his labor—and in its quite un-Marxian emphasis on distributive justice.[89]

This distortion of Marxism was by no means a unique phenomenon in the 1880s, when virtually all European countries were producing vulgarized versions of that system. Few vulgarizations, however, reduced Marxism so completely to the bare bones of economic theory and economic history—in effect, obliterating all traces of Marx's philosophy and sociology— as the English version created by the SDF. Moreover, by interpreting its economic theories in the manner of Ricardian Socialism and early classical economics (as it existed prior to the abandonment of the labor theory of value), the spokesmen of the SDF gave to their theory an archaic, almost ossified quality that made it very vulnerable to criticism from the standpoint of more recent economic theories.[90]

For all this Hyndman was largely responsible. He had specifically and knowingly promoted Ricardian Socialist theory in his books, touting its native Englishness; he had insisted on the continuity of Marxism and early classical economics; and, most surprisingly, he had repeatedly confused Marx's methodology with that of the German historical school of economics (even to the extent of identifying Marx as the "leader" of that school). He also described Marx's methodology in terms that suggested a very naïve form of historical positivism and asserted that this formed the real "scientific" basis of both Marx's Socialism and his own.[91] Thus he

89. Regarding the "right to the whole produce of labour" and Marx's rejection of it (partly because of its implicit individualism), see Menger, *The Right to Whole Produce,* and Marx, *Critique of the Gotha Programme* (1875. Eng. trans. New York, 1938); regarding Marx's repudiation of distributive justice, see esp. R. Tucker, *The Marxian Revolutionary Idea* (New York, 1969), pp. 25 ff., chap. 20.

90. See Henry Collins, "The Marxism of the Social Democratic Federation," in Briggs and Saville, eds., *Essays in Labour History, 1886–1923* (London, 1971).

91. Hyndman, *Historical Basis,* pp. vii–viii, 434–35, 492, and "Socialism in England," *N. Amer. Rev.* 143 (Sept. 1886): 228. The crux of Hyndman's his-

virtually guaranteed the intellectual vulnerability of subsequent Anglo-Marxism, so long as it continued to follow his intellectual lead.

Yet even these were not the most extreme of Hyndman's heresies, for his magnum opus, *The Historical Basis of Socialism in England,* also attempted to synthesize the teachings of Marx with those of Rodbertus and Lassalle. As regards the former, Hyndman's fondness for his work is apparent both in a lengthy appendix devoted to expounding his theory of rent, and in Hyndman's habit, elsewhere in the book, of treating his authority on matters of doctrine as almost equivalent to Marx's,[92] thereby encouraging the widespread English belief that Marx and Rodbertus were Socialists of the same school. Nor is it surprising that the doctrines of the German conservative State Socialist appealed to his English Tory-Radical counterpart: for both had approached Socialism by way of a thoroughgoing opposition to liberal social and political values; both were essentially State Socialists (as Marx was not); and both tended to conceive of Socialism in nationalistic and paternal terms. Such statist, nationalist, and elitist tendencies in Hyndman's thought also suggest affinities with the Socialism of Lassalle, whose iron law of wages, rejected by Marx, was crucial to Hyndman's theory. Hyndman's political tactics, too, were more Lassallean than Marxist: especially his intransigent hostility to Liberal politicians, his optimistic view of parliamentary democ-

---

torical methodology, and thus of his Socialist theory, was his belief that "scientific" historiography consisted in "rigid accuracy in the tabulation of facts," the results of which would form "laws" of social evolution capable of correctly forecasting the "next stages of our growth" (*Historical Basis,* pp. 434–35, 435 n.). His knowledge of the German historical school of economics (from which these views appear to have derived) probably came from his friend, Dr. Rudolf Meyer, a German émigré economist who had served as secretary to Bismarck and as editor of Rodbertus's *Correspondence.* Meyer was the source of Hyndman's initial interest in both Rodbertus and Lassalle. (For doctrines of the German historical school see, e.g., Schumpeter, *History of Economic Analysis,* esp. p. 811, and Rae, *Contemporary Socialism,* pp. 218 ff; regarding Meyer, see Tsuzuki, *Hyndman,* p. 31.)

92. Hyndman, *Historical Basis,* pp. 479–92; chap. 4, esp. pp. 112n., 114n., 126. (Hyndman's knowledge of Rodbertus's economic theories appears to have come from Rudolf Meyer, *Der Emancipationskampf des vierten Standes,* 2 vols. [Berlin, 1874–75].) Marx and Rodbertus were also linked on p. viii.

racy, and his disastrous tendency to wheel and deal with agents of the ruling class.[93]

In these respects, therefore, both Hyndman and the organization he dominated must be regarded as exponents of a heterodox and highly dubious type of "Marxism." But with respect to the most crucial points of later nineteenth-century Marxist doctrine—the points that Eduard Bernstein and the Fabians soon rejected as factually or intellectually untenable—they were unshakably "orthodox." They clung to the labor theory of value in its most rigid form; they believed firmly in the increasing misery of the proletariat and in the inability of trade unions or other agencies to permanently overcome it; and they continued—though not at all consistently—to preach the inevitability of class conflict in a violent and insurrectionary form.[94] Thus the "orthodox" side of their Marxism served to encourage an emphasis on violence and spoliation in their propaganda that, although ill-suited to the otherwise Radical character of their Socialist theory, accorded admirably with their increasingly militant style of rhetoric.

The most obvious source of that rhetorical militancy was the anger inspired in Hyndman and his followers by the poverty and degradation they had witnessed in the London slums. But a more careful examination of their rhetoric indicates that it was not so much poverty per se as the extreme contrast between that poverty and the luxurious habits of the leisure class, "now grown so wanton in their display," that inspired their hatred of the capitalist

---

93. *Historical Basis,* 117 n., 417–18. Hyndman's affinities with Lassalle were widely noted by contemporaries: e.g., Engels called him a "miserable caricature" of Lassalle (G. Mayer, *Friedrich Engels* [London, 1936], p. 250). Hyndman's "wheeling and dealing" was most evident in the "Tory Gold" episode of 1885, in which he accepted money to subsidize three SDF parliamentary candidates from the Tory double agent and trusted ally of Marx and Engels, Maltman Barry. He then approached Joseph Chamberlain with an offer to withhold the SDF candidates in return for a safe seat for himself at Birmingham! (G. B. Shaw to A. Scheu, 17 Dec. 1885, and H. H. Sparling to Scheu, 12 Dec. 1885, Scheu Papers, IISH).

94. Speeches and writings of SDF leaders were not always consistent in affirming these points (see qualifications on p. 106, and in n. 111; also Tsuzuki, *Hyndman,* 55–56), but they nevertheless formed the main thrust of SDF arguments in the middle and late 1880s.

system and gave substance to their revolutionary hope.[95] The hatred of the leisure class, as has been seen in the Introduction, was also the most powerful motivating force behind the English Socialist revival of the 1880s, and SDF Socialism was no exception to that trend. H. H. Champion, for example, flatly equated surplus value with "the total [wealth] absorbed by the whole of the leisure class. . . . The whole of the inhabitants of the wealthy districts and great squares lives on your unpaid labour," he proclaimed, while Hyndman, more shrewdly, pointed to the proliferation of "mere lounger towns, Brighton, Cheltenham, Scarborough and Eastbourne, [which have] sprung up to afford resting places for the growing numbers of indolent wealthy," as evidence that the poverty of the slums was a direct and inescapable result of the existence of a parasitic capitalist-rentier class.[96]

But would the social antagonisms inspired by that class and further abetted by the increasing instability of the capitalist system really prove sufficient to set off a "bloodier revolution than the French one," as Hyndman and his followers asserted?[97] Perhaps the best answer is that they only half believed that claim themselves and never developed a consistent theory of revolution, although they frequently employed the term. For although they expounded a rigidly deterministic version of the dialectic of history —"an historical process grinding on inexorably" toward an "apocalyptic crisis" from which Socialism would automatically result [98]—they tended to regard that "crisis" merely as a political transfer of power, which would be followed by an economic reorganization of society along collectivist lines; and these formed their

95. See p. 12 below. The quotation is from Joseph Chamberlain, "Labourers' and Artisans' Dwellings," *Fort. Rev.* 34 n.s. (1883). For an economic explanation of the late-Victorian expansion of the leisure class, see Eric Hobsbawm, *Industry and Empire*, pp. 96–97, 106.

96. Champion, "Surplus Value," *Chr. Soc.* 10 (March 1884): 155, and Hyndman, *The Coming Revolution in England*, p. 14.

97. E.g. Hyndman, quoted in *The Echo* 9 Feb. 1884, and cf. n. 100, below.

98. See Hyndman, *Historical Basis*, pp. 476–77; W. Sanders, *Early Socialist Days* (London, 1927), p. 29; and W. Kendall, *The Revolutionary Movement in Great Britain: 1900–1921* (London, 1969), pp. 11–12. Hyndman also argued that such revolution must inevitably occur, "whether we want it to or not" (*The Social Reconstruction of England*, p. 30; also *Historical Basis*, pp. 469, 470 *n*.

only serious objectives. In short, they were really reformists in revolutionary garb and used the rhetoric of violent revolution chiefly to stimulate enthusiasm among their sluggish followers and to fill the leisure class with fear. This appeared so obvious to many of Hyndman's opponents within the Socialist movement that they concluded he did not believe in revolution at all and meant to use the SDF only as a "bogie man" to frighten the government.[99] Nevertheless, in his lectures Hyndman continued to insist on the inevitability of a proletarian insurrection (even forecasting it for the centenary of 1789) [100] so that, despite his and his followers' frequent repudiations of violent intentions, their rhetoric led the public at large to associate their movement with violence and to ignore their more pacific protestations.

6. The Problem of Insurrectionary Rhetoric

Given the evidence of popular unrest throughout the middle 1880s —unrest that was repeatedly manifested in the demonstrations of the unemployed organized by the SDF and that spilled over into actual violence in February 1886 and November 1887— the threat of insurrection did not seem so empty as it did before or after those few years, and insurrectionary rhetoric found an unusually respectful audience. Thus Hyndman probably imagined that the threats of violence in his lectures and writings of that period were real and serious and would be received as such; and so, at least initially, did most of the other leaders of the SDF, although the point was soon to lead to serious dissidence. Consequently, throughout the latter part of 1884, Hyndman and his allies built the official teaching of their Federation ever more closely around the doctrines of class war and violent insurrection,

99. See Morris to Mrs. Burne-Jones, 24 Dec. 1884, quoted in Mackail, *Morris*, 2:128. Shaw also described Hyndman's "revolutionary" phrases as mere "stimulants" (Shaw to Scheu, 26 Oct. 1884, Scheu Papers, IISH), and Engels regarded all of Hyndman's rhetoric as "insincere" (quoted in Thompson, *Morris*, pp. 381, 394–95, 402), and cf. the review of Hyndman's *Historical Basis* in *Chr. Soc.* 11 (Apr. 1884), which made a similar point.

100. See Hyndman's threat to the Cambridge Union that "the day will assuredly come when the people you are depriving of their rights will rise against you and scourge you. . . . A bloodier revolution is looming than the French one. Beware!" (*Echo*, 9 Feb. 1884, p. 2e). See also *Justice*, 29 Dec. 1888, predicting a bloody year ahead.

and these, in turn, soon came to be identified with Socialism *as such* in the late-Victorian public mind.[101]

The new outlook of the SDF was thus a product of its leaders' faith in the insurrectionary potential of the English working class —a faith that ultimately proved illusory, but that in the face of mounting unemployment and newspaper exposures of squalor and disease in the great towns that accompanied it must have seemed at least a reasonable possibility in the mid-1880s.[102] Throughout those years, after all, it was common even for Radicals to foresee the possibility of insurrection—the great crowds assembled for the SDF rallies of the unemployed in 1886 suggested this to many contemporary observers—while there were also enough workingmen who warmed to the appeal of blood and thunder to give steady encouragement to the leaders of the SDF. Moreover, the Liberal government itself seemed to fan the flames of discontent by repeatedly sidetracking social reform and leaving the initiative therein to the ultra-Radical and revolutionary fringe.

At the same time, however, the insurrectionary rhetoric of the Federation probably alienated the great majority of the British public. Almost immediately, the popular conception of Socialism, as reflected in the London press, began to change from the rather mechanical idea of state interference in behalf of the weaker classes or the lingering memory of utopian communities to the far more sinister image of an insurrectionary and destructive movement conspiring impatiently for Armageddon. By early 1884 even advanced Radical journals that had previously treated surviving remnants of Owenite Socialism as honorable allies now joined in sounding the alarm. (Their usual opinion, however, was that the SDF was a Tory trick to split the Radical vote.) [103]

101. This was the typical non-Socialist view of SDF teaching, as seen, e.g., in the Radical *Pall Mall Budget* 17 Sept. 1885, pp. 11–12 (an article that also identified SDF adherents as "mostly clerks and shopmen"—i.e., lower middle class).

102. See G. R. Sims's pathbreaking reports on "How the Poor Live," in *Pictorial World* (spring and summer, 1883), and the *Pall Mall Gazette's* great journalistic crusade in support of *The Bitter Cry of Outcast London* (Oct.–Nov. 1883).

103. For general discussion of this question, see Rae, *Contemporary Socialism,* pp. 83–84, and Arthur Bestor, "Evolution of the Socialist Vocabulary," *JHI* (June 1948); for more specific examples, compare the ultra-Radical *Republican* in 1880 and 1884, the Radical *Echo,* Jan.–Feb. 1884, and the Radical *Weekly Dispatch,* Aug.–Sept. 1885.

By 1885, a substantial anti-Socialist literature had developed, and
it probably reflected the opinions of a great many London
Radicals.

For many such Radicals, that change in attitude was set in
motion by the great debate on Socialism between Hyndman and
Bradlaugh in April 1884. There Bradlaugh succeeded in pinning
on Hyndman and his cohorts the label of violent and irresponsible
incendiaries. From their own writings and speeches he derived a
picture of the Socialist menace, armed with dynamite, aiming to
destroy all private property and to reduce life to uniform medi-
ocrity. And although the Hyndmanites repudiated such charges
vigorously (and apparently in good faith), they were unable to
dispel the image Bradlaugh had bestowed upon them.[104] Consequently, the violent and almost unprecedented rioting on 8
February 1886, with which the Federation was indeed connected,
only confirmed that impression in the public mind, leading a
large share of the London press to conclude that "the Social-
Revolutionist gun had gone off too soon," resulting in a flash in
the pan.[105]

Of course, not all the results of the Hyndman–Bradlaugh debate
were damaging to Socialism, as it certainly stimulated discussion
of Socialist ideas in Radical clubs and journals, thereby attracting
a number of intellectuals and self-educated workingmen to the
cause (although not all of them remained for long within the
SDF).[106] But most of the resulting publicity seems to have been

104. The debate was published verbatim in *Justice*, 19 Apr. 1884 and as a
tract, *Will Socialism Benefit the English People?* (London, 1884). For an SDF
rebuttal to Bradlaugh, see J. L. Joynes, "Socialism," *Our Corner* 3 (1884), insisting that Hyndman's dynamite metaphor was not intended to apply to England
and that the real aim of SDF Socialism was "*not* the abolition of private property but its establishment, by means of the emancipation of labour, upon the
only sound basis"—presumably the "right to the whole produce of labour"
(p. 334); also compare *Chr. Soc.* (May 1884), and *Justice,* 7 June 1884, both
affirming that the only revolution intended was "mental." On the contradictions
of SDF rhetoric—its claims to be both revolutionary and peaceable—see *Common
Sense* (1 Mar. 1888), p. 155.

105. S. Olivier, "Perverse Socialism," *To-day* 6 (Aug. 1886): 50. For the most
recent analysis of the 1886 riots, see B. B. Gilbert, *The Evolution of National
Insurance in Britain* (London, 1966), pp. 32 ff.

106. John Burns, Tom Mann, and J. H. Watts were among the Radicals converted to SDF Socialism by that debate (although the first two soon seceded);
other Radical Secularists, including Annie Besant, William Clarke, and Grant
Allen, were drawn to the Fabian Society instead (see chap. 7).

unfavorable and to have helped to innoculate both intellectuals and workingmen against Socialism in the future—a tendency that was further encouraged by the violent rhetoric of Hyndman and his followers. For their praise of violence and confiscation were bound to repel precisely the sorts of skilled workingmen with funds in savings banks who, of all members of the British working class, were likeliest to take the most advanced Radical line in politics and to be most politically active. They were thus precisely the persons, in short, who would otherwise have formed the back bone of the SDF.[107] By continuing to reinforce the impression that bloodshed and spoliation were his aims, therefore, and by his parallel policy of verbally abusing and defaming Radical politicians, Hyndman systematically alienated his most promising source of recruits for Socialism.[108]

That same tendency was also so apparent in *Justice*, the new weekly "organ" of the SDF edited by Hyndman, that Helen Taylor denounced it as "an engine of public demoralisation." "Anonymous and irresponsible journalism is not a Socialist way of working," she pontificated, thus beginning a countermovement from within the SDF.[109] The inevitable upshot was a series of dramatic schisms, beginning with that of Helen Taylor and her followers; for by the summer of 1884 she was the one remaining member of the Executive Council of the SDF who could not accept the doc-

107. See Pelling, *Popular Politics and Society*, pp. 56, 61 (n. 101 above, and Bland, "Editorial Notes," *To-day* [July 1887], p. 3). Such "intelligent artisans" together with clerks and shopkeepers—R. S. Neale's "middling class"—would normally have formed the dominant element in the SDF as they did in most contemporary Radical clubs. (See R. S. Neale, "Class and Class Conciousness in Early Nineteenth Century England," *Vic. Stud.* 12 [Sept. 1968]: 5–32.) In the absence of surviving membership lists, however, it is impossible to determine the precise social character of the SDF, except that it was probably *not* "proletarian" in the Marxist sense. (See Appendix A below.)

108. See William Morris to C. E. Maurice, quoted in Thompson, *Morris*, p. 394, and Annie Besant, *Autobiography* (London, 1893), pp. 299 ff. There was a striking example of that tendency in the failure of SDF speakers to obtain even a hearing from the four or five thousand workingmen at the Radical franchise rallies in Trafalgar Square, in July 1884—chiefly because Hyndman and John Burns so persistently "abused and defamed" the Radical politicians "whom . . . our franchise friends had been worshipping all day" that the assembled workingmen turned against the SDF speakers and attacked them so violently that they had to be rescued by police! (Morris to Scheu, 26 July 1884, Scheu Papers, IISH).

109. Helen Taylor to H. M. Hyndman, [Aug. 1884], M-TC.

trines of class war and insurrection. Her loyalties were still rooted in the Radical past, dominated by the beliefs of her sainted step-father, and her Socialism was therefore of a "traditional" and moralistic type. It was, "in fact, another name for civilisation," and she would have no part in violence or class hatred. Instead, "as Socialism meant the perfection of human existence, it was . . . [continually] in a process of evolution" toward its goal of universal "unselfishness: the strong using their strength to secure the happiness of . . . the weak." But such a transformation must come about gradually, she insisted, and could only be retarded by an "immoral" use of force.[110]

Hyndman himself was not necessarily opposed to such ethical and evolutionary views. Indeed, the gradual, legislative transforma-tion of society continued to form an important part of his Socialist program.[111] But in the summer of 1884 he had become so deter-mined to assert the plenary authority of "Marxism" (as interpreted by himself) , so enthralled by what he saw as insurrectionary possi-bilities, and so hard-pressed by militant demands, that he was in no mood for gradualist arguments from anyone. The resulting quarrel perfectly illustrated his increasing doctrinal rigidity and unwillingness to compromise with the older Radical tradition and the kind of ethical Socialism it could sustain. Hyndman charged Taylor with failure "to go the whole length of our principles"; she, in turn, replied that Hyndman was "as yet only half a Socialist, if indeed half," and, as an "older and truer Socialist" than him-self, claimed to pass judgment on him "from a higher standard." Soon thereafter, she resigned from the SDF, taking her working-class following with her and initiating a trend that continued through the 1880s.[112]

Even before the end of 1884, however, internal antagonisms further split the SDF into opposing camps. Both personal and ideological factors were involved in the schism, but the present

110. Helen Taylor, lecture to the Eleusis Club, in *Justice* (19 Jan. 1884) .

111. Hyndman, *A Commune for London* (1887) —a plea for pure gradualism, in striking contrast with Hyndman's more familiar "revolutionary" style.

112. Hyndman to Helen Taylor, 23 July 1884, M-TC, and Helen Taylor to Hyndman (draft reply), n.d., ibid. Subsequently, Taylor was reported to be running "a halfpenny newspaper [*The Democrat*] with the Henry George Party" (Shaw to Scheu, 14 Oct. 1884, Scheu Papers, IISH) , and land reform again became her chief enthusiasm.

study will be concerned only with the latter, which involved fundamental differences about the meaning and purpose of Socialism. The most recent biographer of Hyndman has characterized the antagonistic forces as representing definite left and right wings of the SDF.[113] The Left, heavily permeated with Anarchism, argued for a more genuinely revolutionary policy and condemned as useless all political activity and reliance on palliative reforms. Real Socialism, it believed, could only take root after a clean sweep of the old, degraded capitalist culture and the establishment of a new moral order. The Right, in contrast, was strongly political, seeking to introduce Socialism through existing parliamentary institutions. It confidently prophesied the outbreak of an insurrection in the near future, sparked by the expected breakdown of the economy, but saw it chiefly as a means of hastening the transfer of political power. Its thought was dominated by the example of the great French Revolution and by the European democratic-revolutionary tradition that stemmed from it,[114] and it regarded each successive instance of distress or public protest in those turbulent years as a possible beginning for that apocalyptic process. (Paradoxically, however, the revolutionary beliefs of the Left did not imply the use of abusive "revolutionary" rhetoric, while the militant rhetoric favored by the Right did not—as has been seen—necessarily imply a serious belief in revolution.)

The leader of the Left, almost in spite of himself, was William Morris, sometimes acting as a mouthpiece for the Austrian émigré Andreas Scheu (who lived in Edinburgh), and for others who were quasi-Anarchists. The leader of the Right, of course, was Hyndman. The issue on which they finally split was essentially one of political "opportunism," compounded by widespread personal distrust of Hyndman, and Hyndman's hostility to Scheu and Edward Aveling.[115] In December 1884, these tensions boiled over to

113. Tsuzuki, *Hyndman*, pp. 57 ff.

114. See Edward Carpenter, *My Days and Dreams* (London, 1916), pp. 246–49; Hyndman, *Social Reconstruction of England;* and "Revolution or Reform," *To-day*, 2 (Aug. 1884): 180–198.

115. Aveling was the common-law husband of Eleanor Marx (see Tsuzuki, *Life of Eleanor Marx*). Regarding charges of opportunism, see n. 93 above. In essence, Hyndman hoped to become the Parnell of the English Left, forcing the government "by threats [of violence] to carry out his wishes." His attempt to make a political deal with Chamberlain adds weight to that view.

produce an open schism. Morris, followed by a majority of the Executive Council, resigned from the SDF to create a new organization, the Socialist League, leaving Hyndman complete control of a greatly weakened SDF. Both of the resulting organizations were thereafter stunted by the mutual hostility and sectarian spirit that accompanied the split, and irreparable damage was inflicted on the image and morale of the Socialist movement. Nor was the great schism of 1884 the last. Almost every year in the late eighties brought forth another schism and the formation of a new Socialist splinter group, so long as Hyndman ruled the SDF.[116]

Meanwhile, the great mass of British workingmen remained untouched by Socialism, while Radical intellectuals tended to regard it as a narrow and sectarian affair. Its doctrines—severed from Radical foundations by emphasis on insurrection and class war—were alien to working-class political traditions, so that despite success in organizing protest demonstrations, its ideology (which offered workingmen no aid in solving their immediate problems) failed to catch on. "Men listen respectfully to socialism," Morris complained, "but are perfectly supine and not in the least inclined to move except along the lines of radicalism and trade unionism." Nor did the SDF's Marxian rhetoric have much appeal for Radical intellectuals educated in liberal and utilitarian habits of thought. So its membership remained small—under 1,000 during the 1880s—and was concentrated chiefly in London, with few men of great ability. All this seemed to bear out a future Fabian essayist's remark that "the English lack the revolutionary temper and will never go in for Socialism *en masse*."[117]

By the end of 1884, therefore, the time was ripe for a new depar-

116. Thus the Tory Gold Scandal of Dec. 1885 (see n. 93) produced a schism and the formation of a new, largely working-class body, the Socialist Union (see its journal, *The Socialist*, July–Dec. 1886); conflict over the usefulness of "revolutionary" rhetoric and the practicability of revolutionary tactics produced another splinter group in 1887, led by Champion (see his journal, *Common Sense*, May 1887–March 1888); the most prominent working-class members of the SDF, Tom Mann and John Burns, defected over the same issue in 1888 (both subsequently joined the Fabian Society); and so it went.

117. William Morris, MS diary, 12 Feb. 1887, BM 45335, and William Clarke to H. D. Lloyd, 24 Oct. 1884, Lloyd Papers, WSHS. H. Bland, "The Need of a New Departure," *To-day* (Nov. 1887): 132, 140, and Annie Besant, quoted in *Prac. Soc.* (Oct. 1886), made the same point.

ture in the Socialist camp, a new approach to winning Radical converts to the faith. In fact, several such departures were made in the middle eighties along five different (but overlapping) lines, which are the chief subjects for the remainder of the present study. Of these five, however, the earliest and most closely linked to SDF experiences were those of Bernard Shaw (who had been allied with Morris in the SDF but had never actually joined that body), and of the very different group of Radical freethinkers and philanthropists, the founders of the Fabian Society, whose ranks Shaw ultimately did join. Through their combined efforts, abetted by the extraordinary group of "converts" who were drawn into that Society in the mid-eighties, an effective Socialist alternative to Marxism was established, grounded in English Radical values. In order to analyze this process properly, however, it will be necessary to isolate and examine separately the chief intellectual traditions represented by the leading "converts" or groups of converts to the Society in the 1880s. In subsequent chapters, therefore, five such intellectual traditions that served as "roads" to Socialism for those converts will be analyzed, using intellectual biography to make each chapter a case study or intellectual portrait of the person or persons who took that road to Socialism.[118]

118. Although those five "roads" were not always logically distinct and overlapped somewhat in content, they were regarded by contemporaries as representing separate and distinct movements. Together, they formed the sources of nearly all the ideas and beliefs that went into the making of Fabian Socialist theory.

Part II
Five Roads to Socialism

4

George Bernard Shaw:
The Radical-Libertarian Road to Socialism

No man is good enough to be another man's master.

WILLIAM MORRIS[1]

On 5 September 1882, when Henry George gave his first London lecture at the Memorial Hall in Farringdon St., a pale, young Irishman, dressed almost too shabbily to be seen in public, slipped late into the meeting and, despite a formidable tendency to criticize, found himself spellbound by the speaker's rhetoric. Because it changed the direction of his life, converting the man who would be England's most widely read Socialist to a lifelong concern with economic problems,[2] it will be useful to retrace the steps that brought George Bernard Shaw to the Memorial Hall that night in such an unexpectedly receptive frame of mind.

1. The Road to Socialism

In the six years since he had come to live in London, Shaw had become, to all outward appearances, a drifter and a social misfit: "unsettled and much in that active but unproductive vein in which an immature man wanders about London at night, plans extravagant social reforms, reads Shelley," and talks in a strain of uncompromising virtue.[3] Only one real point was lacking from that extra-

1. Shaw, quoting William Morris, in "Socialism and Human Nature," lecture, 1890, BM 50683, reprinted in L. Crompton, ed., *The Road to Equality* (Boston, 1971), p. 92, frequently repeated, e.g., as the motto of the William Morris Labour Church in *Major Barbara*, act 3. (Shaw's capitalization and punctuation have been preserved throughout.) Unfortunately, all BM numbers in the Shaw Papers are provisional. They are listed in the following citations as they presently stand, followed by italicized item numbers and folio numbers (as needed).

2. Shaw to Hamlin Garland, 29 Dec. 1904, quoted in A. Henderson, *George Bernard Shaw: Man of the Century* (New York, 1956), p. 215. For the substance of George's lecture, see p. 85.

3. Shaw to Arnold White, 5 Oct. 1879, in D. H. Laurence, ed., *Collected Letters of Bernard Shaw, 1874–1897* (New York, 1965), p. 23.

ordinary self appraisal: that he was also, despite apparent aimlessness, searching continually for an ideological commitment that could focus his abundant energies and give them the direction they lacked. On such an autumn night, therefore, it was his habit to search the city streets for public lectures or debates where the "advanced" ideas of the day were preached, for any new idea might point the way to the salvation he was seeking. Everywhere in London "the air seemed charged with articulate thought," and Bernard Shaw was determined to take in all of it.[4]

As a result of these experiences, Shaw could also describe himself, at twenty-six, as a man of "revolutionary and contradictory temperament": an ultra-Radical with "advanced" opinions on all subjects, except, as yet, on economic ones. Intellectually, he had cut his teeth on classical liberalism (as expounded, for example, in Mill's essay *On Liberty*) and had thrived on the literary classics of social protest (Bunyan, Shelley, Dickens, and Ruskin), and the two strands remained permanently intertwined in his thinking.[5] He was also, by his own account, a "born Communist and Iconoclast": a rebel against every aspect of the genteel, middle-class society that had nurtured him, and against which he now set himself as a new Jeremiah, who would call the respectable classes to repentance by preaching that "respectability founded on property is blasphemy." [6]

Such insights, together with the discontent that underlay them, had come originally from observing his own family, a decayed branch of the Anglo-Irish Ascendancy, who "talked of themselves as the Shaws, as who should say the Bourbons, the Valois, the Hapsburgs," so that snobbery and class consciousness had blighted their lives for generations. Unhappily, that process culminated for young George Bernard Shaw in the economic downfall of his father and the destruction of his own "chance" in life. His father was a former

4. S. Winsten, *Jesting Apostle: The Private Life of Bernard Shaw* (New York, 1957), p. 35. This book contains valuable anecdotal material drawn from extensive conversations with Shaw—the author was his neighbor—but most of its assertions are undocumented and must therefore be used with caution.

5. Shaw to Garland, 29 Dec. 1904, in Henderson, *Man of the Century*, p. 215. For a definition of classical liberalism, see chap. 1, n. 13 above.

6. Shaw, *Immaturity*, standard ed. (London, 1950), preface, p. xix; "born Radical" would have been a more accurate characterization of his beliefs.

civil servant who subsequently failed in business (which, of course, he thought beneath him) and turned so heavily to drink that his family was finally dropped from gatherings of "decent people." Given these circumstances, no money was available to finance the ritual of a gentleman's education for the young Shaw, who in any case showed little inclination for it. Consequently, after enduring the class-conscious humiliation of attending schools with Methodist and Catholic tradesmen's sons until his fifteenth year, his family arranged for his employment in an intensely genteel firm that managed the estates of idle landlords.[7]

Thus "Sonny" Shaw began life as a "downstart." He knew the monotony of office routine from the inside ("I felt myself a born slave"), knew the evils of slum landlordism from managing rent collections, and the spirit of rebellion quickened in him. The first public evidence of such rebelliousness appeared when he was eighteen, in the form of a commentary on the Moody–Sankey revivals that were then taking place in Dublin. Shaw had already dubbed himself an "infidel;" now he ironically demanded that the attentions of those celebrated preachers should be directed to "the rough, the outcasts of the streets," who needed release from the dull routine of hard work, rather than lavished on respectable people whose presence threatened to divert the meetings from their only useful purpose. It was a characteristically Shavian combination of social and religious protest and formed his inauguration as a social critic.[8]

Mounting frustration with his job, where he was under constant pressure to avoid religious arguments, together with a feeling that his talents languished in provincial Dublin, soon convinced the young rebel that he must leave home. In his nineteenth year, therefore, he rejoined his mother, who had already established

7. Ibid, p. xi, and Shaw, *Sixteen Self-Sketches* (London, 1955), pp. 22 ff. Although the Shaws were Anglican Evangelicals (in the Church of Ireland), Bernard Shaw insisted that they were basically irreligious and regarded churchgoing chiefly as a mark of respectability. In any case, he learned to regard organized Christianity with contempt while still in his teens and preserved that attitude throughout the 1880s. For further discussion, see J. Percy Smith, *The Unrepentant Pilgrim* (New York, 1965), pp. 130 ff.; but cf. the caveat in n. 19 below.

8. Shaw, letter to *Public Opinion*, 3 April 1875, quoted in Henderson, *Man of the Century*, pp. 47–48; also Smith, *Unrepentant Pilgrim*, p. 130.

herself in London as a teacher of young ladies' "vocal culture."
There he rapidly took to a pleasant life of concert and lecture going, while attending crammer's classes to prepare him for the civil
service examinations and a highly respectable career. But such ambitions had to be abandoned soon thereafter when he proved to
have no talent for mathematical or linguistic examinations. Consequently, after halfheartedly seeking clerical work in a variety of
situations for which he freely stated his unfitness, he relapsed into
a state of virtual unemployability. For the next five years, with
only brief exceptions, he labored exclusively at developing his
literary talents, producing five novels that were unanimously rejected by the established English publishers.[9]

Despite the failure of Shaw's youthful novels to attract publishers, they are of great importance to his intellectual biography;
for even the earliest of them bristled with idiosyncratic moral
insights that Shaw soon learned to use as verbal darts to pierce the
shield of middle-class respectability. In that manner his early
novels served as vehicles for working out the main themes of his
youthful social observations: the irony of class pretensions and of
snobbishness, and the clashes of personal worth with social status,
of freedom with social convention, and of honest work with aristocratic idleness. All were characteristic Radical attitudes that Shaw
subsequently transformed into the main themes of his Socialist
theory. Yet in its early, fictional form, his criticism lacked clear
focus and direction, and seemed likely to continue to do so until
the fledgling novelist could find some movement or system of
thought to focus his too-scattered insights into a coherent view of
social reconstruction.

The first movement to capture his imagination in that fashion
was the Radical Secularism of Charles Bradlaugh. As a self-proclaimed atheist and social rebel, Shaw was inevitably attracted to

9. Shaw's only prolonged employment in the early eighties involved negotiating
telephone rights of way in east London (Nov. 1879–June 1880); it was one of his
formative experiences. (For details, see the Shaw biographies in the Bibliographical Note, and Laurence, *Collected Letters*, pp. 22 ff.) The five novels were:
Immaturity (1879), *The Irrational Knot* (1880; rev., 1882), *Love Among the
Artists* (1881), *Cashel Byron's Profession* (1882), and, following his reading of
Marx, *An Unsocial Socialist* (1883).

the Secularist Hall of Science, and there found himself spellbound by the lectures of Bradlaugh and his assistant, Annie Besant. At least temporarily, he subscribed to their program of Radical reforms—universal suffrage, complete religious and intellectual freedom, extinction of poverty through birth control—and rejoiced in its affront to the conventions of the polite society. When his new heroes were prosecuted for selling a Malthusian tract in 1877, Shaw sprang to their defense, joining the popular agitation for acquittal and volunteering to sell the tract himself. When his heroes were found guilty, he declared himself an "Anarchist" in protest against the gross injustice of the courts.[10]

Such experiences also helped to channel Shaw's rebellious spirit into Radical and libertarian politics, thus giving him a sense of confrontation with the forces of social tyranny and oppression that left its mark indelibly upon his personality. Fired by his new sense of involvement in a great cause, he began to haunt Radical debating clubs and taught himself stump oratory by speaking out at every opportunity for Radical and Secularist principles and on art and Ireland. His maiden speech was delivered at the London Zetetical Society in October 1880, and from that time he haunted similar debating clubs until the thrust and parry of debate became an almost automatic reflex.[11] These debating societies, in turn, introduced Shaw to a new set of persons from whom his earliest taste for Socialism was acquired. The most important of these was an Alsatian singer and ex-Communard named Richard Deck, who undertook to teach Shaw French and elocution and, at the same time, introduced him to the Anarchism of Proudhon. From the latter, Shaw learned the view that "property is theft" (or, more in accordance with Proudhon's meaning, that property of the sort that lets a man live off the work of others makes him a thief). And this, in turn, reminded Shaw of Ruskin's dictum, to which he frequently referred, that any man who lived without working must

10. See Winsten, *Jesting Apostle*, p. 35, which adds that by "Anarchist" Shaw meant to signify his opposition to all forms of oppressive authority.
11. Autobiographical Notebook, BM 50710A; and cf. *Sixteen Self-Sketches*, p. 56, and chap. 6, n. 6 below. For Shaw's surprisingly radical views on Irish reforms, see *The Radical*, 30 July 1881, report of Zetetical Society.

be "either a thief or a beggar."[12] These two doctrines gave Shaw
his earliest impetus toward Socialism. But for the time being they
seem chiefly to have strengthened the fierce libertarian feelings
that he had previously derived from Godwin, Shelley, and Mill,
and thus to have focused his rebellious discontent more sharply
upon one powerful intellectual-emotional commitment: the commitment to liberty and the opposition to all forms of coercive
authority over mankind.[13]

In the late seventies Shaw found no better outlet for his libertarian zeal than the endless religious warfare of the Secularists. But
the acquittal of Bradlaugh and Besant on appeal took much of the
excitement from that movement, with which, in any case, Shaw
found himself increasingly at odds. At the same time, in the face
of ever-widening distress created by the Great Depression, the
whole agnostic controversy came to seem "barren" and irrele-
vant.[14] At that point, however, his need for a cause that was a
closer touch with curent sources of unrest seemed to be answered
by Henry George and by the wave of interest he aroused among
advanced Radicals everywhere in England.

2. The Sources of Shaw's Socialism

If Shaw was, in fact, searching for a faith on that September
night in 1882, the intense, quasi-religious tone of George's oratory
was perfectly suited to provide it. His moral earnestness, his powerful Radical rhetoric, and, above all, his simple solution to the
problem of poverty immediately captured Shaw's imagination and
opened a new intellectual and moral world to him as nothing else
had since the Bradlaugh trial. Because Shaw was still an economic

12. Shaw was Deck's pupil for nearly a year, ending in May 1881 (BM 50710A).
Only Winsten, *Jesting Apostle*, p. 44, mentions their discussions of Proudhon, but
for Shaw's own tributes to Proudhon and Ruskin, see Shaw, *The Intelligent
Woman's Guide to Socialism and Capitalism* (New York, 1928), pp. 466, 469. The
Ruskin quotation was frequently repeated by Shaw, e.g., in his review of "Andro-
meda," in *Pall Mall Gazette*, Oct. 9, 1885. Cf. his *Rushkin's Politics* (Oxford, 1926),
p. 11.

13. Winsten, *Jesting Apostle*, p. 44, adds that the words from Proudhon's *Confessions*, "whoever lays his hand on me to govern me is a usurper and a tyrant; I
declare him to be my enemy," were "like a cry from Shaw's own heart."

14. Shaw, *Sixteen Self-Sketches*, p. 58.

novice, George's simplified arguments struck him with "the force of revelation": one economic "law" explaining all distress; one common-sense panacea to cure it. "George's logic of the law of rent captured me for life," Shaw wrote, and gave him a new sense of purpose in the world.[15] Somehow he found the cash to purchase *Progress and Poverty* and read through it eagerly, a convert from the start.

The suddenness of that conversion suggests how great Shaw's need had been for it; for he derived from George not just a theory but a Weltanschauung and a new cause to which he could commit himself. Armed with these, he characteristically lost no time in challenging the land monopolists and rentiers to verbal combat. But that inevitably brought him into conflict with his old allies, the Malthusians, as a Georgian was bound to argue that overpopulation was not a cause of poverty and, in defiance of the classical economists, that labor employed capital. (Indeed, Shaw rapidly outstripped his mentor in the latter argument and was soon claiming, in the manner of Proudhon, that labor would have no need of capitalists at all if the latter had not "monopolized" all capital and thus prevented workmen from obtaining it for themselves.) [16] In 1882, however, Shaw was still chiefly bothered by the inequities of rent; and George had outdone even Proudhon in denouncing that as a form of "robbery that is fresh and continuous every day. . . . Because I was robbed yesterday, and the day before, and the day before that, is that any reason to . . . conclude that the robber has acquired a vested interest to rob me?"[17] Thus "robbery" of unearned increments became Shaw's battle cry, blending the Georgian Law of Rent with Proudhon's view of property as theft.

Such sentiments must also have coincided with Shaw's own social

15. Shaw to Garland, in Henderson, *Man of the Century*, p. 215.

16. J. Rothwell (of the Malthusian League) to Shaw, 20 and 25 Nov., 12 Dec. 1882, BM 50509; (I have inferred Shaw's arguments from Rothwell's replies). Shaw adopted Proudhon's argument that interest on loans was evil because it led to the accumulation of large fortunes, which were the instruments of working-class exploitation—a view that he developed more fully in his later writings (see chap. 8, below; also C. Gide and C. Rist, *A History of Economic Doctrines* 2d Eng. ed., trans. R. Richards (London, 1948), pp. 559 ff., 292 ff., and Rothwell to Shaw, 12 Dec. 1882 BM 50509.

17. Henry George, *Progress and Poverty* (London, 1881), pp. 327–28.

observations, for the engineer-hero of his second novel, *The Irrational Knot* (1880), denounces the rentier classes of men, "loafing idly round and spending money that has been made by the sweat of men like myself," as "little better than thieves." In 1880, however, he had only been able to follow up that insight by listing the social anomalies that resulted from the existence of such rentiers:

> They get on with the queerest makeshifts for self-respect. . . . Everything is a sham with them: they have drill and etiquet [*sic*] instead of manners, fashions instead of tastes, . . . [Until, finally, the hero exclaims,] I admit no loafer as my equal. . . . The class that does not work is a class below mine.[18]

Now Georgian economics provided a new conclusion to Shaw's reasoning about the leisure class. For George had shown that the simplest rules of justice, based on classical liberal assumptions, required that landlords must be expropriated and their rents be given to the community. As unearned increment, rent was not rightfully the property of any man. It was socially produced—the result of monopoly conditions that were unavoidable in any populous society—and could only be regained for the community (or "nationalized") by a tax amounting to its whole annual value.

Shaw, therefore, began his journey to Socialism as a land nationalizer. In his first flush of enthusiasm for that cause he joined the Georgian Land Reform Union, and, for nearly a year, worked on its journal, *The Christian Socialist,* through which he made the acquaintance of such early Socialist luminaries as Joynes, Champion, and Frost.[19] These, in turn, encouraged him to attend meetings of the SDF, where, early in 1883, he first heard Hyndman preach the gospel of Karl Marx. Shaw's all-too-characteristic response was to accuse Hyndman of "drawing a red herring across

18. Shaw, *The Irrational Knot* (London, 1905), pp. 338–39.
19. Joynes to Shaw, 22 June, 27 Dec. 1883, and 16 Jan. 1884; also Shaw to Sidney Webb, 11 Aug. 1883, inviting him to join the LRU (BM 50510, 50553). Unfortunately Smith, *Unrepentant Pilgrim*, pp. 137–38, construes Shaw's brief involvement with the *Christian Socialist* set, referred to by Belfort Bax as "Hobnobbing with 'baptized Christians'" (Bax to Shaw, 3 May 1884, BM 50557), as evidence of a new friendliness toward orthodox Christianity; in fact, there is no evidence that Shaw changed his religious opinions during the 1880s.

the track of social regeneration indicated by Mr. Henry George."
For saying this, he was denounced by Hyndman as a novice who
had no right to venture an opinion on economic subjects until
he had mastered Marx. Thus chastened, but with the encouragement of several anti-Hyndmanites with the SDF, Shaw took up the
French translation of the first volume of *Capital* and emerged from
the experience, in his own words, as "a furious Marxist." "It
opened my eyes to the facts of history and civilization, gave me an
entirely fresh conception of the universe, and provided me with a
mission and purpose in life." [20] Thus his long incipient revolt
against bourgeois society crystallized into a Socialist form—but a
form inimical to Hyndman and the official teaching of the SDF.

Yet one may still doubt whether Shaw's Socialist conversion was
really so cataclysmic or the effect of *Capital* upon his mind so powerful as his own account of them suggests; for he could scarcely
have read the translation of that book with any thoroughness in
1883, given his shaky command of French and curious habit of
perusing it in tandem with the score of Wagner's *Tristan und
Isolde*.[21] Moreover, his actual indebtedness to *Capital*, at least with
regard to economic theory, seems to have been chiefly limited to its
first chapter, with its exhaustive elaboration of the principle that
commodities naturally exchange in exact proportion to the quantities of socially necessary labor time embodied in them: "ten hours
for ten hours," and so on. In any case, this was the principle Shaw
seized upon to form the basis of his own Socialist theory. It was a
curious and very limited interpretation of Marx—scarcely "Marxist" at all from the point of view of the SDF—but it was an interpretation for which Shaw was thoroughly prepared by his familiarity with the ideas of Proudhon, Ruskin, and Henry George, all

20. Shaw, "The New Politics," lecture, Dec. 1889, BM 50683, in Crompton, *The
Road to Equality*, pp. 83–84, and as quoted in Hesketh Pearson, *Bernard Shaw*
rev. ed. (London, 1961), p. 68. The most familiar version of this portion of the
"Shaw Legend" is *Sixteen Self-Sketches*, p. 58, but many of the claims made there
(e.g., that other members of the SDF had not read Marx) are untrue. In fact,
Shaw was introduced to the French translation of *Capital* by Robert Banner, an
SDF stalwart (subsequently a Fabian) who had been trained in Marxism by Andreas
Scheu, and for several years thereafter Shaw continued to derive his most important
Socialist ideas from Scheu ("The New Politics," p. 84, and cf. n. 76 below).

21. C. Archer, *William Archer: Life, Work, Friendships* (London, 1931), p. 119.

of whom taught it more clearly than Marx because they derived it as an ethical corollary from their classical liberal assumptions.

For such reasons, these three writers, rather than Marx, were the primary sources of Shaw's Socialist faith. From Proudhon and Ruskin came the original kernel of that faith: the proof that "a *rentier*, living by owning instead of by working, inflicts on society the same injury as a thief," and that to live on the labor of others in that fashion was the primary social sin.[22] Through George's arguments, that insight became part of a reasoned economic system. Marx only completed the process by demonstrating that a capitalist, extracting surplus value, "inflicted on society" the same injury as a landlord. Thus George's attack on property in land was seen to apply equally to the whole economic system that vested ownership of the means of production in a parasitic, exploitative, and nonfunctional leisure class.[23]

Such was the negative side of Shaw's approach to Socialism. His more positive Socialist beliefs followed a similar pattern, blending the teachings of Proudhon, Ruskin, George, and Marx in such a way that the moral ideas of the first three—especially those embodied in Proudhon's and Ruskin's doctrine of the reciprocal exchange of services and in George's theory of rent[24]—were treated as corollaries of Marx's more "scientific" notion of the equal ex-

22. Shaw, *Intelligent Woman's Guide*, p. 466, and cf. Shaw, *Ruskin's Politics*, pp. 11, 17–18. No adequate analysis of Ruskin's influence on Shaw exists (and Shaw himself wrote curiously little about it), but there are useful comments in Sir Kenneth Clark, *Ruskin Today* (Harmondsworth, 1967), p. 269; Eric Bentley, *Bernard Shaw* (London, 1950), pp. 57–58; and J. B. Kaye, *Bernard Shaw and the Nineteenth Century Tradition* (Norman, Okla., 1958), pp. 20 ff. No analysis exists of Proudhon's influence on Shaw, but for Proudhon's economic and moral teachings, see Gide and Rist, *History of Economic Doctrines*, pp. 305–28, and G. Woodcock, *Anarchism* (Harmondsworth, 1963), chap. 5. Marx denounced Proudhon's teachings in *The Poverty of Philosophy* (1847).

23. For the first, quintessentially Shavian public presentation of this argument, see Shaw's speech to the Industrial Remuneration Conference, 1885, reprinted in Pelling, *Challenge of Socialism*, pp. 161–62.

24. For Proudhon's doctrine of reciprocity, or "mutualism" ("mutual respect" requiring mutual and equal performance of services), see P. J. Proudhon, *De la justice dans la Revolution* 3 vols. (Paris, 1858), 1:269, and G. Lichtheim, *Origins of Socialism* (London, 1969), pp. 88–89. For Ruskin's doctrine that "only life was worthy to exchange for life," see *Fors Clavigera*, 4 vols. (London, 1871–84), letter 7 (1871), and cf. the similar argument in E. Carpenter, "England's Ideal," *To-day* (May 1884): 332; also Gide and Rist, *History of Economic Doctrines*, pp. 541–43.

change of labor time. Thus in effect Shaw synthesized what he understood of Marxian economics with a very traditional type of ethical Socialism that remained the permanent foundation of his social faith. This emphasis on the "ethical aspect" of Socialism, which was alien to the SDF, further reinforced the nonscientific character of his economic reasoning, leading him to argue that the true nature of rent and interest lay in the concrete "relations between one man and another"—moral relationships—rather than in the abstract relations between lands of differing fertility or between differing rates of wages, as economists and "scientific" Socialists maintained. Similarly, Shaw understood capital as pure Property, in the Proudhonian sense: a social relationship that was "of a peculiarly abominable kind." [25] Even his tendency to conflate Marx's idea of the equal exchange of labor time with Proudhon's and Ruskin's doctrine of reciprocal services had the effect of emphasizing the human element involved.

Consequently, what impressed Shaw most deeply in his reading of Marx's *Capital* was not its elaborate critique of economic theory, which, he asserted, merely served to obscure the moral nature of the transactions, but its "relentless Jeremiad against the bourgeoisie":

> [Marx's] burning conviction that the old order is one of fraud and murder; that its basis is neither kingcraft nor priestcraft, but the divorce of the laborer from the material without which his labor is barren; and that it is changing and giving place to the new by an inexorable law of development.[26]

More than anything else, it was that "inexorable law"—the dialectic of history—that captured Shaw's imagination in 1883 and made him accept the rest of Marx's analysis. The Great Depression, worsening again in the course of that year, seemed fully to bear out Marx's claim that the cyclical upheavals of capitalism

25. Speech to Industrial Remuneration Conference (in Pelling, *Challenge of Socialism*, p. 162), and "Special Report" of Fabian Conference, 11 June 1886, BLPES, f. 266. Marx also made many of the same points (e.g., in discussing the "fetishism of commodities," in *Capital*, 1:73–74), but they were alien to contemporary Anglo-Marxism.

26. "Karl Marx and *Das Kapital*," *National Reformer* 50 (7 Aug. 1887).

were portents of its imminent destruction, and Shaw began to
eagerly anticipate its end:

> Our profits are vanishing, our machinery is standing idle,
> our workmen are locked out. It pays now to stop the mills and
> fight and crush the unions when the men strike, no longer for
> an advance but against a reduction. . . . The small capitalists
> are left stranded by the ebb; the big ones will follow the tide
> across the water, and rebuild their factories where steam
> power, water power, labor power, and transport are now
> cheaper than in England. . . . As the British factories are shut
> up they will be replaced by villas; the manufacturing districts
> will become fashionable resorts of capitalists living on the
> interest of foreign investments; the farms and sheep runs
> will be cleared for deer forests. . . . [Finally] a vast proletariat,
> beginning with a nucleus of those formerly employed in the
> export trades, with their multiplying progeny, will be out of
> work permanently. They will demand access to the land and
> machinery to produce for themselves. They will be refused
> . . . [Then] they will revolt.[27]

Thus Shaw wrote in his last completed novel, *An Unsocial
Socialist,* the product of his infatuation with Marxism in the spring
and summer of 1883. He had first conceived of it as the beginning
of "a vast work depicting capitalist society in dissolution, with its
downfall as the final grand catastrophe"—a kind of *Capital* in fictional form. As it turned out, the "grand catastrophe" was merely
foretold in marathon speeches, but Shaw remained fully convinced
of its inevitability: "Marx keeps his head like a God," he proclaimed. "The thread of history is in his hand." It is "either Socialism or Smash."[28]

But there was also a more personal reason why Shaw embraced
Socialism so eagerly in 1883. It was revealed in a lecture of the
following year in which he dilated on the harsh prospects facing a

27. *An Unsocial Socialist,* standard ed. (London, 1930), pp. 214–15. For further
discussion of these points, see p. ooo, below.
28. Ibid., Introduction, p. vii. "Karl Marx and *Das Kapital*"; *Unsocial Socialist,*
p. 213.

sensitive young man like himself who was thrown into the commercial world with no resources other than his wits:

> If he be poor, and unable to succeed in a competitive examination for government appointment, he becomes an office boy at fifteen and thenceforth for a pittance . . . counts the money of thieves and gamblers [as Shaw himself had done in Ireland,] . . . they being so absolutely his masters that he dare not write a letter to a newspaper or take part in a public meeting without their approval. . . . All this constitutes what he calls his respectability, which he jealously guards and hands on to his son. . . . I should recommend him to become a Socialist instead [and fight the system openly].[29]

Which was what Shaw had decided he must do in 1883.

3. Shaw's Early Socialist Doctrines

Once that decision was made, Shaw saw that his chief business must be to preach his newfound faith wherever a few persons could be induced to listen: at Radical workingmen's clubs, middle-class debating societies, street corner gatherings, Trafalgar Square rallies, and even at learned societies. Fortunately, the substance of those lectures has been preserved, thanks to Shaw's meticulous care in making and keeping the note cards from which they were delivered, and this has made it possible to chart the changing course of his Socialist ideas during the years most crucial to their development.[30]

The main, almost obsessive theme of those lectures was the contrast between economic honesty and dishonesty: between "theft" and idleness on the one hand, and "honest" labor on the other. The application of this contrast to the landowning and "industrious" classes, respectively, had long been a standard feature of Radical rhetoric. Shaw treated it in much the same way in his

29. "That the Socialist Movement Is Nothing but the Assertion of Our Lost Honesty," lecture, May 1884, BM 50702, f. 155, in Crompton, *The Road to Equality,* pp. 16–17.

30. The note cards for more than forty such lectures, given between Oct. 1884 and Feb. 1888 constitute BM 50700. They are entirely unpublished.

earliest statement of Socialist beliefs, by observing that "a state of things exists whereby a man can live idle if he can force another to work for him," as "every Idler's wealth must be taken from Someone else who has earned . . . it by Labour and has laboured for two." Such was the prevailing dishonesty of contemporary society, and Shaw's immediate response was to declare that it was "absolutely immoral" to allow such rentiers any longer "to confiscate daily the labour of others for whom they did nothing." [31] That principle, he insisted, was the essence of Socialism, which was "loud and earnest just now" precisely because so many "able-bodied persons [were] openly living in luxury and idleness." Thus, restated in more positive terms, the ruling principle of Shavian Socialism was that all "men shall *honestly* labor for those who labor for them, each man replacing what he consumes, none profiting at his fellow's expense, and all profiting alike from the most equitable division of labor." More simply put, "If six hours useful labor exchange for six hours labor . . . without regard for the degree of skill involved, the result is Socialism." Thus the Socialist movement was nothing but "the Assertion of our Lost Honesty": a protest against the "theft" of other men's labor and a plan for restoring integrity to a society that habitually lived by "robbing the poor." [32]

Despite its use of traditional Radical rhetoric, that argument betrays one specific influence that does not fit comfortably into the Radical tradition: the influence of John Ruskin, which was far more powerful than Shaw's biographers have recognized. Like Shaw, Ruskin insisted that Socialism (or "Communism," as he preferred to call it) was a question of "common honesty" with regard to exchange of services; for "wherever material gain follows exchange, . . . precisely what one man acquires the other loses. . . . For every plus there is precisely equal minus." [33] Or, in

31. Shaw to Matthew McNulty, 15 April 1884, BM 50510 (reprinted in Laurence, *Collected Letters*, pp. 81–87), and speech to the Industrial Remuneration Conference, in Pelling, *Challenge*, p. 162.

32. "Our Lost Honesty," pp. 2, 3, 16, 1, and cf. "Exchange: Fair and Unfair" (1885), BM 50700, *10*.

33. John Ruskin, *Unto This Last* (1862; Everyman ed., London, 1907), pp. 110–11; essay 4, p. 173; and cf. W. P. D. Bliss, ed., *The Communism of John Ruskin* (New York, 1891), pp. 5–6, 79.

the words of Edward Carpenter, another contemporary exponent
of the same beliefs, whose words were sometimes almost identical
with Shaw's:

> For every man who consumes more than he creates there must
> of necessity be another man who has to consume less than he
> creates. . . . As far as the palaces of the rich stretch through
> Mayfair and Belgravia, . . . so far (and farther) must the
> hovels of the poor inevitably stretch in the opposite direction
> [,evidences of the social havoc wrought by a system based
> upon dishonesty. For] . . . the Ideal of England to-day [is] to
> live dependent on others, consuming much and creating next
> to nothing. . . . [That] is the source of all England's present
> . . . misery; and honesty and honesty alone will save her.[34]

The more traditional way of making that point, of course, was
to insist that members of the privileged classes who "would not
work" should not expect to eat: an argument Shaw invoked both
frequently and ingeniously in his early lectures, insisting, for example, that under Socialism "not even royal or noble birth"—the
favorite bugbears of old-fashioned Radicals—"would enable anyone to obtain . . . service from a vulgar person without . . . rendering an equivalent service in exchange." With a change of
metaphor, he made the same point by proclaiming that Socialism
converted "Scoundrelism" into "Public Spirit"—Scoundrelism
being the habit of living without working—because under Socialism all antisocial activities, such as idleness and its resulting dishonesty, would be overcome by the pressure of public opinion.
Moreover, there would be no leisure class to back up the idler

---

34. Carpenter, "England's Ideal," *To-day*, 1 n.s. (May 1884) : 324–27, partially
reprinted in *England's Ideal and Other Papers on Social Subjects* (London, 1887) —
an article Shaw almost certainly read and probably utilized in his own writing.
Unfortunately, Carpenter's indebtedness to Ruskin's Socialist theory was not discussed either by Carpenter himself (in *My Days and Dreams*) or in the most
recent analysis of his thought (S. Pierson, "Edward Carpenter," *Vic. Stud.* 13
[1970]: 301 ff.) , but it is evident both in his early Socialist writings, esp. *England's
Ideal*, and in his Manifesto of the Sheffield Socialists (Sheffield, 1886) . For further
evidence cf. Ruskin to Carpenter, 18 May, 27 July 1880, Carpenter Collection,
Sheffield Central Library, MS 386, and in W. H. G. Armytage, "Ruskin as Utopist,"
Notes and Queries 3 n.s. (1956) : 223–24.

against the scorn of the community and no means by which he could remain idle at their expense.[35]

Thus far the teachings of Ruskin and of traditional Radicalism were in agreement. In later years a conflict would emerge between Shaw's Radical and Ruskinian beliefs, and he would move much closer to Ruskin's side, but this was not apparent in his early Socialist writings, which followed a consistently Radical pattern. This pattern may be summarized by noting that all of those writings described the aim of Socialism as the destruction of the class system and the power of social privilege in England—fundamental Radical demands that Radicalism, by itself, had proved unable to achieve—plus the establishment of the workingman's right to the full value of his labor.[36] This last, very traditional Socialist demand was closely linked with the (usually unstated) basis of all Shaw's early Socialist thought, which was his vision of a free trade utopia in which every man would be his own master and all goods and services would exchange "honestly"—at cost price.[37]

However fanciful it may appear, this was the logical culmination of Shaw's reasoning from Radical-individualist premises. It may fairly be described as Radical-individualist utopianism, and Shaw wished to implement it by the equally utopian means of giving all workers free "access" to the means of production and thus the opportunity to "produce for themselves" whatever they needed.[38] For if every person had such an option, he reasoned, no one would be tempted to pay more than the cost price for someone else's product; hence "fair exchange" would follow inevitably. In order to achieve this goal it was only necessary to destroy the "monopoly" ownership of capital, which deprived the workers of

35. *To Provident Landlords and Capitalists*, Fabian Tract No. 3 (London, 1885), and "Socialism and Scoundrelism," lecture, 1885, BM 50700, *4* (paraphrased).

36. This was the implied principle on which Shaw's demand for economic honesty was based; for to receive either more or less than the whole produce of one's own labor was prima facie evidence of inequitable exchange.

37. See Shaw's lectures: "Socialism and Individualism" (1885), "Socialism and Radicalism" (1885), and "Why We Don't Act Up to Our Principles" (1886), BM 50700, *8*:52, *19*:62, and *17*:122; also A. Menger, *The Right to the Whole Produce of Labour*, and chap. 1 above. For further discussion, see sec. 5 below.

38. *Unsocial Socialist*, p. 215, and, much more fully and explicitly, "Exchange: Fair and Unfair," BM 50700, *10*:74.

the means of producing for themselves. Once that monopoly of capital was broken, then the necessary preconditions for equitable exchange—and with them, the "right to the whole produce of labour"—would automatically assert themselves. (See pages 141–42 for further elaboration.)

Such an archaic vision of the good society would be difficult to explain in a British Socialist writer of the 1880s were it not for Shaw's intellectual dependence on Proudhon and the latter's ideal world of independent, self-sufficient peasants and small artisans—which was also, more or less, the world of Shaw's own Irish boyhood.[39] Since coming to England, Shaw had probably seen too little of his new homeland (his ventures beyond London having been limited to coastal watering places) to convince him of the inapplicability of that model to an industrialized society. Moreover, that model had the unique advantage of being the one presupposed by Adam Smith and the classical liberal theory that formed the basis of Shaw's own reasoning about society and that must have seemed plausible to Shaw precisely because of his archaic social assumptions.

At the same time, Shaw's tendency to think in archaic social terms was reinforced by a quite separate set of beliefs regarding life, time, and freedom that formed the usually unstated philosophical foundation of his Socialist theory. Of those three terms, Shaw regarded time as the most fundamental. For life could only be defined in terms of time; freedom could only mean the free disposal of such time; and life without such fundamental freedom was a sham.[40] Together, these ideas formed the basis of Shaw's most characteristic Socialist argument: that the man who lacks the

39. Similarly, where Shaw described the condition of the "proletariat," robbed of its birthright by private appropriation of rent, as "foodless, homeless, shiftless, superflous," he may have fairly described the dispossessed Irish peasantry of his youth but showed no insight into the condition of the industrial working class in England. (See Shaw, "The Basis of Socialism: Economic," in *Fabian Essays* [1889 ed.], p. 9, and G. Lichtheim, *Short History of Socialism*, p. 196.)

40. "On What Is Called the Sacredness of Human Life" and "Capital Punishment," Shaw's earliest (pre-Socialist) lectures, delivered in Feb. and Dec. 1882, BM 50702, *1* and *2*. Both were arguments in favor of capital punishment, urging that it be used for the eugenic improvement of society—an argument that may have been intended as a *reductio ad absurdum* of Malthusian theories (see "The New Politics," p. 83) .

free disposal of his own time and activities because they are controlled by someone else is, in effect, "a Slave"; the man who has
control over another man's time is his "Master"; and "no man,"
as Shaw repeatedly asserted, "is good enough to be another man's
Master." [41] Soon Marx, abetted by George and Proudhon, provided
Shaw with an explanation for the existence of masters and slaves,
and the explanation, thereafter, became the mainstay of his Socialist perorations. It was that capitalism had given a monopoly of
the necessary means of livelihood to the proprietary class, so that
all who lacked a share in that monopoly had to work for the
proprietors and on their terms or starve. Socialism, by insisting
upon economic honesty, now sought to liberate mankind from that
dilemma. By making the workingman's time again his own it
would also make him a "free man": "free to work only to satisfy
his own wants" and dependent on no one for his livelihood. Thus
Socialism would end the conflict of masters and slaves by giving
everyone the means to lead an autonomous existence.[42]

These arguments were far removed from Marxism, as it was
interpreted by Anglo-Marxists in the 1880s. Yet in at least one
respect, despite his individualist and libertarian heresies, Shaw
was in full agreement with Marxian "orthodoxy," and that was in
his belief that revolution was a moral and practical necessity: a
consequence of the inherent injustice of capitalism, which made
it impossible even to ascertain, much less to pay, a workman the
full value of his labor. As the hero of *An Unsocial Socialist* expressed the dilemma,

> The only available standard of compensation was the market
> price, and this he rejected as being fixed by competition
> among capitalists who could only secure profit by obtaining
> from their workmen more products than they paid them for,
> and could only tempt customers by offering a share of the
> unpaid-for part of the products as a reduction in price. Thus
> he found that the system of withholding the indispensable

41. Shaw, "Division of Society into Classes" and "Socialism and Radicalism,"
both lectures, 1885, BM 50700, 6 and 9, and "The New Politics," BM 50683, f. 116.
For the Anarchist implications of such slogans, see pp. 134–35, below.
42. "Socialism and Radicalism," BM 50700, 9.

materials for production and subsistence from the laborers, except on condition of their supporting an idle class, . . . rendered the determination of just ratios of exchange, and consequently the practice of honest dealing, impossible.[43]

Thus Shaw reached the conclusion that society was so thoroughly demoralized by dishonest practices that there no longer remained any basis for honest dealing. Since the basis of modern society was that "the rich habitually lived by robbing the poor," and were praised and envied for so doing, it had become the object of every man's ambition to be supported in a similar idleness.[44] Thus "the principle on which we farm out our national industry to private marauders . . . so corrupts and paralyzes us that we cannot be honest even when we want to. And the reason we bear it so calmly is that very few of us really want to." His solution, therefore, was to make a clean sweep of the entire capitalist order and to begin again on a more honest basis.[45]

4. Shaw's Youthful Anarchism

Such views made Shaw a natural ally of William Morris and his fellow members of the revolutionary wing of English Marxism. Morris, another admirer of Ruskin, looked forward like Shaw to revolution as a means of destroying a decadent and immoral civilization that he loathed and looked to Socialism to provide the basis of a new society in which honesty, spontaneity, and genuine humanity would again be possible.[46] Shaw, of course, had long been sympathetic to Morris as an artist and craftsman whose life

43. *Unsocial Socialist*, pp. 191–92. Shaw subsequently resolved this theoretical dilemma by concluding that the value of a work of art was determined by the number of "simple ideas" it contained—"complex ideas" counting as the multiple of simple ones! ("Art," lecture to Bedford Debating Society, 10 Dec. 1885, BM 50702.)

44. "Socialism," lecture to Liberal and Social Union, Feb. 1885 (reprinted in *Chr. Soc.* [Apr. 1885]) .

45. *Unsocial Socialist*, p. 220, and cf. Shaw's blustering conclusion to Fabian Tract No. 2 (London, 1884) , "That we would rather see a civil war than such another century of suffering as this has been."

46. For analysis of the "militant" faction in the SDF, see Tsuzuki, *Hyndman*, pp. 57 ff. The best short analysis of Morris's Socialism is G. D. H. Cole, *Socialist Thought: Marxism and Anarchism, 1850–1890* (London, 1954) , pp. 415 ff.

was devoted to promoting social regeneration, and he sympathized deeply with Morris's aim of destroying the powerful commercial spirit that degraded popular art and made true craftsmanship impossible. Morris, on the other hand, discovered Shaw in the pages of the Socialist magazine *To-day,* where *An Unsocial Socialist* was serialized in the spring and summer of 1884, and made his acquaintance in June of the same year, when Hyndman arranged a meeting between them to discuss the publication of a story by Shaw in *Justice.*[47] Soon thereafter, Shaw became a regular habitué of Morris's Sunday night suppers and Socialist meetings in Hammersmith. It was here that most of Shaw's new Socialist lectures were tried out on the small but discriminating audience that gathered in Morris's converted carriage house, and Morris himself became Shaw's Socialist mentor.[48]

This state of affairs continued through 1884, while Shaw and Morris remained active workers for the SDF—Shaw as a sympathizer and Socialist lecturer, Morris as a member of the Executive Council. Not unnaturally, Shaw took Morris's side in the internecine struggle between Right and Left within the SDF and developed a strong dislike for Hyndman—a dislike that was powerfully reinforced by Shaw's resentment of Hyndman's domineering habits and revulsion at his style of Socialism.[49] But Shaw's hostility to Hyndman and support for Morris were also motivated

47. Shaw, *William Morris as I Knew Him* (New York, 1936), p. 7, and Hyndman to Shaw, 20 and 30 June 1884, BM 50538. Morris, as usual, was slated to subsidize the venture with a payment of £.10.

48. For further discussion, see E. E. Stokes, Jr, "Shaw and William Morris," *Journal of the William Morris Society* 1 (1961), and J. W. Hulse, *Revolutionists in London* (Oxford, 1970), pp. 122 ff. Sydney Olivier also described Shaw as "Morris' most absorbent disciple" (quoted in M. Olivier, ed., *Sydney Olivier* [London, 1948], p. 75), and Morris's Socialist lectures of the 1880s advocated a form of Radical-individualist utopianism that was very similar to Shaw's. (See E. LeMire, ed., *Unpublished Lectures of William Morris* [Detroit, 1969], esp. pp. 227–28.)

49. Hyndman further alienated Shaw by mutilating the accounts of Secularist meetings Shaw wrote for *Justice* (Hyndman excised all favorable references to Bradlaugh and Besant) and by the insincerity of his political rhetoric: his melodramatic "stories of capitalist greed and oppression," which Shaw believed appealed blatantly to the workers' prejudices and ignored the fact that the workers would do the same thing themselves if the opportunity arose. ("The New Politics," pp. 86–87, and Shaw to Andreas Scheu, 26 Oct. 1884, Scheu Papers, IISH).

by a deeper temperamental tendency that soon polarized feelings throughout the English Left. For Shaw was "at heart an Anarchist," as he confessed to Andreas Scheu in 1884, and as such he could not tolerate the high-handed collectivism of the SDF.

> Of course I know that Collectivism and Anarchism come to the same thing practically when worked out; but I object to any name which might afford a pretext at some intermediate phase of the Revolution, for a Committee of Public Safety composed of the Executive Council of the [S.]D.F.[50]

Above all, Shaw's libertarian conscience rebelled against the dictatorial ambitions that Hyndman was believed to cherish and against the "infallibility" ascribed by collectivists to "their pope, Karl Marx." And since collectivists in England were generally followers of Marx and Hyndman, Shaw declared himself an Anarchist in protest against their "insane disregard" for personal liberty.[51]

In adhering to that point of view, however, he remained in essential agreement with Morris and the other "militant" opponents of Hyndman's rule. All of them shared an anarchistic tendency to oppose political authority, to prefer free, spontaneous activity over any kind of planning, and to identify Socialism with the opposition to tyranny and monopoly in English life. In Shaw's own words,

> We were all out to *ecraser l'infâme,* without in the least knowing how. We had not sorted ourselves out, and were for the moment far more Anarchists than Marxists. We were to break our chains, make a revolution, and live happily ever after.

Morris also provided Shaw with his most uncompromising libertarian slogan: No man is good enough to be another man's master.[52] But Shaw developed the Anarchist implications of that slogan

50. Shaw to Scheu, 26 Oct. 1884 (also quoted in Pelling, *Origins of the Labour Party,* p. 37, n. 2).

51. Shaw, "What's in a Name?" *Anarchist,* March 1885, and "A Word for War," *To-day* (Sept. 1887): 84 n.

52. Shaw, *Morris as I Knew Him,* pp. 5–6, and "Socialism and Human Nature," p. 92.

far more completely than Morris, because he followed such implications and the logic of his opposition to Hyndman almost the
whole way to individualist Anarchism, as propounded by Proudhon and his American disciple, Benjamin Tucker.[53]

The clearest, but also the most disputed, evidence for such conclusions will be found in an obscure Anarchist journal of March
1885 in an article entitled "What's in a Name (How an Anarchist
Might Put It)," and signed George Bernard Shaw. Its position
was one of pure individualist Anarchism—so pure that it might
almost have been borrowed from Tucker, who in fact reprinted
it in his journal, Liberty, in the following month.[54] Its thesis was
that Anarchism is nothing other than the complete and consistent
defense of human freedom, combating monopoly and coercion in
every form. Thus it is the legitimate heir of English Radicalism,
with its traditions of free trade and free competition. Nor did
Shaw hesitate to draw the most extreme applications of those doctrines, for *"laissez-faire,* in spite of all the stumblings it has brought
upon itself by persistently holding its candle to the devil instead
of to its own footsteps, is the torchbearer of Anarchism." The
theories of its prophet, Adam Smith, are still applicable in any
equitably organized society. Monopoly and class privilege are the
real enemies of Socialism, whereas free trade is its natural fulfillment.[55]

Already the "Monopolists" are coming to recognize this fact,
Shaw continued, and are joining forces politically in defense of
their property and privileges. Soon there will not be two parties of
property owners, Whigs and Tories, but "two sorts of Socialists—
Anarchist and Collectivist—confronting one solid body of

53. Tucker, with whom Shaw carried on a mutually admiring correspondence,
was editor of the American Anarchist journal, Liberty, of which Shaw was probably a reader, as the connections between Tucker's individualism and that of Henry
George gave Tucker a readership among the London Georgians. For his doctrine,
see Benjamin Tucker, *Instead of a Book* (London, 1907), and the valuable study,
James J. Martin, *Men Against the State* (New York, 1956).

54. *The Anarchist,* March 1885, reprinted in *Liberty* (11 April 1885), and subsequently republished by H. Seymour as *Anarchism Versus State Socialism* (London,
1889). It has not been published in the twentieth century. Quotes below are from
this issue of *The Anarchist.*

55. There are similar arguments regarding Adam Smith, in "Socialism and
Economics," BM 50700, *24,* esp. f. 149.

Monopolists." Of the two types of Socialists, however, Shaw
argued that

> the Collectivists would drive the money-changers from West-
> minister only to replace them with a central administration,
> committee of public safety, or what not. Instead of "Victoria,
> by the Grace of God," they would give us "the Superinten-
> dant of such and such an Industry, by the authority of the
> Democratic Federation," or whatever body we are to make
> our master under the new dispensation.[56]

In such pronouncements there is still an echo of Shaw's opposition to Hyndman; hence the idea of a "master" particularly
aroused his ire. But the theory of popular government as "trustees
for the people," he asserted, was morally no better. Why not, instead, have an English czar:

> What objection would he be open to that does not apply to
> popular government just as strongly?—nay, more so; for
> should either misbehave, it is easier to remove one man than
> 670 [M.P.s]? The sole valid protest against Czardom, indi-
> vidual or collective, is that of the Anarchist, who would call
> no man Master. Slavery is the complement of authority, and
> must disappear with it. If the slave indeed make the master,
> then the workers are slaves by choice, and to emancipate them
> is tyranny. But if, as we believe, it is the master that makes
> the slave, we shall never get rid of slavery until we have got
> rid of authority.[57]

Despite the flamboyant manner of its presentation, nothing in
this article was inconsistent with the development of Shaw's Socialist ideas in the half-decade preceding 1885. Rather, it represented
the sum of his Radical and Secularist protests against privileged
classes and institutions, raised to the highest peak of intensity. Its
origin may be found in Shaw's youthful enthusiasm for Godwin

56. *The Anarchist* (March 1885).
57. Compare Ruskin on the same subject: "Freemen, indeed! You are slaves, not
to masters of any strength or honor, but to the idlest talkers at that floral end of
Westminster bridge" (*Fors Clavigera*, letter on "Freedom or Slavery").

and Shelley, which was subsequently strengthened by reading Mill, Proudhon, and Henry George,[58] by Anarchist meetings in the early eighties (where Shaw once heard Kropotkin lecture in a basement room) , by friendships with various Anarchists (such as the Fabian, Charlotte Wilson) , and by his whole existence as a rebellious outsider.[59] Thus Anarchism of the sort presented in Shaw's article was the natural culmination of his intellectual development: the most rebellious form of Radicalism and the most complete protest against the existing order.

These conclusions, however, have not found acceptance among contemporary Shaw scholars, both because Shaw himself subsequently denied that he had ever been an Anarchist, and often seemed to be the very opposite, and because the ambiguous subtitle of his article—"How an Anarchist Might Put It"—seemed to imply that it was merely an abstract exercise and did not express his own opinions. The latter impression was also reinforced by a letter Shaw wrote to the editor of *The Anarchist* prior to the publication of his article in which he argued that it was intended chiefly "to shew [his Fabian colleague] Mrs. Wilson my idea of the line that an anarchist paper should take in England." The article was also written at Mrs. Wilson's request to inaugurate a series she had undertaken to edit for *Justice,* "attacking our common enemy, the Collectivists."[60] On the basis of this evidence, the editor of Shaw's *Collected Letters*—the first Shaw scholar to have dealt seriously with the question—has concluded that the article

58. Compare the following with Shaw's Anarchist arguments: "Individualism and Socialism are, in truth, not antagonistic. . . . There is in free trade nothing that conflicts with rational Socialism. On the contrary, we have but to carry the free-trade principle out to its logical conclusion to see that it brings us to such Socialism" (Henry George, *Protection or Free Trade,* p. 308, quoted in Rose, *Henry George,* p. 96) .

59. Regarding Kropotkin, see Winsten, *Jesting Apostle,* pp. 36–40, and Peter Kropotkin, *Memoirs of a Revolutionist* (London, 1908) , pp. 412–13. In addition to Charlotte Wilson (see chap. 5 below) , Shaw was also a close friend of such libertarian Socialists as Andreas Scheu (see n. 76 below) , Packenham Beatty (caricatured as "Erskine," in *Unsocial Socialism*) , and Sergei "Stepniak" Kravchinskii. All four, like Morris, held antiparliamentary views.

60. Shaw to Seymour, 5 Jan. 1885, in Laurence, *Collected Letters,* pp. 109–10, and C. M. Wilson to Shaw, 10 Dec. 1884, BM 50510, adding that "the thought of your long promised contribution to *Justice* being a defence of Anarchism is too entrancing for sober words."

did not express Shaw's own opinions and that Shaw himself was not then an Anarchist.[61]

This argument, however, overlooks Shaw's equally important admission, in the same letter, that "there is nothing in [the article] that I object to commit myself publicly to," through the publication of his signature, provided that the tone and outlook of the journal were not of the insurrectionary sort that would encourage misconstruction of his views. To this, the editor of *The Anarchist*, Henry Seymour, immediately replied, assuring Shaw that his journal was "philosophic" rather than "incendiary" in character, and that his own views were very close to Shaw's.[62] Because Shaw then allowed the publication of his signature, the conclusion seems inescapable that he was "commited publicly" to all the statements in his article. In any case, the article was certainly not an expression of Mrs. Wilson's views—despite having been written at her request—as she was a "communistic Anarchist," in the manner of Kropotkin, and had no sympathy with individualist Anarchism of the sort expounded in Shaw's article.[63] The latter type of Anarchism, however, was entirely consistent with Shaw's other writings in 1883–85. Indeed, one of Shaw's contemporary lectures utilized whole sentences from "What's in a Name?" to proclaim the ultimate desirability of laissez-faire economic arrangements, concluding that although the government might be perfectly capable of running public services and other industries efficiently, the people would do better to run them "for themselves." If they gave the land and industrial machinery to the government the government would become their master and they would again be slaves, and Shaw insisted that there must be no "new Masters."[64] Shortly thereafter, he also described himself to

61. Laurence, *Collected Letters*, p. 109 (editor's introduction to Shaw to Seymour, 5 Jan. 1885).

62. Seymour to Shaw, 5 and 6 Jan. 1885, BM 50511, and cf. H. Seymour, *The Philosophy of Anarchism* (London, 1887). Shortly thereafter, Seymour also became a member of the Fabian Society.

63. See her articles in *Prac. Soc.* (Jan. 1886), and *Freedom* (esp. no. 1, Oct. 1886), which she edited for Kropotkin; and cf. chap. 5, n. 69 and Appendix B.

64. "Retrospect, Circumspect, Prospect," BM 50700, 34, ff. 194–201 (may be dated early 1885 by its reference to the forthcoming "Anarchist paper"), card 8b, under the heading: "The Old Adam (Smith) again." (This was subsequently crossed out and replaced by a more equivocal statement, asking for a united front between Collectivists and Anarchists.)

Andreas Scheu as an "Anarchist and Free Competition man," opposed to the present system chiefly because he believed competition in it "to be the reverse of free"—which was precisely the point made by his article.[65] There can be little doubt, therefore, that the views propounded in Shaw's article were his own and that he considered himself an Anarchist, or anarchistic Socialist, in 1884.

Two major questions remain, however, in the appraisal of Shaw's youthful "Anarchism": how thoroughgoing was it, and how closely did it approximate more orthodox Anarchist teachings? The best way to answer these questions will be to examine Shaw's speeches and writings of the middle eighties for further evidence of Anarchist opinions. One of the clearest evidences of such opinions is Shaw's repeated advocacy of a purified system of economic individualism: a system similar to that proposed by Henry George, but made more efficient by the extinction of interest and of all "artificial monopolies."

In *An Unsocial Socialist,* this point of view is evident in the hero's identification of Socialism with the abolition of monopoly and the establishment of genuine free trade, and in his chief social panacea: making it a felony to pay a workman less than the full value of his labor. But free trade without Socialism—without abolishing monopolies—is self-defeating and will "ruin England," he insists:

> The theory of Free Trade is only applicable to systems of exchange, not to systems of spoliation. Our system is one of spoliation, and if we don't abandon it we must either return to Protection or go to smash [as Marx predicted].

The only real alternative, therefore, is to "reorganize our society socialistically" by destroying monopoly and class privilege.

> When England is made the property of its inhabitants collectively, England becomes socialistic. Artificial inequality will

65. Shaw to Scheu, 26 Oct., 1884, Scheu Papers, IISH. Morris also affirmed in 1887 that Shaw's "real tendencies are towards individualist-anarchism" (quoted in R. P. Arnot, *William Morris: The Man and the Myth* [London, 1964], p. 69), and Sydney Olivier confirmed that opinion in *Freedom* (Oct. 1887).

vanish then before real freedom of contract; freedom of competition, or unhampered emulation, will keep us moving
ahead; and Free Trade will fulfill its promises at last.[66]

In Shaw's contemporary lectures the same themes were further
developed: Socialism was the fulfillment of individualism, the
basis for effective competition, and the next step in the Radical
program. Socialism had "no Advantage in Nobility of Aim," but
only in "Efficiency of Method," Shaw proclaimed. It was based on
self-interest—"if anybody thought the Socialists were against
self-interest he must suppose that they were fools"—and its aims
were identical with those of individualism.[67] But the methods of
individualism are hopelessly inadequate, Shaw argued: left to
itself, mere individualism leads inevitably to its opposite, monopoly, while its slogans, in practice, merely serve to mask existing
monopolistic conditions. Thus the advantages claimed for individualism by its Radical apologists are either mere illusions or they
are neglected by the actual operation of the capitalist system. Only
Socialism can make real individualism possible.[68]

Shaw's treatment of competition was similar. Like self-interest,
he regarded it as an eternal fact of human nature because it "satisfied the most wants with the least trouble." Therefore, it was
pointless to regard competition as immoral, for its morality and
its value to the community depended entirely on the uses to which
it was put. Unless inequality was very great, competition could
do very little harm, Shaw argued. Thus it was only necessary to
destroy the power of privilege and monopoly in order to release
all its potential for good. Nationalize rent, then make competition
completely free—such was Shaw's economic policy in the middle

66. *Unsocial Socialist*, pp. 214, 216. For similar views see "Exchange: Fair and
Unfair," 1886, BM 50700, *10*:74.

67. "The Attitude of Socialists towards Other Bodies," lecture, 1885, BM 50700,
5, and Shaw's reply to the ultra-individualist, Wordsworth Donnisthorpe at the
Fabian Conference, 11 June 1886, with whom he agreed regarding the supremacy
of self interest, only adding that he was a Socialist "because it was in his interest
to be one" ("Special Report" of the Conference, BLPES, f. 263).

68. "Socialism and Individualism," lecture, Nov. 1885, BM 50700, *8*. (This was
probably Shaw's clearest statement on that subject.)

eighties.[69] Moreover, he repeatedly insisted that "since Competition amongst producers admittedly secures to the public the most satisfactory products, the State should compete with all its might in every department of production." He even insisted that the state had "no right to regulate an industry unless it first adopted that trade itself." Such public enterprise should not be carried on for profit, however, but should be used only to stimulate *real* competition among producers.[70] Accordingly, Shaw argued that public enterprise should be extended even into the "sanctuary of the home," where "the State should compete with . . . parents . . . so that every child may have a refuge from the tyranny or neglect of its natural custodians."[71]

Arguments such as this were too eccentric and ambiguous to qualify Shaw as a full-fledged Anarchist, but they do help to underline the fact that his closeness to orthodox Anarchist doctrines varied widely with his subject matter. It was his *economic* doctrines that most closely resembled those of Proudhon and Tucker, while his *political* views remained quite different.[72] For example, Shaw modeled his all-important doctrine of honest exchange largely on that of Proudhon, and, in the middle eighties, actually followed it to the point of advocating an economy based on "equitable labour exchanges," where products would be ex-

69. Shaw must have found competition a tricky subject, as he wrote at least four different versions of his lecture on it between 1884 and 1886 (BM 50700, *1, 3, 7, 18*) ; all took the same point of view. Arguments cited are from BM 50700, ff. 128, 46, 1, 3 (in that order) and from "Points Disputed Among Socialists," BM 50700, *12*: 92–93 (all paraphrased) .

70. *A Manifesto*, Fabian Tract No. 2 (London, 1884; reprinted in Pease, *History of the Fabian Society*, pp. 42–43) , and "The New Radicalism" (1887) , in Crompton, *The Road to Equality*, p. 33. The frequency with which this argument was reiterated in Shaw's lectures of the mid-eighties (e.g., BM 50700, *1, 34, 22, 38*) suggests the great importance he attached to it. H. H. Champion even saw it as the crux of Shavian Socialism (in *Common Sense*, 1 Mar. 1888, p. 155) .

71. *A Manifesto* (in Pease, *History of the Fabian Society*, p. 42) .

72. Like Shaw, Tucker treated Anarchism as part of the Socialist movement, whose goal was the destruction of monopoly and "usury"—rent and interest—in all forms. He defined Anarchism politically as "abolition" of the state and performance of its functions by "individuals or voluntary associations." Economically, he defined it as economic individualism functioning without capitalism. Shaw accepted the latter definition but largely rejected the former. (See Martin, *Men Against the State*, p. 218.)

changed according to time valuations and everyone would be assured the full value of his labor.[73] Shaw's devices for implementing that scheme—particularly his idea of gratuitous credit—were also adapted from Proudhon and Tucker. Gratuitous credit (or "free money," in Tucker's terminology) was intended to make capital available to workingmen without interest so that they could own their own instruments of production. Once this was achieved, Shaw wrote, it would no longer be possible for men to live idly on interest (which resulted from an artificial monopoly of money), or to force other men to work for them because they lacked capital of their own. In fact, the result would be "the very quintessence of free competition." "If any Socialist be moved to demand, aghast, whether I would admit a man's right to own a factory in a Socialist community, I shall reply unhesitatingly in the affirmative," Shaw declared. Such economic arrangements would prevent that person from using his property to exploit his fellow man, since all workmen could obtain the capital with which to erect their own factories if they did not like the terms offered by the owner. Thus Shaw's Socialism would give a man "the right but not the motive to possess more property than he could use himself," and the characteristic system of ownership would be something resembling Guild Socialism or the Proudhonian idea of federated industrial communes.[74]

Full-fledged individualist Anarchists of the Proudhonian school believed such practices would prove so efficacious that no coercive authority would be required thereafter. Benjamin Tucker even argued that the disappearance of the state would, of itself, end the "artificial" monopolies of land and capital, and thus the monopoly rents that they commanded. Shaw, one suspects, lacked the sublime faith in human nature that enabled such theorists to dismiss the state entirely—his view of man was always more skeptical than

73. See "Socialism and Individualism," (BM 50700, 8). The idea of "equitable labour exchanges" was originally Owenite and was actually implemented in London in the 1830s. Subsequently Proudhon made it a part of his system of "mutualism."

74. Shaw, "Concerning Interest," *Our Corner* (Sept. 1887): 205–06, partly borrowed from "Exchange: Fair and Unfair," lecture, 1886, BM 50700, 10. Tucker commented approvingly on this argument in *Liberty* (24 Sept. 1887). Regarding Guild Socialism, see chap. 7, n. 92 below.

that—but he did agree with Anarchists politically to the extent of repudiating "any dependence on . . . parliament," as presently constituted, and he held that under Socialism its functions would be far different than at present. His crucial point of disagreement with the Anarchists, however, derived from his concern with the phenomenon of differential rents, to which he had been introduced by Henry George. It was because he favored the nationalization of such rents—even the "nationalization of rent which arose from the inequalities of personal ability"—that he could not claim to be, "in the technical sense, an Individualist." For such reasons, he also held that there must be a central authority to receive such rents, which properly belonged to society in its collective capacity, while the need for "organization of labour" required society to have "a central organ or brain"—a constitution and a parliament. But it was not essential that it grow out of the present Parliament. "[Instead,] they might start an independent parliament that would compete with the existing one and race it out of the field." [75]

The last suggestion was based on Shaw's pet idea of competition between public and private bodies, but it also served, albeit obscurely, to introduce into his arguments a distinction, derived from Lassalle, between "the government" (repressive) and "the State" (the source of "social freedom"). This distinction made it possible for him to agree with contemporary Anarchists that governments must be abolished, while, at the same time, defending the necessity of a Socialist state.[76] For to vest ownership of land and capital in governments, Shaw argued, would only constitute a "change of Masters;" but the Socialist state—the democratic worker's state envisaged by Lassalle— was altogether different. In the language of Lassalle, who, in the later eighties, chiefly replaced Marx in Shaw's esteem, such a state would form the "highest embodiment of human freedom" for its citizens, and,

75. "Special Report" of the Fabian Conference, 11 June 1886, BLPES, ff. 267, 263–65, 268; and cf. "The Limits of Legislative Duty," and "Socialist Politics" (BM 50700, *41, 22*) for further elaboration of these arguments.

76. This distinction was further developed by Shaw's mentor and correspondent, Andreas Scheu, in his lectures, "Lassalle's Idea of the State," and "The Essence of Freedom and Servitude" (Scheu Papers, IISH); both drew heavily on Lassalle's *Arbeiterprogramm* (1862). Laurence Gronlund's *Co-operative Commonwealth,* which Shaw edited for English publication (London, 1885) also drew a similar distinction.

being thoroughly democratic and egalitarian, would tolerate no "masters" or monopolies of any sort.[77]

Understandably, such pronouncements, balanced precariously between libertarian and authoritarian implications and reconciled only verbally by Hegelian formulas adapted from Lassalle, left men like Benjamin Tucker wishing that Shaw would be "either an Anarchist or a State Socialist a little more consistently." Nevertheless, in 1887 Tucker correctly diagnosed Shaw's outlook as "inclining toward State Socialism" politically, although his economic doctrines still amounted to "pure Anarchism." [78] Or, as Sydney Olivier argued in 1887, Shaw's Socialism was really a form of "mitigated Individualism": individualism mitigated by abolition of monopoly and nationalization of rent, but otherwise wide open to "exploitation" by "men of superior efficiency" or brains.[79] By that time, to be sure, Shaw's anarchistic phase was on the wane (although he never entirely abandoned its ideas, echoes of which continued to recur in plays and essays through the remainder of his life) .[80] But in the mid-eighties, land nationalization and the public functions connected with it formed his only serious deviations from individualist Anarchism. Thus Shaw's Socialism at that stage very nearly approximated the fusion of Smith and Ricardo with

77. Scheu, *loc. cit.* (Shaw's reliance on Lassalle reflects Scheu's increasing influence) , and Shaw, "Retrospect, Circumspect, and Prospect," (BM 50700, *34*) , and "The New Politics," pp. 58–66, the latter drawing much of its doctrine from Lassalle's "Open Letter," of 1862. For a Shavian eulogy of Lassalle, cf. "How the Socialists Have Grown Practical," *Sunday Chronicle,* 16 Nov. 1890.

78. Tucker to Shaw, 4 May and 5 June 1885, BM 50511, and *Liberty* (24 Sept. 1887) . Shaw's shifting libertarian views can also be charted by his varied uses of the motto of Tucker's magazine: "For always in thine eyes, O Liberty, / Shines that high light whereby the world is saved. . . . " Shaw had first used it as the motto of his Fabian *Manifesto* in 1884. For further discussion, see chap. 8, n. 101 below.

79. (S. Olivier) , "A Critic of Anarchism," *Freedom* (Oct. 1887) : 50–51.

80. See Shaw's lecture, "What Socialism Will Be Like," 12 July 1896, reprinted in D. H. Laurence, ed., *Platform and Pulpit* (New York, 1962) , pp. 23 ff., in which Shaw insisted that he never "admitted [to] . . . any contradiction between Individualism and Socialism. I object to the present system because it gives no scope for individuality" (p. 31) ; also sec. 7, "Fabian Individualism," in *Report on Fabian Policy,* Fabian Tract No. 70 (London, 1896) . Such views are also crucial to understanding, e.g., Shaw's conception of Andrew Undershaft, in *Major Barbara,* and his arguments in "Socialism and Superior Brains" (lecture, 1894; reprinted as Fabian Tract No. 146 [London, 1909]) .

Proudhon and Lassalle that Henry George had sought to bring about[81]—with the difference that Shaw's version was more thoroughly antimonopolistic and therefore, in his own terms, more "Socialist" than George's. If the resulting theory was not entirely Anarchist, therefore, it at least inclined heavily in that direction and fully deserved the label of "libertarian."

5. Shavian Socialism and Radicalism

An essential corollary of Shaw's libertarian approach to Socialism and of his insistence that Socialism and individualism were ultimately one was his demand that English Socialists should work more closely with the "other Radical bodies," so as to convince the latter of the need for socialistic methods. In principle, he asserted, there was no real basis for conflict between Radicals and Socialists, since Socialist arguments were essentially Radical in character, were based upon orthodox political economy, and had the establishment of a free and egalitarian society as their end. The Socialist demand to "abolish private property in land and prevent employment of the means of production as capital" was merely the minimum necessary to make the ideal of Radical individualism a reality. Consequently, he solicited the help of all sympathetic Radicals in working out practicable means of instituting that change.[82]

Such opinions, of course, were bound to further alienate Shaw from the Anglo-Marxists of the SDF, although by 1885, when they were first expressed in public, he had already rejected most of the theories that were distinctive of contemporary Anglo-Marxism. Nevertheless, he remained in tune with such Anglo-Marxism to the extent of interpreting Marx's arguments entirely in moral and economic terms, so that even at the peak of his infatuation with the dialectic of history he understood it only in a mechanical sense, as a resultant of economic forces that would ultimately disrupt capitalism and force the proletariat to rebel in order to avoid starvation. If that crisis were averted by timely economic

81. H. George, *Progress and Poverty*, p. xi, quoted and discussed more fully in chap. 3 above.

82. "The Attitude of Socialists towards Other Bodies" (BM 50700, 5) , and lecture to Liberal Social Union, in *Chr. Soc.* (April 1885) .

reforms, however, he knew of no reason to believe the working class would ever develop a revolutionary consciousness—a conclusion that was based upon his own experience with British workingmen.[83] Such workingmen had no desire to overthrow the system of private property, Shaw asserted; they wanted to become small property owners themselves, with the same comforts and values as the bourgeoisie. Given the opportunity, they were also quite ready to become exploiters of their fellow workingmen.[84] Thus capitalists and landlords, as small and easily distinguishable classes, were not the only exploiters of labor; nor were the proletarians the only ones who suffered under the existing system. Instead, Shaw proclaimed, all persons living under capitalism were unavoidably exploiters of labor, and all suffered alike from the prevailing practice of dishonesty.

That was the crux of Shaw's disagreement with Anglo-Marxism, and it was argued most brilliantly in the first of his Socialist *jeux d'esprit,* a letter to Hyndman's paper, *Justice,* signed "G. B. S. Larking." It sought to demonstrate that Hyndman's greedy capitalists and landlords could only succeed in pocketing the full measure of surplus value at times when competition failed to drive prices down to the minimum set by the cost of production. But political economy proved that free competition perpetually tended to drive down prices, and that under such "normal" circumstances it was really the buyer who profited at the laborer's expense.

> But who are the buyers? Editors of *Justice, we* are the buyers: we and our parents, our . . . wives and children. Do these dear ones commit theft whenever they enter a shop? Do you dare assert that the many men of whose probity England is justly proud are systematic thieves? For this is what your theory of surplus value comes to.[85]

83. In his work for the Edison Telephone Co. in 1881. Such firsthand knowledge of working-class life, which was almost unique among contemporary Socialist intellectuals, enabled Shaw to anticipate by some two decades Lenin's discovery that the proletariat was inherently nonrevolutionary.

84. See *Unsocial Socialist,* pp. 142 ff.

85. *Justice,* 15 March 1884. The same theory was expounded at greater length in Shaw to McNulty, 15 April 1884, in Laurence, *Collected Letters,* pp. 81–87, and in *Unsocial Socialist,* pp. 140 ff. Shaw's own comment was that it demonstrated the incompatibility between Marx's theory of value and his theory of exploitation; hence the need to jettison the former ("The New Politics," p. 87).

As usual, Shaw was playing the serious moralist behind his satirical mask, and his point was, perhaps, the most serious he could make in condemning current economic practices: that the system of exchange forced everyone to "purchase the necessaries of life at prices that obviously entail abject poverty on the producers of those necessaries." That is why "we all live by robbing the poor," and why, "as things stand, wealth cannot be enjoyed without dishonor or foregone without misery." [86]

Under such circumstances, what could sensitive, middle-class persons do to set themselves right with society? How could they effectively promote the social and moral revolution that alone could neutralize the power of economic exploitation? And, finally, what form could such a revolution take in quasi-democratic, bourgeois England? Such questions puzzled Shaw while writing *An Unsocial Socialist* and led him to seek new answers that would adjust his highly abstract Socialism more nearly to the realities of modern British society. The result was that the Marxist hero of that novel, who tried to drop out of bourgeois society and live in the proletarian manner, soon abandoned the experiment as a hopeless sham. Through experience with workingmen he came to see that the cause of revolution could not be identified with the proletariat, nor would proletarians themselves ever succeed in generating a new society. Instead, he concluded, the triumph of Socialism could only be brought about by realistic middle-class intellectuals who would utilize superior brains, organization, and political skill to radicalize their own class. Thus the novel's hero found his real work and his hope for the future in converting influential middle-class leaders to the cause—an arrangement that foreshadowed Shaw's subsequent conception of his own function as a Socialist writer and that described the strategy of the Fabian Society, in fictional form, a year before that society was founded.

Shaw's Socialism would therefore be the work of an "enlightened minority," who would have to "overcome [both] the active resistance of the proprietors and the inertia of the masses." Even so, there might still be a proletarian revolution, as Marx predicted, if tyranny and starvation forced the masses to rebel before that

86. Lecture to Liberal Social Union, *Chr. Soc.* (April 1885), and Fabian Tract No. 2.

minority had prepared the groundwork for a new society. But the result of such rebellion would certainly not be anything so just and rational as Socialism, for there was not as yet any proletarian Socialist movement. Instead, Socialism was essentially a middle-class ideal and offered the best hope of future happiness to members of that class, who, if they would only

> educate themselves to understand this question . . . [would] be able to fortify whatever is just in Socialism and to crush whatever is dangerous in it. I trust then that the Middle Class will raise the Socialists above the danger of Coercion, Minor Siege, and consequent Dynamite, by joining them in large numbers. When a Revolution approaches, those who are within the Revolutionary party can do something to avert bloodshed: Those who hold aloof can only provoke it. A party informed at all points by men of gentle habits and trained reasoning powers may achieve a complete Revolution without a single act of violence.[87]

That, of course, was virtually the conclusion Hyndman had reached in 1881—the prophylactic theory of Socialism—only to abandon it as his "Marxism" became more doctrinaire. Shaw's advocacy of it, in 1885, therefore marked the culmination of his reaction against the SDF. For a time, however, he continued to regard Marxian economics as useful to the movement and surplus value as a necessary Socialist concept. In 1884, for example, he wrote off all economic treatises except Marx's as "abominably wicked books" because they failed to recognize that property was theft. After further study of the dismal science, however, he reversed that judgment, concluding that "in economics all roads lead to Socialism." "It is our trump because it condemns the present state of things." [88]

As previous sections have indicated, Shaw's study led him in 1885 to an increasing dependence upon "orthodox" economics—a

87. Lecture to Liberal Social Union, *Chr. Soc.* (April 1885).

88. "Unsocial Socialist," in *To-day* (Oct. 1884): 448–49 (also National Library of Ireland MS 851, f. 285), and *Unsocial Socialist*, as first revised for publication (London, 1887), p. 215; "The Attitude of Socialists towards Other Bodies," lecture, 1885, BM 50700, 5:33.

fact that he first revealed to the world in an article ostensibly devoted to defending Marx against attack by an advocate of Jevons's theory of "final utility." In reality, Shaw's article virtually ignored the value theory of Marx and instead defended the classical cost-of-production theory against the new Jevonian heresy.[89] But that act of apostasy was only a preliminary to Shaw's real shocker: his lecture on Socialism to the Dialectical Society, parts of which have been quoted above. "Though he took an extreme position" in that lecture, *Justice* complained, "the speaker made no reference to surplus value and accepted the laws of the standard economists as represented by Professor Marshall," insisting that the iron law of wages and its Malthusian foundation were not only "substantially sound" but formed the real "scientific" basis of Socialism.[90] For Malthus, Shaw said, had demonstrated that increase of population was the force that ground workers down to the level of subsistence by shifting the "Competition among Masters for Slaves" (which was beneficial) to a "Competition among Slaves for Masters" (which was pernicious) ; and this, together with the Iron Law of Wages, was all that Socialists needed to condemn the capitalist system.[91]

Ironically, there was some resemblance between Shaw's use of classical economics in support of Socialism and that of the Anglo-Marxists—with the crucial difference that Shaw held that Malthus and Ricardo had made Marx's theories unnecessary (see chapter 3, section 5) . The teachings of Malthus and Ricardo also contradicted certain points of Georgian economics, so Shaw largely abandoned the latter in 1886, along with most of his earlier ideological commitments, in favor of complete reliance on classical and neoclassical economics. The following chapters will give an account of the "Marx reading circle" in which Shaw's conversion to that theory was completed. For the present it will be enough to note that in his lecture to the Dialectical Society one may already detect the influence of Sidney Webb supplanting that of

89. Rev. Philip Wicksteed, "*Das Kapital*: a Criticism," *To-day* (Oct. 1884) , based on Jevons's theory of final utility; and Shaw, "The Jevonian Criticism of Marx," *To-day*, Jan. 1885.

90. *Justice*, 31 Jan. 1885. This was a preliminary version of the lecture Shaw subsequently delivered to the Liberal and Social Union, 20 March 1885.

91. "Socialism and Malthusianism," lecture, 1886, BM 50700, *14*.

William Morris. The reference to Alfred Marshall calls attention
to it; for Marshall was Webb's economic mentor in the mid-
eighties, and Webb was a strict Malthusian. In the debate following Shaw's lecture, therefore,

> Mr. Sidney Webb, speaking as a professed economist, said
> that the Socialist position was strictly deducible from the
> standard political economy, and hailed Mr. Shaw as the first
> Socialist who had recognized that Socialism needed no
> heterodox theory to support it.

And, much to Shaw's surprise, Annie Besant, the great woman
orator and Secularist leader, also rose to defend him against the
attacks of other Radicals who had not yet seen the light.[92]

Thus the practical advantages of abandoning Marxism and re-
establishing Socialism on a foundation of "orthodox" economic
theory proved to be very great. Such action could only alienate
the handful of sectarian English Marxists, while it would open the
door of Socialism to the whole body of dissatisfied Radical intellectuals who had been repelled by the obscurity of Marxist theory and
by its advocacy of an insurrectionary class struggle. The immediate
approval of Webb and Annie Besant was only a foretaste of what
such a policy might accomplish, for it was a miniature version of
the future policy of the Fabian Society. Shaw himself joined that
society in the fall of 1884, after his disillusionment with the SDF,
and the intellectual environment he found there made possible
the subsequent development and reformulation of his Socialist
thought.

92. *Justice,* 31 Jan. 1885; and cf. chap. 7 below.

5

The Founding Fabians: The "Ethical" Road to Socialism and Its Tributaries

> The aim of the Society is to help forward the reconstruction of the Social System in accordance with the highest moral possibilities.
> FABIAN SOCIETY MINUTE BOOK, 1883[1]

Previous chapters have been concerned with Socialists who arrived at their new faith by way of active participation in Radical politics, or at least by way of ginger groups on the extreme left. But the scholarly young idealists who gathered in the drawing room of Edward Pease on 4 January 1884 to found the Fabian Society were Radicals of a quite different sort. Few had taken any active part in Radical politics; they had no immediate interest in land reform or in the Irish question; and although the Democratic Federation claimed a handful of them, they were atypical and soon found their Fabian colleagues uncongenial.[2] Instead, the Founding Fabians formed perhaps the purest example in the 1880s of the religious approach to Socialism—or, more specifically, of ethical Freethought reaching out to Socialism as a more complete and satisfactory form of substitute faith. As such, they were also pioneers in the movement from merely "negative" Freethought to a more positive concern with social values and social reconstruction that became a major tendency among Radical intellectuals in the later eighties and nineties.[3]

Like most English Socialists in the eighties, the Founding Fabians were convinced Freethinkers, alienated from conventional

1. The "Aim" of the Fabian Society from its founding until 1887 (Fabian Archive, Nuffield, 7 November 1883).
2. For the fullest account of the founding of the Society, see Pease, *History of the Fabian Society*, pp. 26–36, and p. ooo below.
3. In the later 1880s that tendency was also encouraged by the newly founded ethical societies (for their connections with Socialism see P. Chubb, *On the Religious Frontier* [New York, 1931], pp. 77 ff.), the Positivist societies (see chaps. 2 and 6 below), the Society for Physical Research (see n. 4 below), and the Fabian's less famous twin, the Fellowship of the New Life (see n. 25 below).

religious faith by the new scientific and historical outlook of their time. To a greater extent than most, however, they were unwilling skeptics, having an intense need for personal commitment and belief, which they sought to satisfy through a variety of substitute faiths. Seeking refuge from the "outer darkness of materialism," some had turned to spiritualism—Frank Podmore, J. G. Stapleton, and Rosamund Owen, for example—while others, including Havelock Ellis and his friends, found consolation in the religious philosophy of James Hinton, and still others, including Hubert and Edith Bland, sought it in the "simple life," aestheticism, Christian Socialism, and other quasi-religious tendencies of the period.[4] It was also such religious interests that first brought these people together in 1883 as "disciples" of a Scottish ethical teacher named Thomas Davidson, whose philosophy seemed to offer them a new way to secular salvation.[5]

At the beginning of 1884, however, the Founding Fabians had taken only the most minimal steps toward a clear and consistent view of social reconstruction. As an organized group they were just emerging from the utopian Fellowship of the New Life—the name proposed by Davidson for the company of his followers, whose aim was to form "a perfect character in each and all"—and their wings were still damp from its intense moral idealism. From the New Life they retained an ethical animus against "the blind idol," competition, and a belief that society must be reconstituted "in accordance with the highest moral possibilities." They were intensely earnest about those beliefs and had no idea how to achieve them.[6]

4. Pease, *History of the Fabian Society*, pp. 14–16. Spiritualism and the allied movement for physical research appealed to the younger intellectuals of the 1880s as a means of guaranteeing the reality of spiritual and moral values in the face of the meaningless, materialistic universe implied by contemporary science (see A. O. Gauld, *The Origins of Psychical Research* [London, 1968]). As such they attracted the interest of many early Fabians. See Appendix B for biographical sketches of Podmore, Owen, Ellis, and Hinton. Edith Bland (E. Nesbit), quoted in D. L. Moore, *E. Nesbit: A Biography*, rev. ed. (Philadelphia, 1966), pp. 78, 82. See Appendix B for biographical sketches of the Blands.

5. See W. A. Knight, *Memorials of Thomas Davidson* (London, 1907), and T. Davidson, "Autobiographical Sketch," ed. A. Lataner, *JHI* 18 (Oct. 1957): 532–35; there is no adequate biography of Davidson, and no study of his thought.

6. Pease, *History of the Fabian Society*, pp. 28–30, and Fabian Tract No. 1.

This was the condition in which Shaw discovered the Fabians, still meeting in Pease's drawing room, on 18 May 1884. For some time he had been casting about for an organization that could serve as a stimulus and sounding board for his new Socialist ideas. None of the existing organizations could fill that need, chiefly because they were dominated by personalities more powerful than his own, and because, he averred, they were not up to the level required by his own critical intellect. He was attracted to the Fabians at that juncture by the high-toned classical allusion of their name and by the earnest moral tone of their first tract, entitled "Why Are the Many Poor?" [7] He found them intelligent and congenial—earnest, but still willing to be amused by Shavian ironies—and so concluded that the society was his oyster, which, with all speed, he meant to open with his pen. He joined it formally in September of the same year, intending to convert it straightaway to revolutionary Socialism, as he then understood the term. The original Fabian historian has recorded that "the influence of his intellectual outlook was immediate. Already the era of 'highest moral possibilities' seemed far behind." [8]

Unhappily, the facts are otherwise. Throughout most of 1884 Shaw remained preoccupied with other kinds of work, and his serious contributions to Fabian thought did not really begin until his ideas had been refined by an intensive study of economics, which took place chiefly within the Fabian orbit. In 1884, however, that still lay in the future, and the Fabian Society remained preoccupied with achieving the "highest moral possibilities." It was the spirit of Thomas Davidson—not that of Shaw—that dominated its proceedings.

1. Origins of the Fabian Society

Thomas Davidson, the "wandering scholar" from Aberdeenshire, came to London in the fall of 1882 with the intention of gathering a body of like-minded disciples from among the earnest, young Freethinkers of the metropolis. He was moved to do so by

7. Shaw was recruited for the Fabian Society by Hubert Bland at a Christian Socialist (i.e., land reform) conference in May 1884. Bland sent him the first Fabian Tract (Bland to Shaw, 5 May 1884, BM 50510).

8. Pease, *History of the Fabian Society*, p. 40.

an intensely personal faith in ethical perfection, drawn from his wide knowledge of philosophy and world literature, and by a compulsion to make converts to that faith who would reinforce one another's strivings for "perfection" by living together in an atmosphere of brotherhood. The type of community he envisaged — a secular equivalent of a monastery, based on a nondogmatic, ethical religion and rule of life[9]—has been compared with the Transcendentalist colonies of New England and the Rosminian religious order of northern Italy, with both of which he had close ties. It was also similar to Auguste Comte's ideal social order.[10] But these were only a few aspects of Davidson's amazingly eclectic Weltanschauung, which embraced elements of Positivism, Idealism, and the metaphysics of Aristotle and St. Thomas in a vast, unstable synthesis that had found its latest, but still transitory, inspiration in the work of the Italian Catholic philosopher, Antonio Rosmini-Serbati.[11]

Given such tendencies, it was not surprising that even his own disciples regarded Davidson as "the most inconsistent of men, . . . contesting in the afternoon the very doctrines he had urged in the morning." It scarcely mattered, however, because—always a Scottish Evangelical at heart—the source of his belief remained intuitive and emotional, supported by "the unction of his own fervent conviction," and by the massive earnestness with which he sought to demonstrate that his latest doctrine must be true. Even if a philosophy were true, moreover, he could "easily fail to relish it unless it showed a certain formal nobility and made pretensions to dogmatic finality." [12] Such pretensions were indis-

9. A typical Davidsonian rule of life included injunctions to "unsparingly put aside all prejudice, . . . live openly, . . . banish all selfishness, . . . [and] make no compromise with evil" (Knight, *Memorials*, pp. 21–22).

10. Davidson (1840–1900) had lectured at Bronson Alcott's summer schools in the 1860s and in the early 1880s spent a large part of each year observing the Rosminian Institute of Charity at close range in Domodossola, northern Italy. See T. Davidson, "Autobiographical Sketch," and J. L. Blau, "Rosmini, Domodossola, and Thomas Davidson," *JHI* 18 (1957). Davidson's versions of Comte's *pouvoir spirituel* is briefly sketched in "Moral Aspects of the Economic Problem," in Knight, *Memorials*, pp. 135–36.

11. See T. Davidson, *The Philosophical System of Antonio Rosmini-Serbati* (London, 1882), and "Rosmini," *Fort. Rev.* 30 n.s. (Nov. 1881).

12. W. Clarke, "A Modern Wandering Scholar," *Spectator* (6 Oct. 1900): 453; Ellis, *My Life*, p. 201; and W. James, "Characteristics of Thomas Davidson," *McClure's Magazine* (May 1905): 4–5.

pensable, however, because Davidson looked to the study of philosophy to raise his followers "from the darkness of mere credulity or unbelief into the pure light" of rational moral certainty. And this, above all, was what made him an ideal preacher to a generation of intellectuals who were searching for a new faith that would provide the emotional comfort and security of the old one—especially as Davidson never hesitated to present his teaching as a full-blown religious substitute.[13]

Despite his religious pretensions, however, it was really through education, in the fullest sense, that Davidson hoped to regenerate a world that he found "sadly unspiritual, sadly ignorant, narrow, and frivolous." Through his teaching—and all reports agree that he was a brilliant teacher—he sought to implant a new spirit of moral and social regeneration that, beginning with his own disciples, would grow to transform the social life and institutions of the surrounding world. Such was the larger purpose of the "fellowships" that he established in the 1880s "to bring together men who really and in all earnestness desire to comprehend the world in order that they may better it, and who are ready to consider all questions without prejudice or respect for current and conventional opinions." [14] Ultimately he hoped to turn such "fellowships" into utopian colonies, built around secular churches and schools that would dominate their activities and guide the members toward the achievement of "a perfect character in each and all." "Insight, love, and well-directed labour" would be their guiding principles, and the members, having become "directly conscious of their eternal natures, would lead pure and earnest lives. If anyone wishes to know my creed," he concluded, "there it is." [15]

Such rhetoric must have appealed strongly to both the moral sensibilities and the feelings of boldness and rebellion that stimu-

13. C. M. Bakewell, "Thomas Davidson and His Philosophy," in T. Davidson, *The Education of Wage Earners*, ed. Bakewell (New York, 1904), pp. 1–23; Davidson, "Autobiographical Sketch"; and T. Davidson, *Moral Aspects of the Economic Question* (Boston, 1886), p. 21.

14. Statement of principles for an unidentified fellowship, in Davidson, *Education of Wage Earners*, pp. 20–21, and compare the program for his first London fellowship, quoted in n. 9 above.

15. Davidson, "Moral Aspects," in Knight, *Memorials*, pp. 135–36, and chap. 4; J. Morrison Davidson (brother of Thomas), *The Annals of Toil* (London, 1899), p. 428, and Davidson to Chubb, 17 Feb. 1884, Davidson Papers, Yale. Davidson was remarkably prolific in producing such edifying triads of values.

lated so many younger intellectuals of the eighties to work out new standards of belief and conduct for themselves. But its most powerful appeal probably lay in its eloquent restatement of the values of Evangelical Christianity, to which the young Free-thinkers gathered around Davidson were still committed, despite their loss of formal faith; and many of them desired to see those values defended and even dogmatically propounded, on completely nontheological grounds. Such, at any rate, are the conclusions implied in Davidson's extensive correspondence with his disciples —virtually all of them lapsed Evangelicals[16]—and especially with the earliest and closest of them, Percival Chubb.

Percival Chubb came from a rigidly pious commercial family in Newcastle that had lost most of its money in the current depression but little of its ingrained materialism.[17] Perhaps in reaction against that situation he developed an earnestness so overpowering that he was upset even by "the air of worldliness" that character-ized the civil service, in which he worked. He also yearned to devote himself entirely to intellectual and spiritual pursuits,[18] and Thomas Davidson, whom he encountered at the Aristotelian So-ciety, was precisely the right mentor to guide and encourage such ambitions. Soon Chubb was describing Davidson's vision of the New Life as the "Ideal" that governed all his actions, and though he rejected Davidson's preoccupation with the metaphysical foundations of that ideal he repeatedly professed his zeal to make himself its "justification and recommendation to others," and thus to aid in "the realisation of the social utopia" that they both desired.[19]

16. See nn. 4 and 5 above, and nn. 19 and 69 below. Davidson himself wrote that he could not work with men who had "lost the religious sentiment" (to H. Ellis, 3 Oct. 1883, in Knight, *Memorials,* p. 39) .

17. Chubb to Davidson, 3 Jan. 1883, Davidson Papers, Yale. Chubb (1860–1959) was the longest lived of the original Fabians. He was a founder of the London Ethical Society and emigrated to New York about 1889, where he became pastor of an ethical church. (See his obituary notice in *Manchester Guardian,* 31 March 1960.)

18. Chubb to Davidson, 1 Apr. 1882, Davidson Papers, Yale. His religious posi-tion may be inferred from his intention to write a study of the eighteenth-century deist (and his forebear), Thomas Chubb (ibid.) .

19. Chubb to Davidson, 1 Apr. and 18 June 1882, Davidson Papers, Yale.

With variations in detail, the same description could apply to most of the young men and women who were attracted by David-son's New Life: liberal and Radical intellectuals on the rebound from strict Evangelical training who were still searching for new forms of personal commitment and for a new faith and a new life-style to match. Too middle-class and intellectually sophisticated to join the National Secular Society, several of them flirted briefly with Comtian Positivism in the early eighties (as several Positivists did with Davidson's New Life),[20] while others became active members of the ethical societies that sprang up throughout En-gland in the later 1880s. At the same time Davidson's converts, like Bernard Shaw, belonged to the growing "intellectual pro-letariat" of the late nineteenth century, largely made up of middle or lower middle-class provincial youths who had been drawn to London by their dreams of literary success but who were intellec-tually precocious and ambitious beyond the possibility of their adequate employment in the tight literary world of the metro-polis. Their lives were, therefore, often spent in attic rooms, hungry and lonely, doing hack work for publishers—only the lucky ones got civil service jobs—so that frustration and a kind of alienation were their common lot. Hence their desire to "regen-erate" a world that offered them so little satisfaction and their eager response to the new popular concern for poverty and social crisis that swept over England in the early and mid-1880s.[21]

Interest in social questions among Chubb and his companions, Ernest Rhys, Will Dircks, and Rowland Estcourt,[22] antedated

20. Much to Davidson's annoyance, both Chubb and his friend, Will Dircks, were strongly attracted to Positivism in 1882 (as Davidson himself had been two decades earlier). Dircks, in fact, was a disciple of the Newcastle Positivist, Malcom Quin (Chubb to Davidson, 1 Apr. 1882, 3 Jan. and 11 Mar. 1883; and "Autobiographical Sketch," JHI 18, 532–35). Regarding Positivist flirtations with the New Life, see Davidson to A. Senier (a Positivist), 13 Dec. 1882; J. H. Bridges to Davidson, 18 June 1881; and Chubb to Davidson, 27 Dec. 1882, all in Davidson Papers, Yale.

21. See esp. E. Rhys, *Wales England Wed* (London, 1940), pp. 71 ff. and W. Clarke, "The Fabian Society," *New England Magazine* 16 (1894): 97; regarding Shaw, see chap. 4 above.

22. All were Northerners who had come to London to seek literary careers and who now worked for "emancipation from their present, uncongenial positions" (Chubb to Davidson, 25 May, 4 July 1882, Davidson Papers, Yale). Rhys, the founder of Everyman's Library, Dircks, and Estcourt all subsequently became literary editors.

Davidson's influence over them and was initially reflected in a "manuscript club," formed early in 1882, for which they wrote papers on Positivism, Henry George-ism, and other social movements of that ilk. Once under Davidson's tutelage, however, their ideas took a more utopian turn that led to talk of setting up a colony in the Lake District (!) from which they would attempt to influence public opinion through literary means and thus "set popular discontent in motion." On Davidson's return to London in the fall of 1882 and again in 1883, the group expanded rapidly, attracting several persons of future prominence in Socialism or the world of letters: Frost, Champion, and Joynes, soon to emerge as leaders of the SDF; Havelock Ellis, the sexual reformer; William Archer, the drama critic; William Clarke, the Radical journalist; and such minor literary lights as Henry Salt, the "humanitarian"; Maurice Adams, editor and anthologist; and the future Fabian leaders, Podmore, Bland, and Pease.[23] In all, about thirty men and women—chiefly civil servants, clerks, and freelance journalists, all of them vaguely sympathetic to utopian schemes—were recruited by the fall of 1883, when their more formal meetings were begun.

Given his powerful influence on the formation of that group, which was the origin of the Fabian Society, it is surprising that the latest and most authoritative study of that society denies that Davidson was even its "virtual founder" and contends that he disapproved of it when it was founded.[24] This misconception may spring from the fact that in October 1883, just after the first formal meeting of his followers, Davidson abruptly left London to "sow the seed of the new life" in the warmer climate of Italy, and soon thereafter a schism broke out among his followers concerning the best methods of achieving their high aims. Some of the newer

23. Chubb to Davidson, 25 May, 4 July 1882, Davidson Papers, Yale; chap. 3 above; Ellis, *My Life*, pp. 157–62; H. Burrows and J. Bryce, eds., *William Clarke* (London, 1908), intro.; H. S. Salt, *Seventy Years Among Savages* (London, 1921), pp. 76 ff.; W. J. Jupp, *Wayfarings*, chaps. 6, 7; E. Rhys, *Wales England Wed* and *Everyman Remembers* (London, 1931); and nn. 4 and 5 above. In Davidson's absence their spiritual leader became the unorthodox Congregational minister, W. J. Jupp, of Thornton Heath, Surrey, whose home became the nucleus of a settlement that also included Chubb, Estcourt and Clarke among its members.

24. A. McBriar, *Fabian Socialism and English Politics* (Cambridge, Eng., 1962), p. 3.

recruits, led by Podmore, Bland, and Pease (a young stockbroker friend of Podmore's) wanted an organization that would seek to influence society at large. They were more concerned with "doing than with *being* something," as the unworldly Chubb complained, and their activist tendencies worried the original Davidsonians who remained devoted to the ideal of achieving self-perfection through communal living and fought shy of any formal organization. The new recruits, therefore, proceeded to organize themselves as the Fabian Society—a name devised by Podmore to express his ideal of cautious activism—in January 1884,[25] and the original Davidsonians belatedly followed suit by organizing the Fellowship of the New Life in the spring of the same year.[26] What chiefly separated the two groups, however, were differences of "method and immediate aim," the Fabians believing in the possibility of regenerating society before achieving individual perfection, the New Lifers insisting that they must find salvation for themselves existentially before offering it to the world at large. Despite such differences, both groups were linked by a common core of members and a common ground of social values and beliefs that were their heritage from Thomas Davidson.[27]

The fact that Davidson was spiritually closer to his non-Fabian followers, however, does not substantiate McBriar's conclusion that he disapproved of the Fabian Society when it was founded, for Davidson himself joined the Society "by letter from Italy"

25. Cf. pp. 161–63, below; regarding Pease, see n. 67 below. For fuller accounts of the founding of the Fabian Society, see Pease, *History of the Fabian Society*, pp. 26–36, and Knight, *Memorials*, pp. 16–25 (both incorporate copious documentary evidence), and the Chubb–Davidson correspondence (Davidson Papers, Yale). Pierson, *Marxism and British Socialism*, pp. 108–11, includes further quotations from Davidson's correspondence.

26. Thus the Fellowship of the New Life was technically a secession from the Fabian Society (which inherited the Minute Book of the Davidsonian group). For several years it maintained quasi-communal establishments along Davidsonian lines, first at Thornton Heath, later in Bloomsbury. For further details, see A. Calder-Marshall, *Havelock Ellis* (London, 1959), pp. 86 ff.; H. Ellis, *My Life*, pp. 162 ff.; W. H. G. Armytage, *Heavens Below* (London, 1961), pp. 327 ff.; and Jupp, *Wayfarings*, pp. 75–82.

27. Another meeting ground of Fabians and New Lifers was the Progressive Association, founded by J. C. Foulger, an ultra-Radical printer, who also soon became a Fabian. (See I. Goldberg, *Havelock Ellis* [London, 1926], pp. 96–98, and H. Ellis, *My Life*, pp. 157–58.)

shortly after its founding, and so did Percival Chubb, despite his complaints about the members' spiritual shortcomings.[28] The early leaders of the Society also continued to look upon Davidson as their guide and "founder"; and Davidson, himself, in later years, boasted of having founded the Society, adding that,

> As the name Fabian implied, its purpose was to delay and devote itself to profound study, before undertaking any apostolic work. [And of such aims he heartily approved, as they were also his own.] However, a number of Socialists being unwarily admitted into [the Society] turned it aside from its noble purpose, and committed it to a creed "adopted" on faith. I then, of course, left it.

This is to say that he encouraged the Fabians to study methods of social regeneration but disapproved of any specific Socialist doctrines, chiefly because he regarded Socialism as materialistic and dogmatic and therefore antithetical to a free development of the human mind and spirit.[29]

But it was evident from his arguments that Davidson disapproved specifically only of Marxian Socialism and of the several Marxists who were briefly members of his London group, whereas he showed a strong affinity for the kind of Socialism developed by the early Fabians. He even expounded a form of ethical Socialism himself, insisting that economics must form a branch of ethics and wealth must be utilized to promote public well-being. He praised the similar Socialism of Percival Chubb, who believed that "one of the first acts of ethical consciousness must be to bring about economic reform." [30] But this view also was characteristic of most of the early Fabians, who might well have learned it from

28. Fabian Minute Book (Nuffield), and Chubb to Davidson, 21 Dec. and 25 Oct. 1883, 10 Jan. 1884, Davidson Papers, Yale. Chubb not only remained an active Fabian but attended SDF and (from 1885) Socialist League meetings as well.

29. Podmore to Davidson, 11 Dec. 1884, Davidson Papers, Yale; Davidson to his students, 5 June 1900, in *Education of Wage Earners*, p. 194, and cf. pp. 151, 187–88, and "The Task of the Twentieth Century," 33 ff., 43 ff., in ibid.

30. See Davidson, *Moral Aspects*, and Davidson to H. D. Lloyd, 24 Apr., 1889, Lloyd Papers, WSHS; also Chubb to Davidson, 8 Jan. 1885, Davidson Papers, Yale. For Chubb's own statement of that principle see "The Two Alternatives," *To-day* 8 (Sept. 1887): 73, and "Schismatic Socialism," *To-day* 10 (July, 1888): 4–5.

Davidson himself. For Davidson taught that no moralization of society could be complete or lasting until its economic basis had been transformed. Accordingly, he urged that the "great social task of the future" was the abolition of poverty, no less than of ignorance and vice, and that "communal" (rather than competitive and individualistic) arrangements must become the basis of the new society. Only then, he believed, would it be possible to raise mankind to a new level of "spiritual and cultural freedom," for communal economic arrangements would make possible a true individuality of spirit, whereas the prevailing system of competition could only support a crude materialism. But his abhorrence of "materialism" (which he shared with nearly all the great Victorian moralists) was so intense that any Socialist scheme that gave chief emphasis to economic changes or even to the material improvement of society could only appear to him as crude, "external," and inimical to the achievement of true moral and spiritual "perfection."[31]

Given that perspective, Davidson reacted far less favorably to the Socialist revival of 1883 than did his Fabian disciples. The latter were permanent residents of London and were caught up in its movements of thought, whereas Davidson was only a visitor and remained outside and critical of practically all popular intellectual movements. The Fabians were also more deeply affected than their teacher by the social and economic crises of the early eighties and more predisposed to react favorably to the new currents of Socialist thought that these crises had helped to set in motion. Even Percival Chubb, most Davidsonian of the early Fabians, responded with enthusiasm to the appeal of Henry George, took up land nationalization, extolled the *Christian Socialist* magazine, and gave lectures on *Progress and Poverty*.[32] And what was true of Chubb was also (but in greater measure) true of other founding Fabians: nearly all were enthusiastic supporters of Henry George

31. Davidson, *Education of Wage Earners*, pp. 48–50, 43 ff., and 56–57 (where he defined his final goal as an undogmatic "Socialism of the Spirit").

32. Davidson's influence, however, may be detected in the fact that Chubb's lecture stressed the book's "bearing on the pursuit of knowledge and the acquisition of clear moral views of life" (Chubb to Davidson, 3 Jan. 1883, and cf. June–July 1883, 10 Jan. and 17 Feb. 1884; on the last date, Chubb also mailed a copy of *Progress and Poverty* to Davidson).

and of the ethical-aesthetic Socialism of Ruskin or William Morris.[33]

Finally, the formative meetings of the Society began at a time when interest created by the Socialist revival was at its peak, the fall of 1883. *The Bitter Cry of Outcast London,* then newly published, was stirring the conscience of the entire literate nation against the "sins" of slum landlords and their treatment of the "abject poor." It marshaled strong evidence to demonstrate that "the flood of human misery is gaining on us," while society at present was so little able to cope with the crisis that "the poor can scarcely gain a decent living except through vice." And though its argument was based solely on considerations of Christian philanthropy—the work of Nonconformist parsons appealing to the ingrained religious sentiment of the nation—its powerful conclusion provided a springboard for much of the ethical Socialism of the 1880s: "The State must . . . secure to the poorest their rights of citizenship; the right to live in something better than a fever den, the right to live as something better than . . . brute beasts." [34]

Almost immediately that cry was taken up by the crusading journalism of W. T. Stead, who helped to make it—and the whole question of urban poverty—a national cause célèbre.[35] In the following month, Hyndman published his *Historical Basis of Socialism in England,* which combined German social-democratic theory with the results of recent English work on economic history to produce the first authoritative English exposition of the economic case for collectivism. To most of his readers, newly introduced to social theory by the work of Henry George, its arguments must have seemed current and compelling, as they bristled with evidence that conventional exponents of liberal economics had overlooked or willfully suppressed. Moreover, Hyndman's book

33. Regarding George, see E. Rhys to Davidson, 16 Jan. 1883, and R. Estcourt to Davidson, 27 Mar. 1884, Davidson Papers, Yale; regarding Morris's influence, see sec. 3 below. Ruskin was represented among the Davidsonians by Howard Swan, the son of his most prominent Sheffield disciple.

34. (Rev. A. Mearns), *The Bitter Cry of Outcast London* (London, 1883; reprinted, N.Y., 1970), pp. 2, 15.

35. The *Pall Mall Gazette,* under Stead, published an abridgment of the tract on 16 Oct. 1883, devoted several leading articles to touting it, and printed heated correspondence inspired by it for almost a month thereafter.

effectively drove home the point (which had also been implicit in
The Bitter Cry) that popular unrest and agitation, which were
becoming increasingly apparent, could only be channeled into
peaceful and constructive uses by making immediate collectivist
reforms.[36] Thomas Davidson was not affected by such arguments
and continued to view Socialism with disdain, but his Fabian
disciples were deeply affected by them—not only the early Fabian
Marxists (Champion, Frost, and Joynes) but also such nondoc-
trinaire followers of Davidson as Podmore, Bland, Keddell, and
Pease, who were the leading spirits of the new society. Consequently, by February 1884 Socialism could be described as a new
"fad" among the members and interest in its teachings was
increasing fast.[37]

2. *Early Fabian Doctrines*

Nevertheless, the Fabian Society did not commit itself formally
to Socialism for over a year. Instead, following Davidson's advice,
its founding members preferred to study all the current schemes
of social reconstruction and to commit themselves publicly to
none. This principle was stated in the first of the Society's two
mottoes (devised by Frank Podmore), which argued, in reference
to "the victorious policy of Fabius Cunctator," that the "fruit of
this man's long taking of counsel—and (by the many so deemed)
untimeous delay—was the safe-holding for all men, his fellow-
citizens, of the Common Weal." [38] In the context of 1884, amid
the insecurity and social unrest engendered by the Great Depression, this surely meant that the Fabians intended to "take counsel"
by investigating all current methods of social amelioration so as
to better safeguard English society against the threat of revolu-

36. Hyndman, *Historical Basis*, esp. pp. 448, 464–67, 476–77, and *A Commune for London* (London, 1887) ; also see chap. 3, sec. 3 above for fuller discussion.

37. Chubb to Davidson, 4 Feb. and 21 Apr. 1884, Davidson Papers, Yale; but Chubb himself had already been described as "a strong Socialist" (Clarke to David-son, 8 June 1883, Davidson Papers, Yale) and was certainly active in the movement.

38. The first motto on the title page of Fabian Tract No. 1 (1884) ; its point of view was precisely that expressed by Davidson in the letter quoted on p. 160, above; also Pease, *History of the Fabian Society*, p. 39.

tionary violence.[39] How they did so may be seen in the topics of their meetings during the Society's first year. There were lectures on Anarchism, Marxism, Henry George-ism, and currency reform; no less than three lectures on aspects of utopian Socialism; one lecture and several "reports" on the SDF; and a lecture by an unnamed lady "who held that the human race would be speedily redeemed, if only every member were outfitted with an iron bedstead supplied by the state." [40]

A similar impression also emerges from the earliest references to the Society in the Radical and Socialist press, although such references inevitably reflected the points of view of their respective journals. Thus *Justice,* the organ of the Democratic Federation, first characterized the Fabians as "men of the middle class, who, while they feel sympathy for the poor, are not sure what form that sympathy should take"—certainly they were not Socialists in any sense recognized by the (S) DF!—while the ultra-Radical *Republican,* from its quite different angle of vision, saw the Fabians as "men and women who recognize no class distinctions and are brought together by their discontent with the present social system." [41] In either case, the Fabians appeared merely as Radical philanthropists with vague, melioristic aspirations. And that impression was further reinforced by the remarks of Bernard Shaw, as a new member of the Society, who described his Fabian colleagues in the fall of 1884 as "middle-class philanthropists who believe themselves to be Socialists"—a notion he immediately branded as "erroneous." [42]

If the Fabians really did "believe themselves to be Socialists" at that time, however, they could only have done so in the very

39. This, at least, was Podmore's intention, but he complained to Davidson as early as 11 Dec. 1884, that "the Fabian has by no means kept true to its name [devised by himself]. We have moved precipitately into pamphlet-and-lecturing . . . and our zeal is much more conspicuous than our knowledge" (Davidson Papers, Yale).

40. Fabian Society Minute Book, 1884 (Nuffield); McBriar, *Fabian Socialism,* p. 10 n.; and H. Bland, *Essays by Hubert* (London, 1914), p. 226. The woman in question was probably Mme. de Sales, whose "master key of social reform" attracted attention in Socialist circles in 1884.

41. *Justice,* 8 March 1884, and *The Republican,* July 1884; there is also a similar report in *Newcastle Chronicle,* 14 Oct. 1886.

42. Shaw to Scheu, 26 Oct. 1884, Scheu Papers, IISH.

traditional (by then, almost archaic) sense of fostering moral and cultural regeneration by strengthening the social feelings and habits of cooperation among their fellow men. For they had still not formulated any general theories of collectivism or nationalization and, in practice, showed great reluctance to accept ideas that ran so strongly counter to their traditional liberal bias. This tendency is most apparent in the official pronouncements of the Fabian Society in its early years, beginning with its official "Aim" and "Basis." The former, adopted at the second meeting of the original Davidson group, was almost a distillation of the aims of traditional English Socialism: "[to help forward] the reconstruction of the Social System in accordance with the highest moral possibilities." [43] The latter was more utilitarian in phrasing and more directly concerned with economic problems, but it, too, was restricted to ethical claims and implied no commitments to "state interference."

> The members of the Fabian Society assert that the [system of production for profit instead of production for use] . . . ensures the comfort and happiness of the few at the expense of the sufferings of the many, and that society must be reconstituted in such a manner as will secure the general welfare and happiness.[44]

Both resolutions were passed prior to the founding of the Society and remained its chief articles of faith until the summer of 1887.

A further attempt to formulate the social theories of the Founding Fabians appeared in the first Fabian tract, produced in April 1884. Doctrinally it was eclectic, with phrases suggestive of Owen, Darwin, Comte, Ruskin, and Henry George; but the prevailing tone was unmistakably utopian. In that vein, it identified the chief source of evil in society as competition, which it stigmatized as a "Commercial God" and as a "living swindle," ethically no better than brute force. Like most contemporary Socialists, however, the

---

43. Fabian Society Minute Book, 1883 (Nuffield) ; Pease, *History of the Fabian Society*, p. 19.

44. Ibid. The words in brackets were substituted for "the Competitive System" at the request of Mrs. Wilson.

Fabians vented their strongest hostility on the leisure class,[45] the undeserving beneficiaries of that "swindle," whose economically privileged position enabled them to look "with utter indifference on the struggle for existence that goes on beneath them." In short, the tract sought chiefly to pass moral judgment on the existing social system, while offering no solution to its economic problems other than vague references to "socialization" of capital and an emotional plea to members of the leisure class, urging them to acquire a social conscience:

> You who lead dainty and pleasant lives, reflect that your ease and luxuries are paid for by the want of others! Your superfluities are parents of their poverty! Surely all humanity is not burnt out of you by the gold your fathers left you! Come out from your ease and superfluities and help us!

A similar appeal followed to those who suffered under the system.[46]

Such were the moral tone and theoretical ambiguity of early Fabian propaganda. For although the tract made tentative advances in the direction of collectivism, announcing that the "time approaches when Capital can be made social," it did so only along ethical lines and in such ambiguous terms that its conclusions were compatible with virtually all the current ideologies of a socialistic bent, all of whose remedies the Fabians were still willing to consider.[47] Before the end of 1884, however, the Society did take one decisive step in the direction of collectivism by adding to its established articles of faith the statement that it "looks for the Reconstruction of the Social System in the emancipation of all natural and accumulated wealth from the control of individuals or classes, by placing such wealth in the hands of the Community for the

45. *Why Are the Many Poor?* Fabian Tract No. 1 (London, 1884). See especially its references to the "leisured masher"—a "fop of affected manners" (*OED*), much in evidence in the 1880s, whose reputation for lechery may have offended Fabian sensibilities as much as his idleness.

46. Ibid., pp. 1–3. (Quotations are from the unrevised first edition, which is now very rare. It was subsequently revised stylistically by Shaw.)

47. Fabian Tract No. 2 (by Shaw) had a strong Anarchist flavor (see chap. 4 above), while Fabian Tract No. 4, *What Socialism Is* (London, 1886), offered parallel expositions of Anarchism and Collectivism, both conceived in utopian terms, without expressing a preference for either one. (See chap. 7 sec. 4 below.)

general benefit." It was a small step, however, for the very phrasing of that statement ("emancipation" of wealth rather than
"nationalization," and its vesting in the "community" rather than
the state) was consistent with Anarchist and utopian interpretations and indicated an unwillingness to adopt an unambiguously
collectivist position. Moreover, although that formula was used
in the official "Basis" of the Fabian Society for the next fifty years,
and may even have convinced *Justice* that it should recognize the
Fabians as fellow Socialists, its practical significance was further
reduced by a companion resolution reasserting its moral basis and
intent: "The Fabian Society further endeavours to help forward
the Regeneration and Evolution of Society by insisting that only a
general high sense of duty and subordination of individualistic
aims to the general good can bring about true liberty, and assure
the true dignity of Man." [48] Of those two resolutions, the latter—
echoing the rhetoric of Thomas Davidson—remained the more
important and the more characteristic of prevailing Fabian
opinion.

Fabian Socialism was therefore still in flux at the end of 1884.
Its affirmations, for the most part, were abstractly ethical, suggesting that many Fabians still thought of Socialism less as an economic or sociological doctrine than as a kind of personal faith,
capable of immediate application in their lives. They typically
felt it to be "unsocialist" to ride in anything above a third-class
railway carriage and took the "simple life" as outward evidence
of their faith.[49] Through such acts of personal witness they sought
to "help forward" the transformation of society and to promote the
moral education of their fellow men. Thus the older Davidsonian
outlook persisted in the new Society, continuing to color its Socialist theories with a kind of moral and religious tincture that made
the Fabians distinctive among the Socialists of the 1880s and made

48. From the original Fabian Society card, adopted 30 May 1884, Fabian Archive, Nuffield, and *Justice,* 20 Dec. 1884. The wording of the first resolution was
incorporated directly into the 1887 "Basis" of the Fabian Society, where it has
remained.

49. Bland, *Essays,* pp. 226–27. "When I first called myself a Socialist," Bland
added, "I had all sorts of hopes and aspirations. . . . I seemed to think [it] a widely
inclusive term which embraced anything I particularly wanted. And what was
true of myself, I noted, was true of others."

their Society particularly attractive to renegade Christian Humanitarians, Positivists, Secularists, and the like. This point of view was perfectly summarized by Edward Pease's claim in 1884 that (Fabian) Socialism was a practical "economic" expression of the divine injunction to "love they neighbor," and that it alone could put that commandment into practice in a manner relevant to modern social and economic life.[50]

3. Sources of Early Fabian Doctrines

The Socialist doctrine developed by the Fabians in 1884–85, therefore, owed relatively little to the English Socialist revival and its Marxist prophets and derived most of its inspiration from the older, more religious Socialist tradition that had never quite died out on fringes of the English intellectual Left. The classical exponents of that tradition were Owen, Mill, and the original Christian Socialists, while its more recent spokesmen included Ruskin, Morris, and the Christian Socialists and Humanitarians of the eighties. In a sense, even Thomas Davidson was part of that tradition, for his insistence on moral and cultural regeneration embodied the core of traditional Socialism, and his interest in communal living must have heightened his disciples' interest in the details of earlier Socialist experiments. Thus the first lecture planned for the Davidsonian group in 1883 was to have concerned Robert Owen's experiment at New Harmony, and was to have been given by the great man's granddaughter, Rosamund Dale Owen (who was a founder and an active member of the new society). Three of the lectures during the Society's first year were also concerned with aspects of utopian Socialism.[51]

It is important to emphasize these details because it has been stated authoritatively that the Founding Fabians neither knew nor

50. Pease, "Ethics and Socialism," Fabian lecture, Dec. 1885, reprinted in *Prac. Soc.,* (Jan. 1886), adding that "what we want is a new interpretation of [this] old law adapted to the age in which industry and commerce occupy most of men's thoughts."

51. Fabian Society Minute Book (Nuffield). The three lectures were: "The Two Socialisms" (probably utopian and revolutionary), "English Voluntary Socialism," and Miss Owen's lecture, which was finally delivered a year late, 10 Dec. 1884.

appreciated the Socialist writings of Owen, Mill, and Maurice. Owen's writings, it is said, were too esoteric and prolix to suit their taste and Maurice's too smothered in Christian orthodoxy, while they identified Mill with a defense of laissez-faire that seemed the very opposite of Socialist.[52] If this was actually the case, it is the more important to recognize how familiar the Fabians became with such theories through secondary and tertiary sources. For the aims of Fabian Socialism were precisely those of Owen and his disciples—to build a "new moral world," or an environment that would systematically encourage the development of "social" (or cooperative) qualities and discourage antisocial ones. Its Socialist doctrines also showed a marked affinity with those of John Stuart Mill and his stepdaughter, Helen Taylor, though the Founding Fabians were probably unaware of Mill's Socialist writings at that time. (If so, however, that ignorance was soon remedied by the work of such Fabian converts as Sydney Olivier and Sidney Webb.) [53] In any case, these ideas had been widely enough diffused during the preceding decade to have thoroughly permeated the advanced-Radical intellectual environment inhabited by the Founding Fabians.

There remains the influence of Christian Socialism, which differed from that of Owen and Mill in two crucial respects. Its doctrines, as they were "revived" in the late seventies and early eighties by the self-proclaimed successors of F. D. Maurice, were far more accessible to the Founding Fabians than those of any other form of Socialism and were so similar to those developed by the Fabians that the former may rightly be regarded as the immediate forerunners of the Fabian creed.[54] But the Fabians were also staunch Freethinkers, unlikely to be drawn to doctrines of a clerical cast, while Christian Socialism of the early eighties was ultraclerical and largely Anglo-Catholic in its inspiration—a tradition that was doubly foreign to the outlook of the Founding Fabians, who, as has been shown, were chiefly lapsed Evangelicals.

52. Pease, *History of the Fabian Society*, pp. 22–23, and Shaw, quoted in Mc-Briar, *Fabian Socialism*, p. 274.

53. See chap. 2 above, S. Olivier, "J. S. Mill and Socialism," *To-day* (Nov. 1884), and S. Webb, "Was Mill a Socialist?" *Daily Chronicle*, 11 Mar. 1891.

54. For discussion of Christian Socialist theory (which, ironically, is described as "Fabian"), see Jones, *Christian Socialist Revival*.

The latter problem may be resolved, however, by noting that the Christian Socialists of the eighties presented their ideas to unbelievers in virtually the manner of a secular substitute faith, so different was their teaching from that of conventional Victorian Christianity; and this was particularly true of the Guild of Saint Matthew, the pioneer organization of the Christian Socialist revival, founded in 1877 to minister to Secularists on their home ground and subsequently broadened to include a type of Socialism inspired by Henry George.[55] Its propaganda work, therefore, required the muting of ritualist elements in its creed, so as to stress the secular implication of the Gospels and of what it regarded as the secular mission of the church. Above all, it abjured the tendency to other-worldliness that was so typical of Victorian Christianity, arguing that the church was really a "great Socialistic society for the promotion of righteousness" and social justice and taking care to garnish such effusions with the sort of verbal "unction" that still appealed powerfully to lapsed Evangelicals.[56]

The sort of theory that such doctrines could sustain was first expounded in a little tract, printed by the Guild and called *A Grammar of Socialism,* which was the pioneer exposition of ethical-religious Socialism in the English Socialist revival. Like Ruskin's work, it aimed to formulate the principles of a "social political economy," based on the moral teaching of the Gospels, as an alternative to the antisocial teachings of economic individualism. Accordingly, it focused its attack on the "sin of acquisitiveness" and the resulting extreme disparities of wealth and poverty. Its appeal against these, however, was chiefly directed to the charitable feelings of the well-to-do. For as such evils were essentially internal (reflecting a failure of Christian charity) they could be more readily altered by the "transforming force of public spirit" than by any external reforms; and the rich were, of all

55. See ibid. and F. G. Bettany, *Stewart Headlam* (London, 1926), pp. 217 ff. Headlam, founder of the GSM, was a particularly strong Georgian.

56. Headlam, lecture in 1883, quoted in G. C. Binyon, *The Christian Socialist Movement in England* (London, 1931), p. 122. "It is because we are Christians," he added, "that we feel bound to support all movements which tend to the secular well-being of Humanity."

classes, the best equipped to act in response to such public spirit.[57] Finally, like other contemporary expositions of ethical Socialism, it identified Socialism itself with the operation of that "spirit" as a permanent and essential force in human life. For "even now . . . it is only by virtue of Socialism's mitigating the ferocity of human acquisitiveness that the social fabric escapes destruction."[58]

There, in almost pure form, the early Fabians could have discovered the traditional aims and beliefs of English Socialism— beliefs that they might also have learned (a little less completely) from Thomas Davidson and the English Positivists, but which the Christian Socialists taught in a more bold and forthright manner, making explicit many of the things that were only implicit in earlier theories and openly giving the name of Socialism to their views. Moreover, these Christian Socialists did not attempt to revive the traditional economic panacea of the movement, the self-governing, cooperative workshop, but, instead, sought to adapt the aims and values of traditional Socialism to the new economic methods that were now held to be more "practicable" in the changed circumstances of the 1880s. This was the rationale for the leader of the GSM, Rev. Stewart Headlam's strong advocacy of land reforms derived from Henry George, which, he insisted, were the first steps toward a realization of full Socialism.[59]

Among some groups of Christian Socialists that approach led to an open advocacy of Radical collectivism. Even the *Grammar of Socialism* had argued that an effective Socialist spirit must be expected to bear fruit in such collectivist projects as the public construction of libraries, museums, parks, and housing. The same arguments were developed at greater length by the Rev. Samuel

57. [Rev. T. Wodehouse], *A Grammar of Socialism* (London, 1878; reprinted by the Guild of St. Matthew, 1884). This broadly Ruskinian point of view is especially clear in its three cardinal rules of Socialism. "First: All should work who can. Second: None should consume more than his due share . . . Third: Each should prudently distribute the remainder" (p. 7).

58. Ibid. pp. 5–6, 18. This point of view was also fundamental to the Radical Christian Humanitarianism described in chap. 7 below.

59. Headlam, "A Priest's Political Programme," *Church Reformer* 3, no. 10 (15 Oct. 1884); also ibid. pp. 3, 5. This program was an important forerunner of Fabian gradualism. Appropriately, Headlam himself joined the Fabian Society in 1886, becoming one of its most active members.

Barnett—heir to the mantle of Arnold Toynbee as the leading Radical Christian Humanitarian—in an article entitled "Practicable Socialism," which was widely read in the spring of 1883. It insisted that moderate collectivism would be neither socially disruptive nor burdensome; for the resources, laws, and institutions needed to put it into practice already existed. They only needed to be utilized in a more thorough and systematic fashion and supported by an effective property tax in order to transform English society more thoroughly than any of the revolutionary schemes—"impracticable Socialisms"—that were currently agitating the continental masses.[60]

Such arguments, appearing in a leading Victorian review during 1883, were certainly not lost on the Founding Fabians when they developed their own idea of Socialism. Thus the characteristic Fabian idea of taxing rent and interest to pay for increased social and cultural services may be traced, in part, to Canon Barnett's proposals (echoing the earlier ones of Headlam and Henry George) and to the practical as well as the humanitarian impulses imparted by his work. These, in turn, were supplemented by the more radical views propounded in the *Christian Socialist* magazine in 1883, which, within a few months of its founding (ostensibly in the tradition of F. D. Maurice), was expounding the arguments that land nationalization and public ownership of the means of production were necessary corollaries of Christian social teaching and that the ethics of Jesus and the moral implications of Marxism were identical.[61]

Finally, for a great many of the Founding Fabians, all the foregoing influences were summed up in what was for them the most powerful Socialist inspiration of the early eighties: the social teaching of William Morris. Morris's early Socialist lectures were essentially eclectic, drawing heavily on traditional English and European Socialism, with only a faint tinge of Marx. Thus they consistently identified Socialism with the spirit of "association"

60. *Nin. Cen.* 13 (Apr. 1883): 554 ff. His views and those of the Christian Humanitarianism he partly inspired are further discussed in chap. 7, sec. 1 below.

61. E.g., "Christianity and Socialism are almost interchangeable terms," *Chr. Soc.* (Nov. 1883); its pages were also full of references to early Christian communism, assertions that "because the earth was the Lord's it could not be the landlord's," and so on.

or cooperation, the substitution of social feeling for selfishness, and the practice of human brotherhood. Indeed, the core of Morris's Socialist faith—which, he proclaimed, was "for me, a matter of religion"—was precisely the teaching of the new Christian Socialism: that the "contrasts of rich and poor" fostered by commercial civilization were humanly degrading and "unendurable, and ought not to be endured by either rich or poor."[62] Such contrasts destroyed the practice of brotherhood, in which Morris deeply believed, thereby depriving civilization of its beauty, honesty, and integrity. It was chiefly for the sake of restoring these to modern life that Morris declared himself a Socialist: a believer in cooperation rather than competition.[63] And it was chiefly through his lectures that these ideas first made a deep impression on the early Fabian leaders.

So powerful was the impact of his teaching, in fact, that most of the early leaders of the Fabian Society may be regarded as Morris's followers: Edward Pease, chief organizer of the Society; Hubert Bland, its Honorary Treasurer and leading spirit; Frederick Keddell, its Secretary; and Morris's friend, J. Hunter Watts, were all of that persuasion in 1884, while Bernard Shaw was almost a disciple, and even Percival Chubb was favorably impressed.[64] A large share of Morris's appeal, of course, lay in the charm of his personality and in the vividness of his aesthetic vision. When he identified these with Socialism in 1883, it gave the latter a far more potent attraction for those alienated Radicals of the eighties who had, like himself, come to hate modern civilization for its meanness and ugliness, and who longed to see it replaced by a more humane

62. William Morris, "Art Under Plutocracy," and "Art and Socialism," in *The Collected Works of William Morris*, 24 vols. (London, 1935), 23:167, 172–73, 177, 188, 194. Both lectures were delivered in 1883 and reprinted in 1884. It is also significant that as a new convert to Socialism, Morris "praised Robert Owen immensely" (Mackail, *Morris*, 2:97, and Morris to C. E. Maurice, 1 July 1883, in ibid., p. 106).

63. "I hold that the condition of competition between man and man is bestial, and that of association [or cooperation] only is human" (Morris, "Art Under Plutocracy" (1884), in *Works*, 23:172).

64. Regarding Pease, Bland, Watts, and Keddell, respectively, see: the obituary notice of Pease, *Times* 7 Jan. 1955; Bland, "The Faith I Hold," in *Essays*, p. 222 (also pp. 213–23); Lee and Archbold, *Social-Democracy*, pp. 85–86 (for Watts) and pp. 93, 106 (for Keddell). Chubb and his friends also regularly attended Morris's Sunday night Socialist lectures, as did Shaw.

and satisfying order of life. Thus Hubert Bland's discovery that "if William Morris was a Socialist, whatever else Socialism was it would not be ugly" must have been shared by many of his Fabian colleagues who were searching, more or less consciously, for a way out of the "soul-destroying" drabness of their late-Victorian industrial world.[65] But Morris also presented Socialism in terms of a robust moral idealism, essentially religious in character, that blended easily with the gospel of Thomas Davidson and the visions of utopian community that were inherited by the Founding Fabians. Thus Morris supplemented Davidson's austere high-mindedness with a more masculine ideal of social equality and brotherhood that gave new positive content to the Fabians' vague ethical aspirations.[66]

Of all the Founding Fabians, however, it was Edward Pease, scion of a wealthy Quaker railway family, who in his personal life most fully illustrated the impact of Morris's teaching. As a young stockbroker, afflicted with an uneasy conscience about the nature of his work and the morality of personal wealth, he was strongly attracted by Morris's point of view. Conversion to Socialism followed, wherein he was deeply preoccupied with questions of human brotherhood and of the means by which the love of his fellow men could best be realized in economic terms. After wrestling with such problems for several years, he concluded that he must abandon his "immoral" occupation and take up a manual craft, so as to live by the work of his own hands in complete fellowship with his fellow men. Consequently, in 1886, he moved to Newcastle and became a cabinetmaker in a cooperative workshop nearby.[67]

No other Fabian of the early or middle eighties seems to have responded to Morris's teaching in such a thoroughgoing manner, but its impact was also evident in the outlook of the Fabian Anarchists, most of whom, unlike Shaw, thought of themselves as

65. Bland, *Essays,* pp. 222, 226.

66. See esp. Morris's lecture, "Useful Work *versus* Useless Toil," in *Works,* 23:98–100.

67. Pease, "Ethics and Socialism," *Prac. Soc.* 1: his valedictory to the London Fabians; and cf. *Newcastle Chronicle* (14 Oct. 1886). For a biographical sketch of Pease, see Appendix B.

Anarchist-Communists. Their leading spokesman, Charlotte Wilson, a member of the Fabian Executive Council, was a devoted follower of Morris until about 1886, when her allegiance shifted to Kropotkin. As the wife of a prosperous stockbroker, she too began to feel that she was living on immoral earnings and therefore resolved to become self-supporting by raising poultry at her suburban home in Hampstead. The home itself was also done over in the manner of a rustic farmhouse, in keeping with Morris's ideals of art and the simple life—a common tendency among the more unworldly Fabians (including the Fabian Anarchists), who sought to purge themselves of all the vestiges of an "immoral" commercial civilization. Such persons characteristically cared more about personal witness and a life in keeping with the pure ideals of Socialism than about "external" schemes of economic reform. Hence their Anarchism was, above all, a "faith for the present," resting upon a rejection of the state and, sometimes, of all existing institutions, as morally compromising and therefore unfit to aid in the regeneration of mankind.[68]

Unhappily, few written records of Fabian Anarchism have survived, apart from the excessively florid writings of Charlotte Wilson. In these, her point of view was communistic—even organismic —and her moral outlook was utterly unworldly. The crux of her position was the belief that freedom would release the natural sociability in human nature, reinforcing the "true [or higher] social self," and combating the "lesser sensual self"—the ego—that flourished on the materialistic individualism of the age. More simply stated, her theory was that domination over human beings was the fundamental social evil, destructive of all fruitful relationships. Freedom from domination—whether by government, property, law, or social custom— was therefore necessary to achieve the state of "social union" and the completely social type of personality that Socialism required. As a first step, she urged the Fabians to purge the spirit of domination from their own lives and then to promote the "social revolution," in which all persons who were conscious of their "freedom" would overthrow monopoly and government, seizing the means of production for themselves. (Such an event, however, could not occur until the

68. For a biographical sketch of Charlotte Wilson, see Appendix B.

necessary faith and attitudes had been accepted by the mass of people.) Finally, she foresaw the future organization of society in freely federated communes, each member free to follow his creative impulses, while distribution would approach "complete free communism." This kind of arrangement, she believed, would reconcile all conflict between the individual and society, help to suppress the urge to domination, and reinforce the tendency to cooperation and equal brotherhood, which, she affirmed, were what Socialism was all about.[69]

It will be evident that these views shared little common ground with Shaw's individualist Anarchism apart from their rejection of monopoly and their revolutionary hope. But it is very likely that until about 1886 similar points of view—abhorring dominance, affirming equal brotherhood and "social union," and looking for realization of their aims in a free federation of communes—were held by a great many of the Fabians, whether or not they thought of themselves as Anarchists. Indeed, the most persuasive exponent of that point of view among the early Fabians was not an Anarchist at all in the strict sense, (although contemporaries saw him as "more than half an Anarchist" in temperament), for it was William Morris.[70]

4. The Early Fabians and Marxism

Morris, however, was also a Marxist and an advocate of revolution, which he affirmed even more strongly after his break with Hyndman.[71] Why, then, did the Fabians, and especially *his* Fabian

69. [Charlotte Wilson], "Anarchism," in *What Socialism Is*, Fabian Tract No. 4 (London, 1886), pp. 13–15, and "Social-Democracy and Anarchism," *Prac. Soc.* 1 (Jan. 1886); also her lead article in *Freedom*, no. 1 (Oct. 1886).

70. For further discussion of the Anarchist tendencies in Morris's Socialist writings, see Cole, *Marxism and Anarchism*, pp. 415–16; Woodcock, *Anarchism*, pp. 417–18; and Hulse, *Revolutionists in London*, pp. 90 ff. Also see W. Morris, *News from Nowhere* (London, 1890), his quasi-Anarchist utopia.

71. Morris's espousal of Marxian economics has been argued (with, perhaps, an excess of partisan zeal) in E. P. Thompson, *Morris*, pp. 736–46 and pp. 886–99; but Thompson has not sufficiently noted the eclectic and utopian character of Morris's early Socialist lectures, which were what chiefly influenced the early Fabians.

followers, not follow his lead to similar conclusions? Perhaps the commonest answer to that question was that they did: Shaw repeatedly asserted that "the Fabian Society was warlike in its origin" and that peaceful, constitutional methods developed only at a later stage.[72] Unhappily, that judgment conflicted with his own contemporary observation that his fellow Fabians were "middle-class philanthropists" whom he intended to convert to his own revolutionary point of view. In the event, of course, the exact opposite transpired, and Shaw's intransigence was soon replaced by the peaceful methods of the Fabians.[73] This is not to say that there was no "warlike" faction among the Founding Fabians, however, but only to insist that the "practical (or non-revolutionary) party" was always "much the strongest." Apart from Shaw and Charlotte Wilson it is impossible even to identify the "warlike" members. In any case, contemporary records agree that as early as 1885–86 "the Society definitely declared for constitutional methods of reform . . . and began to evolve [toward] . . . permeation." [74] One result was that, in 1885, Shaw himself was won over to peaceful and constitutional methods, while such active, politically minded Radicals as Sidney Webb, Sydney Olivier, and Annie Besant were simultaneously drawn into the Society as converts. Their combined influence was probably decisive in insuring that the Society would adhere to parliamentary tactics (in contrast to the antiparliamentary views of Morris and the

72. Shaw, *The Fabian Society* . . . , Fabian Tract No. 41 (London, 1892), pp. 3–4. Shaw's account is notoriously untrustworthy as history but provides important insights into his own attitudes and beliefs.

73. Shaw to Scheu, 24 Oct. 1884, Scheu Papers, IISH. Shaw based a further argument on a Fabian resolution of 29 Feb. 1884, praising "the good and useful work" of the (S)DF; but the caveat attached to that resolution, explicitly disavowing "the statements and phrases used in the pamphlets of the Democratic Federation and the speeches of Mr. Hyndman," makes it clear that even then the society's differences from the (S)DF were not "latent" (as Shaw contended) but explicit (Fabian Society Minute Book, Nuffield; Pease, *History of the Fabian Society,* p. 38; and Fabian Tract No. 41, p. 4).

74. Edith Bland, quoted in Moore, *E. Nesbit,* pp. 65–66; Pease, quoted in *Newcastle Chronicle* (14 Oct. 1886), and in J. Burgess, ed., *Will Lloyd George Supplant Ramsay MacDonald?* (London, 1926), p. 138; also G. Wallas to Pease, 4 Feb. 1916, Fabian Archive, Nuffield.

Anarchists) and would develop a strong battery of arguments against the insurrectionary rhetoric of the SDF.[75]

Despite such developments, interest in Marx's theories remained strong among the Fabians in the middle eighties. Current events, beginning with the Socialist revival in the fall of 1883, helped to give those theories a new intellectual vogue, which is reflected in the fact that several of the Fabians are said to have purchased copies of *Capital* (volume 1) in French translation at that time, although it is probable that none went so far as actually to read the volume then.[76] Many of them, however, did read Hyndman's *Historical Basis of Socialism,* which disseminated the key ideas of Anglo-Marxism so widely that the effort of reading them at their presumed source was probably not deemed necessary. Consequently, such phrases as "surplus value" and "the exploitation of labor" passed freely among the Socialists of the 1880s without implying any firsthand knowledge of the theories that lay behind them. Nevertheless, the intellectual prestige of Marx remained high, and it was probably as a result of that prestige that a group of interested Fabians (including Shaw and Charlotte Wilson) established an informal "reading circle" in the winter of 1884–85 to promote study of the first volume of *Capital* and invited other Radicals and Socialists to attend. They were economic novices and felt strongly the need to master the "scientific" arguments—especially those concerning surplus value—upon which the Socialist case was supposed to rest; and they surely expected to find themselves in full accord with Marx, once they had mastered his intricate economic reasoning. Such, however, was not the outcome of their debates, chiefly because the technical skill and economic mastery of the anti-Marxists, including such serious economists as F. Y. Edgeworth and Philip Wicksteed, and such future Fabian luminaries as Webb, Olivier, and Wallas, won an easy victory

75. These typically followed the pragmatic line of arguing that no insurrection could possibly succeed against the military resources of the modern state (which appeared to be borne out by the events of "Bloody Sunday," 13 Nov. 1887, when an illegal Socialist demonstration was overwhelmingly routed by police), and that it would not even be supported by a significant portion of the working class. See S. Olivier, "Perverse Socialism," *To-day* 6 (Aug. 1886): 50, and Fabian Tract No. 41; also *Times,* 14 Nov. 1887, pp. 6–7.

76. Pease, *History of the Fabian Society,* pp. 24–25.

over amateurish partisans of Marx such as Hyndman, Bax, and, at the beginning, Shaw.[77]

That victory by no means stopped the Fabians from using the language of surplus value; nor did it put an end to their interest in the works of Marx.[78] But it did help to emancipate them from the influence of the SDF and from its claim that the only road to Socialism was by way of Marxian-Lassallean economics and the rhetoric of class war. Thereafter, the Fabians felt more free to find their own economic road to Socialism by way of the Ricardian law of rent (which Marx had ignored) and of Jevons's theory of "final utility." These will be discussed more fully in subsequent chapters.[79] Here it will be sufficient to note that the resulting theory of differential rent enabled the Fabians to radically revise the Anglo-Marxist theory of surplus value (the chief theoretical foundation of SDF Socialism), and thus to arrive at very different social and political conclusions from those of the SDF. Briefly stated, the Fabian theory of rent held that all the elements of what Marx had called surplus value—rent, interest, and wages and salaries above the minimum level—were determined in the same manner as the rent of land: by the difference in yield between the poorest land (or capital, or human skills) actually in use and the yield of a superior example of the same. Hence the different rates of rent, interest, and wages that actually prevailed were the results of inherent inequalities in productivity that were bound to occur under any economic system. Socialism, therefore, could not simply abolish the results of such inherent inequalities, as Anglo-Marxists thought it possible to abolish surplus value; it could only change the recipients of the resulting rent and the uses to which it was put, by making it into public property and

77. For further discussion, see chap. 6, sec. 4 below; also G. Wallas, *Men and Ideas* (London, 1940), p. 103, and Shaw's MS Diary for 1884–85 (BLPES).

78. Shaw, in particular, resumed that study in the summer of 1885 under circumstances that deserve retelling in Sidney Webb's own words. "I have begun to teach German to G. B. Shaw, the embryo novelist [Webb wrote to Sydney Olivier, 7 July, 1885]. He knows 'and' and 'the' only. We began Marx, Kapital, vol. two— not the easiest of books—[and] read two pages in two hours, accompanying each word with a philological dissertation" (Passfield Papers, pt. 2, BLPES).

79. The Fabian theory of differential rent is more fully discussed on pp. 200–02, 209.

using it for public advantage. But these were things Socialists could achieve quite as effectively by piecemeal reform as by a sudden revolution. Consequently, the logic of the Fabians' economic theory required that they support any sort of land tax, death duty, graduated income tax, or the like that promised to recover for the nation at least part of the rent that was now privately appropriated; and this reinforced their antirevolutionary tendencies by encouraging them to treat as "questions of more or less" the economic problems that Anglo-Marxists treated in terms of "all or nothing."[80] This, in turn, made their approach to Socialism fully compatible with the type of current Radical politics that gave top priority to social reforms. Because it enabled the Fabian theorists to make common cause with such potential allies as cooperators, trades unionists, and ordinary Radical workingmen, that new approach to Socialism also laid the foundation for the great increase in the number of converts from Radicalism to Socialism (though not necessarily to the Fabian Society) that occurred in the late eighties and early nineties.[81]

The most important immediate result of that new approach to Socialism, however, was that it drew into the Fabian Society the group of brilliant young Radicals—Sidney Webb, Sydney Olivier, Graham Wallas, and their friends—who had led the attack on Marx at the Hampstead meetings and subsequently took over the leadership of the Society itself (see chapters 6–8). Having converted most of the Society to neoclassical economics (and, more specifically, to the expanded theories of rent and final utility that will be discussed in the following chapter), they themselves joined the Society and, in company with Shaw, became its best known intellectual spokesmen. Their "conversions," in turn, prepared the way for further conversions of Radical intellectuals, including those of Annie Besant and William Clarke, and thereby set the pattern for future Fabian propaganda.

Thereafter, the Society moved steadily toward the type of Radical collectivism that had first been developed and then played down by the Democratic Federation in the early eighties. Along with that doctrine, it also adopted the hope of converting large

80. Wallas to Pease, 10 Jan. and 4 Feb. 1916, Nuffield.
81. This is further discussed in chap. 7 below.

segments of English Radicalism to Socialism through its reformist, evolutionary arguments. Such arguments, however, had only a small place in the intellectual armory of the Founding Fabians. Instead, it was the new converts of the mid-eighties—Webb, Olivier, Wallas, Besant, and Clarke—who revived such evolutionary arguments, developed them in a distinctively Fabian way, and made them the dominant note of Fabian theory in the 1890s. Indeed, "classical" Fabian theory—the theory of the *Fabian Essays* —was almost entirely the work of such converts, plus Shaw and Hubert Bland. And of that company of converts the most important and most widely known was surely Sidney Webb.

6

Sidney Webb: The Positivist Road to Socialism

> Sidney Webb used to say that the most obvious modern application
> of Comte's "law of the three stages," is that Comtism is the metaphy-
> sical stage of Collectivism, and Collectivism is the positive stage of
> Comtism.
>
> GEORGE BERNARD SHAW, "The Illusions of Socialism"[1]

On 20 March 1885 Sidney Webb began his long association with
the Fabian Society by delivering a lecture entitled "The Way
Out." Contrary to all that readers of his later writings might have
expected, however, it was a full-scale exposition of the methods
of social reconstruction taught by Auguste Comte, stressing the
latter's concepts of "trusteeship" and "moralisation," and it concluded with a declaration that "Socialists are on the wrong track
even with regard to the question of expediency: they will find it
easier to moralise the monopolist than to expropriate him."[2] The
trouble with Socialism, Webb explained, was that the advance in
public morality required to make it practicable would be so
vast that all its social goals would have been attained before the
system could be effectively established. Thus, as he argued in his
next Fabian lecture, "Socialism will only be possible when it is
unnecessary"; therefore, "moralisation" of the capitalists offered
the more hopeful and more practical method for creating public
happiness.[3]

Such were Webb's views in early 1885, and there is no evidence

1. In Edward Carpenter, ed., *Forecasts of the Coming Century* (Manchester,
1897) , 153 n.
2. Sidney Webb, "The Way Out," lecture to the Argosy Society, 1884, and to
the Fabian Society, 20 March 1885, complete MS, PP VI, *19*, 47. (Citations from
the Passfield Papers consist of section [in roman numerals], subsection numbers
[if any], item numbers [in italics], plus folio numbers, if relevant.) McBriar,
Fabian Socialiam, p. 14, erroneously notes that there is "no record" of this lecture,
but as that book was written without reference to the Passfield Papers, all of its
statements regarding Webb are more or less untrustworthy.
3. "Socialism and Economics," delivered, September 1885, PP, VI, *22*.

that they changed within the year. When he joined the Fabian Society on 1 May 1885, he did so as an avowed exponent of Comtian Positivism, and his conversion to Socialism, which occurred belatedly in the following year, involved little more than giving a new and more popular name to the social aims and values he had learned from Comte.

These claims, however, are entirely at odds with the conventional view of Webb, who has more often been depicted, in Shaw's words, as an "orthodox" follower of John Stuart Mill who followed him in converting to Socialism; or, in G. D. H. Cole's description, as an unemotional civil servant who "did not trouble himself much about any underlying philosophy," but thought only of "translating every idea into . . . the machinery needed to give it effect." [4] But the evidence in Webb's letters, essays, and lecture drafts makes it clear that he fitted neither of these stereotypes in his early life. Instead, his early intellectual work, including his social theories, was colored by intense social and religious feeling and by keen interest in philosophy, and his strongest intellectual tendency was toward the Positivism of Comte and Spencer—not toward Mill.

Such conclusions necessitate a thorough reinterpretation of Webb's early intellectual career, which has hitherto been virtually ignored. Indeed, for a person of such national prominence extraordinarily little accurate information has been available regarding any aspect of his life and opinions. He has not yet received a full-length biography (although one is currently being written), and the present chapter is, in fact, the first study of his early years that has made systematic use of his personal papers. (All other accounts of those years, in contrast, have been based chiefly on the reminiscences of his wife and Bernard Shaw.) [5] Yet the years before Webb began his "partnership" with Beatrice Potter and, above

4. Shaw, quoted in Margaret Cole, ed., *The Webbs and Their Work* (London, 1949), pp. 4, 6; also Shaw, *Sixteen Self-Sketches*, p. 108, and G. D. H. Cole, *The Second International*, p. 210.

5. The best existing biography is M. A. Hamilton, "Sidney Webb," in *DNB, 1941–50*, pp. 935 ff. (far superior to the same author's *Sidney and Beatrice Webb* [London, 1934], chap. 2, which is untrustworthy), supplemented by M. Cole, *Beatrice Webb* (London, 1934), chap. 5; Kitty Muggeridge and Ruth Adam, *Beatrice Webb: A Life* (London, 1967), pp. 120–22; and Beatrice Webb, *Our Partnership* (London, 1948), pp. 3–11. An official biography is presently being written by Prof. Royden Harrison of Warwick University.

all, the early and middle eighties were precisely the most crucial period for the formation of his Socialist theories. The ideas, beliefs, and values that he formulated then remained the basis—though sometimes an inconspicuous one—of all his subsequent social thought, and the Fabian Society was their heir.

1. The Making of a Positivist

The earliest record of Sidney Webb's political opinions was preserved in the reports of a Radical, middle-class debating society entitled the Zetetical ("[truth]-seeking"), of which both he and Shaw were active members in the early eighties. Its stated purpose was to "search for truth in all matters affecting the interest of the human race," and its outlook was thoroughly "advanced," agnostic, and emancipated.[6] Within that heady atmosphere, however, Webb first appeared as the defender of a very straightlaced form of liberal-Radicalism. He had serious scruples about government interference with labor; he was a strict Malthusian; and his ideal of social reconstruction was limited to the "moral elevation" of the working class—an idea that was equally congenial to Positivists and Evangelicals.[7] Thus when a Radical lecturer advocated extension of the factory acts to give fuller protection to women's labor, Webb questioned whether such protection was compatible with liberal values. And at a subsequent meeting he argued against the formidable Helen Taylor, currently speaking for the Irish Land League, that the growth of Irish population would have to be repressed and Catholics converted to Malthusianism before a useful purpose would be served by land reform.[8]

In the early eighties, therefore, Webb was still essentially an orthodox political Radical, in the manner of John Morley and John Stuart Mill—individualistic, earnest, and high-minded. But

6. Prospectus of the Zetetical Society (PP, VI, 4), and cf. Henderson, *Man of the Century*, pp. 136–37, and *The Radical*, 28 May 1881–30 July 1881. The name Zetetical had been associated with London Radicalism since the early nineteenth century, when Richard Carlile's "Zetetic Societies" taught self-educated artisans the rational skepticism of the Enlightenment (see E. P. Thompson, *Making of the English Working Class*, p. 727).

7. The social morality of Positivism and Evangelicalism were closely akin and tended to reinforce each other; for further discussion, see pp. 195–97.

8. *The Radical*, 16 and 30 July 1881, reporting meetings of 30 June and 19 July 1881; Shaw also spoke on Ireland at the latter meeting.

the manner and phraseology of his speeches also revealed traces of an earlier involvement with Evangelical religion—especially apparent in his fondness for homiletic and even scriptural language, in his overt use of social morality as a substitute faith, charged with the familiar phrases of Evangelical piety, and in the studied cautiousness of his approach to social change. All these elements went into the formation of his social faith, and all were largely products of his home and family environment, reinforced by his education and by his choice of a career.

His family was lower middle class—shopkeepers and clerical workers "in a small way," who lived, in the early eighties, in a slightly shabby neighborhood just west of Russell Square. They were by no means intellectuals, although they valued education enough to send their two sons to Switzerland and Germany for a year of language study (which paid off handsomely in subsequent examinations) . Otherwise, they gave their children standard "commercial" educations and sent them to work as junior clerks at fifteen. Thereafter, Sidney's schooling was restricted to night classes, but through intensive study and an exceptional performance on examinations he moved steadily to higher levels of employment. Within a few years he was offered a share in the brokerage firm in which he worked, an inducement to stay in the business, but he turned down the offer because he cared more for public service than for wealth (according to Graham Wallas) . His public spirit, plus his desire to "have time for his own intellectual work," consequently led him to the Civil Service, where, by 1882, competitive examinations had placed him in the First Class, Administrative Grade, on a par with recent university graduates. In 1883, his studiousness was further rewarded with a scholarship in international law at Cambridge. But professional and financial pressures prevented him from leaving work for the three years required for such a course of study, so that, instead, he studied law at London University at night, becoming Barrister of Gray's Inn in 1885, and obtaining his LL.B. the following year.[9]

9. Webb Memorabilia, PP, I; Hamilton, "Sidney Webb," *DNB: 1941–50*, pp. 935–36; memoir of Webb by Graham Wallas, Wallas Papers, BLPES; Beatrice Webb's typescript Diary, 26 April 1890 (14:34, PP.) and notes on Sidney Webb by his brother, Charles Webb, 30 June 1948 (copy in Tawney Papers, BLPES, box containing material for Tawney's proposed biography of Webb. I owe this last reference to the kindness of Dr. Jay Winter.)

Despite his striking professional success—still rare for someone of his origins—Webb's social and political values continued to reflect the outlook of his family. His politics were an inheritance from his father, a devoted metropolitan Radical who had worked in 1865 as an election agent for John Stuart Mill, and for years had served on the local vestry and the Board of Guardians. Indeed, the bulk of his time was spent on public service, so that the family became accustomed to giving public welfare priority over personal interests.[10] It was also a *"happy* family," as Sidney confessed in a rare mood of nostalgia, but it was "always in the thick of the fight." Consequently, "one of the great influences I have missed is [the] peace" of quiet provincial life.[11]

His mother, on the other hand, raised her children on strict, Evangelical piety, taking them every Sunday to some metropolitan church or chapel, where she searched for "an eloquent preacher, free from sacerdotalism." [12] Such training made a deep impression on young Sidney that long outlasted his phase of orthodox belief; for it created the basis of his subsequent conversion-in-reverse and of the moral faith that underlay his Positivism and Socialism. In the early eighties he became a strong "Rationalist" or "Free-thinker," but by 1885 he had gained enough humorous detachment from religion to write that he had "dutifully" accompanied his mother to church "—for the first time in years—and had as reward a very dull sermon about God hardening himself to the proud, etc., which I took to [mean] myself." In fact, his personality was fundamentally too placid—even, as the tone of his letters demonstrates, too open, warm, and genial—to become permanently enmeshed in the Calvinist scheme of guilt and redemption. Instead, his world view was derived almost entirely from the Enlightenment. He held that "calm reason" was "highest and best in the world," although it brought him nothing but un-

10. B. Webb, *Our Partnership,* pp. 2–3; also Sidney Webb, "Reminiscences," *St. Martin's Review* (Oct. 1928) ; and SW to Beatrice Potter, 22 July 1891, PP, II: 3i, *18.*

11. Webb to Olivier, 17 July 1885 PP. II: 2, *9.* Characteristically, however, when Webb visited such a quiet provincial haven in 1885, its wretched "courts and alleys" soon turned his thoughts to "the bitter cry of outcast Salisbury. I remembered in time whence came the (cathedral) Close revenues, and my radicalism revived," he wrote in ibid.

12. B. Webb, *Our Partnership,* p. 5.

happiness, and even went so far as to justify his break with an inamorata on the ground that her "theism" and irrationality were incompatible with such beliefs.[13]

As a convert to rational Freethought Webb followed a path already worn smooth by generations of liberal intellectuals, from earnest Evangelical piety to an equally earnest but secular substitute faith—a process that Beatrice Webb later described as a "conscious and overt transferral of the impulse to self-subordinating service from God to man."[14] In the Freethought lectures and debates that formed his major intellectual outlet in the early eighties he defended Mill's doctrine that enduring happiness could only be obtained by service to a higher cause, and he claimed that the selfless service of "Humanity" formed the only cause that could be worthy of man's highest and noblest efforts. In a militantly secular vein, he went on to insist that all theistic rationalizations of that impulse were both unnecessary and inferior to the simple creed of altruism. This belief was common to Secularism, Positivism, Ethical Culture, and, indeed, to practically all forms of secularized Christianity in the late nineteenth century, but it found its most elaborate and systematic exposition in the Positive philosophy of Auguste Comte.[15]

Webb's road to Positivism was a familiar one for liberal intellectuals of the eighties, for it led by way of an early enthusiasm for "the new learning of the nineteenth century"—the evolutionary sciences, whose prophets were Spencer, Comte, and Huxley— to his own synthetic blending of those systems. His earliest commitment was to Spencer, the Bacon of the new scientific era, he believed, who had "unified" all knowledge in a synthesis that Webb expected to endure for "many generations." At the same

13. Webb to Wallis, 28 June and 2 July 1885, PP, II: 2. Webb also recalled calmly reasoning his way out of an intense childhood fear of hell (*Our Partnership*, pp. 10–11).

14. B. Webb, *My Apprenticeship* (London, 1926), p. 123.

15. Webb, "The Ethics of Existence," PP, VI, *3*, and "On Serving God," PP, VI, *1*, 15, 17, 19, 20; both were written ca. 1880. It is also significant that Webb found his "ethical ideal" most perfectly expressed in George Eliot's Positivist hymn, "O may I join the Choir Invisible" ("Ethics of Existence," p. 59), and specially praised her novels for their inspiring "ideal of devoted service" ("George Eliot's Works," PP, VI, *6* written ca. 1882.

time he professed continuing respect for Comte and Mill as
Spencer's predecessors and continued to draw upon them for
ideas. From Comte he took the hierarchy of the sciences and the
law of the three stages, the core of the Positive philosophy, though
he maintained that Spencer and not Comte had finally brought
social science to its positive stage. Mill, on the other hand, he saw
as "the latest philosopher of the pre-scientific age" and a continuing inspiration to Radicals through his "uniformly progressive
opinions." Only his work in logic and economics still had relevance, however, because those fields alone were unaffected by the
influence of biology; but wherever biological analogies had had
great impact, as in sociology and religion, he held that Spencer's
influence was paramount.[16] Finally, Webb's acceptance of a broadly positivist world view was decisively encouraged by the avante-
garde debating societies (including the Zetetical and Dialectical)
that he frequented in the early eighties. There the works of his
new idols were openly revered—Huxley, Tyndall, and George
Eliot (to say nothing of Mill and Spencer) were on all the members' shelves—and young members were encouraged to draw from
them the most advanced religious and philosophical conclusions.
In such an environment it was only natural for Webb to declare
himself a "positivist"—a scientific thinker in the line of descent
from Hume and Mill—and to profess the deep concern for
social progress and reform that this faith implied among his
peers.[17]

Nevertheless, Webb was still far from being a Positivist in the
full Comtian sense,[18] and his systematic study of Comte's writings
probably began only in 1882, when Sydney Olivier, his fellow

16. "The New Learning of the Nineteenth Century and Its Influence on Philosophy," lecture, ca. 1880, PP, VI, 2, 11–12 verso, 16, 2 verso, 10. Webb also demonstrated his enthusiasm for Spencer through persistent use of such Spencerian
metaphors as "social organism" and "specialised political tissue," and through his
defense of Spencer's religious doctrine of "the Absolute Unknowable" (ibid.) .

17. Ibid. ff. 17, 20v, 24–25, and Shaw, *Sixteen Self–Sketches*, p. 56. Webb also
identified the key doctrines of such "positivism" as "the relativity of all knowledge"
and the "certainty of invariable causation."

18. Webb must have been acquainted with Comte's system in 1882, however,
from lectures by Positivists at the debating societies he attended: e.g., Dr. Congreve, at the Zetetical Society, 26 Oct. 1881, and Dr. Bridges, at the Argosy
Society, 11 May 1882.

resident clerk at the Colonial Office, encouraged Webb to join him and Graham Wallas (Olivier's closest friend from Oxford) in discussing the "principle works" of Comte and attending Positivist meetings.[19] Olivier's enthusiasm extended to all aspects of Comte's system, embracing even its religious creed and catechism, and he especially praised its "comprehensiveness." Webb, on the other hand, proceeded more warily in his approach to Comte and expressed far more ambivalence about his teachings. For while he warmly praised Comte's social theory, he also noted that it was "unfortunately by him enveloped in a dense mass of other doctrines which have impeded its progress." [20] But what he learned from Comte he kept far longer than Olivier or Wallas, and it became the lasting basis of his social faith.

The evidence of Webb's infatuation with Positivism is diverse, ranging from paeans to "Humanity" and vows of "thankfulness for the great unnamed dead" (showing that even Comte's religion obtained a foothold in the door of his imagination) [21] to an extended use of Comtian sociology and ultimate acceptance of its approach to social reconstruction. An interest in social reconstruction was also, in all likelihood, what first attracted Webb to Comte and caused him to break away from Herbert Spencer. For Spencer's antimeliorist, ultra-individualist polemics, which denied virtually all hope of social regeneration, must have offended Webb's moral sensibilities, whereas Comte's *social* point of view would have sustained them and would have agreed as well with the public-spirited and self-sacrificing values of his family and its

19. S. Olivier to M. Cox, 22 Jan. 1884, in M. Oliver, *Sydney Olivier* (London, 1948), p. 62; also pp. 60–61. The "principal works" of Comte that they read must have included: *A General View of Positivism*, trans. J. H. Bridges (London, 1865, 1885); *Catechism of the Positivist Religion*, trans. R. Congreve (London, 1858); *The Positive Philosophy*, trans. and abridged by H. Martineau (London, 1853, 1873); and *The System of Positive Polity*, trans. Bridges et al. (London, 1875–77).

20. "The Economic Function of the Middle Classes," Lecture to the Argosy Debating Society, Feb. 1885, PP, VI, 20, 37; an abridged version appeared in *Church Reformer* (March 1885). Further evidence bearing on this point will be found below.

21. "On Serving God," and "The Way Out," f. 31. For further evidence, see Webb's discussion of dedicating himself "to Humanity," and his espousal of Comte's doctrine of womanhood (which he applied to his future wife): SW to Beatrice Potter, 13/14 July, 30 May, 24 June 1890, PP, II: 3i.

faith.[22] In any case, the social values he derived from Comte were the very opposite of Spencer's, and it was from them that he acquired his earliest taste for collectivism, and thus the nucleus of his Socialist faith.

Webb's acceptance of Comte's sociology was first apparent in a series of lectures on social and economic history that he delivered throughout the middle eighties.[23] Such history, as he conceived of it, was the "ultimate science": a study of the "natural law" according to which social organisms were born, modified, multiplied, and died. In short, it was really sociology, conceived on ultrapositivist lines.[24] For Webb held that its "laws" were entirely comparable with the law of gravity and were no less universal in their application. In proof, he cited anthropological evidence that "the human mind has progressed, and is progressing, much in the same way all over the globe." That argument, of course, formed part of Comte's "law of the three stages," which could be utilized to predict future developments. Webb, therefore, offered the prediction (which was probably also his first statement of the "inevitability of gradualness") that the Western world was moving toward "a new organization of humanity" that would be characterized by an organic "social unity" and by perpetually increasing "social consciousness."[25] He justified that belief by arguing, in a

22. See Herbert Spencer, "Reasons for Dissenting from M. Comte," in *Essays: Scientific, Political and Speculative,* 3 vols. (London, 1891), vol. 2, and Philip Abrams, *The Origins of British Sociology: 1834–1914* (Chicago, 1968), pp. 73, 77. Webb probably derived the language of social organism from Spencer, but he soon recognized that its implications were contrary to Spencer's mechanistic world view, whereas Comte's *veu d' ensemble* was genuinely organismic, and Comte explicitly recognized that the social organism had "a life [of its own] . . . apart from that of any of the individuals in it" (Webb, "History of Economic Theory," lecture, early 1890s, PP, VI, *64*, 39–41).

23. "Feudalism," "The Growth of Industrialism," "The Reformation," and "The Economic History of Society in England," PP, VI, *10*, *11*, *12*, *17*, respectively, lectures either to the Sunday Lecture Society or to the London Working Men's College, 1883–85.

24. "Economic History of Society," f. 9; for Webb's "ultra-positivism," see his insistence that scientific laws must be "exactly true of every individual case [—not statistical probabilities—] . . . everlasting, ubiquitous and unbroken" (lecture to British Association, 16 Sept. 1889, PP, VI, *41*).

25. "On Serving God," f. 7, and "The Reformation," ff. 59–61. On the relation between "the inevitability of gradualism" and nineteenth-century Evolutionary Positivism, see J. W. Burrow, *Evolution and Society* (Cambridge, Eng., 1966), esp. p. 187.

virtual paraphrase of Comte's law of increasing social sympathies; that:

> the progress of industrialism has bound every one of us into one great army of workers, in which each one . . . no longer fights for himself, but for the whole, and receives no longer what he individually produces, but a share of the whole. We fight the battle of life shoulder to shoulder throughout the whole universe: . . . [a] marvellous system of unconscious industrial co-operation.[26]

In similarly Comtian (or Saint-Simonian) terms, Webb also argued that the intellectual "anarchy" of the modern era, which was especially evident in the "critical period" of the nineteenth century, must soon be superseded by a new organic synthesis of knowledge—a synthesis that was already taking shape and soon would form the basis for a "higher type of social structure, based on the consciousness of Humanity alone." In other words, he held that history itself was bent on social regeneration and was bringing it about through an increase in social (or altruistic) feelings so great that men would finally lose all sense of individual identity. In an almost Calvinistic fashion, however, such knowledge of the predestined course of history only stimulated Webb to preach more fervently the need to "break down all remnants of isolated individualism still left among us." "Before men can be thoroughly social society must doubtless be organised," he wrote, "but before it can be organised man must have become conscious of himself, not as an individual but as a unit of the larger whole."[27] And he devoted his best efforts in the middle eighties to promoting the development of that state of consciousness.

26. "Growth of Industrialism," ff. 63–64. This was one of Comte's most fundamental sociological generalizations: see, e.g., *Cours de philosophie positive*, 2d ed. (Paris, 1864) , 6:721; *Positive Polity*, 2:134–44, 320–21, 3:55–58; and E. Caird, *The Social Philosophy and Religion of Comte* (London, 1885) , pp. 36–39. For Webb's elaboration, see n. 64 below.

27. "The Reformation," ff. 59–60; "Growth of Industrialism," f. 54; "The Reformation," 60–61; Webb's other historical generalizations, e.g., that the Reformation broke the "organic" unity of the middle ages and impelled western civilization toward individualist "anarchy" ("The Reformation," f. 54) , were cut from the same Comtian cloth.

2. Positivism and Socialism

Such was the essence both of Webb's Positivism and of his subsequent Socialist creed, in which the doctrines of social solidarity and interdependence, expounded above, became the basis of his mature collectivism. Slightly expanded they also formed the basis of his Fabian essay in 1889, in which Comte (together with Darwin and Spencer) was acknowledged as the source of the intellectual tendencies leading to modern Socialism—and of Webb's version of them, in particular.[28] Further expanded, they formed the basis of all Webb's Socialist writings of the later eighties.

But such conclusions should not be restricted to Webb alone, for they apply in varying degrees to the majority of his Fabian colleagues in the early eighties, when Positivist influence was at its peak in England: [29]

All the young men [of that decade] who were interested in progressive thought studied the works of Comte and learned from them the idea of a complete reconstruction of the social system. Positivism was then a growing creed, and it was the rise of English Socialism that put a sudden end to its expansion.

So wrote Edward Pease, secretary and historian of the early Fabian Society, and ample evidence supports his argument, despite reluctance of the latest historian of Positivism to grant such widespread influence to Comte.[30] In fact, Positivism formed a way

28. "The Basis of Socialism: Historic," in G. B. Shaw, ed., *Fabian Essays in Socialism*, jubilee ed. (London, 1948), pp. 31–32, 43, 53–54; and cf. chap. 8, sec. 3, below.

29. The peak of British interest in Comte's teachings probably occurred about 1879, as a result of the journalistic debate begun by W. H. Mallock's attack on Positivism in *Is Life Worth Living?* (London, 1879). See Amy Cruse, *After the Victorians* (London, 1938), pp. 24–25, and compare Mallock's earlier satirical novel, *New Paul and Virginia; or Positivism on an Island* (London, 1878).

30. Edward Pease, "Recent English Socialism," in T. Kirkup, *History of Socialism*, 5th ed. rev. by E. Pease (London, 1913), p. 375; also Pease, *History of the Fabian Society*, pp. 14, 18; and for the most recent (but much too narrowly conceived) discussion of Comte and English Socialism, see Simon, *European Positivism*. In contrast to the latter, George Lichtheim, *A Short History of Socialism* (New York, 1970), pp. 171–81, greatly exaggerates the importance of Positivism as a source of Fabian doctrine, although his claims are largely true of the Webbs.

station for almost all the early Fabians about whom much evidence survives, and Socialism, arriving later on the scene but armed with greater popular appeal, did surely steal most of its thunder. Few of those embryonic Socialists, of course, ever advanced beyond the stage of "incomplete" Positivism, where they were influenced more by Comte's methods, aims, and social ideals than by the religious cult or the prescriptions for a new society that were the marks of his complete adherents.[31] But their involvement with his teaching was still powerful enough to color their subsequent Socialism and even, in large measure, to determine the type of Socialist faith they would adopt.

Because of the present low regard for the theories of Auguste Comte, it is seldom recognized that both in England and throughout much of Latin Europe his social teaching was the most powerful non-Marxist source of Socialist doctrines in the 1880s and 1890s. In England this was a result both of the remarkable "fit" between Comte's teachings and the intellectual and emotional requirements of the age, and of the apparent appropriateness of his teachings to the current crises of English society. For Positivism offered the most systematic criticism of liberal capitalism that was readily available to young English Radicals who were disenchanted by the way that economic system had succumbed to the Great Depression, and by the inability of classical economics to prevent or cure it. Positivism was also ideally equipped to tap the revulsion against the "anarchy" and wastefulness of commercial competition that was felt by increasing numbers of sensitive late Victorians. Of course, it also supported capitalism in a modified and moralized form (and such support was probably essential to its widespread diffusion at that time). But its view of society was, nevertheless, semi-Socialist, as it repudiated competition, insisted on

31. For further distinctions between "complete" and "incomplete" Positivists, see Royden Harrison, "Professor Beesly . . . ," in Briggs and Saville, eds., *Essays in Labour History*, pp. 206–07. In the present study "complete Positivists" will refer both to those who sought to form a Positivist church (Congrevians) and to those who sought chiefly to disseminate the principles of Positivism (Harrisonians); "incomplete Positivists" will refer to persons attracted by Comte's method of social reconstruction and his idea of science. In contrast to such usage, Simon, *European Positivism*, unnecessarily limits his study to complete Positivists, thus excluding from consideration much of the movement's real influence in England.

the dominance of ethical over economic considerations, and offered its votaries an ultimate vision of social harmony and solidarity that was essentially Socialist in character.[32]

Unlike late-nineteenth-century Socialism, however, Positivism presented such visions as the outcome of a full-fledged secular religion; and it was precisely the religious character of its teaching that seems to have made the strongest *initial* appeal to the class of liberal intellectuals from whose ranks the English Socialist converts were chiefly recruited (though few of the latter went so far as to embrace that religion openly). If few such intellectuals accepted *complete* Positivism, however, a great many were seriously attracted by its claims to have based religion on science in a manner compatible with the current vogue of Darwinism,[33] to have reconciled the conflicts of science and religious emotion, and to have shown the way to the regeneration of mankind through the systematic encouragement of love and altruism. All these claims answered real, often pressing, emotional needs of the temperamentally unskeptical skeptics of the 1880s who were unable either to accept a religion that contradicted the current doctrines of science or a scientific world view that excluded religious hope. But most urgently, the former Evangelicals needed an outlet for their Evangelically inspired impulse to self-subordinating service; and the altruistic creed of Positivism, reinforced by its demonstration of the inevitable victory of altruism over egoism, provided this more effectively than any of its competitors—so effectively, in fact, that Beatrice Webb dubbed it the "logical culmination" of the whole Victorian tendency to secularize religious emotion by transferring it from God to man. Accordingly, she classified the majority of her intellectual peers as "Positivists" (though of a singularly

32. Pease, *History of the Fabian Society*, pp. 14–18. For further discussion of the relations betwen Positivism and Socialism, see R. Harrison, *Before the Socialists* (London, 1965), pp. 333 ff., and G. Lichtheim, *Short History of Socialism*, pp. 171 ff. For evidence of popular disenchantment with orthodox economics, see Abrams, *Origins of British Sociology*, pp. 77 ff., and Webb, "Economic Function," p. 70. For further discussion of Comte's English influence, see J. Buckley, *The Victorian Temper* (Cambridge, Mass., 1951), pp. 192–95.

33. Thus, e.g., G. Gissing, *Workers in the Dawn* (London, 1880; Garden City, N.Y., 1935), p. 216, presents the Positive philosophy as the true "supplement to Darwin; the theories of both point to the same result."

incomplete variety) because "we all make the service of man the leading doctrine of our lives." [34]

If the religious aspect of Comte's teaching was what first excited widespread interest in Positivism, however, such interest was most likely to be sustained by its intellectual pretensions: its claims to have overcome the major intellectual crises of the age—crises over the declining credibility of classical economics and of the utilitarian psychology on which it rested (which seemed to presage the breakup of the whole liberal world view), and crises resulting from the fragmentation of knowledge in an age of specialization, which had heightened the already considerable fear of moral relativism.[35] The last of these considerations was also perhaps the most ambiguous, for Positivism itself embodied a type of intellectual relativism that would remain until all knowledge had reached its final, "scientific" form. But Comte also claimed to have given such form to the most crucial branches of human knowledge, sociology, and ethics, where need for public certainty was felt most keenly, while the future society toward which he showed humanity progressing involved a virtual apotheosis of the conventional moral creed—a doctrine that must have given comfort to countless troubled consciences. In similar fashion, Comte claimed to have overcome the current fragmentation of knowledge by having made scientific method its sole basis, and to have guaranteed its essential unity by showing that every science and every social system progressed through the same stages of development, in the same sequence, and was therefore headed for the same ultimate goal. (This was, of course, the teaching of the celebrated "law of the three stages," which as a quasi-religious doctrine had the additional advantage of showing that a glorious future awaited all mankind as a result of its journey to scientific maturity.) Finally, on a more practical level, Comte's sociology provided an attractive alternative to the world view of liberalism and classical economics, and, in contrast to the near fatalism of the latter, put

34. B. Webb, *My Apprenticeship*, pp. 129, 124. For an impressive statement of what such a Victorian bluestocking might find in Comte, see "Helen Norman's Diary," in Gissing, *Workers in the Dawn*, pp. 215–16.

35. See Abrams, *Origins of British Sociology*, pp. 54 ff.; regarding the "spectre of relativism" haunting nineteenth-century social thought, see R. Grew, in *Comparative Studies* 11 (July 1969): 358, and Burrow, *Evolution and Society*, pp. 98–99.

forward a comprehensive "scientific" method for accomplishing the reconstruction of society.[36]

In the early eighties the Positivist method of social reconstruction was the part of Comte's teaching that attracted the greatest popular support, since many Radical intellectuals who had lost faith in the power of liberal remedies to cope with the distress accompanying the Great Depression saw Positivism as a "hopeful solution" to that problem.[37] In contrast to the discredited liberal remedies, Positivism proposed to begin by transforming the moral basis of society: rooting out the ingrained habits of selfishness, together with the laws and institutions that sustained them, while stimulating the growth of social sympathies and altruism, which alone could effectively regenerate mankind. Such a process, it was thought, would gradually "infuse society with social duty from top to bottom," until all capitalists were "moralised" and functioned as disinterested trustees (or civil servants), paying themselves only a modest wage for the social services they performed. Thereafter, although the means of production would legally belong to individual owners, all capital would be treated as a public trust and would be administered solely in the public interest. The working classes would also learn to treat their work as social service, without thought of personal gain. Thus the cash nexus would lose its power at all levels of society, and the ills of capitalism would be cured without the need for "any revolution in the social mechanism."[38]

Inevitably, few of those who were drawn to the social teaching of Positivism accepted Comte's whole scheme of social reconstruction, but its basic method of moralization and its demand for a systematic cultivation of social sentiments and a reorganization of social institutions on an altruistic basis found widespread endorsement—especially among free-thinking journalists, scientists, and ci-

36. Comte, *Positive Philosophy*, bk. 1, chap. 1, and bk. 6.
37. See M. Olivier, *Sydney Olivier*, pp. 60–61.
38. Comte, *General View of Positivism*, pp. 166–75, 203–07; *Positive Polity*, vol. 2, chap. 2, 129 ff.; and Webb, "The Way Out," f. 37. For popular, contemporary expositions of such views, cf. Positivist Henry Ellis's article, "Can the Capitalist Be Moralised?" *To-day* (Aug.–Sept. 1885), and F. Harrison's address to the Industrial Remuneration Conference, 1885 (reprinted in *National and Social Problems* [London, 1908]), which was a particular favorite of Webb's.

vil servants of an advanced liberal persuasion. Even their leading
oracle, T. H. Huxley, who was usually overtly hostile to Comte,
agreed that the latter's social aims were "not only possible but
inevitable," and formed "the only political object at all worth
fighting for." [39] There was also just enough common sense in
Comte's social theories to make them appealing to young intellectuals who had not yet found their social bearings but could respond warmly to the high-mindedness, the ambiguous mixture of
conservative and radical proposals, and the combination of organismic theory with liberal political policies that characterized the
English Positivist movement. Finally, its affirmation of Christian
social values gave Positivism an edge over Marxism and Social
Darwinism, its chief rivals, by making it more attractive to that
large class of skeptics who were not yet fully weaned from
Christianity.

Briefly stated, these were the chief sources of Positivism's appeal
to the Socialist generation of the early eighties; and of no one was
this more true than Sidney Webb.

3. Webb's Gospel of Social Positivism

Webb's own response to that appeal was to embark on a virtual
campaign of social evangelism in the debating societies he attended, drawing his arguments from a mixture of Positivism and
classical economics. This combination (which accurately reflected
his own point of view) was theoretically contrary to Comte's
teaching but was actually accepted by the leading English Positivists with the proviso that economic arguments must be treated
as a part of sociology. And that was also Webb's intention, although his purely economic interests often got the upper hand.
Reinforced by his own Evangelical asceticism, he derived from the
classical economists both an obsession with the need for "abstinence"—for capitalists to live modestly and save their income
for the sake of reinvestment—that neatly dovetailed with Positivist
demands for moralization and trusteeship, and a strong belief in
the Ricardian law of differential rent as elaborated by the con-

39. T. H. Huxley, "Scientific Aspects of Positivism," in *Lay Sermons* (London,
1893), p. 149.

temporary economists, Marshall and Walker.⁴⁰ From Positivism, on the other hand, he took a broadly social and organismic point of view (the expression of Comte's *esprit d'ensemble*), which had as its corollaries a belief in the interdependence of all men and the consequent need for all to subordinate their "personal" aims to those of social integration, plus the economic doctrine that "wealth is social in its origin and should be so also in its application." In Webb's own synthesis, however, all those doctrines were woven into the central (and very Positivist) argument that wealth must be regarded as a public trust, not for consumption but for investment in the public interest.

So vigorously did Webb drive home that point that his resulting rhetoric virtually made personal consumption the chief touchstone of morality: "We are the cause of the misery of the poor by consumption of more than our share of the produce," he pontificated to his debating comrades in 1885. And he urged on them the strict moral duty to live frugally, to save, and to invest for the public good, even insisting that "one should never enjoy luxury without guilt." For "extravagence is waste, and waste is always a national crime." Therefore, like Shaw and Ruskin, Webb found "nothing . . . more sickening than the current middle-class morality concerning irresponsible consumption"—the morality, par excellence, of the leisure class—which set up virtual "endowments for idleness," diverting the revenues of land and capital from public to "personal," selfish, and unproductive ends. And insofar as private appropriation of rent and interest led to that result, Webb did not hesitate to call it "robbery." ⁴¹

In all such arguments, however, conspicuous consumption by the idle rich and their sheer unproductiveness emerged as the chief objects of Webb's wrath. "What the upper classes cost the world is not the money incomes they receive, but what they consume," he insisted time and again—"especially their expenditure

40. See S. Webb, introductory lecture on political economy [to the London Working Men's College], Oct. 1883, PP, VI, *9*, 4. Regarding Webb's praise of "abstinence" and "Social asceticism," see "The Way Out," f. 56, and "Economic Function." Regarding Marshall and Walker, see nn. 44 and 49 below.

41. "The Need of Capital," Fabian Lecture, 1886, PP, VI, *28*, 14), and "Economic Function," pp. 29 ff., 32, 50—the last actually quoting from Henry George, *Progress and Poverty*, p. 258 (see p. 90 above).

beyond service rendered to the world." It was a quasi-Socialist line of argument, but Webb's conclusion was the characteristically Positivist one of making the "monopolist," who, as a rent receiver, must exist in some form, more keenly aware of his social duty to save and reinvest the wealth with which he had been entrusted by society. If he performed such duties faithfully, Webb argued, the capitalist justified his role, for society could not manage its saving and investment so efficiently by any other means. Therefore, Webb did not "even blame Vanderbilt for his life." But "it is obviously not necessary to hand over 850 millions to that incubus in order that 150 millions may be saved." Thus, if capitalists did not reform themselves they could be easily replaced by others who would do their job of saving without so much consuming.[42]

If these arrangements were to work smoothly, however, someone was needed to keep an eye on the capitalists, and Webb assigned that function to the middle classes, arguing that they had a dual responsibility: to act both as a conscience of the capitalists (since only when "we [have brought] these Monopolists to extend their trusteeship from $\frac{1}{4}$ or $\frac{1}{3}$ up to the whole of monopoly profits" will the economy begin to function equitably), and as trustees of the tribute society paid to them for their own "monopolies" of skill and knowledge, which Webb labeled the "rent of exceptional ability."[43] The reason for the latter was that, like land and capital, all socially necessary skills and abilities constituted a monopoly that was either socially formed (through education) or was the result of an accident of birth and whose income was differentially structured.[44] Hence, like the rent of land and the

42. "Economic Function," ff. 87 ff., 58 ff., 91; and Webb, quoted in *Prac. Soc.* 2 (Feb. 1886) : 28. See also Webb, "Socialism and Economics," and "Some Economic Errors of Socialists," *Prac. Soc.* (Feb. 1887) , for similar views. Webb achieved instant notoriety by arguing that Vanderbilt, as investor, should be regarded as a public benefactor.

43. "Economic Function." Webb also argued that such practice of trusteeship made it possible for middle-class people to fulfill "in a little way" the "collectivist ideal" ("The Way Out," ff. 51–52) .

44. Webb derived the phrase "*rent* of rare natural abilities" from Alfred and Mary P. Marshall, *The Economics of Industry* (London, 1879) , p. 144, where it formed part of an analysis of "the earnings of management" (chap. 12) . Marshall subsequently modified that concept by treating it only as a form of "quasi-rent" (in

interest on capital, the remuneration that such skills obtained in excess of "economic wages" constituted a form of differential rent, of which society alone was the appropriate beneficiary. In its name, Webb eagerly exhorted his fellow debaters to "recognize that thy ability, produced *by* society, is due *to* society, to whom [as a trustee] thou owest the uttermost farthing paid [thee] for its use." [45]

To many of his hearers and beholders such social evangelism must have seemed at least slightly humorous. Picture an earnest, intense little man, with a cockney accent, an oversized head, and a profile "suggestive of Napoleon III,"[46] preaching the virtues of austerity and altruism to audiences of clerks and civil servants, urging that the social salvation of England depended upon the stewardship of their small incomes. Yet such "sermons" were also skillfully contrived to touch the religious and moral sensibilities of the audiences by blending traditional Radical and Evangelical catch phrases within a matrix of Positivist analysis. Thus they awakened echoes of the Nonconformist conscience by reiterating the sacred incantation that "if any man would not work, neither should he eat," and recalled the tradition of Radical Jeremiads against idle "monopolists and owners of the soil"—but with the difference that Webb (like Shaw) now sought to extend such opprobrium to all rentiers and to the entire leisure class. Indeed, he extended it further to include the entire middle class and even skilled laborers, on the ground that all received "rent of ability." All must, therefore, be prepared to give an account of their economic "stewardship;" otherwise "the long suffering masses, roused

---

Principles of Economics [London, 1890], pp. 492–502, 608–10) —a partial retreat from the position he had taken in 1879; but by that time Webb had already developed his own theory of "economic rent" (see n. 49 below), which was more comprehensive than Marshall's. "Economic wages," in contrast, were determined solely by the level of subsistence and contained no rent (see p. 209 above).

45. "Economic Function," f. 49: part of a larger plea for a graduated income tax. The whole paragraph is couched in pseudo-biblical phraseology.

46. Shaw, quoted in Henderson, *Man of the Century*, p. 211. For another view of Webb as public speaker, see the roman a clef, *Transition,* by the Fabian novelist Emma Brooke (London, 1895), pp. 100–01. Sheridan, the hero, is Sidney Webb: a small lean man "with a fine, rugged head . . . and the air of a student." But "the main quality [of his public persona] was burning conviction and absolute sincerity."

at last from their ignorant patience, . . . [will one day] cry of your class, . . . 'cut it down, why cumbereth it the ground?' " [47]

The most intellectually impressive feature of those lectures was the theory of "economic rent," mentioned above, which Webb held to be a real "natural law," in contrast to such "artificial" economic maxims as free trade.[48] This kind of rent may be briefly defined as the income resulting from any sort of differential economic advantage, whether of land, capital, or exceptional ability. Because all three forms of rent were aspects of the same economic phenomenon, Webb held that they were all analyzable by the same Ricardian "law" that rent equals the difference between the income of a superior piece of land and that of one at the margin of cultivation.[49] Such a theory was ideally suited to his polemical purposes because, in effect, it tapped the moral resources of the land nationalization movement—already popular among his Radical audiences—and extended them by a logical process to other forms of wealth. Hence Webb's repeated insistence that the return on invested capital fell into the moral category of "unearned increment," and that the same was true of managerial and administrative salaries. All belonged rightfully to the entire community, and no individual had any moral claim on

47. That biblical quotation was used repeatedly in the mid-eighties to conclude Webb's lectures, whether of a Positivist or (ostensibly) Socialist persuasion, namely, "The Way Out," f. 62; "Economic Function," f. 92; and "What Socialism Means: A Call to the Unconverted," *Prac. Soc.* 6 (June 1886) : 93.

48. Introductory lecture, f. 1. For this reason, Webb regarded the law of rent as the chief theoretical foundation of economic science.

49. See David Ricardo, *Principles of Political Economy and Taxation*, ed. P. Sraffa (Cambridge, Eng., 1951) , chap. 2, and Webb's lectures: "The Way Out," "Economic Function," and "Rent, Interest, and Wages: A Critique of Karl Marx," (PP VI, *19;* VI, *20,* and VII, *4,* respectively) ; also "The Rate of Interest and the Laws of Distribution," *QJE* (Jan. 1888) , which extended that theory by adding a fourth type of rent, windfall profits. The chief sources of Webb's theory of economic rent were Alfred Marshall (see n. 44 above) , and F. A. Walker, *A Brief Text-book of Political Economy* (London, 1885) , pp. 204 ff., and *Political Economy* (New York, 1883; no English edition) . The theory of economic rent was first formulated in Archbishop Richard Whately, *Elements of Logic* (London, 1826) , appendix. Walker subsequently elaborated his version of that theory in "The Source of Business Profits," *QJE* (April 1887) , to which Webb replied in "Rate of Interest," (Jan. 1888) . For further discussion, cf. McBriar, *Fabian Socialism*, pp. 36–40, and G. D. H. Cole, *Second International*, p. 312; the fullest and most recent study (unfortunately lacking in historical perspective) is D. M. Ricci, "Fabian Socialism: The Theory of Rent as Exploitation," *JBS* 9 (Nov. 1969) .

them except as a "trustee." The immediate, practical significance of such arguments, however, was that they could be used to justify extending the steep rate of taxation that Mill had advocated for the "unearned increments" of land value to the apparently "earned" income from capital and exceptional ability. Stated more programmatically, Webb's chief objective was to greatly reduce the amount of rent, interest, and wages of superintendence (estimated by him as jointly constituting more than two-thirds of the gross national product) that was currently received by the middle and upper classes, and to redistribute it through social services, public investments, and increased wages. So far as Webb was concerned, that object could be achieved either by a greatly increased, steeply graduated income tax or by a process of voluntary moralization,[50] but the full implications of that argument were more far-reaching than he then recognized—at least as long as he remained a kind of Positivist.

4. Webb's Critique of Socialism

In fact, Webb's arguments were in every way better suited to a Socialist (or collectivist) theory than to a Positivist one, but his powerful and very common Radical bias against public ownership made him slow to see that. For several years, therefore, he clung obstinately to his Positivist via media, unshaken by the Socialist revival of 1883, or by the ground swell of Socialist activity that followed it and swept his closest friends, including Wallas and Olivier, into the ranks of the new faith. Instead, he viewed that heresy with a stern and condescending opposition. He announced in 1885:

50. "Economic Function," f. 92, and "Need of Capital," *Prac. Soc.* (June 1886) : 22. With regard to the possibility of increasing wages at the expense of profits, see "Rate of Interest," *QJE* (Jan. 1888) . It should be added that a graduated income tax was widely regarded as "communistic" in the 1880s. McBriar, *Fabian Socialism*, p. 33, however, misses the point of this argument in suggesting that Webb's theory of rent was intended to show that "even an ideal capitalist society is unjust." That was more nearly the argument of Shaw and the SDF, whereas Webb's intention was to show how capitalism could be made ideally just through "socialistic" reforms and the concurrent growth of "social feeling" (see esp. "Economic Function," ff. 42–43, and chap. 7, below) .

I am, I am sorry to say, no believer in State Socialism, the
impossibility of which I need not even attempt to demonstrate. I am not even a believer in Land Nationalisation in
the ordinary sense. . . . Instead, I am a sincerely orthodox
believer in Political Economy, as propounded, say, by Marshall
and Walker [the chief sources of his analysis of rent].

And he continued to praise free competition as the system that
would lead to greatest happiness all round. He agreed with Socialists that it would be nice if the government owned the land and
capital, "provided it leased them to individuals [for management];
but it can't presently get either one except through the inadmis-
sible plan of taking from the present possessors." In any case, mere
ownership mattered little, so long as it was possible to limit the
extent of individual wealth through taxation and moralization.[51]
    Nor did he "follow Mill's conversion [to Socialism]," as Shaw
repeatedly asserted. Instead, Webb rapidly outgrew his early reliance on Mill's economic theories, and his mature relationship to
"the Saint of Rationalism" was far more ambivalent than Shaw's
remark suggested. In the mid-eighties, Webb's economic allegiance
went not to Mill but to the current theorists in the neoclassical
tradition—to Marshall and Walker, together with Jevons and the
current sociological and "historical" schools[52]—whereas he held
that Mill and his orthodox disciples had reached a dead end in
economic theory. They had carried Ricardian arguments as far as
possible along deductive lines and had "succeeded fairly well" in
freeing their work from the class bias of most nineteenth-century
economics. But further advances in that science now depended
upon "shifting the economic point of view" and on making more

51. "Economic Function," ff. 28, 41.
52. Shaw, quoted in M. Cole, *Webbs and Their Work*, pp. 4, 6, and cf. n. 41
above. Both Marshall and Walker atempted to integrate historical methodology into
their versions of neoclassical theory, while the English Positivists were particularly
keen supporters of the historical method, tracing its origins (erroneously) to Comte.
See the complete Positivist J. K. Ingram's article, "Political Economy," in *Encyclo-
paedia Britannica*, 8th ed. (London, 1886)—cited frequently by Webb as the work
of a "convinced Socialist"—and his very influential presidential address to the British
Association, Section F, *The Present Position and Prospects of Political Economy*
(London and Dublin, 1878), reprinted in Abrams, *Origins of British Sociology*, pp.
177 ff.

use of sociological methods. As to Socialism, Mill had demonstrated that it was "economically possible" on a theoretical basis but had never succeeded in demonstrating its practicability or its application to the "art of politics." Thus Mill's acceptance of Socialism in theory had simply made him an "unsafe Social utopian, from the bourgeois point of view." [53]

To Mill, as to the entire English Socialist tradition, the essence of Socialism was the practice of "association" and the claim that cooperation represented a higher moral stage than competition. It is not clear, however, whether Webb understood this fact in 1885, although his characterization of Mill as a "Social utopian" suggests that he did. If so, he forgot or overlooked it some years later when he claimed Mill as a forerunner of Fabian collectivism. A more crucial problem was that Mill himself had treated Socialism as impossible on any large scale until men reached the stage in moral development "when it will neither be, nor thought to be, impossible for human beings to exert themselves strenuously in procuring benefits which are not to be exclusively their own, but to be shared with the society they belong to." But Webb, in Positivist fashion, replied that when such a time arrived—and Positivists saw it as inevitable—men would no longer need Socialist institutions, which would "only be possible when [they had] become unnecessary." Instead, as mankind progressed intellectually and socially the aim of Socialism would be replaced by the more "scientific" scheme of industrial hierarchy, controlled and moralized by the force of a thoroughly "social" public opinion.[54]

Webb's Positivist view of Socialism was not free from ambiguity, however, since Positivism itself was a form of "moral and religious Socialism." At the same time, Positivists loudly denounced the type of revolutionary Socialism that appeared in England in 1884 and 1885. Thus Positivists used the term in two quite different senses. The first, which Frederic Harrison described as "true and sincere Socialism," was really Positivism plus the idea of "association": an attempt to moralize society that was mistaken in its methods but laudable in its aims. Unhappily, it was now extinct. The more usual meaning of the term, the "real and dangerous

53. "Economic Function," ff. 52 ff., 67–68.
54. Mill, *Autobiography*, p. 162, and Webb, "Socialism and Economics."

Socialism" of current vogue, on the other hand, was applied by
Harrison to all the recent crop of English Socialist societies, which
he stigmatized as products of an alien (mostly German) movement
that advocated evil and destructive methods for promoting the
social goals that Positivism sought to achieve in peaceful, evolutionary ways.[55]

In 1885 Harrison's condemnation would have been immediately
recognized as a characterization of SDF "Marxism," which was the
only kind of Socialism that currently received much publicity in
England. At the same time, Marx was being read, or at any rate
discussed, by so many of Webb's Radical and Socialist friends that
Webb could not long have avoided reading him also—if only out
of self-defense. In the event, it was Shaw who first induced him
to read *Capital* and then to join the "Marx reading circle" in
Hampstead, mentioned in the previous chapter, where persons
of various Radical and Socialist persuasions met to debate Marx's
economic arguments.[56] It was Webb's introduction to the Socialist
movement and his first activity within the Fabian orbit.

Fortunately, both Shaw and Webb have left descriptions of
"Mrs Wilson's economic tea parties" and of the verbal battles that
took place there. Shaw reported that the first chapters of *Capital*—
on which most of their attention was concentrated—were "of
extraordinary efficacy in setting us by the ears," so that quarreling
usually began before the reader for the evening "had gone far
enough to feel seriously fatigued." [57] Webb noted that the tendency began at the first meeting, when Professor Edgeworth, as
the guest of honor, began discussion by loudly "snorting" his
"contempt for Karl [Marx] and all his works."

The company—most of whom were apparently under the
impression that we were assembled . . . [to] drink in the
wisdom of some great seer—were speechless with amazement.
Edgeworth's voice was followed by a silence . . . thick enough

55. Frederic Harrison, *National and Social Problems* (London, 1908), pp. 28–30,
and "Moral and Religious Socialism," esp. p. 429: "Positivism is . . . Socialism
founded on science and inspired by religion."
56. Shaw, quoted in M. Cole, *Webbs and Their Work*, p. 6, and cf. chap. 5, nn.
83–85 above. (With rather less credibility, Shaw also claimed that Webb read
through all of *Capital*, vol. 1, within an hour.)
57. Shaw, "Bluffing the Value Theory," *To-day* (May 1887) .

> to have been cut with a knife. In despair, he appealed to me. I rushed in, and the rest of the evening was a kind of Scottish reel *"à deux,"* Edgeworth and I gaily dancing on the unfortunate K[arl] M[arx].

Such was the triumph of neoclassical analysis over Marx, who had no English defenders with similar economic expertise. Fearing demoralization of the group, however, Webb importuned Shaw (who had been truant) to come and give an utterly "unscrupulous" defense of Marx. Otherwise, "we shall have discarded *Le Capital* within a month and [will] be found studying the gospel of Ricardo!" [58]

Soon most of the future Fabian leaders were drawn into the fray, where Webb, assisted by Olivier, systematically impregnated them with his economic views, which soon became the official theories of the Fabian Society. Even Shaw—despite his "brazen" and "unscrupulous" defense of Marx—was gradually weaned from his infatuation with *"Le Capital"* and became an exponent of something like neoclassical economics. Happily, the arguments by which Webb brought about that change may be inferred from the critique of Marxian Socialism that he developed in his lectures during 1885 and 1886. Its main theme was that, despite its claims to scientific status, such Socialism lacked any real scientific basis, "either in economics or in ethics," and had added nothing to "economic science." Webb's meaning was essentially twofold: first, that Socialism, properly speaking, was not a question of science at all, but a "theory as to the social structure most likely to conduce to human happiness." Its recommendations were therefore "rules of art"—aspects of "a new experiment in the great Art of Living" that only posed as scientific.[59] And second, Webb argued that Marxian economics was methodologically outmoded—a reversion to the theoretical level of the early classical school, as seen in its "abstract-intuitive" (or purely deductive) methodology and in its reliance on an empirically false model of human behavior under capitalism, which took account only of acquisitive motives. It was therefore incapable of adding to the

---

58. Webb to Shaw, 11 Nov. 1884, Shaw Papers, BM 50553.

59. "On Economic Method," lecture, ca. 1884–85, PP, VI, 25, esp. 24 ff., and "Socialism and Economics."

development of science and was not even practically useful, being both less empirical and more cumbersome than the current neoclassical theory.[60] But, for the time being, Webb did not treat even the latter as the last word in economic doctrine; instead, he looked to the application of new sociological methods (of the sort advocated by English Positivists) to bring economic science to its full development. Consequently, he charged that Marxism, through its old-fashioned methodology and its unrealistic assumptions, ran directly counter to the chief requirement of modern "economic science": the creation of "Economic Sociology," which alone could give that science the relevance and credibility it needed to regain public confidence.[61]

To a generation accustomed, as ours is, to view Marx as a sociologist, these charges must sound very curious. But they at least make clear the fact that Webb interpreted Marx in the current English manner: as an economist in the classical tradition whose major theoretical achievement had been surplus value. Unlike the English Marxists, however, Webb and Olivier regarded that theory, together with the labor theory of value on which it rested, as the most vulnerable features of Marxian analysis. In contrast, even Ricardo's version of the labor theory of value was less rigid and more empirical. Consequently, the Fabian criticism of Marx followed the path laid down by Ricardo himself, who had conceded (in contrast to Marx's more rigid teaching) that the special advantages of superior capitals, sites, and skills, in fact, prevented equal quantities of labor time from producing equal economic values. And it was precisely because of that fact, Olivier

60. See Webb, "On Economic Method," ff. 2–19 and esp. 17 ff., and "Rent, Interest, and Wages," ff. 4–7 (MS. annotated by Olivier), and Olivier, "Idols of the Sty," pt. I, *To-day* (Aug. 1886). There was a fundamental inconsistency in Webb's arguments: in the earlier ones ("Economic Method," 1884) he unfavorably contrasted the abstract method of "Marx, Engels and Rodbertus" with the "concrete-deductive" method of Mill and the neoclassical school, whereas in the later ones ("Rent, Interest, and Wages," 1886), he lumped both Mill and Marx together in the "concrete-deductive" school and contrasted it with a new type of economic theory based on sociological "natural laws" ("History of Economic Theory," PP VI, *64*).

61. Webb, introductory lecture, f. 4, and "Economic History of Society," ff. 1, 19; and cf. "History of Economic Theory," ff. 50–55, and "Economic Function," f. 70 for further arguments that economics should be subordinated to sociology.

concluded, that surplus value arose at all.[62] For surplus value, properly understood, was only another name for economic rent: the unavoidable result of the special economic advantages incidental to production and distribution. Marxian analysis left these out of account, although, as Olivier insisted, they were bound to occur even under conditions of the most perfect communism. Consequently, a modified neoclassical analysis, using the theory of differential rent, explained that phenomenon both more efficiently and more realistically than Marxism. Moreover, such a theory also emphasized the socially all-important fact that every class above the level of subsistence wage earners received *some* surplus value, whether in the form of land rent, interest on capital, or the "rent" of abilities and skills. In short, the "exploiting" classes were far more numerous than Marxian theory implied, for they included even semiskilled laborers, who, because they had at least a marginal share in the "monopoly" of skill, received at least a modicum of rent. Only completely unskilled labor, living at the level of subsistence (in other words, on "economic wages"), was not to some extent monopolized and therefore received no rent. Nevertheless, the rents received by the other classes did not constitute exploitation of unskilled labor, because they were abstracted not from the produce of such laborers alone, but from that of the entire society. (Since rent, as such, was always the result of social or natural factors, moreover, it could never be the result of individual or class efforts.) Thus society collectively, rather than any individual or class, was "robbed" by individual appropriation of economic rent, and only society as a whole had a just claim to its restoration.

Despite the collectivist implications of this argument, Webb continued to combine it with the belief, endorsed by Mill and Comte, that a reformed and moralized system of private property would be most beneficial to all classes—a system of private property as it might become "under the impact of noneconomic motives . . . with a proper administration of the national share of the

---

62. Olivier, "Perverse Socialism," *To-day* (Aug.–Sept. 1886), and Ricardo, *Principles of Political Economy*, pp. 11, 30, 36, 38; also H. Barkai, "Ricardo's 97% Labour Theory of Value," *Economica* 24, (1967): 418 ff. Olivier went far beyond Ricardo, however, in reviving Adam Smith's argument that rent was an independent element in the determination of value.

product, and . . . a greater influence of the higher feelings." [63] In short, he envisaged a quasi-Positivist, mixed economy in which systematically applied pressure of the social sympathies and altruism—the "higher feelings"—would eliminate the evils in the present social system. Marx had provided no defense against such contentions, Webb insisted, because his arguments were based entirely on the model of "economic man" and took account only of material considerations. Consequently, Marx had ignored the influence of all the noneconomic motives in human behavior that Webb (and Comte) insisted were "daily increasing in power" over mankind, and, with them, the possibility of regenerating society by "moral" means.[64] Marx's materialism and emphasis on class conflict—both red herrings to Victorian moralists—could only retard the operation of such emotional forces, and thus would actually hinder the reconstruction of society. As a result, Positivism would prove easier than Marxism to put into practice; its results would be more impressive (because of enlisting men's higher natures) ; and it would prove more liberal in practice, being free of the regimentation and coercion that Webb regarded as inseparable from Socialist schemes. Moreover, Webb claimed, Positivist methods were more immediately practicable than those of Socialism and Anarchism because they did not require such radical changes in human nature—they "need not wait for the conversion of the wife-beater" to do some good (!) —nor would they put as much strain on sluggish and inefficient government as collectivism and land nationalization. Above all, their good effects would be immediately apparent. In a society seething with discontent, "we can [not] wait to do justice," Webb declared, and only moralization could generate justice fast enough to overcome the threat of

63. See the end of chap. 5 above for further elaboration of this point. For discussion of Fabian theories of economic rent and wages, see pp. 201–02, 209 above; Webb, "Rent, Interest, and Wages"; and Olivier, "Perverse Socialism."

64. Webb, "Economic Function," pp. 20–21, and "Rent, Interest, and Wages," p. 20, and compare Mill, *Autobiography* (Coss ed.) , pp. 162–63. Regarding Comte's law of the increasing power of social sympathies, see n. 27 above; for Webb's own version of that law, see "The Way Out," ff. 46–47, and his parallel claim that (Comte's) sociology showed that "no man or woman . . . could have grown up in that society infinitely selfish, without [also] becoming more or less sympathetic with his neighbours" (MS, "Special Report" of Fabian Conference, 11 June 1886, BLPES, f. 230) .

revolution. In any case, "even if Socialism is to come we have to do our duty in the meantime." [65]

5. Webb's Conversion to Socialism

These were Webb's guiding beliefs in the spring of 1885, when he became a member of the Fabian Society, and so, in essence, they remained throughout his first year of membership. In the course of that year, however, his hard line against Socialism gradually softened, so that in each successive lecture he treated it a little more favorably and saw it as more closely approximating his own Positivist ideal. Thus when the Fabians abandoned their flirtation with Marxian theories in the latter part of 1885 (owing largely to Webb's persuasiveness), he probably concluded that there was nothing significant separating their views from his, while Fabian Socialism, purged of its Marxian accretions, might prove to be a more effective name than Positivism for his distinctive social theories. In effect, therefore, he dropped from his idea of Socialism all the features he had found objectionable in its Anglo-Marxist form and transferred the social aims and values he had advocated as a Positivist to a new home in the Socialist movement.

The latter process may be best illustrated in the lecture on "The Economics of a Positivist Community," which Webb delivered to the Fabians on 14 January 1886—the first occasion on which he publicly identified himself as a Socialist. His explanation of that remark, however, indicated that there had been no real break with his earlier views. "I call myself a Socialist," he explained, "because I am desirous to remove from the capitalist the temptation to use his capital for his own exclusive ends. Still, the capitalist may do good by accumulation." In the same lecture he also treated Positivism as one of the three basic forms of Socialism (the others being Anarchism and collectivism) and insisted that the choice between public ownership of capital and moralization of the capitalists remained "an open question for Socialists." Finally, in subsequent lectures, he described Socialism as "the call to frugal and

65. Webb, "The Way Out," ff. 38–39, 50–52, 59; and compare Comte, *General View*, pp. 162–63, 170.

earnest living" and "a judgment of morality on the facts of life"—
phrases that almost reiterated his old plea for moralization.[66]

Not unnaturally, some of his hearers asked whether he was still
a disciple of Comte. By 1886, however, Webb had decided that he
was not. "I am by no means sure that the capitalist can be moralised," he explained, for by itself the process would be "too slow,"
and "economic rent would remain unaltered." Hence moralization
would have to be supplemented by Socialist legislation—taxation
of the three forms of rent and regulation of industry in the public
interest—so as to "enforce" the social duties of the capitalists and
make them less tempted to squander wealth upon themselves. Indeed, "the enforcement of [that] social duty" was now seen as the
chief "mission of Socialism."[67] But Webb's conversion was not
really complete until he also transferred to Socialism what had
been his strongest practical argument for Positivism: the claim that
it would stave off the threat of revolution by moralizing society
from within. Henceforth the Socialists would also undertake that
task, and "there is work in plenty for all to do," he insisted. "We
must bring home to the monopolist the sense of his trusteeship,"
and to begin that work, "no one need wait for the millennium—
each one can begin it for himself. . . . The Kingdom of God is
at hand." [68]

How, then, did Webb's Socialism differ from his earlier social
Positivism? In its emphasis on taxation and its more perfect understanding of the laws of social evolution, he replied in 1887. Comte
had been unable to see beyond the stage of society based upon wage
labor, whereas a recognition of the transitoriness of such society
and of the necessity of moving on to ever "higher stages of social
evolution" was precisely what now distinguished Socialists from
Positivists and other advanced Radicals. Webb also labeled Comte

66. "The Economics of a Positivist Community," *Prac. Soc.* 2 (Feb. 1886)—the
community described therein was virtually an embodiment of all the social reforms
that Webb had advocated in past lectures—"The Need of Capital," June 1886, PP,
VI, 28; summarized in *Prac. Soc.*, July 1886, and "What Socialism Means."

67. Discussion at Fabian meeting, 14 Jan. 1886, in *Prac. Soc.* (Feb. 1886): 28,
38–39, and "The Need of Capital," p. 23. Webb still insisted that the "keynote" of
Socialism was "extreme social asceticism" and that "voluntary moralisation" was the
best method of achieving it ("The Need of Capital," p. 24).

68. "Economics of a Positivist Community," *Prac. Soc.* 2 (Feb. 1886): 39.

"utopian" because he had not seen the necessity for continuous social change, whereas Socialism, as he now understood the term, was nonutopian, precisely because it offered no blueprints for social reconstruction and was always in a state of evolution. Consequently, "there will never come a moment when we can say '*now* Socialism is established.' The principles of social organisation must already have secured [at least] partial adoption [for a society to function at all] . . . and the progress of Socialism is but their more complete recognition and their conscious acceptance as the line of advance upon which social improvement depends."

These laws of social evolution had originally been proclaimed by Comte but were not fully understood by him because they really led beyond Positivism to Socialism.[69] That was why Webb called "Comtism" the "metaphysical stage of Collectivism," and why he saw collectivism as the real "positive stage of Comtism." In 1886 and 1887, however, while Webb was still making his transition to collectivism, he continued to see the role of Socialism as virtually that of Positivism writ large:[70] the complete moralization of society by means of a "revolution . . . in opinion" regarding the social sources and uses of wealth. "Think how changed will be the House of Commons," Webb wrote in illustration of that principle,

> when Members realise the teachings of the economists as the Socialists realize [*sic*] them—when economic rent and interest are clearly and consistently regarded as tolls levied upon labour by monopolists, taking what should belong to the whole community. What a different aspect is placed upon public provision of museums, parks, [and] picture-galleries for the multitude: on free education and on universal technical training [when these are seen] as means to secure at last to the whole people that real free choice of occupation [and intellectual development] . . . now enjoyed only by a small class.[71]

69. "The Economic Basis of Socialism," lecture, 1887, PP, VI, *33*, 17, 18, 6.
70. See n. 1 above, and chap. 8, sec. 3, for fuller discussion of the Positivist character of Webb's collectivism. (Webb did not begin to call himself a collectivist until about 1888, however.)
71. "What Socialism Means," p. 92.

Thus it is clear that Webb expected broadly humanitarian results to follow from the acceptance of his Socialist principles, although in 1886 he was never quite successful in stating what those principles were. In programmatic terms, however, his Socialism was practically reducible to a demand for taxation of "economic rent" so as to finance social services on a greatly expanded scale. And this was also the meaning of Socialism implied by most of the Radical Humanitarians of the eighties, from Arnold Toynbee to Joseph Chamberlain, who greatly increased the popularity of the term by calling their reform programs "socialistic." But although Webb's Socialism pointed to such humanitarian ends, they were not the whole of it, since, properly speaking, his Socialism was a complete Weltanschauung: a vision of a new moral world, where social or altruistic motives would prevail over selfish or "personal" ones. Or—as he finally stated the matter in 1889— Socialism, on its "ethical side" (which he always regarded as paramount), implied "the general recognition of fraternity, the universal obligation of personal service, and the subordination of personal ambition to the common good." [72] No Positivist could object to anything in that, but it also reflected the more immediate influence of the new humanitarian feeling of the eighties, which was an equally powerful force in shaping the emerging theories of Fabian Socialism.

72. *Socialism in England* (Baltimore, 1889), p. 12.

7

Fabian Converts of the Mid-Eighties: The Christian-Humanitarian and Secularist Roads to Socialism

> Once let a man be embarked on his profession, and the feeling that he is doing his duty so grows upon him that it will often . . . consti-tute . . . the chief motive of his conduct. . . . It is this powerful, all-pervading and easily excited sentiment which we Socialists believe to be almost entirely wasted under the present system, and which we would endeavour to turn, both in ourselves and others, to good effect. . . . We rely on that as the motive power that will drive our engine of reform.
>
> GRAHAM WALLAS[1]

In 1885 and 1886 the Fabian Society received its most important body of recruits: the persons who, with the aid of Shaw and Bland, produced the *Fabian Essays* and gave the Society its first taste of fame. In their careers two further roads to Socialism are apparent: Radical Christian Humanitarianism and Secularism—movements that overlapped both with each other and with Positivism, which shared with them a common core of social values and beliefs. The appeal of the first (like that of Positivism) was chiefly to the edu-cated middle class—the group that also provided converts for the Christian Socialist and Ethical movements. The second was lower middle class in orientation and served to mediate some of the aims of both Positivism and the new Humanitarianism to its much more extensive following. Among the Fabian converts of the middle eighties, the Christian-Humanitarian road is best illustrated by the careers of Sydney Olivier and Graham Wallas, both Oxford men and sons of the Establishment, while the Secularist road is illus-trated by Annie Besant and William Clarke, déclassé intellectuals of middle-class origins, both of whom suffered a traumatic loss of

1. Graham Wallas, "Personal Duty Under the Present System," *Prac. Soc.* 1, no. 7 (July 1886): 119, and "The Motive Power of Socialism," *Sunday Chronicle*, 7 Dec. 1890.

social and economic status and found in Socialism a form of emotional redress.[2]

Unlike the Founding Fabians, all the leading converts of the middle and later eighties were active in Radical politics before their conversions and their links with the Radical tradition and, above all, with the Radicalism of John Stuart Mill, were closer and more apparent than those of the earlier Fabians. At least one of their number, Sydney Olivier, really did "follow Mill" in his conversion to Socialism, and several others retained a distinctively Millite quality in their subsequent Socialist writings. In their careers the transition from advanced Radicalism of the Millite variety to Socialism in the Fabian sense can be seen with greatest clarity.

1. Sydney Olivier

Radical Christian Humanitarianism, whose best-known symbol was the university settlement house,[3] was the most conspicuous result of the great awakening of social feeling among the English educated classes in the early 1880s. In its earliest stages such humanitarianism was stimulated by the appalling social conditions that accompanied the Great Depression and by the sensational publicity that they received in the *Bitter Cry of Outcast London* and the newspaper exposés that followed it. These, in turn, quickened the latent sense of social obligation in the English middle class, instilled through generations of religious training, to produce feelings of guilt and contrition such as those expressed by Arnold Toynbee, the most perfect embodiment of all that the

2. There were similar differences between Christian Socialist and Secularist recruits to the early SDF, as noted in chap. 3 and Appendix A. Radical Christian Humanitarianism (also called "philanthropy" by contemporaries) and Secularism are more fully discussed below. The best recent studies are Melvin Richter, *The Politics of Conscience: T. H. Green and His Age* (Cambridge, Mass., 1964), and Susan Budd, "The Loss of Faith: Reasons for Unbelief Among Members of the Secular Movement in England, 1850–1950," *Past and Present* 36 (1967): 106–25.

3. The earliest and most influential settlement house was Toynbee Hall, founded in 1884 by S. H. Barnett. See H. O. Barnett, *Canon Barnett: His Life, Work and Friends*, 2 vols. (Boston, 1919), 1: 307–13, and K. S. Inglis, *Churches and the Working Class in Victorian England* (London, 1963), pp. 145 ff., 162 ff.

movement stood for, in his confession to the working class that

> we have neglected you; . . . we have wronged you; we have
> sinned against you grievously . . . ; but if you will forgive
> us . . . we will serve you, we will devote our lives to your
> service, . . . [asking only] one thing in return [: that] . . . if
> you get a better life, you will really lead a better life.[4]

Similar principles had already been expounded, more obscurely if more philosophically, by Toynbee's Oxford mentor, T. H. Green and were subsequently disseminated far more widely by Mrs. Humphry Ward's immensely successful novel, *Robert Elsmere* (1888). In the early eighties, however, such teachings were still the special property of the more sensitive offspring of the affluent middle class, smitten by what Beatrice Webb described as a new "class-consciousness of sin":[5] a consciousness of injury done to the poor by their whole social order, and of the need for expiation through some form of penitential service. And the various projects of personal and public philanthropy proposed by Toynbee and his followers, including the settlement house that bore his name, had precisely that as their objective.

On the level of national politics this humanitarian feeling was most eloquently expressed in the rhetóric and personality of Joseph Chamberlain, a man in whom the "desire to serve the many [had] . . . become a passion absorbing within itself his whole nature,"[6] and who was thus able to impart to Radical politics a greatly intensified current of social feeling. Repeatedly, in his campaign for the Unauthorised Programme, Chamberlain defined Radical politics as "the science of human happiness," and his own aim as a politician as "increas[ing] the happiness of those who are less fortunate among us." Thus he sought to turn his electoral campaign in 1885 into a great humanitarian crusade—a novel tactic for an excabinet minister hoping to return to power—and its chief proposals were,

---

4. Arnold Toynbee, *"Progress and Poverty": A Criticism of Mr. H. George* (London, 1883), p. 53, originally a lecture delivered in Nov. 1883, with Sydney Olivier in the audience (M. Olivier, ed., *Sydney Olivier: Letters and Selected Writings* [London, 1948], p. 53; also Richter, *Politics of Conscience*, pp. 322 ff.).

5. B. Webb, *My Apprenticeship*, pp. 155 ff., quoting Samuel Barnett.

6. B. Webb's Diary, 12 Jan. 1884, quoted in ibid., p. 107. (She was quite intimately acquainted with Chamberlain in the mid-eighties.)

in fact, the very things Canon Barnett had christened "Practicable Socialism":

> We can . . . secure to every member of the community the enjoyments which are the chief prize of the existence of the cultivated and educated rich man. We can give them free education; we can put their feet upon the ladder which leads up to a storehouse of knowledge. . . . We can by galleries and museums cultivate their taste for art and . . . science. [And] . . . by these same measures of wise co-operation, which some call communistic, but which seem to me to be simply co-operative, we can make the poor man's cottage as healthy as the palace of the rich.[7]

Through such proposals the new humanitarian tendencies passed into the realm of what was commonly called Socialism. Toynbee and Barnett, for example, both called themselves "Socialists" in that special sense, and Chamberlain also employed the term, adding by way of clarification that "the Poor Law is Socialism; the Education Act is Socialism, . . . and every kindly act of legislation by which the community has sought to discharge its responsibilities . . . to the poor is Socialism." It was also in the latter sense of the term that Henry Sidgwick, the Cambridge philosopher, described "socialistic enthusiasm" as "the main current of new feeling among thoughtful young men during the last few years . . . [especially as regards] the relations between rich and poor." [8] This idea of Socialism was far more congenial to the early Fabians than the one that was currently propagated by the SDF;

7. Joseph Chamberlain, speech at Glasgow, 15 Sept. 1885, in *Mr. Chamberlain's Speeches*, ed. C. W. Boyd (Boston, 1914), pp. 195, 199–200, and cf. J. L. Garvin, *Life of Joseph Chamberlain, 1885–1895* (London, 1933), pp. 66 ff., for commentary. For Barnett's views, see Rev. and Mrs. S. A. Barnett, *Practicable Socialism* (London, 1888), chaps. 6, 12.

8. Chamberlain, speech at Warrington, 8 Sept. 1885, quoted in Garvin, *Chamberlain, 1885–1895*, p. 78, and Henry Sidgwick's Diary, 1886, quoted in Arthur Sidgwick, ed., *Henry Sidgwick: A Memoir* (London, 1906), p. 440. Also compare Frederic Harrison's judgment: "Socialism, meaning a general desire to have all arrangements of society . . . controlled by social considerations and reformed to meet paramount obligations—this kind of Socialism is now powerfully ascendant" (*National and Social Problems*, p. 424).

consequently, most of the Fabian converts of the eighties first called themselves Socialists in that broad, humanitarian sense and embellished their Socialist pronouncements with heavy applications of the new humanitarian rhetoric.

Such rhetoric, for example, was apparent even in the lectures of Sidney Webb, whom we have already seen appealing to the new class consciousness of sin in his insistence that "we [the middle class] are the cause of the misery of the poor by consumption of more than our share of the produce," and in his appeals for "earnest and frugal living" as a means of compensation. It was also apparent in the Fabian J. B. Bright's proposal for a "Ransom Society" (presumably inspired by Chamberlain's "Ransom Speech"), which would enable "members of the . . . leisure class" to "redeem" themselves from the sin of affluence by giving "money and personal services" to the poor.[9] But the most thoroughgoing exponents of such attitudes among the Fabian converts of the middle eighties—perhaps because they conformed most closely to the upper-middle-class Establishmentarian norm of the new humanitarianism—were Sydney Olivier and Graham Wallas.[10] Both were sons of Anglican clergymen of a severely Evangelical persuasion.[11] Both were sent, as a matter of course, through public school

9. J. B. Bright, "A Ransom Society," *Prac. Soc.* (Sept. 1886) : 138; it was also intended to coordinate the philanthropic attack on "sweated labour" by directing money away from "unproductive . . . attempts to cure the mere symptoms of misery."

10. Significantly, however, the respects in which they conformed most closely to the Toynbee Hall—Humanitarian social norm (especially in their comparative wealth) were also the respects in which they diverged most clearly from the Fabian norm. Thus while the Olivier family spent long periods abroad, living on unearned income, and Wallas inherited an annual income of nearly £100 from his family, most of the early Fabians (including even the Oxford and Cambridge graduates) came from less affluent backgrounds and lived entirely on the earnings of their own labor. (M. Olivier, *Sydney Olivier,* p. 30, and G. Slater, reminiscences of Wallas, WP, box 32.)

11. See M. Olivier, *Sydney Olivier,* pp. 49 ff., and a sermon preached in 1863 by the Rev. Gilbert I. Wallas (father of Graham), invoking the terrors of the orthodox Day of Judgment as a warning to sinners (reprinted in *N. Devon Journal* [Barnstable], 23 Oct. 1913). Yet the Wallas family was also said to have been warm and close-knit, something that must have been facilitated by a tendency to season orthodoxy with humor, as in a recurring family "debate" over whether it was better to eat first the rice or the currants in a rice-and-currant pudding, the currant advocates maintaining that if the fruit were not eaten immediately the Day of Judgment

and university, where they distinguished themselves by winning scholarships in open competition. At Oxford, they became close friends, sharing the same college (Corpus Christi), the same tutor (Thomas Case), and many of the same intellectual interests, which were impressively wide-ranging. There also they were infected with the germ of "infidelity" by way of the utilitarian philosophy that still flourished in their college, as a result of which they took John Stuart Mill as their intellectual master and were regarded locally as "pretty extreme Radicals." [12]

Such a fall from grace was not accepted without loud protestations from orthodox parents, however, so that for about three years after his graduation the elder Oliviers launched recurring campaigns to lure young Sydney back into the Christian fold.[13] In Wallas's case, the results must have been still more painful, as he had originally intended to go into the church,[14] and, in the manner of "clergymen gone wrong (or rather right)," in John Morley's characteristic phrase, he felt it necessary to maintain his infidelity in an uncompromising manner. The latter trait was most

---

might intervene and the chance be lost forever, while their opponents argued for the pleasure of *anticipating* the fruit! (Slater, reminiscences, WP, box 32). One suspects that the future Utilitarian took the latter side and argued for deferred gratification.

12. M. Olivier, *Sydney Olivier*, pp. 26–27, 47, 49, and *Sunday Chronicle*, 7 Dec. 1890. The "tutorial world" of Oxford, and especially of Corpus Christi College in the 1860s and 1870s, "was dominated by Utilitarian philosophy and Whig politics. . . . Its religious views were mildly sceptical, tending toward the theology of Strauss and Renan and the scepticism of Comte and Mill," though without encouraging any open break with orthodoxy (Bishop Knox, "Memories of Corpus Christi College," *Pelican Register* 20, no. 6 [June, 1932]: 140–41). Such tendencies were strengthened for Wallas and Olivier by their tutor, Thomas Case, an outspoken empiricist and exponent of Mill's *Logic*, whose influence also kept Corpus free of Idealism through the early eighties. Paradoxically, however, his philosophy of Realism, like the current Oxford Idealism, was intended to provide a secure foundation for a Christian moral life. See T. Case, *Realism in Morals* [Oxford, 1877], and Wallas, "Education," lecture, Feb. 1886, WP, box 22, f. 21, sec. 3. For further discussion, see M. J. Wiener, *Between Two Worlds: The Political Thought of Graham Wallas* (Oxford, 1971), chap. 1. This is the only full-length study of Wallas's thought.

13. M. Olivier, *Sydney Olivier*, pp. 49, 51, 56; and cf. his characteristic comment on parental orthodoxy: "Why do these people plague and torment themselves with their infernal religion or perversion thereof?" (ibid., p. 57).

14. H. Carey (former student) to Wallas, 9 Aug. 1886 (WP, box 1).

impressively displayed in 1885 when, in the tradition of the great Victorian agnostics, he resigned a school mastership in Highgate, rather than conform to religious practices in which he could not believe.[15] Religious convictions, therefore, were not matters to be taken lightly by these earnest young Radicals. But, like so many of their Fabian colleagues, the most lasting consequence of their fall from grace was that it helped to transfer the impulse to self-subordinating service that was so often nurtured in an Evangelical conscience from God to all mankind.

The result was an unusually powerful development of the "class-consciousness of sin," which, in Olivier's case, was intensified by a growing alienation from the rich, "respectable," and privileged society into which he had been born—a condition that matched (and, perhaps, derived from) his religious alienation. Like many similar youths who came down from Oxford in those years, "burning to save their souls" through dedicated service, he soon found his way into settlement-house work at Toynbee Hall and into the parallel movement, organized by the sister of Arnold Toynbee, to bring "sanitary aid" to London slum dwellers.[16] These, in turn, served to introduce him not so much to Socialism itself—although Canon Barnett, the founder of Toynbee Hall, professed a mild, humanitarian form of "Practicable Socialism"—as to the kind of people who became Socialists and the kinds of organizations in which Socialism was spawned during the middle eighties.

Among such persons, the most important to the development of Olivier's ideas was his future brother-in-law and former schoolmate, Harold Cox: a Cambridge Radical of "advanced and eccentric opinions," who, even better than Olivier, exemplified the "class-consciousness of sin" and showed what kind of dedication it could produce. Between 1882 and 1885 he was successively an extension lecturer on economics to Yorkshire workingmen (in which capacity he deeply influenced Olivier's economic views), promoter of an experiment in cooperative farming inspired by

15. Miss May Wallas has confirmed that this practice was obligatory Holy Communion (letter to the author, 17 Dec. 1970), contrary to the more fanciful conjecture in Fremantle, *Little Band of Prophets*, p. 46.

16. M. Olivier, *Sydney Olivier*, pp. 25, 67, 35, 63–64; and cf. Miss Gertrude Toynbee's letter in *Pall Mall Gazette*, 9 Nov. 1883.

Ruskin and Edward Carpenter, a settlement-house worker under the direction of Canon Barnett, and a persistent agitator for Radical political reforms.[17] Somehow, in the process, he came to call himself a Socialist in a vague, philanthropic sense and undertook lecturing for the Democratic Federation. He also brought Olivier into contact with the Barnetts and their work of "social reconciliation," for the sake of which Olivier moved, in the spring of 1884, to lodgings in the Whitechapel slum, and encouraged his first interest in the Democratic Federation.[18]

But other forces were also drawing Olivier in the same direction in 1884, of which the most important were land nationalization, as preached by Henry George, the Christian Socialism of his English followers, and the Positivism of Auguste Comte. Olivier's attitude to George was ambivalent: "a rhapsodic and unchastened style, strongly suggestive of the pulpit," he wrote of *Progress and Poverty*, mocking its tendency to deduce "the immortality of the soul from the sound theory of property in land." But, at the same time, George's doctrine of land nationalization appealed to him on Radical grounds, both as an extension of Mill's theory of unearned increment and as "a doctrine . . . which Herbert Spencer habitually treats as a foregone conclusion."[19] Such an appeal could scarcely be resisted by an ultra-Radical utilitarian, so Olivier joined the (Georgian) Land Reform Union in 1883 and soon was aiding its leading spirits, Champion and Joynes, in editing *The Christian Socialist*—first in the interest of land reform and then, increasingly,

17. See "Harold Cox," *DNB, 1931–40*, pp. 195–96, and his obituary in the *Times*, 2 May 1936. He was the son of a wealthy circuit court judge. As an undergraduate he was president of the Cambridge Union, and, following his Socialist phase, he became editor of the (Whig) *Edinburg Review*. His agricultural venture (which, after early crop failures, culminated in the attempted manufacture of radish jam!) is described with suitable hilarity in Winsten, *Salt and His Circle*, p. 53; Shaw, "The New Politics" (BM 50683) ; and E. Carpenter, *My Days and Dreams*, p. 124.

18. He was listed as an SDF speaker in *Justice* from May 1884, and in that capacity Olivier heard him deliver a Hyde Park harangue on 27 October 1884 "about Socialism and Second Chambers, etc." that his befuddled listeners took as a denunciation of "the luxurious habits of those who live in more than one room" (M. Olivier, *Sydney Olivier*, p. 68). See ibid., pp. 35, 61, 71, for his introduction to the Barnetts, and cf. *Justice*, 19 Jan. 1884, where Olivier is listed among members and sympathizers of the (S) DF.

19. Olivier to Wallas, 15 Nov. 1882, in M. Olivier, *Sydney Olivier*, p. 54.

in support of the Democratic Federation and of Marxism in a very moralistic sense.[20]

His lack of sympathy with the materialist and insurrectionary character of Anglo-Marxism, however, may be judged from the fact that, in the same years, he became deeply involved with the Positive philosophy and religion of Auguste Comte. As already noted, he was abetted in this enterprise by Webb and Wallas—the former as his fellow resident at the Colonial Office, where both were First Division clerks. Together, the three of them studied "the basic works of Comte" and professed to find in them a "hopeful solution" to the social and religious crises of their time.[21] Unlike Webb, however, Olivier was chiefly drawn to the metaphysical aspects of Comte's doctrine and never developed a strong commitment to the Positivist method of social reconstruction. Instead, he continually debated the respective merits of Socialism (as interpreted, perhaps, by Harold Cox or by his Christian Socialist coworkers) with those of Positivism as a competing social creed. And for a time he found himself unable to judge decisively between them. On the one hand, he concluded that

> a great advance in the direction of Socialism must be the next move, if only for the purpose of educating the future controllers of labour. And on purely economic grounds it seems to me advisable as the only means of organising production [so as to avoid the waste resulting from trade cycles and unnecessary competition among employers].

At the same time, he rebuked Hyndman and the Anglo-Marxists for overlooking the "possibilities for good" in a rationalized and improved system of capitalism, such as that envisaged by Comte or Mill, concluding that capitalism, "if moralised" in a Positivist fashion, would probably be "economically superior" to Socialism.[22]

20. Ibid., p. 36, and chap. 3, sec. 3 above.
21. Ibid., p. 60, and chap. 6, sec. 3 above.
22. Olivier to Margaret Cox (his future wife), 28 Oct. 1883 and 18 Feb. 1884, in ibid., pp. 61 and 64. In Feb. 1884 he also took a characteristically Positivist view of "the inevitable evils of a Socialist system, [if] organized without as thorough a revolution morality as would suffice to obviate the evils of capitalism" (ibid., p. 64).

Socialism, on the other hand, would be *ethically* superior to any conceivable form of capitalism.

The one thing about which Olivier was certain, however, was that for anyone intellectually abreast of his time, the only "conceivable solutions to the problems of Capital and Labour" were Positivism and Socialism, because they alone embodied a genuinely "social" point of view and made explicit the fact that the old individualism was now dead.[23] This was the basis of all Olivier's subsequent reasoning about social questions. Unlike Webb, however, he did not proceed from that point to a fuller acceptance of Comte's social teaching (perhaps because his view of Positivism was always more abstractly intellectual than Webb's). Instead, the ethical appeal of Socialism, with its religious overtones, exerted the stronger pull. But this made it almost inevitable that the Socialism Olivier adopted would be of a highly traditional and idealized variety— "the opposite and antidote to all forms of Individualism," as he defined it, insisting that the "one indispensable part of Socialist teaching" was its doctrine of "the social nature and propensities of man." He even went so far as to endorse the chief panacea of traditional English Socialism, the self-governing co-operative workshop, and to describe the system of "placing the machinery of government under democratic management by the whole body of workers interested" as the essence of Socialism in practice. In some of his writings of the late eighties, he also advocated an equal division of the product of labor and aspired to an ultimate state of utopian communism.[24] In every case, however, he insisted that

> the complete Socialist criticism of our economy is, not that it is capitalistic, but that it is individualistic. Capitalism is [only] one among the many forms of exploitation which are the inevitable outcome of the unchecked individualistic struggle. [Socialism must seek to overcome them all.][25]

23. "Perverse Socialism," *To-day* 6 (Aug. 1886) : 50, and "A Critic of Anarchism." *Freedom* (Oct. 1887) : 50–51.

24. "John Stuart Mill on Socialism," *To-day* 2 (Nov. 1884) : esp. 497, and *Freedom* (July 1887) : 39. The last two points are discussed more fully on p. 227 below.

25. "Perverse Socialism," pt. 2, *To-day* 6 (Sept. 1886) : 112.

Such were the doctrines of "the larger Socialism," an essentially ethical Socialism, which Olivier vigorously contrasted with the "narrow," negative, and merely anticapitalist teaching of the SDF:

> The larger Socialism, as distinguished from mere anti-Capitalism, insists that it is useless to expect the abatement, even of economic evils, by any . . . revolution other than a revolution in economic *motive*. Individualist considerations may prompt the establishment of a co-operative form of production or distribution, but only the true spirit of co-operation can ensure its working satisfactorily.[26]

What such Socialism sought to bring about, therefore, was a complete change of heart: a new spirit of social conscience, brotherhood, and cooperation, which Olivier went so far as to describe as "the perfect human religion which, alone, can make society whole." Fortunately, as Comte's sociology had taught, that spirit was "yearly increasing now and seems likely to increase still faster in the future,"[27] and Olivier rested much of his case for Socialism on that belief.

Given such beliefs, it was inevitable that Olivier's Socialist theories would conflict with those of Mill and Marx, which were rooted in individualist and competitive assumptions that Olivier regarded as inherently un-Socialist. Of the two, however, he found Mill much closer to the spirit of the larger Socialism. For despite his "fatal notion that sociological laws could be deduced from . . . the probable workings of the desire for wealth," the "whole feeling [of his work was] . . . social," and on almost all questions of "social economy" his opinions were "uniformly progressive." For these reasons, and because in his last years Mill had also turned more openly toward Socialism, Olivier concluded that his work formed the most powerful inspiration for the English Socialist movement. His *Political Economy* . . . put [more] men on the track" of Socialism than all the avowedly Socialist books written since. Moreover, it was only necessary to separate the genuinely

---

26. Ibid., pp. 113–14; he also endorsed Mazzini's teaching that "nothing can supplant the individualist motives for exertion save the new social religion" (ibid.).

27. "The Motive Power of Socialism," *Sunday Chronicle*, 7 Dec. 1890.

social kernel of its teaching from the individualist chaff in order to
arrive at an approach to Socialism that was very much like Olivier's
own.[28]

To a far greater extent than Webb, therefore, Olivier really did
"follow Mill" in his conversion to Socialism, drawing out and
making explicit what the latter had left merely implicit and demanding for here and now what Mill had proposed only for the
distant future. He was also the first Fabian to draw his colleagues'
attention to Mill's Socialist leanings, and thus to lend the respectability of the latter's name to the developing doctrines of the Fabian
Society.

Marx, on the other hand, was seen by Olivier in a very different
light: as an essentially non-Socialist, even "reactionary," writer,
because his reliance on "individualist motives" was unrelieved by
even the underlying "social feeling" of Mill's work. *Capital*, volume one, and the other "fragments" of Marx's writings that were
then available in England were merely anticapitalist polemics that
did not "teach Socialism" at all, while Anglo-Marxism, with its
narrowly economic focus and its blatant appeal to class warfare,
pointed toward a barren struggle for economic advantage that was
the very opposite of Socialist. This was doubly unfortunate because
"outside the proletariat, there are thousands ready for the larger
Socialism who are repelled . . . by the reactionary tendency of
[Socialism's] loudest preachings."[29] These were the persons Olivier
especially sought to reach.

Such persons were presumably potential recruits for (if not
already members of) the Fabian Society, and one might also rea-
sonably suppose that the "larger Socialism" itself was Fabianism in
embryonic form. This was not so, however, as a comparison of
Oliver's beliefs with those of contemporary Fabian colleagues,
such as Webb, will indicate. For if Olivier agreed wholeheartedly
with the latter regarding the impossibility of revolution, he disagreed regarding both the reality of class war (which he held to be

28. "Mill on Socialism," *To-day* 2 (Nov. 1884): 493, 495–96, 503.
29. "Perverse Socialism," *To-day* 6 (Aug., Sept. 1886): esp. 51, 54, 112–14; and
compare the almost identical verdict of Morris's disciple, J. B. Glasier, on Hyndman's lectures, in J. B. Glasier, *William Morris and the Early Days of the Socialist
Movement* (London, 1921), p. 30, and in L. Thompson, *The Enthusiasts* (London,
1971), p. 90.

an inevitable product of unbridled economic competition) and the means of restoring social peace. In keeping with the theory of economic rent (discussed in chapter 6), he viewed such "war" as a "mutual pillage" of all classes in which the proletariat, lacking the protection of even a semimonopolistic position, "necessarily came out emptiest." His remedy, however, was to insist more strongly on the complete extinction of competitive individualism, and on its replacement by a frank acceptance of the organic inter-dependence of modern societies, in which economic value (the "produce of labour") was inevitably a social product—both the power and the opportunities for creating it being due to society as a whole.

> Who then but society itself has any claim of right to the prod-uct of those powers and opportunities? What claim has any man to demand . . . a higher reward than his brothers? . . . Every man who appropriates more than his brother . . . [by virtue of some special] advantage in the competitive struggle . . . is just as much in receipt of surplus value, just as much an exploiter of his fellows' labour, as the ideal capitalist of Marx.[30]

In short, complete equality of remuneration was the only policy compatible with a Socialist repudiation of economic individual-ism—a conclusion very few of Olivier's Fabian colleagues shared. But Olivier went further still, by arguing that for a mature Social-ist society—"for fully socialised and moralised humanity"—this must be interpreted to mean: "From each according to his abilities, to each according to his needs,"[31] which was utopian communism of the purest water.

This was the theoretical basis for Olivier's habit, in Fabian de-bates of the later eighties and nineties (when he was not away on troubleshooting missions for the Colonial Office), of taking the

30. "Perverse Socialism," and "A Champion of the Perverse," *To-day* 6 (Sept., Nov. 1886): 176, 111, 113–14, and *Freedom* (July 1887): 39; the theoretical basis for these arguments, which was jointly worked out by Olivier and Webb, is more fully explained in chap. 6 above. The final point is also virtually identical with Shaw's "G. B. S. Larking" argument (see chap. 4, n. 84 above).

31. *Freedom* (July 1887): 39–40. (The article is signed "S.O.")

most radical position on all issues, so that he remained, well into middle age, the irrepressible enfant terrible of the Society. No other Fabian of the eighties, save Shaw, was so consistently utopian and revolutionary (and Olivier was merciless in his attacks on Shaw's implicit individualism). Thus, despite apparent personal dissimilarities and the fact that Olivier remained a Fabian and a civil servant, his Socialist theory went far beyond the conventional Fabian orbit and into the revolutionary-utopian one of Morris and Kropotkin.[32]

2. Graham Wallas

Graham Wallas, in contrast, has been described as the "least revolutionary" and most "instinctive[ly] gradualist" among the early Fabians.[33] He was also the most firmly committed of that group to the values of Radical Christian Humanitarianism and became more firm in that commitment in the later eighties while Olivier became less so. Nevertheless, Wallas's intellectual development paralleled Olivier's so closely that it will not be necessary to provide a similarly detailed account of his progress to Socialism. Instead, it will be sufficient to note that after graduating from Oxford in 1881, he spent several years coaching wealthy youths for public school scholarships at a preparatory school near Maidenhead-on-Thames—a place close enough to London for easy communication but distant enough to prevent him from participating in the round of Humanitarian and Socialist activities that absorbed Olivier's energies in those years. His correspondence with Olivier, however, reveals a keen sympathy with such activities and, more importantly, an interest in the doctrines of Positivism and Socialism that kept pace with Olivier's own. (He was even converted to Socialism by the books Olivier sent to him at Maidenhead.)[34] Finally, in December 1884, he obtained a post as assistant master at the Highgate School in north London—a location that

32. See E. Hobsbawm, "The Lesser Fabians," in W. P. Munby, ed, *The Luddites and Other Essays* (London, 1971), and Hulse, *Revolutionists in London*.

33. See Slater, reminiscences, WP, box 32, and Wallas, "Education" (WP, box 16, f. 35); and cf. Munby, *Luddites*, p. 238.

34. Wallas, *Men and Ideas*, p. 11 (Vita); *The Art of Thought* (London, 1926), pp. 238, 261 n.; M. Olivier, *Sydney Olivier;* and *Sunday Chronicle*, 7 Dec. 1890.

was particularly advantageous for allowing him to join Olivier, Webb, Shaw, and their Fabian friends at the Marx discussions that were held across the Heath in Hampstead. Unhappily, the arrangement was short-lived. Before the end of the following year religious scruples intervened: Wallas refused to take communion as required by the school, and therefore resigned his post, going abroad for a year of study in Germany. There he encountered a Socialist movement far more extensive and well organized than the embryonic one in England. Some of his German friends were deeply sympathetic to the movement, and his interest in it continued to develop.[35] Consequently, when he returned to England in the Spring of 1886, he joined the Fabian Society as a professed Socialist.

The Socialist theory that emerged in his earliest Fabian lectures, however, owed far more to his Evangelical religious temperament and training, and to the similarly inspired teachings of Ruskin, Toynbee, and the Oxford Idealists,[36] than to any German or English school of Socialism. From the first, Wallas proclaimed that the Socialist "idea" was for him a "new religion," free from doctrinal entanglements of the old one, but endowed with all its moral teachings and taboos. Thus he took "personal duty," the most powerful vestige of the Evangelical conscience, as the keynote of his teaching, urging his fellow Fabians to maintain a scrupulous stewardship of their time and resources for the service of their fellow men. For "every step which leads to increased happiness, education, and leisure for our fellow men is a step forward for our Cause," he argued, so that the duty to work for such aims was inescapable in any person who called himself a Socialist. And in terms explicitly evoking the class consciousness of sin, he reminded his fellow Fabians that their educations had cost money enough to have "raised several poor lads from ignorance and despair." Hence they owed heavy obligations to society in return for the special advantages they had enjoyed—obligations that Wallas expressed

35. See J. Deimling (German friend) to Wallas, 17 July 1885, referring to the Socialists as "apostles of the poor and oppressed" (WP, box 1) .

36. Although Wallas remained ignorant of T. H. Green's Idealist philosophy while at Oxford, he did profess an "intense respect . . . for the Hegelian philosophers" as persons (*Prac. Soc.* [July 1886]: 119, and see n. 12 above), and the similarity of outlook between himself, Green, and Toynbee—a form of Puritan asceticism transmuted into social conscience—is unmistakable.

economically as a form of "rent." Such rent was partially payable by spending only "a socially just income" and devoting one's remaining wealth to public purposes, but was payable in full only by giving personal and devoted service to the poor.[37]

That was also Wallas's answer to the burning question among the early Fabians of "how best to live the Socialist life." But to those seeking more practical advice, he especially urged the work of school managership—a form of voluntary service that he himself had undertaken and that he followed up with settlement work and social investigation in the early nineties. Finally, he urged his hearers to lose no opportunity of preaching the "Socialist idea," and of "working upon the conscience of the comfortable classes" until they were imbued with the spirit of social duty. For it was precisely

> this powerful, all pervading . . . sentiment, which we Socialists
> believe to be almost entirely wasted under the present system,
> . . . which we would endeavour to turn . . . to good effect [by
> preaching and by example]. . . . We rejoice that this common
> social feeling . . . is yearly increasing now and seems likely to
> increase still faster in the future. We rely on that as the motive
> power that will drive our engine of reform.[38]

This kind of rhetoric identified Wallas as the most deeply moralistic and humanitarian of the early Fabians, as well as the one most persistently inclined to "preach."[39] As already noted, however,

37. "Tithes" and "The Morals of Interest," WP, box 16, and "Personal Duty Under the Present System," *Prac. Soc.* (July–Aug. 1886): 119–20, 124–25. The emphasis on simplicity of living and on spending only a socially just income are suggestive of Ruskin, who strongly influenced Wallas while the latter was at Oxford (*Men and Ideas*, p. 80), although his influence on Wallas's Socialist theory was marginal.

38. Wallas, "Socialists and the School Board," *To-day* 10 (Nov. 1888): 131–32; biographical sketch, *Woman's Signal* (22 Feb., 1894): 123; T. Woodham to Wallas, 10 Nov., 1887 (WP, box 1); *Prac. Soc.* (July 1886): 119; and *Sunday Chronicle*, 7 Dec., 1890. Wallas subsequently acknowledged the Positivist origin of his "motive power" argument in a lecture, "The Social Motive," *Fabian News* (May 1913): 42–43.

39. See B. Webb, *Our Partnership*, p. 37. But Wallas was uniquely gifted among Fabians as a speaker who could "move [working-class] audiences" by his "evident candour and moral passion" (W. S. Sanders, *Early Socialist Days* [London, 1927], pp. 36–37).

he did not outgrow those qualities like Olivier, but instead intensified them in the later eighties and nineties, becoming closely associated with Toynbee Hall and University Hall—the chief centers
of Christian Humanitarianism in London—and with the guiding
spirits of both institutions.[40] Somewhat more surprisingly, he also
arranged to lecture on the duties of citizenship under the auspices
of Toynbee Hall and the Charity Organisation Society (COS).
This is surprising because, despite its broadly Humanitarian outlook, the COS was adamantly opposed to Socialism and took an
extreme individualist view of the causes of poverty.[41] And it is
clear from his letters that Wallas agreed with the COS on at least
some of the issues that divided it from contemporary Socialists. For
example, he believed strongly in the need to morally rehabilitate
the poor, teaching them "self-sacrifice and duty" (although he
preferred to leave the latter job to men more perfect than himself), and he seems also to have accepted the COS policy of sup-
pressing outdoor relief and encouraging self-reliance for the sake
of making the poor into good citizens.[42]

These considerations raise serious questions about the nature
of Wallas's Socialism—especially the question of whether it was,
like Webb's, chiefly a new name for essentially pre-Socialist (Positivist or Humanitarian) beliefs. To this question, his Fabian essay,
"Property Under Socialism," appears to give the clearest answer:
an explicit, if unenthusiastic affirmation of gradualism and collectivism, encompassing the common program of the Fabian "Old

40. See Wallas's correspondence with Canon Barnett, C. S. Loch, and Mrs.
Humphry Ward (WP, box 1). University Hall was founded in 1890 by Mrs. Ward
to implement the teachings of her novel, *Robert Elsmere* (1888), and Wallas was
closely involved with it from the beginning.

41. C. S. Loch to Wallas, 18 Aug., 10 and 18 Sept., 1890, 28 Feb., 6 and 13 June,
1891, WP, box 1. His citizenship lectures were jointly sponsored by the COS and
the University Extension Society (see R. D. Roberts, its secretary, to Wallas, 29
Nov., 1890, ibid.) Although the latter eventually became his sole sponsor, all his
early arrangements were made with Loch and the COS. For discussion of COS
principles, see Richter, *Politics of Conscience*, pp. 330 ff., and C. L. Mowat, *The
Charity Organization Society, 1869–1913* (London, 1961), chap. 4 and p. 101 ff.

42. See esp. Loch to Wallas, 10 and 18 Sept., 1890, pronouncing Wallas "sound
as to O[utdoor] R[elief]," etc. (WP, box 1); and cf. *Prac. Soc.* (Aug. 1886): 125,
regarding the need to moralize the poor (a point of view that was also explicit in
Toynbee's demand that the poor "really lead a better life," quoted on p. 217 above).

Guard."[43] Its chief significance for Wallas, however, lay in the "hope" that such policies would bring "education, refinement, and leisure," together with "the arts which humanise life," within range of the whole population. "Then, at last, such a life will be possible for *all* as not even the richest and most powerful can live today."[44] Such aspirations, of course, were shared by most contemporary Humanitarians, but Wallas went beyond them in seeking not only to mitigate the evils of the class system by urging the "classes who compose society to do their duty to each other," but to end it by promoting real equality of opportunity. This was the basis of his claim that, whereas the Humanitarians offered only a "balm for the sufferings of our fellows," the Socialists showed that "those sufferings can be cured" by making a fuller and freer life *equally* available to all. Such was the "hope" he offered to the world under the name of Socialism,[45] and his devotion to it fully justifies his designation as the most consistently Radical and Humanitarian of the early Fabian leaders.

3. Annie Besant

Many of the same ideas were also taught by the English Secularist movement, though typically in a less elegant form, and, next to Charles Bradlaugh, its most prominent leader in the 1880s was Mrs. Annie Besant. She was also by far the most widely known and influential Fabian convert of that decade.[46] At the time of her

43. Wallas, "Property Under Socialism," in G. B. Shaw, ed., *Fabian Essays in Socialism* (London, 1889), but Wallas characteristically added that this "tentative and limited Social-Democracy" was only a necessary step toward the "better life" proclaimed by Socialism, and not that life itself (p. 147–48). (Unless otherwise noted, reference is to 1889 edition of *Fabian Essays*.) "Education," WP, box 16, and Shaw, *Fabian Essays*, p. 148.

44. "Education," WP, box 16, and Shaw, *Fabian Essays*, p. 148.

45. *Sunday Chronicle*, 7 Dec., 1890), and Shaw, *Fabian Essays*, pp. 132, 149—esp. the idea of "equal rights" to the good things of life. Cf. Wallas, *Men and Ideas*, p. 107.

46. See *Annie Besant, an Autobiography*, (London, 1893); Gertrude M. Williams, *The Passionate Pilgrim* (New York, 1931), still the shrewdest interpretation of her life; and Arthur Nethercot, *The First Five Lives of Annie Besant* (New York, 1961), the most recent. Unfortunately, no collections of her correspondence are known to exist. For recent discussions of Secularism, see Budd, "The Loss of Faith," and P. Thompson, *Socialists, Liberals, and Labour: The Struggle for London* (London, 1967), pp. 31–33. For older works, see the Bibliographical Note.

conversion she was a vice-president of the National Secular Society, co-editor of its weekly paper, *The National Reformer,* and
publisher of a more personal monthly called *Our Corner.* Through
such media she had built up a personal following throughout England and Scotland, which, added to her close association with
Bradlaugh, gave her a position of substantial influence in working-
class Radical politics. By common consent, she was also the greatest
woman orator of her time. Thus her accession was not a prize to
be taken lightly by a fledgling society whose members, though
bright and talented enough, were still unknown outside a very restricted circle of London Radicals. It was Annie Besant who gave
them national publicity and national connections for the first time,
and she was by no means unaware of the importance of that gift.
Almost from her accession, therefore, she was given a place in the
inner circle of the Society's leaders and soon began to exercise
powerful influence in the formation of its policies.

Despite her national prominence and the fact that she was
somewhat older than most of her Fabian colleagues, Annie Besant's
personality and origins were very typical of the society in its early
years. Yet she embodied those typical Fabian qualities in an extreme and slightly outlandish form. She was intensely (even neu-
rotically) religious, and a powerful religious impulse with strong
sexual overtones ran throughout her varied intellectual commitments. Indeed, her religious odyssey was almost a parody of the
Victorian theme of the loss of faith and search for a substitute.
Though educated in an atmosphere of intense Evangelical piety,
she showed an early fondness for ritualism and the mysteries of the
Anglo-Catholic faith. In late adolescence her emotional life became
fixated upon prayer, fasting, self-mortification, and adoration of
the saints, while the "figure of the Christ" became the focal point
of all her nubile hopes and longings. Thus inspired, she sought to
"prove [her] love by sacrifice," and even martyrdom—should that
prove possible—so as to "turn my passionate gratitude into active
service." And these were impulses that she rightly concluded
formed the "keynote" of her entire life.[47]

Soon her exemplary piety captivated a young curate, and the
resulting marriage became her first and chief disaster. She had

47. Besant, *Autobiography,* p. 57. Characteristically, she never seems to have
recognized the evidence of displaced sexuality in such confessions.

yearned to be the bride of Christ, as one astute observer noted, and the Reverend Frank Besant "was hardly an adequate substitute." [48] Within a few years the inevitable disenchantment with a stiff-necked husband and his restrictive notions of marriage began to blend subtly with the doubts about the validity of her faith that were never far from the surface in such an intense Victorian bluestocking. The inevitable breakaway occurred when, in the tradition of George Eliot, she refused to remain present during the Eucharist, in which she could no longer believe. In Besant's case, however, no reconciliation followed. She left her husband permanently, and in due time their children were taken from her by the courts. Fortunately, she had already found some friends among a talented group of London Freethinkers, and through their good offices she learned to make a new life as a professional writer of skeptical, anti-Christian tracts.

It is doubtful whether such an arrangement, focusing all her energies on the narrow and essentially negative writing of Freethought polemics, would have lasted very long had she not come under the spell of Charles Bradlaugh's powerful and very masculine personality. Once under that spell, however, both her spiritual and emotional life found a new focus, and she was soon pouring into the work of Bradlaugh's National Secular Society all the love, enthusiasm, and hero-worship she had formerly channeled into the Anglo-Catholic faith. Following Bradlaugh's lead, she declared herself an "atheist" and sought to make such atheism into a complete religion, with service to humanity as its keynote. Atheists, she proclaimed, were "the pioneers of progress, who in their zeal to improve earth have forgotten heaven and in their zeal for man have forgotten God." And for her creed, she proclaimed: "I believe in Man. In man's redeeming power; in man's remoulding energy; in man's approaching triumph through knowledge, love, and work." [49]

Fortunately, Secularism itself retained the rudiments of an organized religious cult from its origin in the teachings of Robert

48. W. T. Stead, quoted in Nethercot, *First Five Lives*, p. 42.

49. *The Gospel of Atheism* (1876), and *Why I Do Not Believe in God* (1887), quoted in Besant, *Autobiography*, 151–52, 146.

Owen and its earlier leadership by G. J. Holyoake. From that legacy it still utilized such outward trappings of sectarian Christianity as Sunday meetings in Halls of Science, vaguely imitating the order of an Evangelical service, and a creed that, in effect, was Positivism watered down for mass consumption. As expounded by Holyoake its chief articles of faith were: a belief in altruism— "that the good of others is the highest aim of man"; the belief that such aims can only be achieved by the material improvement of *this* life; and the belief that science is "the Providence available for man's use" and the only means to his ultimate regeneration. Its highest aims, he proclaimed, were to promote the "moralisation of this world, which Christianity has proven ineffectual to accomplish," and to infuse an "ethical passion" into all of social life.[50]

The ethical doctrine taught by Secularism was strictly utilitarian, but in the altruistic manner of Mill's later years, so that it contained much of the social teaching of Comte in secondhand form. Through her acceptance of that teaching, Annie Besant may be regarded as yet another Fabian in the Millite-Positivist tradition.[51] Her chief problem as a Secularist, however, was to breathe a more vital, religious spirit into its threadbare and—in Bradlaugh's hands—decidedly arid creed. In her period of deepest involvement, therefore, she sought to show that the worship of science itself could sustain a genuine religious experience:

As we bow our heads before the laws of the universe . . . a strong, calm peace steal[s] over our hearts, a perfect trust in the ultimate triumph of right, a quiet determination to "make our lives sublime." . . . The contemplation of the ideal [—and especially, of the ideal expressed in noble human lives from

50. George Jacob Holyoake, *English Secularism* (Chicago, 1896), pp. 35, 36, 73, 124—based chiefly on the same author's earlier *Secularism . . . a Religion for the People* (London, 1854). J. M. Robertson, Secularist leader and historian, noted even more explicitly that "if ever two parties existed with something like a common creed it is they [the Positivists] and we" (*National Reformer* [16 Nov., 1884]: 322).

51. Her own ethical doctrines were Utilitarian, but she also studied Comte extensively in 1875 and expounded his teachings in a series of articles for the *National Reformer* that were favorable to his ethical views but repudiated the authoritarianism of the *Positive Polity*.

the past—] is true prayer; it inspires, it strengthens, it en-
nobles. The other part of prayer is work.[52]

And work was provided in ample measure by the intense activism
of the Secular Society, always at the forefront of ultra-Radical
causes.

Significantly, Annie Besant confessed that she could only value
the results of such work insofar as they contributed to the "moralisation" of those who participated, creating a sense of "true
fraternity, true brotherhood, . . . heart to heart, in . . . loyal service
to the common need, and generous self-sacrifice to the common
good." [53] In short, she sought within the Secular Society a true
religious fellowship and an outlet for her compulsion to self-
sacrifice. Unhappily, its prosaic atmosphere was not well suited
to such needs. "Temperamentally," it has been said, "she had
never for a moment belonged" in such a narrowly intellectual and
combative company, and by the mid-eighties the truth of that claim
was becoming unmistakable.[54] She was again restless, and that
restlessness soon led to an increasing interest in the new phenomenon of English Socialism.

At first, however, she was "put off" Socialism by the "bitter and
unfair attacks" its spokesmen made against Bradlaugh and her
fellow Radicals. But she followed the rash of Socialist activities in
1884 with avid interest, including the much publicized debates,
and her writings in the latter part of that year indicate that some
of the new ideas were seeping in. She was moving steadily toward
the outer fringes of traditional Radical politics and toward collectivist reforms of the type that Hyndman and his allies propagated:
free schools and school lunches, protection of factory labor, and
the eight-hour day. By the end of 1884 this process had taken
her to the point of constructing cautious arguments in favor of
such collectivism.[55] She was ready for conversion to Socialism,
provided it could be offered to her in an appropriate manner.

Hyndman's Socialism, of course, would never do; she was al-

52. *Gospel of Atheism* (1876), in Besant *Autobiography*, p. 152. The apostrophes
to Humanity and the references to "Collective Immortality" are characteristic of
Positivist teaching.
53. *The True Basis of Morality* (1874), in Besant *Autobiography*, p. 156.
54. Williams, *Passionate Pilgrim*, pp. 140–50.
55. See esp. "Daybreak," *National Reformer* 64 n.s. (21 Dec., 1884): 427, and
ibid., 65 n.s. (25 Jan., 1885); also Nethercot, *First Five Lives*, pp. 218 ff.

ready too antagonistic toward it. But the Fabians, who openly courted the support of Radical Secularists, offered a more appealing gospel, and Shaw, the scourge of Hyndmanism, offered it in the most appealing form of all. Hence it was only natural that Annie Besant's first public defense of Socialism occurred at Shaw's lecture to the Dialectical Society in February 1885 and that she joined the Fabian Society, some two months later, as Shaw's protégée.[56] Her conversion, however, really began with an impassioned lecture by the French Anarchist-Communist, Louise Michel in 1883, whose vivid portrayal of the starving women and children of the Paris slums and plea for human brotherhood first aroused her sympathy for Socialism.[57] When these were combined with the apparently hard-nosed political and economic reasoning of Shaw, she found the mixture irresistible. In an essentially accurate summary of the factors in her Socialist conversion, she wrote:

> Its splendid ideal appealed to my heart, while the economic soundness of its basis convinced my head. All my life was turned toward the progress of the people, the helping of man; [now] it leaped forward to meet the stronger hope, the lofty ideal of social brotherhood, the rendering possible to all of a freer life.[58]

In short, she was now to seek in Socialism precisely the kind of religious faith and fellowship that she had never adequately found in Secularism. It was to be her new Religion of Humanity, and some of her verbal effusions of the next few years said so quite explicitly. Socialism was to be

> the Gospel of Man's Redemption, . . . a social union closer than any brotherhood the world has known, . . . the Golden Age which poets have chanted . . . [and] martyrs have died for: . . . that new Republic of Man, which exists now in our hope and . . . faith and shall exist in reality on earth.[59]

56. See the end of chap. 4, regarding Shaw's lecture.
57. See "Daybreak," *National Reformer* 61 n.s. (21 Jan., 1883) , and cf. Nethercot *First Five Lives*, p. 227.
58. Besant, *Autobiography*, p. 304.
59. *Modern Socialism* (London, 1886) , p. 51; "The Co-operative Commonwealth." *Our Corner* (Sept. 1885) : 163; and *The Evolution of Society* (London, 1885) .

Finally, as she wrote in her most popular Socialist tract, Socialism was

> the one name which is recognized all the world over as the name of those who are opposed to political, religious and social tyranny in every land; . . . who see a brother in every worker, a friend in every lover of the people.[60]

In effect, she had transferred to the Socialist movement all the social aims and aspirations and the intensely emotional humanitarianism that she had cherished as a Secularist. Her Socialism was essentially old Secularism glorified and expanded to an international scale, but still laced with all the quirks and political reforms that she had fought for as a Secularist-Radical. The Fabian Society was her obvious choice of a new spiritual home, because it shared so many of her Radical aims and values.[61] Of all the London Socialist societies, it most nearly shared her quasi-religious view of the movement and conceived of Socialism in moral and humanitarian terms that could do no violence to the exalted character of her social feelings. Even the "class consciousness of sin," which was so widely felt among the early Fabians, found echoes in her writing:

> In sober truth, I love the poor—those rough, coarse people, who have paid their lives for our culture and refinement, & I feel that the devotion to them of [my] abilities cultivated at their cost is the mere base debt that I owe, *for my class,* to them.[62]

Through the Fabian Society she now found the means of channeling such feelings into "practical work" that was congenial to her temperament and was enriched by the company of kindred spirits. It was to be her spiritual home for the next half decade.

60. *Why I Am a Socialist* (London, 1886), p. 2.
61. This was especially true of Shaw, whose overt friendliness to Radicals and insistence that Socialism was the real fulfillment of Radical individualism were precisely the doctrines best suited to her needs. Shaw also worked very hard to bring her into the Society in the spring of 1885. Fortunately, Besant was fascinated by Shaw almost from their first meeting and soon began to regard him as a possible replacement for Bradlaugh in her emotional life.
62. Annie Besant to J. W. Ashman (first American member of the Fabian Society), 13 Mar., 1887, in Nethercot, *First Five Lives,* p. 400 (emphasis added).

4. William Clarke

The second convert deriving from the Secularist tradition was William Clarke, a person far less prominent than Annie Besant, but, in the later eighties and nineties widely known and respected as a Radical journalist.[63] His impact on Fabian thought was slight, but he exemplified more perfectly than any other convert of the eighties the progress of a thoroughgoing political Radical toward Socialism. In the early eighties he had come very close to being one of the Founding Fabians. He was a member of the original Davidsonian group and by temperament was strongly attracted both to the "New Fellowship" and to its founder and prophet, Thomas Davidson. He did not, however, join either the fellowship or the Fabian Society in its first years, being, perhaps, too much of a "loner" for such organizations. But although he remained outside the Socialist ferment of the early eighties, he viewed its rise, and the concomitant rise of working-class concern about social problems, with a sympathy that owed much of its force to his personal misfortunes.

His origins were typically Fabian. He was born in Norwich to a commercial, middle-class family, partly of Scottish extraction, and his early life was suffused with Nonconformist religion of an intensely Evangelical type.[64] His early politics were also an outgrowth of that milieu, as they followed the Nonconformist style of Radicalism that had become a powerful force in many provincial cities[65]—a type of politics to which Clarke remained faithful long after its religious foundations had eroded away. Even before entering Cambridge University as an overage, noncollegiate student

63. There is no biography of Clarke, but see the biographical sketches by Herbert Burrows and Lord Bryce in *William Clarke: A Collection of His Writings* (London 1908), and the collection of his letters to H. D. Lloyd, in the Lloyd Papers, WSHS.

64. Some of his ancestors were Covenanters, and in his youth he believed "in the Biblical millennium" (Burrows and Bryce, *William Clarke*, pp. xi, xxvi–xxvii). I can find nothing, however, to justify the assertion in Hobsbawm, "Fabianism and the Fabians, 1884–1914" (Ph.D. thesis, Cambridge, 1950), pp. 90 ff., that his family inherited a native "Jacobin" tradition.

65. Regarding the latter, see (W. H. White), *The Autobiography of Mark Rutherford* (London, 1881), and the discussion of Clarke's native Norwich in H. J. Massingham, ed., *H. W. M.: A Selection from the Writings of H. W. Massingham* (London, n.d.), pp. 322 ff. Norwich was a notable stronghold of Nonconformist Radicalism.

already used to working as a junior clerk, he had passed through the usual phases of Victorian doubt and had emerged as a Unitarian with a strong mystical streak and a hatred of dogma. Typically Nonconformist political causes such as temperance, disestablishment, and complete religious equality were also the focuses of his extracurricular activities. He defended them vigorously in the university debating societies as an undergraduate, and, after graduation, continued the work as a journalist in the local Nonconformist press.

From such Nonconformist, ultra-Radical beginnings it was only a step to the Radicalism of the Secular Society, and one that was almost inevitable when the last vestiges of his Evangelical faith had vanished. By the early eighties, therefore, after settling as a freelance journalist in London, Clarke became a strong supporter of Charles Bradlaugh, a Republican, a Freethinker, an intense admirer of American democracy, and a crusader for Irish independence. Such were the political principles from which his evolution to Socialism began. His first step toward the latter goal may be seen in his support for Bradlaugh's land reform movement, which soon broadened out into more general support for land nationalization following Henry George's campaign of 1882. Though not himself a Socialist, he viewed the Socialist ferment and accompanying agitation of 1884 with deep sympathy, which was reflected in the articles he wrote concurrently for the *Boston Advertiser* and *Springfield Republican*. But, most of all, his enthusiasm was fired by Bradlaugh's campaign against the parliamentary oath, which roused the Secularists for their last great nineteenth-century attack on the Establishment.[66]

Unlike Annie Besant, however, Clarke was unable to find even a temporary spiritual haven among the organized Secularists. He always felt "the emptiness of merely anti-religious propaganda" and yearned for some form of contact with a "higher reality" in the universe.[67] As a result he passed through stages of infatuation

66. Clarke to Lloyd, 8 Jan., 1884, Lloyd Papers, WSHS, and cf. Walter Arnstein, *The Bradlaugh Case: A Study in Late Victorian Opinion and Politics* (New York, 1965). His articles from London (signed "C") appeared roughly bimonthly in *The Boston Advertiser* in 1883 and 1884.

67. Clarke to Lloyd, 23 Nov., 1888, Lloyd Papers, WSHS.

with the various transcendentalisms then in vogue: that of Emerson (which also gratified his doctrinaire Republican views), that of Mazzini, and finally the "neo-Hegelianism" of the Oxford Idealist school. None of these satisfied him permanently; but of the three it was the political religion of Mazzini that had the most profound effect upon his intellectual development in the eighties. By temperament he was ideally suited to accept the latter's doctrine that "political questions could not be separated from religious [ones]" [68]—a belief that underlay all his Radical politics. In the manner of both Mazzini and the original Fabians, he believed it was the function of politics to serve as a "true exponent of the inner life." Without such inspiration he found all politics sordid, whereas, inspired by an adequate "ideal of human life," political pursuits could become a virtual religion for him—and the "only religion I [now] have," as he confessed in 1888.[69]

Such attitudes, of course, were nurtured by the crusading spirit of Nonconformist and Secularist politics long before Clarke found new inspiration for them in the idealism of Mazzini. They had inspired his original support for Bradlaugh and the Freethought cause, and his letters of the period dripped with unction about "avoiding the compromises and commonplaces of what we call practical politics." Ironically, it was on the latter ground that one of his Freethought idols, John Morley, fell from grace in 1883, lured "by the bait of office," Clarke believed, to "sacrifice his manliness" by taking the oath that Bradlaugh had refused.[70] In three more years, however, Bradlaugh himself fell in the same way, absorbed innocuously into the great Gladstonian party, and there seemed nothing left worth fighting for in the old Radical bag of tricks. Such a disillusionment with Radicalism, as the party lay broken by Chamberlain's defection, Tory victory, and the fall of its major idols, was a common feeling among intellectuals in 1886. The following chapter deals with this disillusionment as a political problem. On a personal level, it sent Clarke out in search

68. W. Clarke, Introduction to *Essays: Selected from the Writings of Joseph Mazzini*, ed. by W. Clarke (London, 1887), p. xxvii; and cf. Stopford Brook's analysis of Clarke's political religion, in "Biog. Sketch," in *William Clarke*, xxvi.

69. Clarke to Lloyd, 23 Nov., 1888, Lloyd Papers, WSHS; but cf. his sad confession in the same letter that he could no longer "feel as Mazzini felt" about life.

70. Clarke to Lloyd, 23 May, 1883, Lloyd Papers, WSHS.

of a new political faith, and the result was his conversion to Socialism and his membership in the Fabian Society.

Like Annie Besant, he was first attracted by the moralistic and religious side of Fabianism—its promise of human brotherhood, social regeneration, and the universal practice of cooperation. In that form, however, his Socialism amounted to little more than a restatement of Mazzini's social idealism. For, although Clarke was well acquainted with Positivism (having frequented Frederic Harrison's house in the early eighties), it was chiefly from Mazzini that he learned to take a "social" view of man and society and to abandon the assumptions of Radical individualism. As Clarke himself noted, Mazzini had taught that the individual alone "cannot create" anything lasting, and that the "new birth" of society "can only proceed from the collective life." [71] Thus Clarke concluded that Mazzini's social aims were not "fundamentally divergent" from those of present-day Socialists, though he had doubts about the means by which Mazzini sought to fulfill them.[72]

Finally, such belief was reinforced, in the late eighties, by a close association with the younger exponents of Oxford Idealism, D. G. Ritchie and J. H. Muirhead, who shared with Clarke the task of lecturing on social problems to the recently founded London Ethical Society.[73] In that manner Clarke came into contact with the philosophical tradition that had been nurtured in England by T. H. Green. Green's teaching sometimes paralleled that of the Fabians, but Clarke was probably the first among them to make serious use of it. Through that philosophy, he seemed, at last, to have found the basis of a viable faith, and joyfully exchanged the "old, hard, crude, Secularist agnosticism," for the "new, deeper, richer social idealism" of Oxford and the Ethical Society.[74]

71. *Writings of Mazzini*, pp. xxi-xxii. For a brief analysis of Mazzini's Socialism see Richard Hostetter, *The Italian Socialist Movement: Origins, 1860–1882* (Princeton, 1958), pp. 38–46.

72. This was Clarke's conclusion in *Writings of Mazzini*, p. xxiv, but he later wrote that Mazzini sought to bring about Socialism through "What is called 'Cooperation,' . . . and every economist knows this is absolutely chimerical" (Clarke to Lloyd, 23 Nov., 1888, Lloyd Papers, WSHS).

73. See the typed letter, Clarke to W. Salter, 3 Nov., 1887, Lloyd Papers, WSHS.

74. Ibid.

Ironically, however, Clarke did not approach Socialism solely in Idealist terms; for he was, at the same time, the most outspoken exponent of Marxism among the early Fabians. Two factors, his American experiences and his own financial anxiety, were chiefly responsible for that fact. Like most English Radicals he tended to idealize American democracy from a distance, but several trips to the promised land during the eighties, plus a close friendship with the American muckraker, H. D. Lloyd, turned admiration to disgust and convinced him of the "failure of mere . . . [democracy] to solve a single one of the pressing problems" of industrial society. Instead,

> the great fact of the division between rich and poor, millionaires at one end, tramps at the other, a growth of monopolies unparalleled, crises producing abject poverty just as in Europe proved to men clearly that new institutions were of no use with the old forms of property,[75]

and laid the foundations for a Marxian analysis of economic evolution.

"I do not subscribe to the whole of Marx," he wrote in 1887, about a year after joining the Fabian Society, "but I do contend that his . . . analysis of value and explanation of economic development are true in general. . . . We say that there is robbery by the capitalist of the produce of . . . labour, and that *this* is the cause of poverty." And he cited American trusts, unemployment, and embattled strikers to prove that the evident polarization of capitalist society and the increasing misery of the proletariat therein were rapidly bringing events to a revolutionary climax. Indeed, in 1887 he held that such revolution was strictly "inevitable:"

> [The] necessary evolution of capitalism itself prevented any "peaceful solution of the social problem." My own belief is that we are in for a fierce, bloody struggle . . . and possibly even absolute social anarchy (though I hope not) . . . . What

75. William Clarke, "The Fabian Society," in Shaw, *Fabian Essays in Socialism*, American ed. (Boston, 1908), p. xxiv.

I fear most is that there may be serious strife before the
workers are well prepared for it.[76]

The explanation for such opinions lies chiefly in Clarke's temperamental differences from the other Fabians. He was given to
pessimism and deep fits of depression, whereas they seem to have
been inveterate social optimists. But above all, it was increasing
anxiety about his career, his financial solvency, and the future of
society that nurtured his deep pessimism in the later eighties.

> . . . I am only fit for anything productive about one day in
> five [he complained, in 1888]. . . . I can only write on a few
> unpopular subjects on which I hold unpopular opinions that
> do not pay. . . . I cannot get a living by my pen: I know no
> profession and am too old to learn. . . . I have tried for thir-
> teen weary years and I have had enough of it. . . . At 36,
> when I ought to be in a good position for life, I am next
> door to being a pauper.[77]

Such despair also formed a recurrent theme in his correspondence
throughout the eighties, leading him to exclaim in moments of
particular stress that society must be "either idiotic or diabolical"
to treat her brainworkers so harshly. To a great extent, it also
explained his conviction that social conditions had become "in-
tolerable" and capitalism too "ruthless" to be endured, and that
both must therefore be overthrown.

Hence also his conclusion that social harmony could never be
brought about by moral persuasion (as Wallas and Olivier had
taught), or even by judicious application of "palliatives." [78] Both
conclusions were the more remarkable because Clarke himself was,
at heart, a gradualist who had declared himself willing to "accept
or even work for any palliative (providing it is genuine)," and
because he took an active part in the sort of ethical preaching that

76. Clarke to Salter, 3 Nov., 1887, Lloyd Papers, WSHS, emphasis in original.
77. Clarke to Lloyd, 23 Nov., 1888, and cf. his repeated pleas for money or work,
8 Jan., 1884 and 2 Feb., 1885, Lloyd Papers, WSHS.
78. Viz,, Clarke's rebuke to those who think that economic problems can be solved
"by the preaching of morality," although he also insisted that economic problems
were essentially moral (*Writings of Mazzini*, pp. xxiv–xxv) .

was intended to arouse the conscience of the comfortable classes.[79] But so long as his pessimistic feelings lasted, Clarke could only conclude that nothing of that sort would ultimately succeed. The "ruthlessness" of the "plutocratic classes" was so intense, their hearts were so hardened against all morality, and the condition of the poor was so "desparate" that no amount of amelioration could be expected to stave off the revolution.[80]

5. Fabian Theory in 1886

The prevailing Fabian opinion to the contrary was based upon a mixture of ingrained social optimism, belief in an historical tendency for inequalities to be modified by law, and faith in the evolutionary "laws" of sociology of Auguste Comte: especially the law that men were bound to become more social as industrial civilization advanced (see chapter 6, note 26). These were the chief Fabian alternatives to Marxist theories of history. They were stated and their Socialist implications were developed with greatest clarity in the Introduction to Fabian Tract Number 4, *What Socialism Is*. This document, which has never been reprinted, provides the most comprehensive view of Fabian Socialist theory in the spring of 1886.[81] After a brief survey of modern economic history it concludes that

> [the] evolution of economic conditions . . . [that are] degrading alike to the idle and to the working population, has brought with it tendencies which are an earnest of remedy.

79. Clarke to Slater, 3 Nov., 1887, Lloyd Papers, WSHS.

80. It is only fair to add that in 1888, perhaps in response to the new current of Fabian collectivism, he modified his views sufficiently to conclude that "socialistic legislation . . . prevents in England the wilder developments of revolutionary socialism with which the world is familiar in the case of France and Germany" ("The Influence of Socialism on English Politics," *Political Science Quarterly* [Dec. 1888]).

81. *What Socialism Is*, Fabian Tract No. 4 (London, 1886). Most studies of the Fabian Society have noted only its eccentricity in presenting two rival views of Socialism, Anarchism and collectivism (both exceedingly utopian), without endorsing either one. But the Society did endorse the brief introduction to the tract, and that is its most important section. It was the work of a committee headed by Annie Besant. ("Socialist Notes," *Our Corner* [April 1886]).

The Great Industry, . . . rendering all branches of production mutually interdependent, has socialised labour and paved
the way for co-operation.

That, in turn, had spurred a "conscious growth of social feeling"
among the people. Backed up by the "inevitable development" of
democratic institutions, such feeling was fostering a steady trend
toward "State interference on behalf of the exploited class. Education and political power" had further suggested to this class
the "possibility of changing their social condition by legal methods, and in this direction such English Socialism as exists has
hitherto mainly moved." [82]
Thus the Fabian Society officially endorsed the view that "social
feeling" was the basis of Socialism. It was the Fabians' chief
antidote to class war, and they believed firmly that the evolution
of industrial society would strengthen it and help it to bear fruit
in the form of ameliorative legislation. Further evidence of such
beliefs may be found throughout contemporary Fabian writings,
as in the same tract's reference to "the mass of socialistic feeling
not yet fully conscious of itself as Socialist," which the Fabians
would make it their special business to develop, and in Tract
Number 5's contention that the Socialist remedy must be applied
through "the growth of social sympathies, promoted by accompanying cessation of class distinctions." The same tract also treated
legislative reforms as the inevitable consequence of such moral
tendencies.[83]
The most thoroughgoing statement of that view, however, was
contained in the Fabian report on *Unemployed Labour,* which
was printed "for the information of members" in the spring of
1886. The keystone of its argument was that "a Socialist State
presupposes the predominance of the social instincts" (or social
sympathies) and that "to secure that predominance we have to
unlearn the lesson of the last hundred years, and to realise that
Society is not a fortuitous concurrence of competing greed . . . but
a synthesis of interrelated parts, co-operating in an ordered har-

82. *What Socialism Is,* pp. 4–5.
83. Ibid., pp. 5–6, and *Facts for Socialists,* Fabian Tract No. 5 (London, 1887),
sec. 12 (in 1887 ed. only). In an apparent contradiction to this argument, sec. 10
of this tract was entitled "the Class War," but the remedies proposed therein were
the opposite of warlike.

mony." For that purpose, new social habits were required. Fortunately, "government undertakings surpass all others" in providing
the necessary "social education," by enabling those so employed
to feel "bound together in an organic whole." Thus by greatly
increasing the scope of public service (and its near equivalent,
military service), "the relatively backward social instincts might
be so far developed as to be made adequate to the requirements
of the Socialist State."[84]

That was also the doctrine the Fabians propounded at the conference of Radical and Socialist societies that they organized in the
summer of 1886,[85] and Webb supplied it with a "scientific" foundation by arguing that (Comte's) "Sociology" showed that even in
such an intensely "selfish" society as their own everyone was bound
to become "more or less sympathetic with his neighbour."[86] As
such social sympathies increased, in response to the increasing in-
terconnectedness and interdependence of advanced industrial
society, belief in Socialism would also increase, aided by the new
humanitarian tendencies of the time. "Dawning conscience" was
already bringing the sons of rich and selfish capitalists "to our
ranks," Webb wrote, and the growth of social sympathies and
social conscience could be expected to act even more powerfully
in that direction in the future, providing the necessary motive
power to drive the Fabians' "engine of [humanitarian] reform." [87]

84. *The Government Organization of Unemployed Labour: Report Made by a
Committee of the Fabian Society and Ordered to Be Printed for the Information of
Members* (London, 1886), p. 23. It was written by both Webb and Podmore (Pease,
History of the Fabian Society, p. 57), and betrays strong influence of J. S. Mill in its
repeated insistence that a highly developed "social consciousness" is "indispensible"
to "the evolution of a Socialist State" (p. 21). (Compare Mill, *Autobiography*,
p. 163.)

85. "In order to make any changes in the basis of our social system permanent
we must counteract the abnormal development of the self-regarding instincts by
which the system is now upheld. A Socialist State presupposes the predominance of
the social instincts" ("Special Report" of the Fabian Conference, 9-11 June, 1886,
BLPES).

86. Webb, replying to Wordsworth Donisthorpe, 11 June, 1886, in ibid., f. 230.

87. Webb, "What Socialism Means," *Prac. Soc.* (June 1886), and G. Wallas, "The
Motive Power of Socialism." Similarly, Annie Besant wrote that Socialism "relies
for its progress" on the fuller development of the "instinct of benevolence," the
"joy in creative work," and the many other social instincts that would flourish
when livelihood was made secure. Through the development of such "instincts" men
would learn to "identify their interests with those of the community" (Shaw,
Fabian Essays, pp. 168–69).

Happily, such reform was bound to stimulate more intense social
feeling, which, in turn, would stimulate new social reforms until,
by a kind of chain reaction, the whole society would be moralized
and regenerated. Thus the internal transformation of society by
the spread of social feelings and its external transformation by
means of legislative reforms were seen to be complementary aspects of a continuous social process whose end product would be
Socialism. This was the earliest Fabian doctrine of the inevitability
of gradualness.

It was also, in essence, what Webb had meant by stating that
Socialism aimed to bring about a "gradual revolution" in public
opinion that would result in a vast extension of social welfare
legislation, thereby making possible the maximum freedom,
richness, and diversity of human development at all levels of
society.[88] This thoroughly liberal and humanitarian view of the
aims of Socialism was also shared by most of the early Fabian
leaders. Wallas has already been quoted to this effect, and Olivier's
views were similar, as he insisted that the aim of Socialism was
to open the educational and cultural resources of the community
to all, "with sufficient leisure for all to enjoy [them]." [89] But this
point of view was probably most clearly stated in Annie Besant's
summation of "the Social[ist] Ideal" as "enough of work, of leisure, of joy," to which she added that "the greatness of a nation
depends not on the number of its great proprietors, on the wealth
of its great capitalists, or the splendour of its great nobles, but on
the absence of poverty among its people, on the education and
refinement of its masses, on the universality of enjoyment in
life." [90] Thus the business of practical Socialism, as these early
Fabians saw it, was to establish the social and economic conditions

88. Webb, "What Socialism Means," and cf. p. 213 above.

89. S. Olivier, "Idols of the Sty," pt. 2, *To-day* (Oct. 1888): 98; also [S. Olivier],
Capital and Land, Fabian Tract no. 7 (London, 1888), p. 16, and cf. W. Clarke,
"An Examination of Some Criticisms of Democracy," *To-day* (Dec. 1888). Olivier
also argued that such demands would prove useless without a national minimum
standard of life for all citizens—a notion that subsequently became one of the most
prominent Fabian reform proposals.

90. Besant, *The Evolution of Society* pp. 19–20; and cf. her exposition of "The
Socialist Ideal," in *The Socialist Movement* (London, 1887), p. 22, and "Industry
Under Socialism," in Shaw, *Fabian Essays*, esp. p. 169.

under which such humanitarian aims could be most fully realized.

How, then, did this Socialism differ from other Radical faiths of that decade? The Fabian answer was that it differed in its uncompromising insistence upon a "social" point of view and in its methods of translating that point of view, and the values appropriate to it, into social institutions for the future. What such institutions would be and what they would entail was not so clear, as the Fabians, for the most part, retained a tendency to distrust collectivism and to imagine that the social institutions of the future would "organize themselves" in the form of "freely-federated" industrial communes (a term that persisted in Fabian literature for many years) .[91] These, in turn, were expected to consist of federated "associations" of workmen, fulfilling the old ideal of the self-governing workshop on the larger scale required by the modern industry—a striking anticipation of early twentieth-century Guild Socialism.[92] Thus many Fabians continued to believe that the perils of big government could be overcome and the competing claims of the individual and society could be reconciled within a framework that would give full scope to the development of the "higher" social feelings.

In propounding such views in 1886, the Fabians came closest to the teaching of John Stuart Mill and his version of the English Socialist tradition. Both he and they regarded Socialism as the outcome of a high level of moral and cultural development whose achievement constituted the highest aim of human progress, but both (as liberals) were unwilling to risk any large measure of coercion for the sake of bringing it about. Hence the strong localizing tendency in early Fabian writing, and the tendency to idealize the community (or "commune") rather than the state. Hence also the strong emphasis on Socialist education and the desire to work through public opinion for the advancement of

91. This view was repeatedly expressed at the Fabian conference in June 1886, in Tract No. 4 (section on "Collectivism") , and in the Fabian essays of Shaw and Besant ("Industry Under Socialism" and "The Transition," respectively.)

92. That early Fabian tendancy toward Guild Socialism has not been sufficiently recognized, but it is quite explicit, e.g., in the expositions of both Anarchism and collectivism in Tract No. 4, and in Annie Besant's Socialist writings (including her Fabian essay) . (The best recent study of Guild Socialism is S. Glass, *The Responsible Society* [London, 1967].)

their social aims, seeking to transform the moral outlook of the populace until it was fully ready for the Socialist state, while putting Mill's theory of unearned increment to work through economic reforms in a more vigorous fashion than Mill himself would have wished. But the Fabian publications of 1886 also marked the high point of similarity between the early Fabians and Mill. Thereafter, as they developed a more complete commitment to the idea of collectivism, they necessarily moved further from Mill's idea of Socialism and closer to the idea of Socialism that had been propounded by the Democratic Federation in the early eighties. Despite that tendency, however, they never entirely lost sight of the moral and cultural aims that had originally drawn them to Socialism; and they never abandoned the implicit commitment to liberal values that continued to separate them, in practice, from their fellow collectivists of the SDF.

8

The Final Stage in the Development of
Fabian Doctrine: The Theory of Collectivism

> Socialism is the outcome, the legitimate and necessary outcome, of
> Radicalism; . . . the main current of Radical legislation, despite little
> eddies and backwaters, sets toward Socialism; . . . just as Evolution,
> taking up the chaos of biological facts, set them forth as an intel-
> ligible and correlated order, so Socialism, dealing with the chaos of
> sociological facts, brings a unifying principle, which turns Radicalism
> from a mere empirical system into a reasoned, coherent, and scientific
> whole.
>
> ANNIE BESANT, *Radicalism and Socialism*[1]

The early Fabians were Radicals both by inclination and early
training, and some, including most of the converts of the mid-
eighties, had been active in Radical politics prior to becoming
Socialists. Thus a smooth transition to the kind of Radical collectivism that is evident throughout much of the *Fabian Essays*
would appear to have been their natural course. In 1886, however,
few of the leading Fabians were favorably disposed to such collectivism, and none were willing to make it the basis of their faith.
Sidney Webb, for example, proclaimed that "it would be no more
fair to identify Socialism with Collectivism than to identify Christianity with Primitive Methodism"; Sydney Olivier complained
that the public too often "misunderstood" Socialism in the sense
of "national collectivism"; and Graham Wallas accepted the idea
of public ownership only as a means of preventing property from
falling into the hands of unmoralized stockholders.[2] Finally,
though he was less strongly inclined toward Anarchism than he
had been in 1885, Bernard Shaw still regarded collectivists as the

---

1. From the London, 1887 ed., p. 4. Hyndman had also advanced a similar argument in "The Radicals and Socialism," *Nin. Cen.* (Nov. 1885), pp. 833 ff.

2. S. Webb, "What Socialism Means," *Prac. Soc.* (July 1886); S. Olivier, "Idols of
the Sty," pt. 2, *To-day* (October 1888); and G. Wallas, "Morals of Interest," WP,
box 16. (For discussion of the concept of moralization, see chap. 6.) Wallas cautiously added that collectivism should be avoided wherever it would involve the
loss of over 75 percent of present interest.

"Torys" of Socialism and collectivism as a doctrine incompatible with his libertarian beliefs.[3]

Thus the leading Fabians in 1886 seem to have taken a position very similar to that of John Stuart Mill, holding that while, on grounds of abstract justice, the state might do anything necessary or desirable for public welfare, in practice, its actions must be restrained by considerations of expedience.[4] And to judge from their report, *Government Organization of Unemployed Labour,* the Fabians had no higher opinion of the expedience of collectivism than Mill himself. They praised the social and moral advantages of public employment, but regarded it as so "notoriously inefficient" and so inherently uneconomic that in the end they could only approve of the public ownership and management of such restricted activities as the sale of liquor and the supply of gas and water—both proposals endorsed by Joseph Chamberlain—the railways, tobacco cultivation, and the organization of rural "land armies" (the last being a form of make-work for the unemployed). All were traditional Radical proposals (some of them endorsed by Mill as early as 1848), so that only by combining all of them in one program could the Fabians be said to stand in advance even of the "New Radicalism" of their time.[5] In 1886, however, they were not inclined to work vigorously even for that much, because they regarded such proposals as a very subordinate part of Socialism.

1. Radical Collectivism in Fabian Theory

There was, however, one influential voice within the Fabian Society that consistently urged the opposite point of view, and for that reason Annie Besant must be regarded as the original archi-

3. G. B. Shaw, "Points Disputed Among Socialists," lecture, 1886, BM 50698.

4. See, e.g., P. Chubb, "Schismatic Socialism," *To-day* (July 1888) : 4.

5. *The Government Organisation of Unemployed Labour* (1886). The "Gothenburg Programme" of public liquor sale had long been advocated by the temperance wing of the Radical Party; railway nationalization had been advocated by another wing, headed by Sir Rowland Hill (see E. E. Barry, *Nationalisation in Great Britain* [Stanford, 1965], pp. 85–88) ; tobacco culture was virtually unknown in England and was therefore a good experimental field for public enterprise; and municipalization of gas and water was advocated by Radicals in many urban areas (and already widely implemented there by the late 1880s) .

tect of Fabian collectivism. From the beginning of 1886 she took the initiative in drawing the Fabian Society into greater involvement with Radical politics, which, in turn, inspired a greater emphasis on Radical collectivism as the means of making Fabian Socialism meaningful and "practicable" in current political terms. (And these were precisely the grounds on which the Fabian Society eventually adopted a collectivist program.) Such an approach was also a very appropriate one for Annie Besant. Of all the Fabian converts of the mid-eighties, she was the most politically experienced and the most actively involved in Radical politics. As we have seen, she had also come to Socialism by way of an increasing acceptance of advanced Radical social reforms, which gradually drew her to collectivism. Thus of all the Fabians whose writings have survived she was the most ready to identify Socialism with collectivism and the most anxious to bring Socialists into Radical politics in its support.[6]

She was not alone in that enterprise, however, since almost from the time she joined the Society she was strongly supported by two coworkers whose contributions to Fabian collectivism were almost as important as her own. They were Hubert Bland, Honorary Treasurer of the Society, and Thomas Bolas, publisher of its unofficial journal, the *Practical Socialist*. Bland (as mentioned in chapter 5) was Tory-Radical in politics and brought to Fabian discussions of Socialism the same attitude of noblesse oblige and temperamental sympathy for collectivism that Hyndman and his coworkers had imparted to the SDF (of which Bland and his wife were very briefly members).[7] But the Fabian Society was his more natural habitat, both because of its middle-class intellectual character, which he shared, and because he almost immediately established himself as its dominant personality. In the latter capacity he utilized his powerful persuasive skills to promote a combination

6. Regarding her conversion, see pp. 236–37 above. Her views are set forth in a remarkable series of pamphlets published between 1885 and 1887 and collected as *Essays on Socialism* (London, 1887).

7. The Blands were SDF members only from the beginning of 1885 to the "Tory Gold" scandal of Dec. 1885 (see H. W. Lee and E. Archbold, *Social Democracy in Great Britain* [London, 1935], p. 93). For Bland's beliefs and attitudes, see H. Bland, *Essays by Hubert* (London, 1914), and *With the Eyes of a Man* (London, 1905); for a biographical sketch, see Appendix B.

of Radical collectivism and independent Socialist politics that made him a natural ally of Annie Besant. Bolas's political origins are more obscure, but it is clear that he came to Socialism by way of a rather cranky obsession with railway nationalization, and therefore as a collectivist.[8] The early issues of the *Practical Socialist* (one of a series of little magazines he printed at his "chemical, electrical, and technological laboratories" in Chiswick) consistently identified Socialism with Radical collectivism, even to the extent of heaping praise on Joseph Chamberlain as the "fearless and outspoken exponent of the main essentials of Socialism," and of insisting editorially that every step that made public authority and regulation more acceptable to the public was a step forward for the Socialist cause. It also strongly favored a working alliance with the Radical Party to promote such aims.[9]

Fortunately, political circumstances in the early months of 1886 were exceptionally favorable to the promotion of such policies. Eighteen-eighty-five had been a kind of annus mirabilis for the Radical Party, suffused with the popular excitement generated by Chamberlain's "Unauthorised Programme," and with the expectation that a genuine Radical government would soon be installed in Westminster. As a result, popular interest in Radical reform reached a new peak of intensity, and great changes were thought to be forthcoming. In contrast, 1886 was a Radical year of despair. The party was virtually shattered by Chamberlain's "defection"—his dramatic break with Gladstone—and all the bright hopes of social reconstruction were dashed against the unexpected obstacle of Home Rule. Such disasters, added to the political annihilation of Sir Charles Dilke, most popular of the London Radicals,[10] and the Liberal-Radical defeat in the General Election of 1886—all within the space of a few months—left the Radical Party not only leaderless but also demoralized and disor-

---

8. See *The Railway Reformer* (1883–84) and the Railway Reform Leaflets that he published in that interest; also Barry, *Nationalisation in Great Britain*, pp. 93 ff.

9. *Prac. Soc.* 1 (Jan., Feb., March 1886) ; its editorials also spoke well of Bismarck! Bolas subsequently founded and edited *The Socialist* (July–Dec. 1888) which shared offices with the Anarchist paper, *Freedom*, and eventually drifted into the Socialist League.

10. He was named co-respondent in the most widely publicized divorce trial of the century (see R. Jenkins, *Dilke: A Victorian Tragedy*) . For Chamberlain's "defection," see Garvin, *Chamberlain, 1885–1895*, pp. 159–97.

ganized. These circumstances, therefore, created uniquely favorable opportunities for Socialist infiltration of the Radical ranks
and raised hopes of marshaling the Radical rank-and-file behind
a Socialist-inspired leadership.

This course appeared especially promising in London, where
Chamberlain had never established an effective power base and
where the caucus system (or its centralization through the National Liberal Federation) had not yet been effectively built up.[11]
As a result, the real centers of Radical politics in London remained
intensely independent and schismatic. The most important of
them were the nearly three hundred Radical workingmens' clubs,
which combined political and social functions in various pro-
portions. In 1881, it will be recalled, the Democratic Federation
had attempted to give them unified direction and leadership, but
on terms that were unacceptable to most of the clubs, which continued to cherish a deep respect for Mr. Gladstone. In 1884, with
somewhat greater success, a loose "Radical Federation" was formed
under the leadership of London workingmen, and early in 1886
(following what was, for London Radicals, the disastrous election
of 1885) that was broadened into a Metropolitan Radical Federation, under which name it flourished for about a decade as one of
the foci of the London Radical renaissance.[12]

The other foci were the London Municipal Reform League,
a pressure group demanding full local government for London,
whose origins went back to the efforts to secure metropolitan
Home Rule by John Stuart Mill and his political patron, James
Beal,[13] and the newly organized London Liberal and Radical

11. See National Liberal Federation, *Annual Reports* (Birmingham, 1880–85):
very few London caucuses were represented in the NLF before 1886 and Chamberlain was generally unpopular in London (a fact partially confirmed by the 1885
election).

12. Regarding the Radical Clubs, see H. J. Hanham, *The Reformed Electoral
System* (London, 1968), pp. 20–23, and P. Thompson, *Socialists, Liberals and
Labour* (London, 1967), pp. 91–95; also S. Webb, *Wanted, a Programme* (London,
1888), and R. A. Woods, *English Social Movements* (New York, 1891), pp. 56–57.
For the MRF, see *The Radical* (May, 1887), and *Republican* (Feb., 1886); these
serve to correct the account in Thompson, *op. cit.*, pp. 93–94.

13. More accurately, Beal's Metropolitan Municipal Association was merged with
the Municipal Reform League in the early eighties, when the latter began to catch
on conspicuously among middle-class Radical leaders (McBriar, *Fabian Socialism*,
pp. 189–90). Webb and other Fabians were attracted to this movement but never
formally joined it.

Union. The former was the chief source of proposals for "gas and water Socialism" in London, whose lead the Fabians were at first content to follow. The latter was chiefly a coalition of the caucuses that were belatedly organized in London, chiefly under Gladstonian auspices, in 1886 and after. Its president was John Morley —a rigid and uncompromising Gladstonian from 1886 onward— but many of its rank and file were of a more radical persuasion, and in the late eighties the organization showed a marked preference for advanced Radical proposals, well to the left of those accepted by the (now Gladstonian) National Liberal Federation.[14]

Such was the political situation among London Radicals when Besant, Bland, and Bolas began their campaign to draw the Fabians more actively into politics as a ginger group on the Radical Left. Their first significant achievement was the Fabian sponsorship of a three-day conference in June 1886 designed to bring together Radical and Socialist societies of all persuasions, with the avowedly political aim of "finding some common basis on which Radicals, Socialists, and Social Reformers of all kinds can cooperate for practical work in and out of Parliament."[15] And although the reports of that conference suggest that its results were meager—certainly no new "Democratic organization" resulted therefrom—Mrs. Besant found them highly encouraging:

> On Land we found common ground: on Capital we found none: on Democratic Policy differences were fairly put and . . . there is a likelihood of agreement. There was a strong unity of feeling against the idle class; a declaration that it was the duty of all to work; a determination to destroy class difference; a belief that poverty resulted from bad social conditions and was a remediable evil.

These points, she believed, formed the necessary "basis of common action" among Radicals and Socialists, thus laying the foundation

14. For a discussion of London Radical politics, see P. Thompson, *Socialists, Liberals and Labour*, pp. 90 ff. and cf. McBriar, *Fabian Socialism*, pp. 237–39, and Webb's optimistic view in *Wanted, a Programme* and *Socialism in England*, pp. 68–69.

15. Quoted in "Fabian Notes," *Our Corner* (March, 1886) : 189. Significantly, Thomas Bolas was co-chairman of the conference committee.

for the Radicals' conversion to the Socialist faith. For having come that far, she argued, Radicals had only to follow their accepted principles logically and consistently in order to become full-fledged Socialists.[16]

In that sense, Socialism was simply the "next step in the Radical program," as Shaw (who soon became one of Annie Besant's chief supporters) proclaimed in 1887: "The new Radicalism is Socialism. [But] to call it so would be needless cruelty to the many progressively minded persons who cannot bear the name, though they are clamoring for the thing more or less intelligently at every political discussion . . . in England." But, Shaw insisted, the New Radicalism was also "practical Socialism as opposed to . . . catastrophic," because it looked to a peaceful and gradual extension of collectivist measures to accomplish the renovation of society.[17] Thus the business of "practical Socialists"—the only "realistic" politicians in Shaw's view—was to encourage that tendency among Radicals at every opportunity, always working for the great day when the merely individualist Liberals—Morley, Harcourt, Gladstone, and their ilk—would be driven into the Tory camp and the genuine Radicals would unite in a "real Party of Progress" (the "Democratic" alliance forseen by Annie Besant) that would have "practical Socialism," or collectivism, as its creed.[18]

Happily, the ultra-Radical press was equally enthusiastic. Some of its organs even exceeded Shaw and Besant in their demands for Radical-Socialist cooperation, while welcoming the Fabians warmly into the ranks of Radical politics.[19] Thus the Society quickly achieved a unique and prominent standing in advanced

16. Annie Besant, report of the conference, in *To-day* 6 (July 1886) : 14. Briefer reports of the conference were carried in *Our Corner* and *Christian Socialist* of the same month, and there is a complete longhand "Special Report" of the proceedings in BLPES.

17. Shaw, "The New Radicalism," lecture, Oct. 1887, in Crompton, *The Road to Equality*, pp. 19, 29. As evidence that such views were gaining in popularity Shaw also cited Joseph Chamberlain's recent "discovery that the Root of the Matter (i.e., Radicalism) is Socialism."

18. Shaw, letter to *The Star*, 1 April 1889, in reply to Hyndman, and compare Besant's similar view in *Radicalism and Socialism*. For Shaw's conversion to collectivism, which owed a good deal to the influence of Annie Besant, see sec. 5 below.

19. *The Radical*, Sept. 1886, editorial, citing Annie Besant, and cf. ibid. (April 1886) for earlier favorable comments on the Fabians.

Radical circles, making it that much easier for it to carry out its celebrated policy of "permeation," or infiltration. The latter strategy was intended primarily to give it influence over the Liberal and Radical associations of the metropolis, together with the Radical workingmen's clubs and their federation, which Fabian activists characteristically regarded as the powerhouses of metropolitan Radical politics.[20] Thus, in a somewhat more subtle fashion, the early Fabians revived the original ambitions of the Democratic Federation, seeking to implement them with the same historical arguments and the same (by now quite standard) collectivist proposals. Hence the policy of "permeating" Radical politics with Socialist-inspired reform proposals—the Socialist adaptation of a much older Radical tactic[21]—became the most important channel through which collectivism entered the mainstream of Fabian Socialism (see Appendix C).

This is not the place to attempt a full-scale assessment of the policy of permeation (which has been done adequately elsewhere), but the misconceptions created by some recent discussions of that subject do at least require a brief rebuttal.[22] The commonest of these misconceptions is that permeation was a policy fundamentally opposed to independent labor and Socialist politics. On the contrary, however, all known Fabian discussions in the 1880s treated the tactics of permeation, the running of independent Socialist candidates, and the eventual organization of a labor-based Socialist party (when and where sufficient popular support could be found) as complementary and mutually supportive policies. (Unlike the SDF, Fabians did not advocate the founding of a Socialist party or the running of Socialist candidates where adequate electoral support did *not* exist.)[23] As the manifesto of the Fabian

20. See Besant in *The Link*, 7 April 1888, and compare Webb's claim that "the Liberal Association . . . is the elementary form out of which all revolutions grow" (Webb to Beatrice Potter, 26 Aug. 1890. PP, II, 3, 14).

21. Sir Charles Dilke, quoted in *Pall Mall Budget*, 12 Jan. 1882.

22. It is discussed most fully in McBriar, *Fabian Socialism*, esp. pp. 95–97, 234–35, 245–48. Misconceptions are found in P. Thompson, *Socialists, Liberals and Labour*, pp. 138–42, and E. Hobsbawn, "The Lesser Fabians," in Munby, ed., *The Luddites*, pp. 233–34. For further discussion, see Appendix C.

23. This was most notoriously done by the SDF in the General Election of 1885, when all SDF candidates lost their deposits. (See chap. 3 below).

Parliamentary League (FPL), which expressed the political views of the majority of Fabians, announced in 1887:

> Until a fitting opportunity arises for putting forward Socialist candidates to form the nucleus of a Socialist party in Parliament, [the FPL will] . . . support . . . those candidates who will go furthest in the direction of Socialism. . . . In . . . local elections, the League will, as it finds itself strong enough, run candidates of its own [as in 1888]. . . . By steady work on these and similar lines, Socialists will increase their power in the community, and will before long be able to influence effectively the course of public opinion.[24]

This point of view was also presented with near unanimity in a series of articles by leading Fabians, published between 1886 and 1888,[25] which further elaborated the basic idea that infiltrating Radical organizations with Socialist ideas and programs was the best means of preparing the way for the establishment of a labor-based Socialist party. For the latter could only become a meaningful possibility when a sufficient number of Radicals—and especially of "intelligent artisans," who were now overwhelmingly organized as Radicals—had acquired a Socialist outlook. Annie Besant, the acknowledged Fabian authority on labor politics, summed up this view by insisting that "the capture of Radical organizations already existing should be the first object of the Labour Party"—a party that as yet scarcely existed—for the Radical "caucus . . . is the one effective means of organizing the [po-

24. FPL Manifesto in *Prac. Soc.* (Apr. 1887): 42; also Pease, *History of the Fabian Society*, pp. 68–69, and p. 260 below. Regarding Fabian participation in the 1888 London School Board election, see the appendix below.

25. These articles, grouped by journals in which they appeared, were: *Practical Socialist*: H. Bland, "The Socialist Party in Relation to Politics" (Oct. 1886) ; J. B. Bright, "English Possibilists" (Jan. 1887) ; H. Bland, "The Socialist Party in Relation to Politics (II) ," (Feb. 1887). *To-day*: [S. Webb] "The Present Crisis in the Socialist Movement" (June 1887) ; E. R. Pease, "The Labour Federation," (June 1887) ; [H. Bland] Editorial Notes (July 1887) ; H. Bland, "The Need of a New Departure" (Nov. 1887) ; P. Chubb, "The Two Alternatives" (Sept. 1887) . *Our Corner*: articles by Annie Besant cited in chap. 7 above. *The Link*: lead articles by Annie Besant, esp. 7 April, 1888. References to the Fabian debate on Socialist politics contained in these articles by, e.g., McBriar and Hobsbawm, have failed to note the high degree of consensus that they reveal.

tential] Labour majority," and thus of creating a viable basis for future Socialist politics.[26] Significantly, this policy of permeation closely approximated the method of promoting Socialist politics that was advocated by Karl Marx, in sharp contrast to the methods actually employed by the SDF.[27]

Fabian acceptance of permeation, however, was never quite complete in the late eighties, due to continued opposition from the Fabian Anarchists, who were opposed both to political activity and to collectivism of any kind. That opposition was taken very seriously by Shaw, who tended to exaggerate its magnitude, it inspired all of Bland's early counter-arguments in favor of Fabian involvement in politics,[28] and so long as it lasted the society was inhibited from adopting a clear statement in favor of collectivism. The impasse was finally resolved in the fall of 1886 when Bland and Besant promoted the establishment of a separate Fabian Parliamentary League with the purpose of bringing "Socialism to bear on current politics, and organizing the Socialist vote." This ad hoc organization, created to outflank the Fabian Anarchists, then became the major seedbed of both Fabian politics and Fabian collectivism, remaining throughout the 1880s the only branch of the Society to which collectivist objectives were specifically ascribed:

> Now that the doctrine of *laissez-faire* has fallen into disrepute, and the right of the State to compete with private enterprise is admitted and acted upon [stated the new Fabian "Basis" of 1887], the Fabian Parliamentary League sees a peaceful and expeditious path to Socialism, through such measures as

26. *Link,* lead article, 7 Apr. 1888. The term "Labour Party" (used almost interchangeably with "Socialist party") referred merely to a (mostly unorganized) "movement of men and women," working by "common methods" toward the "common end" of labor emancipation. (See H. Bland, "The Need of a New Departure," *To-day* 8, p. 132.)

27. See Henry Collins, "The Marxism of the SDF," in Briggs and Saville, eds., *Essays in Labour History, 1886–1923* (London, 1971), p. 47. For further discussion of permeation, see the Appendix C.

28. Bland to Shaw, 25 Sept. 1886 (BM 50511). Bland's early political writings were also strenuously anti-Anarchist.

Nationalisation of Railways, Municipalisation of Ground Rents and of industries connected with local transit, and with supply of gas and water in the towns.[29]

No other Fabian statement of the eighties was so explicit about collectivism or about the "path" by which it might be reached. But it is equally significant that the items to be "collectivised" in the FPL program remained virtually unchanged from the Fabian report on unemployment of 1886. They were still the standard measures of Radical collectivism, now moved from the background to the foreground of Fabian reform programs—or rather they reached the foreground of Fabian programs a year later when the Society as a whole was merged with the FPL and quietly accepted its political objectives. If the Fabians of the late eighties differed programmatically from advanced Radicals such as Dilke, Labouchere, or the members of the London Municipal Reform League,[30] therefore, it was chiefly with regard to their ultimate ambitions and in their belief that piecemeal reforms would carry them by degrees to a fully collectivised economy. This, at least, was the implication of their rhetoric, but it remains doubtful whether many of the early Fabians ever accepted that vision in its integrity. Instead, they regarded the projected Socialist consummation as so distant that it became fashionable to argue that it need never arrive in any full-fledged form.[31] Thus the Fabians' acceptance of collectivism was never so complete as it appeared to be in the more sweeping examples of their rhetoric.

29. Revised Fabian Basis, in "Socialist Notes," *Our Corner* (July 1887). Regarding the founding of FPL, see *Prac. Soc.* (Oct., Nov. 1886), and Pease, *History of the Fabian Society*, pp. 67–69.

30. Dilke was politically quarantined in the late eighties but was developing into a moderate Socialist; Labouchere advocated, perhaps, the most advanced Radical program of any M.P. in 1885–86: severe death duties and a steeply graduated income tax ("The Three Programmes, No. 3," *Fort. Rev.* [Oct. 1885]); the LMRL advocated municipalization of public utilities, including transport (which was subsequently the policy of the London Progressive Party).

31. See esp. Shaw, "The Illusions of Socialism," in Carpenter, ed., *Forecasts of the Coming Century* (Manchester, 1897), also reprinted in Laurence, ed., *Selected Non-Dramatic Writings*, pp. 406–26, and Bland's complaints in his Fabian essay (1889 ed., pp. 211–14), which turned out to be thoroughly justified.

2. *Social Darwinism and Fabian Theory: Besant's Doctrine of Collectivism*

Most of the Fabian arguments for collectivism in the late eighties rested (perhaps unconsciously) on the fundamental ambiguity that pervaded the use of that term (and of the term Socialism) in its commonest sense.[32] For the public regulation of specific industrial functions and a fully collectivised economy were, in reality, two quite different things. But the same term was so commonly used in reference to both, and it was so frequently asserted by enemies of state interference that every extension of public authority helped to push the nation closer to the brink of Socialism, that it seemed merely commonplace to conclude that the difference between complete collectivism and a limited (but increasing) tendency to state interference *was* only a matter of degree.[33] It was also almost as commonplace to argue, as Besant did, that "the main current of Radical legislation . . . sets toward Socialism"—an argument that she might have borrowed either from Hyndman or from Herbert Spencer in the early eighties.[34] Nevertheless, the historical argument for Socialism was ultimately unsatisfactory in that form, as it suggested no compelling reason why collectivism should be consciously extended to the point of complete ownership of the means of production and distribution. Hence the need for a new and more elaborate theory to link collectivism more closely with the most popular intellectual tendencies of the age. And that work, too, was first undertaken by Annie Besant, in her Socialist pamphlets of 1885–87.

As a theorist she tended chiefly to present Socialism in terms of the currently popular Darwinian sociology. "I am a Socialist be-

---

32. *OED,* 2:621, defines collectivism, as understood in the 1880's, as the "socialistic theory of collective ownership *or control* of the means of production" (emphasis added). The word was an English neologism, recently borrowed from France, where it chiefly served as a synonym for Marxism. For further discussion, see chap. 1, n. 44 above.

33. That was, of course, the conclusion reached by Herbert Spencer in *The Man Versus the State* (London, 1884), and endlessly reiterated in the pamphlets and paper (*Jus*) of the Liberty and Property Defence League.

34. Besant, *Radicalism and Socialism,* p. 4. For comparison, see chap. 1, sec. 1 above. Spencer, of course, opposed that tendency vociferously.

cause I am a believer in Evolution," she wrote in her most popular Socialist tract, arguing that Socialism performed for politics and sociology the same function that Darwinian evolution had performed for biology: "[it] brings a unifying principle [to political theory] which turns Radicalism from a mere empirical system into a reasoned, coherent, and scientific whole." And it was this attempt to present Socialism "scientifically," as the necessary outcome of social evolution, that dominated her theoretical writing in the late eighties. For "Science," she insisted,

> can grasp tendencies of the present, and recognising the conditions of social growth of the past, can see how the present has been moulded and along which lines its further development must inevitably pass. Now the progress of society has been from individualistic anarchy to associated order; from universal, unrestricted competition to competition regulated and restrained by law, and even to partial co-operation in lieu thereof.[35]

In terms that were almost a paraphrase of Herbert Spencer, she also concluded that society was steadily "evolving towards a more highly developed individuality of units, and towards their closer co-ordination." (For good measure, it was also "evolving towards a more generous brotherhood, a more real equality, a fuller liberty.") [36]

Thus she professed to see in Spencer's "law of the integration of matter" the "scientific" basis of Socialism: the proof "that [human] progress must lie in the direction of closer social union," and in the development of centralized, collective organs of administration that such a "union" necessarily implied. Spencer, of course, had arbitrarily modified his premises rather than accept the socialistic implications of that law and of the organismic analogy on

35. *Why I Am a Socialist* (London, 1886), pp. 2 and 3 and *Radicalism and Socialism*, p. 4.

36. *The Evolution of Society* (London, 1885), p. 24; and compare Herbert Spencer's universal law of evolution: "a change from an incoherent homogeneity to a coherent heterogeneity, accompanying the dissipation of motion and the integration of matter" (*First Principles* [London, 1862], p. 291).

which it rested.[37] But among sociologists in the eighties the dominant tendency was to reject Spencer's arbitrary revisions of his own
theory and to treat the increasing integration of social units into
a more "definite and coherent" organic form as a real evolutionary
law. Such "anti-Spencerian Spencerism" obviously owed a heavy
debt to Comte's law of socialization, and another to the more popular teaching of T. H. Huxley, who insisted that the special feature
of human evolution was its conscious use of plan and forethought
to direct the progress of society.[38] Both were reflected in Annie
Besant's conclusion that society, as an evolving organism, "must
either integrate yet further," or else disintegrate. Thus, she concluded, a "closer social union," such as that proclaimed by Socialism, was the necessary means to survival and to continued material
progress for an advanced, industrial nation such as England had
become. It alone could prevent the antisocial tendencies in man—
so long encouraged by the spirit of unlimited competition—from
destroying the social organism through the struggle of conflicting
interests. Indeed, Socialism was simply a name for all the "inte-
grating" forces in society, in opposition to the "disintegrating"
ones that were a survival of "the brute." And the ultimate stage
of social integration would be collectivism itself, wherein all land
and means of production would be "property of the social union,"
"controlled" by the community for its general benefit.[39]

Such use of Social Darwinism as a foundation for collectivism
was Annie Besant's chief theoretical achievement, and it was a
natural one for a leader of the National Secular Society, where
Spencer and Huxley were regarded as oracles and evolution was

37. See W. M. Simon, "Spencer and the Social Organism," *JHI* 21 (1960) : 296.
For a defense of Spencer's use of organism, however, see J. D. Y. Peel, *Herbert
Spencer* (New York, 1971), chap. 7, esp. pp. 185 ff.

38. For the term "anti-Spencerian Spencerism" (and the debt to Comte that it
implied), see A. W. Small, *Origins of Sociology* (Chicago, 1924), p. 316. Huxley's
arguments were most fully developed in *Evolution and Ethics* (London, 1893), but
most of them were expounded earlier in "The Struggle for Existence: A Programme," *Nin. Cen.* 23 (Feb. 1888), esp. pp. 161–63, and some dated back nearly
twenty years to "Administrative Nihilism" (1871). For the impact of these articles
on Webb, see sec. 4 below.

39. *The Evolution of Society*, pp. 15–20, picturing history as a "contest" between
the "savage desire for personal accumulation" and the "social desires . . . to subordinate the individual to the general good"; and cf. *Why I Am a Socialist*, p. 2.

a sacred and unquestioned dogma.[40] Annie Besant was probably also the first English Socialist to use Social Darwinism in such a fashion; but she was preceded in that regard by at least one American, Laurence Gronlund, whose *Co-operative Common-wealth* would have been known to her, if only because Shaw was its English editor. In any case, she obtained and read that book for review just before producing her main series of Socialist tracts, and the results were immediately apparent.[41] Within a month she had adopted Gronlund's Spencerian arguments as her own, and had greatly widened her idea of "the sphere of the state" and of the feasibility of a centralized economy. Gronlund's American examples, which showed industry already centralized and administered by salaried managers to an extent still almost unknown in England, demonstrated to her that massive, centralized production was more efficient than the sort of individualistic production, organized in small firms, that was still the norm of English industry. Because it was so profitable, such centralization was the inevitable tendency of industrial growth; but the "social union" rather than the individual capitalist should be its beneficiary. Thus Besant found the "chief merit" of Gronlund's book in its proofs that "we have already growing in our midst the seeds of Socialism, and that the English nation has in working order many institutions which can readily be transformed into Socialistic centers of business." In short, she learned the lesson of economic gradualism and the idea of the managerial state from Gronlund—in spite of the fact that Gronlund, himself, in his first edition, had insisted on the necessity of revolution.[42]

40. See, e.g., E. Aveling, *The Gospel of Evolution* (part of The Atheist's Platform, published by Bradlaugh and Besant [London, 1884]).

41. Laurence Gronlund, *The Cooperative Commonwealth in its Outlines: An Exposition of Modern Socialism* (Boston and New York, 1884); English edition, revised by G. B. Shaw (London, 1885). Shaw's revisions were extensive but only stylistic. Now see the new critical edition, with an introduction by Stow Persons (Cambridge, Mass., 1965). "Publisher's Corner," *Our Corner* (July 1885) lists the book as received for reviewing. The same month began the serialization of "The Evolution of Society," the first of Besant's Socialist essays to employ organismic arguments.

42. Besant, review of *The Cooperative Commonwealth*, in *Our Corner* 6 (Sept. 1885): 162–65, and cf. S. Persons' introduction to *The Cooperative Commonwealth* (Cambridge, Mass., 1965), pp. xxiv–xxv. The second edition was gradualist.

It is less clear how such arguments impressed other Fabians. Gronlund's book was widely read in 1885 and 1886, but apart from Besant's comments, only Shaw's and Wallas's have come to light, and their comments were both disparaging.[43] Nevertheless, many of Gronlund's arguments about the role of middle-class intellectuals—for example, that they must provide the necessary motive power for social transformation and mold public opinion into a form capable of sustaining the Socialist state—suggest beliefs that Fabians themselves were currently developing and must, at least, have provided reinforcement for their own ideas.

Gronlund's work, however, was essentially a popularization of German Social-Democratic theory, much modified by his American experience and humanitarian outlook, but still (in the first edition) well within the tradition of vulgarized Marxism. And that bias undoubtedly reduced its appeal for the Fabian converts who, after 1886, were to take the leading role in fashioning the Society's doctrines: Shaw, Webb, Olivier, and Wallas. Their ideas, in contrast, came not so much from Gronlund, or from any existing school of Socialist theory, as from four broad intellectual tendencies that were characteristic products of the new British climate of opinion of the 1880s. Briefly, these were: (1) the social theory of Comte, especially as it stood for a moral equivalent of collectivism; (2) the tendency to anti-Spencerian Spencerism in contemporary sociology, which drew heavily on Comte, especially in the work of Lester Frank Ward; (3) the tendency to reject laissez-faire and to take a broadly social view of economic policy, characteristic of the new economic movement of the late eighties; and (4) the Neo-Idealist philosophy emanating from Oxford. All were fundamentally evolutionary and historical in character—that was the distinctive feature of the new climate of opinion—and all except the last derived their original impetus from Comte.

3. Sources of the Fabian Theory of Collectivism

Throughout the 1880s Comte's teaching remained the most powerful intellectual influence on the formation of Fabian theory.

43. Shaw regarded *The Cooperative Commonwealth* as a "clever book" but unoriginal, and complained that Gronlund had "no adequate notion of . . . the extent to which ideas he evidently regards as startling novelties have become common property here" (*Justice*, 13 July 1885). Wallas criticized Gronlund in *Fabian Essays*, pp. 131, 133; also p. 137.

As Pease noted, it "offered solutions for all the problems that faced us. It suggested a new heaven, of a sort, and it proposed a new earth, free from all the inequalities of wealth, the preventable suffering, the reckless waste of effort, which we saw around us." [44] In the event, very few of the early Fabians accepted Comte's method of social reconstruction—Webb was, for a time, almost unique as a Fabian spokesman for that—but they were deeply influenced by Comte's fundamental concepts and by his approach to the problems of society. Most of the leading Fabians in the eighties derived from Comte the idea of a "scientific" social reconstruction conceived on evolutionary lines and sought to find in his new social science the means of bringing it about. From Comte, too, many of them learned the first lesson of Socialist theory: that traditional individualism was conceptually inadequate—a mere "abstraction" belonging to the "metaphysical stage" of intellectual development—and that it must be superceded by a theory with a broader social focus: the community or even "Humanity" as a whole. Comte's theory also made society itself into a "real universal": a living organism with its own purposes and laws of historical development, a seat of values in its own right, and the appropriate standard of judgment for all social and economic issues.[45] And to such arguments, finally, it added the appeal of its evolutionary basis and the sanction of historical inevitability.

It is, therefore, not inaccurate to say that the Fabian theory of collectivism in the late eighties derived its conceptual framework largely from Positivism, and that its main ideas were those of Comte, recast but still in recognizable form. This is especially true of the moral aspect of collectivism, whose essence was the subordination of individual advantage to the common good. Even "sanitary regulation," Comte wrote (anticipating one of Sidney Webb's favorite examples), "is ennobled by knowing that the object of it is to make us . . . more fit for the service of others," for it is by such means that we become "habituated to the feeling

44. Pease, *History of the Fabian Society*, p. 18, and cf. chap. 6, sec. 2 above for a fuller discussion of Comte's influence in the 1880s; also G. Wallas, "The Social Motive," *Fabian News* (May 1915): 42–43, and R. Harrison, *Before the Socialists* (London, 1965), pp. 333 ff.

45. See H. Marcuse, *Reason and Revolution*, 2d ed. (New York, 1954), p. 359; and for further discussion of Comte's "collectivism," cf. F. A. Hayek, *The Counter-Revolution in Science* (Glencoe, Ill., 1952), pt. 2, chap. 6, and pt. 3, passim.

of subordination to Humanity." [46] In more conventional economic terms, he also taught that "all material wealth is the common product of society . . . and is never merely an individual creation;" and although he drew from that doctrine the conclusion that "moralised" capitalists should henceforth act as trustees for the wealth of the community (without ceasing to be property owners), it amounted, nevertheless, to a *moral* equivalent of collectivism. Finally, that collectivist tendency in Comte's teaching was also reinforced by his sociological principle that society alone is real— the individual is a mere abstraction—and by his political tendency to expand the functions of the state to "the greatest [possible] extent," as Herbert Spencer complained. [47] The Positivist theory of industrial society also emphasized the advantages of economic centralization (a concept closely allied with collectivism), and praised the greater efficiency made possible by mass production, increased concentration of capital (oligopoly), and the resulting elimination of wasteful competition [48]—all points that Webb, at least, was quick to develop in his own writing. And while none of the latter arguments overtly advocated collectivism, all helped to create the oligopolistic–bureaucratic economic ideal on which the Fabian theory of collectivism largely rested. [49]

Such were also the intellectual foundations of Sidney Webb's claim that collectivism was "the positive stage of Comtism." [50] For the collectivist implications of Comte's social teaching were unmistakable, however much the English Positivists might deny them, and Webb's idea of collectivism in the late 1880s was almost entirely derived from them. This was at least partially evident in his Fabian essay, where the arguments for collectivism showed a

46. Comte, *General View*, p. 104, and cf. Webb, *Socialism in England*, p. 12.

47. Comte, *Cours de philosophie positive*, ed. E. Littré, 6 vols., 2d ed. (Paris, 1864), 6:590, and cf. F. Harrison, *National and Social Problems*, p. 429, and chap. 6 above. Spencer is quoted in Abrams, *Origins of British Sociology*, p. 56.

48. See, e.g., the Positivist J. H. Bridges's claim that "to us the concentration of wealth in a small number of holders is absolutely essential to its efficiency," quoted in F. Maxse, *Causes of Social Revolt* (London, 1872), p. 50 n., and cf. R. Harrison, *Before the Socialists*, pp. 269–72.

49. Hayek, *Counter-Revolution*, pp. 58, 91–92, also argues that Comte's social holism was "methodologically collectivist" and led, in practice, to political collectivism. (Cf. p. 53 for a definition of "methodological collectivism.")

50. For the full quotation see the epigraph to chap. 6 above, and Carpenter, ed., *Forecasts of the Coming Century*, p. 153 n.

heavy indebtedness to Comte.[51] Moreover, Webb's very notion of collectivism was an elaboration of Comte's idea of economic trusteeship, now transferred from individual captains of industry (in Comte's version) to the elected representatives of the community at large. In effect, this was a restatement of the Positivist social ideal in democratic terms, giving to elected officeholders the powers that Comte had reserved to a privileged class. It was, therefore, through his belief in democracy that Webb diverged most significantly from Comte, whose teaching otherwise remained his social inspiration. It was because Comte had rejected democracy and had trusted, instead, in the sanctions of an organized religious cult that "Comtism" could be no more than the "metaphysical stage of Collectivism." And it was precisely because modern collectivism was grounded on Radical democracy—the mainspring of modern political evolution, as Webb saw it—that it had become the "positive stage of Comtism." [52]

Among the early Fabians such direct derivation of collectivist beliefs from Comte was probably limited to Webb, but nearly all of them found important reinforcement for their theories of collectivism in Comte's organismic concept of society.[53] For if society was indeed an organism with a central brain and nervous system controlling its subordinate organs, none of which could survive apart from the organism as a whole, this made the case

51. At the outset of his Fabian essay, e.g., Webb went out of his way to describe Comte as a founder of the trends in modern thought that led to Socialism: the evolutionary and organismic tendencies later developed by Darwin, Spencer, and Huxley. Webb's view of history, the conceptual basis of his essay, was also derived from Comte, being based on an alternation of "organic" and critical (or, in Webb's phrase, "anarchical") stages of intellectual history, leading ultimately to a new age of science. Finally, Webb's idea of social organism was essentially Comtian (and entirely anti-Spencerian in its applications). See Shaw, *Fabian Essays*, (jubilee ed.), pp. 53–56, 31–32, 43, and Webb, *Socialism in England*, pp. 11–12, 44.

52. Shaw, *Fabian Essays*, (jubilee ed.), pp. 31 ff., 57, and cf. Webb's repeated references to J. K. Ingram, complete Positivist and author of the article "Political Economy," in *Encyclopedia Britannica*, 9th ed., vol. 19, as an "avowed Socialist," and to his Positivist-inspired arguments as bulwarks of Socialist theory. (See Webb, *English Progress Toward Social Democracy*, p. 3, and Webb, *Socialism in England*, pp. 47, 49.)

53. Regarding Olivier, Wallas, and Besant, see chap. 7 above, and Harrison, *Before the Socialists*, pp. 337–41. For discussion of Comte's organismic concept, see *Cours*, 4:235–53, 417, and F. W. Coker, *Organismic Concepts of the State* (New York, 1910), pp. 115–16, 123–24.

for political collectivism seem almost irresistible. Spencer, as has been seen, denied that the organismic analogy had such implications, and even Comte demurred to the extent of firmly separating the spiritual and temporal powers in a curiously medieval fashion. But the organismic analogy itself provided no grounds for making such a separation. Rather, its most obvious political implication was that all social functions should be subordinated to one central power, the state. And that became the dominant tendency of British sociological thinking in the 1880s—especially after Herbert Spencer's brief English influence went into eclipse. Thereafter, British sociology developed generally along the lines marked out by Comte: melioristic, evolutionary, and increasingly collectivist in outlook. And while it avoided any of Comte's specific social remedies, it applied the organismic analogy with a degree of literalness and comprehensiveness that was undreamed of even in Comte's doctrinaire philosophy.[54] Such was the tendency, especially powerful in England in the later eighties and nineties, that seemed to place the stamp of social science on the emerging Fabian doctrines of collectivism.[55]

Curiously, however, the sociologist who most fully elaborated the Comtian and anti-Spencerian tendencies outlined above, and whose thinking most closely resembled that of the early Fabians, was not British at all. He was the American, Lester Frank Ward, whose *Dynamic Sociology,* published in 1883, began to make an impact in Fabian circles some three years later.[56] His argument

54. See, e.g., Leslie Stephen, *The Science of Ethics* (London, 1882), whose extravagant organismic analogies must have influenced many Fabians; also the work of L. T. Hobhouse. (See Abrams, *Origins,* pp. 57–58, 84 ff.). Derivation of the (anti-Spencerian) organismic analogy from Comte rather than from the various German sociologists who developed it more elaborately is predicated on Fabian ignorance of such German scholarship—with the exception of A. Schaeffle, *The Quintessence of Socialism,* trans. under supervision of B. Bosanquet (London, 1889), which was widely and approvingly read by Fabians.

55. Conversely, Fabian writing of the later 1880s also *contributed* to the development of this tendency in sociological thought—esp. in the work of L. T. Hobhouse (a close friend of the Webbs), whose characteristic social views were largely anticipated by the early Fabians.

56. Lester F. Ward, *Dynamic Sociology,* 2 vols. (New York, 1883). There was no English edition. For commentary, see R. Hofstader, *Social Darwinism in American Life* (New York, 1944). Sociologists of the late nineteenth century characteristically treated social reconstruction as the implicit object of their study.

that society possessed a "collective mind" which directed and was capable of modifying its evolution so as better to fulfill its basic needs—the theory of "telic" or purposeful evolution—strongly influenced some of the early Fabians. Happily, both England and America in the 1880s had entered upon the "telic" evolutionary phase, wherein "man is just as able to control society for his own good as he has been able to control other parts of nature," as a Fabian exponent of Ward's theory argued in 1887. Socialism, in that writer's view, was simply the purposeful and scientifically directed use of "group feelings" and the "collective mind" to produce a planned and intelligently controlled evolution, rather than the haphazard, "anarchic" evolution of the past. Thus, with some justification, Fabians could proclaim that collectivism, implemented gradually and intelligently, was a "direct result" of the new tendencies in sociology, and "the logical outcome of the scientific progress of mankind." [57]

Thereafter, the only remaining obstacles to a theory of collectivism seemed to lie in the domain of economics, in the traditional objections of economic theory to any systematic reliance on the state. Especially among the younger economists of the 1880s, however, new intellectual tendencies were at work, and in the late eighties these seemed to flow together from all sides to form a "new school," imbued with the sociological and humanitarian attitudes of the decade. Orthodox Positivists were quick to claim that the influence of Comte had been decisive in its formation— especially as one of its hallmarks was subordination of strict economic aims to broader social and ethical considerations: to sociology, in fact.[58] But that tendency may be more properly traced

57. W. H. Utley, "Scientific Aspects of Socialism," *Our Corner* 9 (Feb. 1887) : 82 ff. citing Ward, *Dynamic Sociology*. Ward himself scarcely went that far. He was not a Socialist, but he clearly opposed laissez-faire and advocated greatly increased state interference. Huxley's similar arguments were another source of such ideas (see Huxley, "Struggle for Existence," *Nin. Cen.* 23 [1888], and Comte, *General View*, p. 165) .

58. Of the extensive contemporary literature on the "new school," see esp.: H. S. Foxwell, "The Economic Movement in England," *QJE* 2 (1887) (the journal itself also strongly supported the "new school") ; C. H. Dunbar, "The Reaction in Political Economy," *QJE* 1 (1886) ; E. Caird, "Political Economy, Old and New," *QJE* 2 (1887) ; W. Smart, "The Old Economy and the New," *Fort. Rev.* 52 n.s. (Sept. 1891) ; and R. T. Ely, *The Past and Present of Political Economy* (Baltimore, 1884) , chap. 4.

to Mill and to his insistence on the primacy of social values, while, in the eighties, it was reinforced by practically all schools of British social reformers: by English Positivists, by humanitarians such as Arnold Toynbee and Canon Barnett, by moralists such as Ruskin and Thomas Davidson, by Christian Socialists, and by the English historical school of economics, one of whose chief objectives was the redirection of economic theory to a greater concern with positive social welfare.[59]

By the late eighties the impact of the "new school" on the direction of economic thinking had become very evident among the younger economists and their professors. Indeed, the most influential economic teachers of the decade—the recognized leaders of the new movement—were Marshall, Walker, and Jevons: precisely the men whose theory most successfully combined historical, humanitarian, and social reforming tendencies in economic thought with renewed devotion to abstract theory. (They were also the economists who most deeply influenced Fabian thought.) Marshall, in fact, regarded the hope of social amelioration as the central purpose of economic study, and, in contrast to the older watchword of laissez-faire, coined the slogan, "let the state be up and doing." And the other leaders of the new economic movement were scarcely less emphatic in insisting on the need for public initiative to resolve deep-rooted social problems.[60]

None of these arguments, in the eyes of their exponents, con-

59. See J. K. Ingram, *History of Political Economy* (Edinburgh, 1888; rev. ed., London, 1915), pp. 191 ff., and F. Harrison, *National and Social Problems*, p. 407 (both by Positivists); T. Davidson, *Moral Aspects of the Economic Question*, pp. 11, 20, and A. Toynbee, "Ricardo and the Old Political Economy," in *Industrial Revolution*, pp. 163–64; T. Wodehouse, *A Grammar of Socialism*; A. W. Coats, "The Historical Reaction in English Political Economy," *Economica* (1954); also, for examples of the latter, see T. E. Cliffe Leslie, *Essays* (London, 1879), David Syme, *Outlines of an Industrial Science* (London, 1875), and J. Rae, *Contemporary Socialism*, pp. 200–20.

60. Foxwell, "Economic Movement in England," p. 100; also E. Caird, "Political Economy," *QJE* 2, (1887) pp. 213–15; A. Marshall, "The Present Position of Economics" (1885), in A. C. Pigou, ed., *Memorials of Alfred Marshall* (London, 1925), pp. 173–74; and Pigou, in ibid., p. 84. Also Hutchinson, *Review of Economic Doctrines*, pp. 9, 46 ff., 66–67. For Walker, see his "Recent Progress in Economics," in *Publications of the American Economic Association*, 4 (Baltimore, 1889): 17–39, and, for W. S. Jevons, *The State in Relation to Labour* (London, 1882) —a book much quoted by Fabians.

stituted Socialism (although Marshall, at least, admitted that economists could gain important insights from the older Socialist tradition) .[61] But in popular usage, almost anything that was not strict individualism might be called Socialism—the "we are all Socialists now" syndrome—and no distinction was commonly made in terminology between state interference and complete central-ization. It was, therefore, in this loose, popular sense that Fabians such as Webb sought to prove "that all the younger [economists] are now Socialists, with many of their professors," and to imply that, by extension, this gave scientific support to the Fabian theories of collectivism.[62] Webb even went so far as to write to Alfred Marshall, urging him to declare himself Socialist. "I believe we agree absolutely in economics and practically in politics," Webb concluded. "I am accepted by the Socialists as one of them," and Marshall, presumably, would be accepted also.[63] If Webb was, in fact, a Socialist only in the loose sense in which the term might have been applied to Marshall, and to such younger economists as Edwin Cannan,[64] it is a fact of no small significance. For the present, however, it will be enough to note that the "new school" of economics helped to create a climate of opinion in the late eighties that was more favorable to the propagation and develop-ment of collectivist ideas; and the Fabians were among the first to benefit from it.

Finally, the new philosophy of British Idealism is evident in Fabian writing of the late eighties—the latest and least conspicu-ous of the new intellectual tendencies. In a watered-down and idiosyncratic form some elements of Idealism had been injected

61. Marshall, "Present Position of Economics," in Pigou, ed., *Memorials of Alfred Marshall*, pp. 156, 173; also J. M. Keynes, "Alfred Marshall," in ibid., pp. 20, 50.

62. *Socialism in England*, p. 46; also Webb's claim that "the scientific difference between the 'orthodox' economists and the economic Socialists has now become mainly one of relative stress" (ibid.) .

63. Webb to Marshall, 28 Feb. 1889, PP, II—probably an extension of the argu-ment quoted above.

64. Cannan, who subsequently became professor of economics at the London School of Economics, was cautiously favorable to collectivism. (See his Fabian lecture, "Economics and Socialism" [1889], in Cannan Collection, BLPES.) Conse-quently, Webb also wrote to him that he "followed Mill in calling myself a Socialist. Don't you?" (Webb to Cannan, [1889], ibid.)

into Fabian theory through the work of Thomas Davidson, and were reinforced by the popularity of Mazzini among early Fabian converts. But Idealist key words and modes of thought became conspicuous in Fabian writing only about 1888; and then they emanated chiefly from the second generation of Oxford Idealists —from D. G. Ritchie and Bernard Bosanquet (both Fabians in the early nineties), and from J. H. Muirhead (Wallas's flatmate) and his colleague in the London Ethical Society (a hotbed of Idealism), William Clarke.[65] What they passed on to Fabian theory, however, amounted to little more than terminology— "Zeitgeist," "the Social Ideal," and "the State" (which still had foreign overtones in English)[66]—plus new ways of stating the already commonplace doctrine of social evolution. The main function of that philosophy, then, was to reinforce the tendencies already set in motion by Positivism, Darwinism (especially in its sociological form), and the "new" economics: the already pervasive view that the "State" was a real "moral organism," with its citizens indissolubly bound together as "members one of another," so that, from its very nature, it had the duty of removing hindrances to public welfare and of creating the positive opportunities that individuals required to develop to their fullest stature.[67] To such essentially liberal teachings, Idealism seemed to add a higher philosophic sanction than they had previously enjoyed.

65. Ritchie's *Darwinism and Politics* (London, 1889), a reply to Herbert Spencer's ultra-individualism, was originally presented as lectures to the Fabian Society in the summer of 1888. Bosanquet lectured to the Fabian Society in February 1890 on his theory of "moral Collectivism" (see "Individualism and Socialism Philosophically Considered," *Charity Organization Review*, 69 [Sept. 1890]), and he also noted that the Fabians were becoming more influenced by "German ideas" (to F. Peters, 18 July 1890, in J. H. Muirhead, ed., *Bernard Bosanquet and His Friends* [London, 1935], p. 74).

66. See G. Sabine, *A History of Political Theory*, rev. ed. (New York, 1956), p. 739; A. Ulam, *Philosophical Foundations of English Socialism* (Cambridge, Mass., 1951), p. 31; and M. Arnold, *Culture and Anarchy* (1869. Cambridge, Eng., 1960), p. 75. As if to emphasize its foreignness, the word "State" was frequently capitalized and put between quotation marks in English writing of the 1880s.

67. The classic statements of these views are B. Bosanquet, *The Philosophical Theory of the State* (London, 1899), and D. G. Ritchie, *The Principles of State Interference* (London, 1891). For recent commentaries, see Richter, *Politics of Conscience*, pp. 332–33, and S. R. Letwin, *The Pursuit of Certainty* (Cambridge, Eng., 1965), pp. 338–41; and cf. nn. 92 and 93 below.

4. Webb's Doctrine of Collectivism

The evidence of such Idealism in Fabian writing of the eighties was probably clearest in Sidney Webb's doctrine of collectivism, which became the focus of his Socialist theory in 1888–89. It may be seen especially in his tendency to view Socialism–collectivism as a kind of world-historical idea, progressively manifesting itself through changes in the thought and institutions of the present age and drawing nourishment from all its chief intellectual tendencies. (The endless instances of public regulations that he cited in those years, in lists that often extended over a page, were offered as evidence of that tendency, demonstrating its broad pervasiveness.) [68] A further Idealist influence may be seen in Webb's adaptation of the Hegelian idea of freedom (which he partially disguised by the language of Social Darwinism) in his statement that the fullest freedom is found in spontaneous acceptance of laws and regulations that are for the public good, through a complete internalization of the "social instinct embodied in the law." [69] A still more diffuse Idealist influence may be seen in the occasionally authoritarian rhetoric with which Webb elaborated his belief in the moral and practical necessity of subordinating individuals to the higher needs and purposes of society—a belief that became the foundation of his mature doctrine of collectivism.

Such teachings were not, of course, the exclusive property of Idealist philosophy (although Webb's indebtedness to that philosophy was clear from several explicit references in his writings) .[70] But Idealism did constitute at least one of the major strands in Webb's mature Socialist theory, and it was a crucially important strand because the core of his theory was the Idealist notion of collectivism as a moral concept (almost a Platonic or Hegelian

68. See, e.g., Shaw *Fabian Essays*, pp. 47 ff., Webb, *Socialism in England*, and *English Progress Toward Social Democracy*, Fabian Tract No. 15, pp. 13–14.

69. "Anarchism," PP, VI, f. 12b, concluding that men would be perfectly free when they had fully internalized all the restraints imposed by law. Thus "the amount of individual liberty to do other than the *right* course . . . is a measure of society's ignorance," Webb added.

70. See, e.g., the paradoxical reference to the master "bound" and slave "free," in "Rome," *Our Corner* 12 (Aug. 1888) : 89—a direct borrowing from Hegel's *Phenomenology of Mind*, IV A 3 c (trans. J. B. Baillie [London, 1910], pp. 184–88) .

idea), underlying and interpenetrating external, institutional changes, but never wholly identifiable with them. And it was always in this special, philosophic sense rather than in the ordinary, economic one, that Webb expounded the idea of collectivism. For example, in his correspondence with a Fabian colleague in 1888, he wrote that my theory of life is

> to feel at every moment that I am acting as a member of a committee and for that committee. . . . But I aspire *never* to act alone or for myself. This theoretically combined action involves rules, deliberation . . . and the disregard of one's own impulses, and in fact *is Collectivism*.

Elsewhere, even more pointedly, he wrote that the essence of collectivism was the "subordination of personal interest to the general good," so that every action that encouraged or embodied that tendency should be regarded as a practical manifestation of collectivism.[71]

It is probable, however, that Idealism had more to do with the form than with the substance of this doctrine, which may also be seen as an elaboration of Webb's earlier, Positivist-inspired plea for a greater consciousness of social unity, powerful enough to "break down the remnants of isolated individualism still left among us," which was already collectivist in principle. On quite a different level, it was also closely related to the "spirit of social duty" extolled by Wallas and Olivier.[72] But Webb's mature doctrine of collectivism extended beyond both the Victorian idea of duty and the Positivist idea of social solidarity to form something like a complete Weltanschauung and rule of life. These were first elaborated in a lecture to what had been the Hampstead "Marx Circle" (now renamed the Hampstead Society for the Study of Socialism) in 1888 entitled "Rome: A Sermon in Sociology." In effect, it

71. Webb to Margery Davidson (soon to become Mrs. Edward Pease), 12–13 Dec. 1888, PP, II: 2, 27, f. 69, making specific reference to the argument in "Rome" (cited in n. 73 below); and *Socialism in England*, p. 12.

72. "The Reformation," PP VI, *12*, f. 60f; and cf. chap. 6 above. See, e.g., Webb to Sir H. Bacon, 5 Aug. 1880. PP, II: 2, *24*, and Webb to Beatrice Potter, 21 Sept. 1890, PP, II: 3, *18* (notebook diary), arguing that the best way to create a spirit of collectivism was by ceaseless preaching of public duty.

made the practice of collectivism (as Webb now defined the term) into a moral imperative, amounting almost to the whole duty of man. "If the progress of Humanity be our ultimate end, and not merely our own personal happiness," he wrote, revealing the continuity of his Positivist and Humanitarian beliefs,

> we must take even more care to improve the Social Organism of which we form a part than to improve our own, individual developments. . . . [For] the perfect . . . development of each individual [consists] . . . in filling, in the best possible way, his humble function in the great social machine. . . . We must abandon the self-conceit of imagining that we are independent units and bend our proud minds, absorbed in their own cultivation, to this subjection to the higher end, the Common Weal.[73]

Such were the conclusions Webb drew from the experience of "Roman Collectivism"—the Roman sense of civic duty and of devotion to the state—and he summed them up cogently in the maxim that "man's perfect state is constant subjection." "Thou shalt renounce (*'Entbehren sollst du!'*)," he quoted approvingly (if mistakenly) from *Faust*,[74] adding that

> the perfectly socialised man puts constraint on himself in every direction. Our wrongheaded refusal willingly to bow the neck to this yoke is the one unpardonable social sin; the obstinate "will to live" an individual life, which is a survival of the brute in man. . . . If the whole organism—social or biological—is to be kept alive and in health, . . . [individual]

---

73. *Our Corner* 12 (Aug. 1888) : 87–88, one of a series of lectures on the development of the "Social Ideal" in history. Its main point was the superiority of Roman "collectivism" over Athenian individualism. Parts of it were reprinted in Webb's Fabian essay.

74. Goethe, *Faust*, pt. 1, sc. 4. Webb strangely misinterprets this line that really expresses Faust's unhappiness over "doing without" (*entbehren*), not his approval of it. Webb's reading probably reflects the influence of Carlyle, who eloquently attributed the gospel of "Renunciation" (*entsagen*) to Goethe (in *Sartor Resartus* [London, 1897 reprint], pp. 153–54). In any case, it was a very "Calvinistic"—or Evangelical—reading of Goethe. (See W. H. Bruford, "Goethe's English Reputation," *Publications of the English Goethe Society*, n.s. 18 [1948]: 34 ff.) .

development must be rigidly subordinated to the welfare of
the whole.

That was what Webb meant by collectivism. Its opposite, he
insisted, was "logically Anarchism," and must be rooted out wherever it appeared.[75]

This became an almost obsessive theme for Webb in the later
eighties: collectivism was unselfish social behavior, self-subordinating service to the common weal; Anarchism was selfish, antisocial
individualism. Moreover, Webb argued, such individualism was
based on an illogical premise (the premise of Mill's *Liberty*) that
there were "practically self-regarding" spheres of action concerning which the individual was accountable only to himself, whereas,
he now insisted, "there are no purely self-regarding acts. Every
act . . . affects the universe for good or evil, everlastingly [and]
irreparably. There is no forgiveness of sins."[76] Thus Webb
aligned himself entirely with Comte on the great question of
freedom versus social responsibility (and, therefore, of individualism versus collectivism).

In the same secularized Evangelical vein he also wrote to his
future wife, "What shall it profit a man to save his own soul if
thereby even one jot less good is done in the world"—an indica-
tion of the displaced religious feeling that lay behind his sweeping
claims in favor of collectivism.[77] (For if the typical Evangelical
tendency was toward individualism, it could be redirected toward
collectivism by emphasizing, as Webb did, the ideas of social
obligation and unselfish service that also lay at the heart of the
Evangelical creed.)

Even Webb's theory of differential rent was intended to provide
support for that doctrine of collectivism; for (as has been shown)
Webb and his Fabian colleagues saw in that theory the implication
that society as a whole was the rightful possessor of all such rent

75. "Rome," pp. 89, 83; "History of Economic Theory," PP, VI, *64*, ff. 42–43, and
Webb to M. Davidson, 12–13 Dec. 1888, PP, II: 2, 27. To his future wife he added
more pointedly, "We have no *right* to live our own lives. Not what I am best
fitted for but what the public welfare demands of me—is what one seeks" (to B.
Potter, 29 June 1890, PP, II: 3, 7).

76. "Anarchism," PP, VI, *18;* and compare Shaw, *Fabian Essays*, pp. 58 ff.

77. Webb to Beatrice Potter, 29 June 1890, PP, II: 3, 7.

(including land rents, interest on capital, and salaries and wages above the minimal level), on the ground that it was intrinsically unearned.[78] This argument radically altered the moral significance of the doctrine of surplus value (now defined as consisting of the three main forms of rent) by showing that neither individuals nor a class but, rather, society as a whole was "robbed" by its private appropriation. The economic side of collectivism, therefore, consisted in the restoration of such rent to society, chiefly by means of taxation, and its disbursement in the manner best suited to promote the welfare of the entire community.

Finally, Webb gave his case for collectivism a more contemporary tone by expressing it in the language of Social Darwinism, thus bringing the evolutionary and social implications of Positivism and Idealism into a more "scientific" focus. "We now know that in natural selection, at the stage of development where the existence of civilised man is at stake, the units selected from are not individuals but societies," he wrote. And the attribute which determined the outcome of such social selection was "social organisation," as reflected in the adaptability and suitability to social needs of a nation's "specialised political tissue."

> Natural selection . . . is influenced most strongly by different characteristics at different stages of development: [first, "physical strength," then "mental cunning," etc.] . . . but we do not yet thoroughly realise that this has [now] been superceded . . . by social organisation. . . . The French nation was beaten in the last war [1871] . . . because the German Social Organism was, for purposes of the time, superior in *efficiency* to the French.[79]

Here, for the first time, Webb made explicit his belief in the need to strengthen England's "national efficiency" if she was to survive

78. See chap. 6 above, for discussion of Webb's theory of rent. Contrary to McBriar, *Fabian Socialism*, pp. 41–42, the differential character of this theory *was* essential to Webb's argument that rent was inherently unearned—by anyone. It might be assumed a priori that an idle landlord's rent was unearned, but the differential argument was essential to show that it was also unearned even by the cultivator, because it was not properly the result of any human effort.

79. "Rome," pp. 87–88, emphasis added.

as a great industrial power and transmit her culture to posterity. Such "external social Darwinism" had recently been popularized by T. H. Huxley in a brilliant attack on the ultra-individualism of Herbert Spencer.[80] Webb followed Huxley's lead in making a strong plea for greatly expanded technical education (which remained a lifelong enthusiasm) ;[81] more widely available secondary and university education; sanitary, health, and housing legislation; the eight-hour day, more stringent regulation of factories; free school lunches; public bathhouses—in short, all the usual items of Radical collectivism, which he now justified as the means of making England technically and physically "efficient" enough to compete with the growing industrial power of Germany and America. Soon this too became an obsessive theme, as Webb urged repeatedly that collectivism alone could reverse England's declining economic position and restore her national greatness. In a remarkable anticipation of the ideology of national efficiency that flourished in the next two decades he insisted that only the "socially fittest societies" would be able to survive the coming world crisis, and that such social fitness would be determined chiefly by the health, industrial efficiency, and moral solidarity of the nation as a whole.[82]

Such were the practical conclusions Webb drew from his Social Darwinist approach to collectivism. Fortunately, despite the ominousness of some of his rhetoric, his actual proposals were far removed from those propounded by persons of a more genuinely authoritarian bent. For Webb never suggested that the state itself should become more coercive; rather, a greater sense of cohesion

80. T. H. Huxley, "The Struggle for Existence," pp. 161 ff.

81. He was subsequently, e.g., chairman of the Technical Education Committee of the London County Council. His contemporary arguments for technical education are found in: "The Way Out" (1885) PP, VI, *19*, f. 46; "Some Economic Errors of Socialists," *Prac. Soc.* (Feb., Mar. 1887) ; 14 ff., 31 ff.; "The Need of Capital" (1886) , PP, VI, *28;* and "What the Government Labour Bureau Might Do," *To-day* 8 (Dec. 1887) ; 159 ff.

82. See esp. "Rome," and compare Huxley in "The Struggle for Existence," esp. pp. 175 ff., which laid the foundation for the subsequent theory of national efficiency. For the latter, see G. R. Searle, *The Quest for National Efficiency* (Berkeley and Los Angeles, 1971) , which, however, does not mention Huxley. Important as the "efficiency" arguments were, however, they were not (as Eric Hobsbawn has alleged, in "Fabians and Fabianism" [Ph.D. thesis, Cambridge Univ., 1950]) the basis of Webb's Socialist theory, which remained primarily moral.

and commitment should develop from within it in response to the appeal of social duty—a belief Webb shared with J. S. Mill and many early Socialists who saw such a growth of social feeling as the necessary precondition to the establishment of a Socialist society.[83] Moreover, it was the current phase of social evolution—the phase of "moral anarchy" inspired by the revolutionary era—that required the heavy emphasis on social unity at the expense of individuality. For "it is the relative development of the Social Organism that shows the type: having got a good type of organism, . . . and not til then, can the individual usefully advance." Only when the English social organism had built up the "collective" cells and tissues required for coping with the new industrial order could the persons making up that society fully develop their individual potentials. But it was always implicit in such arguments that the individual would again "advance"—would "improve" as a moral and intellectual being—as a result of the new social organization, whereas without it, all individuals would eventually regress through the revolutionary anarchy that such society would be powerless to prevent.[84] The crucial point, however, was that individual self-development remained the goal and purpose of all social progress:

> The real test of any proposed change is whether or not it will result, in fact, in stimulating and developing the aggregate of individual faculty and individual responsibility, which alone make up the strength and force [efficiency?] of the community.[85]

It is, nevertheless, undeniable that from about 1888 Webb's collectivist arguments took a sharply authoritarian turn, somewhat like Mill's in the early 1830s, or those of the contemporary Marxist theorist, E. B. Bax,[86] so that for a time—chiefly the 1890s—his

83. Mill, *Autobiography*, p. 163.

84. "Rome," pp. 87–89; also *Fabian Essays*, pp. 57–58.

85. Webb, in *Cambridge Modern History* (Cambridge, Eng., 1909), vol. 12, subsequently reprinted as *Towards Social Democracy* (London, 1919), p. 43.

86. See chap. 2, n. 40 above. Bax, resident philosopher of the SDF and Socialist League, contended that Socialism required a "conscious sacrifice of the individual to the social whole" (*The Ethics of Socialism* [London, 1887], pp. 18–21, 28–29), and cf. S. Pierson, "Ernest Belfort Bax: 1854–1926," *Vic. Stud.* 12 [Nov. 1972]: 39–60).

commitment to national efficiency and to ensuring the survival of the British social organism seemed to override the more basic liberal commitments that permeated his writings (as in the above quotation) in other periods. What seems most curious from the present perspective, however, is the apparent disparity between Webb's sweeping theoretical arguments (where his new "authoritarianism" was to be found) and the rather modest reform proposals that they were intended to sustain. This was a result, in part, of the threat to the survival of the social organism that Webb perceived in Anarchism and laissez-faire individualism—both infamous things that must be intellectually crushed before real social progress could occur—and a result, in part, of the quasi-religious function of Webb's collectivism as a substitute faith, intended to transform the lives of its individual believers. Both considerations encouraged Webb to state his collectivist theory in the most sweeping terms. Yet his actual reform proposals, the outward and visible manifestations of his collectivist faith, were conceived along such moderate lines that they did not extend even to the nationalization of all the means of production and distribution or to workers' control of industry, which Webb later denounced as a mere "shibboleth." [87]

In this respect, Webb's Socialist theory invites comparison with that of his sometime Fabian colleague, the Idealist philosopher, Bernard Bosanquet, who also combined a sweeping assertion of the moral authority of the state—the "higher self" of every citizen— with a cautious defense of individual liberty and the economics of free trade. Bosanquet, to be sure, went much further than Webb in his insistence on economic individualism, something Webb had not attempted to defend since 1885, but his arguments will still serve to illustrate the way in which a theory of "moral Socialism" that was intensely authoritarian in tone could be paired with a political and economic program that was intensely liberal. [88]

87. Webb at Labour Party Annual Conference, 1918, quoted in T. Nairn, "The Nature of the Labour Party," in P. Anderson and R. Blackburn, eds., *Toward Socialism* (London, 1965), pp. 184–85.

88. See, e.g., Bosanquet, "Individualism and Socialism Philosophically Considered," and Letwin, *Pursuit of Certainty*, pp. 338–39. To be sure, Bosanquet professed himself ready to accept "any amount of collectivism" that was expedient, but he thought that would prove to be very little.

Webb's commitment to liberal *collectivism,* on the other hand, suggests a comparison with another Oxford Idealist and sometime Fabian, D. G. Ritchie, who appealed to both Darwin and Hegel in support of a policy of moderate "state interference." Ritchie's discussion of the obligations of the citizen to the state was very similar to Webb's, and the practical applications of his collectivism were equally moderate.[89] Thus Webb's combination of authoritarian rhetoric with essentially liberal reforms was by no means unique—especially for a theorist who found part of his inspiration in the teachings of Idealist philosophy.

In any case, the very limited character of Webb's Socialist program followed almost inevitably from his characteristic way of defining Socialism, which was threefold: politically, it implied "collective control over and ultimate administration of the means of production for public advantage"; economically, it implied "collective administration of rent and interest"; and ethically, as has been seen, it implied individual subordination to the community and its needs.[90] But the ethical side alone was conceived in unequivocal terms, whereas the "collective control" that was required politically might mean little more than statutory regulation, and "ultimate administration" of industry might be realized only in the distant future. Consequently, Webb's practical efforts to promote reform (like those of Shaw and most other Fabians) went chiefly into projects to obtain a larger share of rent and interest for public purposes, including the promotion of national health and "efficiency." This was what, in most cases, the early Fabians meant by "nationalisation," and their devices for bringing it about were the standard Radical ones: death duties, heavy property taxes, a graduated income tax. Indeed, Shaw argued quite explicitly (like the Henry-Georgian he was), that such taxation fulfilled all the economic requirements of Socialism in the most convenient way; "literal" public ownership would merely be a

89. Ritchie, *Principles of State Interference,* and *Darwinism and Politics,* and cf. Letwin, *Pursuit of Certainty,* pp. 340–41. Ritchie, subsequently professor of moral philosophy at St. Andrews, was a Fabian from 1889 to 1893. A similar comparison might be made with the liberal social theory of L. T. Hobhouse (which was also mildly collectivist), except that most of the latter appeared after 1889 and was probably heavily influenced by Webb's writing.

90. Webb, *Socialism in England,* p. 12, and cf. sec. 3 above.

burden. And it was also Shaw—though he spoke for Webb and all the Fabian "Old Gang"—who stated most clearly the underlying Fabian belief that long before full economic collectivism had been achieved the work of Socialism would be complete and the tide would recede, leaving much industry still in private hands.[91]

5. Shaw's Doctrine of Collectivism

Shaw was the last of the Fabian "Old Gang" to accept collectivism, and his devotion to the individualist view of Socialism died hard. When he finally accepted the new theory, therefore, it may be taken as evidence that the last significant resistance within the Fabian Society had crumbled. In 1886 and 1887, however, Shaw was in a period of uncertain transition between the Anarchist and collectivist poles of Socialist doctrine, unable to accept either one wholeheartedly. In that transitional mood he characterized the thoroughgoing collectivist as the "Conservative of Socialism," because he stood for comprehensive regulation of society; whereas the thoroughgoing Anarchist was the old-fashioned "Whig" or "Liberal." Each in his own way sought to promote liberty, the characteristic error of the former being to forget that power corrupts, and of the latter, to forget that law and order may enhance liberty. What Shaw desired, in effect, was a compromise position that he could characterize as "realistic" (or "scientific") Socialism: Socialism based solidly on economic and social science, that would take human nature as it existed—vain, selfish, and competitive—rather than try to remold it according to some ideal plan.[92] Accordingly, he proceeded to define a "scientific Socialist," in 1887, as a hard-nosed realist who bases his idea of Socialism squarely on self interest. He will, therefore, accept competition and reject price-fixing by the government (except in cases of essential public monopolies), will not forbid interest and will "permit the

91. Shaw, "The Basis of Socialism: Economic," in *Fabian Essays* (jubilee ed.), pp. 24–25, and "Illusions of Socialism," in Carpenter, ed., *Forecasts of the Coming Century*.

92. Shaw's notion of realism was most fully expounded in *The Quintessence of Ibsenism* (London, 1891), and was applied to politics in, e.g., "Socialism and Human Nature," in Crompton, ed., *Road to Equality*, Chap. 5, and "How the Socialists Have Grown Practical," *Sun. Chronicle* (16 Nov. 1890).

clever man to take what he can get." He will insist only on public ownership of land and accumulated capital and on genuinely representative governmental institutions. Above all, he is "in a hurry to start political work" and, at least in England, entirely repudiates "catastrophic change." [93]

Despite its ambiguities this position was a very attractive one for Shaw—so attractive that he continued to repeat it at intervals over the next two decades—because it enabled him to preserve the fullest measure of individual liberty and the productive stimulus of competition by resisting collectivism at every point where natural monopoly and its offspring, "rent," did not require it to protect the public interest. His more decisive shift toward collectivism in 1887–88, like that of the Fabian Society at large, therefore, derived not so much from ideological considerations as from the practical consequences of his new political activism (reflected, for example, in his statement about being "in a hurry to start political work"). This activism characteristically took such forms as supporting Annie Besant's political campaigns in the late eighties—it was Besant who drew Shaw into politics and turned him toward "parliamentarism"—spreading the Socialist gospel by lectures at Radical clubs and caucuses, and serving as "permeative Fabian" on his local Liberal and Radical Association.[94] As a matter of practical necessity, all these activities encouraged increased reliance on Radical collectivism and increased hostility toward the antipolitical attitudes of Anarchists and followers of William Morris, whom Shaw had previously counted among his allies in the Socialist cause.

In 1886 Shaw's intellectual view of Anarchism also underwent a drastic alteration. The change may have been initiated by the discussions of Proudhon to which the Hampstead "Marx circle" turned early in that year, and for which Shaw read (or reread) large parts of *What Is Property?* It is likely that those discussions

93. "Socialist Politics" (lecture, 1887), BM 50700, 22 (paraphrased). This line of argument was more fully developed in *Socialism and Superior Brains*.

94. Regarding Shaw's shift to "parliamentarism," see Morris to Mahon, 15 Jan. 1886, in R.P. Arnot, *William Morris*, p. 56; regarding his political work, see Shaw's statement in Pease, *History of the Fabian Society*, p. 112 n., and Shaw to Hyndman, 22 June 1888, BM 50538 (not in Laurence, *Collected Letters*), where he offered a pragmatic justification for it.

had the same effect on his view of Proudhon that the earlier discussions had had on his view of Marx.[95] In any case, there is
evidence of such changing opinions as early as June 1886, when
Shaw "spoke against Anarchists" at the Dialectical Society, following a lecture by Charlotte Wilson. Thereafter he became increasingly critical of Anarchism in all his public utterances,
especially with regard to its antipolitical posture and its rejection
of the state.[96]

   This shift in outlook was immediately reflected in a number of
autobiographical passages written by Shaw in the late eighties—
most notably his comment on the lines from John Hay's "Liberty"
that he had earlier used to head his Socialist *Manifesto* (Fabian
Tract Number 2), in 1884. In his 1886 revision of *The Irrational
Knot,* however, Shaw flatly repudiated those lines, making his
hero (who usually expressed his own beliefs) call freedom "a
fool's dream":

> I once thought . . . that freedom was the one condition to be
> gained at all cost. . . . My favorite psalm was that nonsense
> of John Hay's:
>> For always in thine eyes, O Liberty,
>> Shines that high light whereby the world is saved;
>> And though thou slay us, we will trust in thee.
> And she does slay us. Now I aim at the greatest attainable
> justice, which involves the least endurable liberty.[97]

Thus "justice," especially in the sense of equitable exchange, con-

95. Shaw, typescript diary (BLPES), 20, 22 Jan. 1886; also 13 Mar. 1856. Webb
was also a participant in those discussions and even translated Proudhon for Charlotte Wilson's paper, *Freedom.* For his criticisms of Anarchism, which are likely to
have powerfully influenced Shaw, see "Considerations on Anarchism," PP, VI, *18,*
and sec. 4, above.

96. Shaw, typescript diary, 2 June 1886. Shaw's earliest criticisms of Anarchism
followed the quasi-Lassallean line of arguing that the state and collective ownership
of property were necessary to guarantee real "social" freedom. See "Retrospect,
Circumspect, Prospect," BM 50700 (34), and chap. 4, n. 64 above.

97. "The Irrational Knot" revised MS (National Library of Ireland, MS 845, f.
641), printed in *Our Corner* 9 (Feb. 1887): 81. In the later published version of the
novel (New York and London, 1905), Shaw further altered the last lines, in keeping
with his new enthusiasm for Nietzsche, to read: "now I am for the fullest attainable
life, which involves the least liberty."

tinued to be the watchword of Shaw's Socialist theory, while
freedom was reduced to the rank of an expedient that was valuable
only insofar as it was useful in the struggle for equality. Under the
influence of Webb and Lassalle,[98] moreover, Shaw came to see
the state as an essential instrument for achieving equality and
justice, both as receiver of (socially created) rents and as organizer
of the national economy. He even argued in 1887 that, by a law
of historic development, communities tended inevitably to become
more highly organized, thus perpetually increasing the functions
of the state—a clear reversal of his earlier position. And he added
ominously that the only alternative to political democracy was a
despotism by the strongest and cleverest individuals.[99] Finally,
in a brief summary of his own changing attitudes toward Anarchism (which was characteristically disguised as an historical
account), Shaw argued that

> When Anarchism was first heard of . . . in England, it was
> welcomed . . . [by himself] as a protest against the insane dis-
> regard of . . . personal liberty, apparent in some Collectivist
> ideals. But it has since [sic] developed into a doctrine of
> unmitigated individualism, having for its economic basis an
> invincible ignorance of the law of rent. As such, it is no
> longer welcome, or even tolerable, to Socialists.[100]

What emerges most clearly from such arguments is that Shaw's
quarrel was solely with Individualist Anarchism, which he persistently identified with Anarchism in general. Communistic Anarchism of the Kropotkin variety, on the other hand, he viewed far
more favorably, arguing that it was not really Anarchism at all,
and even conceding to Charlotte Wilson that "free [i.e., Anarchist]
communism will probably evolve" as the ultimate stage of Social-

98. For Lassalle's influence on Shaw in the mid-1880s, see chap. 4 above, and n.
108 below.

99. "Socialist Politics," lecture, 1887, BM 50700 (22). The influence of Webb's
new, Positivist-inspired authoritarian teachings (see sec. 5 above) is very evident in
such statements.

100. "A Word for War," To-day 8 (Sept. 1887): 84 n., and cf. Olivier's reply to
Shaw in Freedom (Oct. 1887). Shaw's statement is best understood as autobiographical.

ism.[101] He also insisted that he had no quarrel with the theory of
Anarchism but only with its practical results; and he defended
collectivism and the enhanced role of the state on the similarly
"practical" grounds that they were essential to the efficient operation of the national economy and to eliminating idlers.[102] Because
Anarchism could not effectively achieve those goals it must be
abandoned as a practical expedient, however desirable it might
be as an ultimate ideal.

Curiously, however, Shaw continued to expound Anarchist
economic theories for more than a year after he repudiated Anarchist politics, and only ceased to do so when he was driven to
abandon the logical foundation of those theories—his belief in the
labor theory of value and its Socialist corollary, the right to the
whole produce of labor—and thus to rebuild his own theory of
rent upon a new foundation.[103] That new foundation was provided by Jevons's theory of final utility, as expounded by the
clergyman-economist, Philip Wicksteed; but Shaw sat at Wicksteed's feet as a member of a fortnightly "economic circle" for
almost a year before abandoning the Ricardian theory of value,
upon which his original case for Socialism had rested, and accepting the Jevonian one instead. And his chief reason for accepting
Jevons's theory, even then, was probably that it gave him a new
stick with which to beat the English Marxists—a new means of
demonstrating that their economic theories were unscientific and
that their politics were misguided.[104]

A more important consequence of accepting that theory, however, was that it gave Shaw a decisive theoretical reason for accept-

101. C. M. Wilson to Shaw, 16 Feb. 1887, BM 50511. In "Technical Socialism"
(MS draft of a proposed "textbook" on Socialism, 1888, BM 50667, ff. 17–18, 20–21),
Shaw argued that Anarchist-Communists should not be distinguished from com-
munists in general. For further discussion see J. W. Hulse, *Revolutionists in London*
(Oxford, 1970), pp. 111–37.

102. Shaw, *Why I Am a Social-Democrat* (London, 1894), p. 3, and "Technical
Socialism," BM 50667, f. 13.

103. See "On Interest," *Our Corner* 10 (Sept.–Oct. 1887), and "Technical Socialism," BM 50667, ff. 9–10, where Shaw specifically repudiated the right to the whole
produce of labor as "utopian."

104. For Shaw's part in "Beeton's Economic Circle," see C. H. Herford, *Philip
Wicksteed: His Life and Work* (London, 1931). Shaw first used Jevons against Marx
in "Karl Marx and *Das Kapital*," *National Reformer* 50 (1887).

ing the doctrine of collectivism that his friend, Sidney Webb, was currently promoting—a reason, moreover, that perfectly complemented his long-standing advocacy of Henry George's theory of rent. What Jevons's and George's theories had in common was chiefly an emphasis on the social determination of economic values —commodity values in the case of Jevons; land rents in the case of George[105]—in contrast to the strict labor theory of value in which Shaw had formerly believed. Both Jevons and George argued that the pressure of public demand against the margin of supply, rather than the labor of individuals or classes, was the chief factor in determining such economic values. By accepting such arguments, Shaw soon reached Webb's conclusion that society collectively should have the benefit of the values it had collectively created, and this made him a collectivist. That was why there was "something whole-hearted" about his conversion to final utility (or "marginalist") economics, for he believed that he could not justify collectivism so effectively on any other theoretical basis.[106]

Perhaps the only surprising feature of that argument was Shaw's slowness in adopting it (for there is no evidence of it prior to 1888) ; and the explanation for that is surely that so long as Shaw believed in the labor theory of value it prevented him from seeing such implications in the theory of rent. Webb, on the other hand, having approached that theory from a point of view strongly colored by Positivism, saw things in a mere "collective" light from the beginning.[107]

105. George specifically defined rent as "the value of land" (in *Progress and Poverty*, bk. 5, chap. 2) , although in other respects he was an exponent of the labor theory of value.

106. See McBriar, *Fabian Socialism*, p. 33, and cf. chap. 6 above for a fuller discussion of this argument for collectivism. Such economic reasoning also led Shaw to accept Webb's argument that interest was "unavoidable in the nature of the case," and so ought to be publicly appropriated, like any other form of rent. (See "The Basis of Socialism: Economic," in *Fabian Essays*, and cf. Webb, "The Rate of Interest and the Laws of Distribution," *QJE* [Jan. 1888].)

107. Shaw read Walker's theory of rent in 1886 (diary, 16 Mar. 1886) , but the implications of the idea only took hold slowly. Shaw was probably never seriously influenced by Positivism, but he did concede that the "modern idea . . . that social organization is paramount . . . was originally confined to Positivists, who, however, corrupted it with visions of a restored Holy Roman Empire" (review of *Pine and Palm*, in *Pall Mall Gazette*, 14 Mar. 1888) .

Once Shaw grasped the full implication of Webb's theory, however, he treated it as a complete refutation of Anarchism and lost
no time in launching full-scale attacks on his former allies from
his new, collectivist standpoint. The root of all the "absurdities"
perpetrated by "American Individualist Anarchists and Proud-
honists," he proclaimed, was their "invincible ignorance of the
law of rent." "Once admit their quibble . . . that rent [in all its
forms] does not enter into price," and you are lost.[108] Once em-
barked on that line of reasoning, Shaw characteristically found
no stopping place short of a complete endorsement of collectivism,
which he now held to be the one "realistic" road to Socialism
(although the particular form of collectivism he promoted remained curiously archaic and utopian).[109] Soon he abandoned
the last vestige of his former individualism by issuing unprecedented pronouncements to the effect that "every man's property
is property of the State, which it can dispose of as it pleases," although, for the sake of expediency, "the State will naturally secure
his welfare at the least trouble to itself." Echoing Webb's theory
of collectivism, he also insisted that since no actions can be merely
"self-regarding" or socially indifferent (in the sense propounded
by J. S. Mill) all men must limit their actions so as not to injure
the community. "Conscientious and educated men seek [to do that]
. . . throughout their lives and never for a moment think of themselves as free agents." Indeed, such freedom was merely a "dialectical figment." [110]

As a result of such arguments, Shaw went on to define Socialism
in collectivist terms that were, if anything, more thoroughgoing

108. Shaw, "A Word for War," p. 84 n.; review of Gonner's *University Economics*,
in *Pall Mall Gazette*, Nov. 1888; and "A Refutation of Anarchism," *Our Corner* 11
(June, 1888) , subsequently expanded and published as *The Impossibilities of Anarchism*, Fabian Tract No. 45 (London, 1893) .

109. "Technical Socialism," BM 50667. Shaw continued throughout the late 1880s
to endorse Lassalle's version of collectivism: state-subsidized, self-governing cooperative workshops. He also saw Lassalle as the supreme political "realist" and regarded
his Workers' Program of 1862 as analogous to the emerging Fabian program of
municipal collectivism. (See "The New Politics," BM 50683, ff. 25–26, and "How the
Socialists Have Grown Practical," *Sunday Chronicle*, 16 Nov. 1890.)

110. "Socialism and Property," essay, 1888, BM 50690, reprinted as "Freedom and
the State," in Crompton, *The Road to Equality*, pp. 41, 38–39, and cf. Webb's contemporary arguments in "Rome," quoted in sec. 4 above.

than Webb's, arguing that any person who favored extending collectivism far enough to "make it the predominant and characteristic system in this country," should be called a Socialist.[111] By the time the *Fabian Essays* were in preparation for the press, early in 1889, he was determined to carry out that "collectivism" even to the extent of removing his name, as editor, from the title page, on the ground that an individual editor was "an individualist throwback." [112] Thus Shaw began his career as a militant enemy of individualism in every form—an attitude that made him sometimes talk as if the mere act of nationalization constituted Socialism, and as if public ownership in itself would solve the problems of society. These were by no means consistent positions with Shaw, as he never entirely abandoned his fondness for libertarian ideals, but they were voiced so loudly and persistently over the next few decades that they soon came to be regarded as authoritative Fabian attitudes by his wide reading and listening public. And once disseminated, that impression proved impossible to dispel.[113]

111. Technical Socialism," BM 50667, chap. 2. (This was the MS of a textbook on Socialism begun by Shaw in 1888.)

112. Circular letter, Shaw to all the Fabian essayists, 10 Jan. 1889, BM 50515. An amusing correspondence followed as other essayists denied Shaw's claim.

113. See, e.g., J. B. Kaye, *Bernard Shaw and the Nineteenth Century Tradition* (Norman, Okla., 1958). The argument, however, is only partly true, as indicated by the persistence of Anarchist ideas in Shaw's writing. (See chap. 4, n. 80.)

Conclusion

With Shaw's conversion to collectivism, the development of classical Fabian theory as set forth in *Fabian Essays*[1] was complete, and subsequent publication of those essays in December 1889 soon established the Society's reputation as an intellectual constellation of the first magnitude. Indeed, the popularity of the essays was so great,[2] and the Fabians were so accomplished in the art of self-advertisement, that their society soon came to be regarded as a national institution: an apotheosis symbolized by such varied events as the appearance of lead articles devoted to its affairs in metropolitan newspapers, a rash of Fabian romans à clef, and a highly visible tendency in the early 1890s for intellectuals from all branches of the British Left to join the Society and take the plunge into avowed Socialism.[3] The last point also illustrates what was probably the most important immediate achievement of the essays: their dissemination of a Socialist doctrine that appealed powerfully to British Radical intellectuals (and was favorably reviewed by a wide variety of Liberal and Radical journals),[4] thus providing the necessary theoretical basis for such intellectuals' conversion to

1. The common core of theory in *Fabian Essays*, which was the nearest thing to an official doctrine that the early Fabian Society produced, was evolved at regular meetings of the essayists (minus Bland) between 1886 and 1888. (See correspondence in WP, BLPES.)

2. The first edition was sold out within a month, and over 27,000 copies were sold during the first year and a half (Pease, *History of the Fabian Society*, p. 88). No Socialist publication in England had ever previously approached such popular success.

3. See, e.g., *Daily Chronicle* leaders, Oct. 29, 30, 1893, commenting on the new Fabian manifesto. The most notable Fabian novels were Mrs. Humphry Ward, *Marcella* (London, 1893), the work of the leading popularizer of fashionable ideas in late Victorian literature, and Emma Brooke, *Transition* (London, 1895), a fictionalization of Sidney Webb's career written from within the society. For a list of eminent Fabian recruits, see W. Clarke, "The Fabian Society," *New England Magazine*, 10 n.s. (Mar. 1894).

4. Strongly favorable reviews were carried by, e.g., the (Liberal) *Speaker*, *Daily News*, *Athenaeum*, *Nonconformist*, the (Radical) *Star*, and *Co-operative News*; even the (Tory) *Methodist Times* and *Stock Exchange* urged their readers to "read and ponder these most important" essays. (Reviews are reprinted in publisher's blurb, Fabian Archive, Nuffield.)

Socialism. As a result, the early Fabians were able not only to make Socialism "respectable," as they often claimed, but even to make it fashionable among British intellectuals of the Left. This was an important achievement, because it laid the foundation for the alliance between these intellectuals and the Labour Party, itself heavily permeated with Fabian ideas, that has been such a notable feature of twentieth-century British politics. Without *Fabian Essays,* on the other hand, it is doubtful whether that alliance would so soon (if ever) have come into being.

What those essays actually propounded, however, was little more than a loose synthesis of the Radical intellectual tendencies analyzed in chapters 4 through 8—a synthesis so loose that each essay still virtually adopted its own approach to Socialism. Thus, in Olivier's essay, Socialism was presented as an expression of the growing moral sense of the community, made potent by the inevitable increase of social feelings in the modern, industrial world, while in Webb's it was seen as the outgrowth of the most distinctively "modern" intellectual trends and the implicit tendency of recent social legislation—"the next step in the Radical programme"—and in Shaw's it was identified with the public appropriation of differential rent (the theory of which was also elaborately restated). In a similar fashion, Socialism was identified both with collectivism of a narrowly mechanical sort and with the culmination and fulfillment of individualism.[5] Happily, such diversity seems not to have weakened the appeal of Fabian Socialism, but rather to have reinforced the useful impression that it offered something for (almost) everyone—an impression that was surely one of the chief sources of its attractiveness to contemporary intellectuals of the Left.

What chiefly distinguished *Fabian Essays* from earlier Fabian writing, however, was precisely the new emphasis on collectivism and collectivist reforms. This was most clearly reflected in the fact that all seven of the essayists followed Shaw in at least formally identifying Socialism with a type of collectivism that was defined

5. See esp. Shaw's definition of Social-Democracy in the introduction to *Fabian Essays,* p. iv, and Olivier's contention that "Socialism is merely Individualism rationalised, organised, clothed, and in its right mind" (p. 105).

solely in economic and political terms.[6] This had the advantage of imparting much-needed theoretical coherence to the essays, but at the same time it produced a drastic narrowing of the Society's field of vision, pushing the earlier preoccupation with ethical and religious values to the periphery of that field, because such things no longer seemed directly relevant to the new preoccupation with collectivist reforms.[7]

In effect, this amounted to a major reorientation of Fabian theory: the culmination of the process analyzed in chapter 8, whereby the goals and values of Fabian Socialism were bound ever more tightly to the needs of Radical politics. This had the great advantage of placing such Socialism firmly within the existing structure of English politics, and so laid the foundation for the reformist, evolutionary Socialism of the twentieth-century Labour Party. Within the realm of theory it also had the advantage of replacing the appeal to moral principles—increasingly unfashionable among secularized intellectuals in the 1890s—with the more "scientific" appeal to political and economic expediency. At the same time, however, this reorientation had the equally great disadvantage of threatening to purge Fabian Socialism of precisely the moral values, quasi-religious commitments, and visions of a world transformed that had drawn most of the Fabians to Socialism in the first place, and which continued to inspire most of their activities.

In the event, that threat remained largely unrealized [8] because

6. E.g., "vesting the organisation of industry and the material of production in a State identified with the whole people by complete Democracy" (*Fabian Essays*, p. iv). Webb's more moralistic and more authoritarian version of collectivism, in contrast, was not mentioned in the *Essays*, although it made a shadowy appearance on pp. 56–60 as "The New Synthesis."

7. Clayton, *Rise and Decline of Socialism in Great Britain*, sees this change as marking the shift from Socialism to mere "Labourism" (cf. Chap. 1, n. 41). For the Socialist movement as a whole, however, he places it at the much later date of Labour's coming to power (1922–24).

8. Stanley Pierson, *Marxism and British Socialism*, argues the contrary, but his argument depends too exclusively on the views of Shaw and Webb (who were not the whole Fabian Society) and overstresses the importance of official manifestos, such as Tract No. 70 (by Shaw), in contrast to the lectures and writings of other leading Fabians, whose Socialism retained more of the ethical-religious imprint.

most of the leading Fabians still continued to conceive of Socialism
in ethical and religious terms and therefore only halfheartedly
accepted the redefinition of Socialism in economic and political
terms (and of Socialist theory in terms of mere expediency) that
accompanied the new emphasis on collectivism. Thus the reorientation of Fabian theory was far less thoroughgoing than it appeared
to be—a point that is confirmed even by internal evidence in the
essays, all of which, except Shaw's, continued to expound Socialism
in at least partially moral and religious terms, while a few of them
remained primarily committed to that perspective.[9] Moreover, the
essays also revealed a fundamental conflict over how the doctrine
of collectivism should be applied, Bland and Clarke insisting on
the necessity of full public ownership of the means of production,
whereas the majority of essayists (Webb, Wallas, Olivier, and
Shaw) adopted the more moderate (and more Radical) policy of
progressively taxing rent and interest for the support of welfare
and public investment programs.[10] Continuing distrust of outright
nationalization was also evident in the arguments in support of
cooperative workshops and publicly organized industrial "communes," in the essays of Shaw and Besant, while several essayists
went so far as to assert that collectivism itself could be no more
than a step toward the more complete and radical regeneration of
society that was still their primary objective.[11] Thus, despite the
formal reorientation of Fabian theory, the traditional goal of
social regeneration and the parallel tendency to identify Socialism
with the triumph of social feelings and the building of a new
moral world persisted in both the Fabian essays and in Fabian

9. See the essays of Olivier (esp. pp. 103–04, 111–12, 124–28), Wallas (esp. pp.
132, 146–49), Besant (esp. pp. 167–69); also Webb (pp. 56–60), Bland (pp. 219–20),
and Clarke (pp. 99, 101), in *Fabian Essays*. Shaw, in contrast, based his arguments
for Socialism entirely on expediency (or "realism") —a tendency he developed much
more fully in essays of the 1890s, such as "Socialism and Human Nature," (in
Crompton, *Road to Equality*, chap. 5).

10. See esp. Bland (pp. 211–15) and Clarke (pp. 99–101, which however seems
to place the collectivist *denouement* at a very remote period of time), in *Fabian
Essays*. The majority position was closer in spirit to that of the 1887 Fabian "Basis."

11. See Shaw (pp. 190–99), and Besant (pp. 152–66), and the references to Olivier,
Wallas, and Besant, in n. 9, above—esp. Wallas's claim that "the tentative and limited
Social-Democracy [common to all the essays] which I have sketched is the necessary
and certain step to that better life which we hope for. . . . [It] is not itself such a
life," however, and so it too must be superceded by a higher stage of development in
which, at last, the goals of traditional Socialism would be realized (ibid., 147–48).

lectures of the 1890s;[12] and the combination of such views (which were especially clear in the essays of Olivier, Wallas, and Besant) with the hard-nosed economic reasoning of Shaw and Clarke did much to give the essays their exceptionally wide-ranging appeal.

Such facts must be emphasized, not only because they highlight the underlying continuity of Fabian theory throughout the 1880s, but also because they are crucial to understanding the wider significance of that theory in the 1890s and after, when its influence spread rapidly beyond the small class of Radical intellectuals who had formed its earliest and most characteristic converts to become the chief intellectual leaven of the working-class and lower-middle-class Socialism of the Independent Labour Party (ILP) and the Labour churches in the industrial north of England. Two separate strands of influence must be distinguished at this point, however: the influence of Fabian research and of formal Fabian theory, on the one hand, and the equally important continuity between the Ethical Socialism of the Fabians in the 1880s and that of the ILP in the 1890s, on the other. It has long been recognized that Fabian facts and figures and even more abstract types of Fabian theory circulated widely among ILP Socialists in the 1890s, and that, having little head for theory themselves, such Socialists were often content simply to adapt Fabian theories to their own needs.[13] In contrast, the continuity between the Ethical Socialism of the early Fabians and that of the ILP and subsequent Labour Party has been far less widely recognized. Thus it may be useful to list some of the strands of Fabian theory from the 1880s that reappeared in subsequent decades in the utterances of rank-and-file Labour Party Socialists in places as distant as Yorkshire. These strands included the Social Darwinist approach to Socialism, with its characteristic comparison of social with organic evolution, the (Positivist) belief in a "law of progress" inherent in the development

12. This was especially true of Webb, who, as has been seen, conceived of collectivism in primarily ethical terms (see chap. 8, sec. 4 above) : cf. his later references to the "humanitarian basis of Socialism" and to "translat[ing] our [Socialist] faith into our lives," in his lecture, *The Fabian Society* (Netherfield, Notts., 1891) , and his repeated references to the religious character of the Socialist movement (e.g., in letters to his future wife: Webb to B. Potter, 26 Aug. 1890, PP, II, BLPES) .

13. See McBriar, *Fabian Socialism*, chap. 10; also Pierson, *Marxism and British Socialism*, pp. 204–06, 211–13.

of modern industry that was steadily moving British society toward Socialism (which would thus be achieved without any "radical surgery"), and the belief that the intellectual and moral conscious-ness of the mass of Englishmen must first be transformed in order to make possible the achievement of such Socialism. In a manner strongly reminiscent of the early Fabians, and of J. S. Mill before them, these Labour Socialists aimed to reform both capitalists and workingmen, so as to educate both in the new social ideals that (they believed) industrial progress was now increasingly bringing to fulfillment.[14]

To be sure, there is not sufficient evidence to claim specifically Fabian derivation for arguments that were so manifestly "in the air" in the 1890s and after; but the continuity between such argu-ments and those of the early Fabians, who were also, in most cases, the first to formulate and disseminate them in England, is unmistakable. Indeed, if such arguments were "in the air" by the 1890s, it was largely because the early Fabians had put them there; and the same Fabians—to a far greater extent than William Morris or his disciples—were also the pioneers of the ethical-religious type of Socialism that was subsequently adopted by the ILP.[15] Moreover, the most articulate leaders of the ILP and the closely allied Labour churches—Keir Hardie, Ramsay MacDonald, John Trevor, and many of the women lecturers for the ILP [16]—were themselves Fabians in the 1890s and were saturated with early Fabian ideas and attitudes.[17] This was especially true of MacDon-

14. See Bernard Barker, "Anatomy of Reformism: The Social and Political Ideas of the Labour Leadership in Yorkshire," *International Review of Social History* 18 (1973) : 1, 12–14.

15. Morris's lectures lacked the elements of Evangelical morality and biblical allusion that characterized much ILP rhetoric in the 1890s, and ILP lectures (other than Bruce Glasier's) lacked the aesthetic orientation of Morris's Socialism. In a general way, Morris was an inspiration both to the early Fabians and to the early ILP Socialists, but early Fabian Socialism was much the closer than Morris's, in both style and content, to the Socialism of the ILP.

16. For a discussion of the ILP lecturers, Margaret McMillan, Katherine St. John Conway, Enid Stacy, and Carolyn Martyn, see Pierson, *Marxism and British Social-ism*, pp. 161 ff. The last two were closest in outlook to the Fabian Essayists.

17. Paradoxically, their continued adherence to such ideas brought them into frequent conflict with Webb and Shaw, who, as chief spokesmen for the new orienta-tion of Fabian theory, were increasingly intolerant of ethical and religious rhetoric in the 1890s, but it by no means damaged their relations with other Fabians who preserved a more traditional point of view.

ald, whose early writings reveal an almost ultra-Fabian point of view, and who elaborated many of the arguments cited above in his own subsequent writings; but it is also true of Trevor, who openly borrowed most of the Socialist theory for his Labour churches from the Fabians,[18] and only slightly less true of Hardie, whose Socialist rhetoric in the 1890s, heavily weighted with Evangelical morality and biblical allusions, was strongly reminiscent of the early Socialist lectures of Webb, Besant, and Pease. Through his political oratory, which included such moralistic slogans as "labour and liquor don't mix," [19] the marriage of Radicalism and Socialism that had first been undertaken by the Fabians was fully consummated, and the transfer of Radical beliefs and loyalties to the Socialist movement, at the popular level, was effectively begun. Such Socialism was unmistakably "old Radicalism writ large," and the conversion of traditionally Radical working men was its primary objective. Thus the preaching of such ILP and Labour Party Socialists (who, like the early Fabians, were irresistibly inclined to preach) continued the development of early Fabian ideas and beliefs, and, after combining them with a smattering of later Fabian facts and arguments, made them an integral part of the ideology of the politically conscious labor movement that was fast growing to maturity in the last decade of the nineteenth century.

18. See MacDonald, "A Rock Ahead," *To-day* 7 (Mar. 1887) —a plea for gradualist Socialism led by the educated classes—and the evidence cited in McBriar, *Fabian Socialism,* pp. 293–94; also B. Barker, ed., *Ramsay MacDonald's Political Writings* (New York, 1972), pp. 10–48. For discussions of Trevor's Socialism, see Pierson, *Marxism and British Socialism,* pp. 226 ff., and Pelling, *Origins,* 132 ff. Fabians frequently preached in Labour churches, and even a few specifically Fabian churches were formed in the 1890s: e.g., one at West Hampstead (N. London) and a more flourishing one at Victoria Park (E. London). See *Workman's Times,* 22 Sept. 1893, and the "Manifesto" of the Victoria Park Fabian Church (Fabian Archive, Nuffield).

19. See Pelling, *Origins,* pp. 68, 140–41, 143, and compare Hardie's claim that "Socialism" is the embodiment of Christianity in our industrial system" (ibid., p. 140) with, e.g., Pease, "Ethics and Socialism," *Prac. Soc.,* (Jan. 1886). Fred Ried, "Kier Hardie's Conversion to Socialism," in Briggs and Saville, eds., *Essays in Labour History, 1886–1923,* chap. 2, is the best account of his early intellectual development.

Appendix A: Early Recruits to the Democratic Federation

Early recruits to the (S)DF came chiefly by way of the Christian Socialist movement (which, in practice, meant by way of a heavy emphasis on the teaching of Ruskin and Henry George) or by way of the Freethought movement (including, but not limited to, Charles Bradlaugh's National Secular Society). The most notable recruits of the former sort were: H. H. Champion, R. P. B. Frost, J. L. Joynes, and William Morris. As noted in chapter 3, all came from affluent backgrounds and inherited incomes large enough to enable them to devote their time and energies largely to Socialism. They also shared a common background in the established church and public schools, and (with the exception of Morris) continued to take an active part in Christian Socialist organizations and in preaching Socialism to clerical gatherings throughout the 1880s. (See sources cited in chapter 3, nn. 77, 80, and Joynes to Shaw, 16 Jan. 1884, BM 50510. Regarding subsequent biographical sketches, see Lee and Archbold, *Social-Democracy*, chaps. 8 and 9; Shaw, "The New Politics," in Crompton, *The Road to Equality*, pp. 81–87.)

Champion (1859–1928), the son of a major general, had been an artillery officer in India and Egypt until invalided out in 1882. His father then advanced him the capital to become a publisher, in which capacity he published much of the literature of the English Socialist revival. Frost (c. 1859–?) had been Champion's schoolmate at Marlborough and lived on fashionable Woburn Place. He was the son of a country clergyman and was heavily endowed with Evangelical earnestness. Joynes (1853–93), son of an Eton master, himself held a mastership there until Dec. 1882, when he was fired because of his support for Henry George and his increasingly Radical opinions. Thereafter, he became a free-lance journalist and eventually studied medicine with the intention of practicing in the slums (Joynes to H. George, 4 Nov. and 7 Dec. 1882; 13 and 28 Feb. and 25 Mar. 1883, George Papers, NYPL; also S. Winsten, *Salt and His Circle*, pp. 38–81). Morris (1834–96), a generation older than the others, had already established an international reputation as a poet and designer before joining the Federation and was easily the most famous convert of the Socialist revival. He must be classed among the Christian Socialist recruits both because of the strong religious orientation of his Socialism, which was grounded on an essentially Christian ideal of brotherhood, and because of his heavy reliance on Ruskin's social teaching. (For his numerous biographies, see the Bibliographical Note below; regarding his conversion to Socialism, see Mackail, *Morris*, 2: 97, and "How I Became a Socialist," *Justice* [16 June, 1894].)

Recruits to Socialism from the Freethought movement were characteristically less affluent than those from Christian Socialism, and typically came from Nonconformist families of much lower social standing. Thus of the four most notable recruits from that source—E. Belfort Bax, Herbert Burrows, Edward Aveling, and Eleanor Marx Aveling—only Bax (1854–1926) was wealthy in the manner of Champion, Frost, or Morris, and his family was Nonconformist. He was probably also the first native English Marxist, having come to Marx by way of Hegel while studying philosophy in Germany in the late seventies. By 1883 he had become a free-lance journalist specializing in history and philosophy, though he continued to live on his inherited income. (See Bax, *Reminiscences and Reflexions of a Mid and Late Victorian* [London, 1918].) Burrows (1845–92), a civil servant in the Indland Revenue Department, son of a Methodist parson, and sometime noncollegiate student at Cambridge, was in 1883 a follower of Helen Taylor and a vocal partisan of Secularism, Irish independence, and women's rights. (See A. H. Nethercot, *The First Five Lives of Annie Besant* [Chicago, 1960], pp. 264–65.) Aveling (1851–98) was also the son of a Nonconformist parson and was vice-president of the National Secular Society before joining the SDF in 1884. He had a doctorate in science and was employed as a lecturer on chemistry and anatomy in London teaching hospitals. He was generally regarded as an unsavory character. (For the fullest account of his life and of Eleanor Marx Aveling's, see C. Tsuzuki, *The Life of Eleanor Marx* [Oxford, 1967].) Eleanor Marx Aveling (1855–98), the brilliant daughter of Karl Marx, was the common-law wife of Edward Aveling. Before joining the SDF with her "husband" she had been an aspiring actress and drama critic and had been involved in the international Socialist movement for many years as an informal secretary for her father. She took little discernible part in the SDF during her brief membership but, with her "husband," formed the nucleus of the anti-Hyndman Marx "family group."

Most of the more prominent early working-class recruits to the SDF also derived from Freethought traditions: John Burns (engineer) from the National Secular Society branch in Battersea, Joseph Lane (a carter by trade, but virtually a professional propagandist) from the ultra-Radical Secularism of Stratford (E. London), J. L. Mahon (engineer) and Robert Banner (bookbinder) from Scottish Freethought, and Jack Williams (dock laborer) and James Macdonald (fancy tailor) from Radical clubs with strong Secularist leanings. It is also noteworthy that most of those recruits were self-educated, "respectable," skilled artisans of the sort that are most usefully classified in the "middling class": the social strata immediately below the middle class proper (see chapter 3, n. 109). Nevertheless, none except Lane are known to have taken part in shaping the early policies or ideology of the SDF. Instead, the latter were almost entirely the work of the middle-class leaders of the SDF who have been described above, and the only role that working-class members of the SDF are known to have played was one of vigorous opposition to the "Marxist" ideology that was adopted for them by the middle-class leadership. (See Engels to Bebel, 30 August 1883, in Marx and Engles, *Correspondence* [London, 1934], p. 419.)

The Social Composition of the SDF in the 1880s

If the policies and ideology of the early SDF reflect predominantly middle-class influence, then to what extent can that organization be called "proletarian"? In the absence of surviving membership records that question cannot be answered with any certainty, but some clues may be considered. As indicated in chapter 3, the original working-class following of the Federation was rapidly alienated, and middle-class supporters assumed a preponderant influence. Some contemporary reports indicate that subsequent recruits were drawn largely from the lower middle-class ("mostly clerks and shopmen," according to the *Pall Mall Budget* [17 Sept. 1885]: 11–12) and from skilled artisans, plus day laborers in heavily working-class areas (see W. S. Sanders, *Early Socialist Days* [London, 1927], p. 17, describing the Battersea Branch of the SDF, and evidence cited in P. Thompson, *Socialists, Liberals and Labour,* p. 216). Thus, although the social composition of SDF branches must have varied widely in different neighborhoods, its recruits seem to have come predominantly from the "middling class" (see above) —a conclusion that is reinforced by Stanley Pierson's similar findings with regard to Socialist League branches whose membership records have survived (see *Marxism and British Socialism,* p. 88), and by Charles Booth's sociological investigations in the 1890s (quoted in Thompson, *Socialists, Liberals and Labour,* p. 216). There is, however, also some merit in the alternative view that the SDF appealed primarily to Tory workingmen, as the SDF record of alienating Radical workingmen is so strong that Tories (especially in London and S. Lancashire) formed the most obvious alternative source of recruits. (See P. F. Clarke, *Lancashire and the New Liberalism* [Cambridge, Eng., 1971], p. 41.)

Appendix B: Biographical Sketches of Early Fabians

Frank Podmore (1856–1910), active founder of both the Fabian Society and the Society for Psychical Research (SPR), was the son of an Evangelical clergyman turned public-school headmaster. He graduated from Haileybury and Oxford, became a first-class clerk in the Postmaster General's Office, and was subsequently the author of numerous studies of psychic phenomena and of Robert Owen (*Robert Owen,* 2 vols. [London, 1906]). His rooms in the Dean's Yard, Westminster, served as the first headquarters of both the Fabian Society and the SPR. (See E. J. Dingwall's introduction to F. Podmore, *Mediums of the Nineteenth Century,* ed. Dingwall 2 vols. [New Hyde Park, N. Y., 1963].)

Rosamund Dale Owen was born in New Harmony, Ind., in 1846, to Robert Owen's eldest son, a U.S. Senator from Indiana. She came to England in 1883 to lecture to the remnants of the Owenite movement, by then largely given over to Spiritualism, on her own unorthodox blend of Evangelical Christianity and Spiritualism. She met Podmore at the SPR and he brought her to the Fabian Society, of which she became a founding member. In 1888 she married the eccentric writer and reformer, Laurence Oliphant (see R. D. Oliphant, *My Perilous Life in Palestine* [London, 1928]).

Nothing is known of **J. G. Stapleton** except that he was the oldest and probably also the wealthiest of the Founding Fabians.

[Henry] Havelock Ellis (1859–1939), literary critic and scientific student of sex, was born into a strongly Evangelical, middle-class family in the London suburbs. In his teens he became an agnostic with strong pantheist tendencies inspired by the philosophy of James Hinton (below), which also led him to study medicine in the early eighties, with the intention of combining it with a literary career. His friends at the early "New Life" meetings included the widow of James Hinton and her sister, Caroline Haddon, who were engaged with Ellis in editing Hinton's works (see H. Ellis, *My Life* [London, 1940], and *DNB, 5th supp.* [1931–40], pp. 258–60).

James Hinton's (1825–75) muddled and diffuse philosophy, which combined elements of scientific Freethought, Idealist metaphysics, and the altruistic ethics of Positivism, was precisely the sort of intellectual concoction that was likely to appeal to the unskeptical skeptics of the 1880s. Beginning with the revolt against materialism, it "turned the latter around by seeing matter as a form of spirit," thus producing a kind of poetic pantheism integrated with science. To this it added a belief in self-transcendence and unity with God through unselfish service to others, and a belief in sexual emancipation—a combination that appealed strongly to several of the early Fabians (see *DNB*, Vol. *9*, 898–900; J. Hinton, *Life in Nature*, edited and with an introduction by H. Ellis [London, 1932]; C. Haddon, ed. *The Larger Life* [London, 1886]; and for his influence, see W. J. Jupp, *Wayfarings* [London, 1918], pp. 64 ff., and Ellis, *My Life*, pp. 130 ff., 142 ff.].

Hubert and **Edith Bland** were the most "aesthetic" of the Founding Fabians. Hubert Bland (1856–1914), Hon. Treasurer of the Society, was also its most religiously orthodox member (he soon converted to Catholicism), and one of its few Tory Socialists. By his own account, he was born into an old Tory family and educated for the army until his mother's influence diverted him to a business career. Unhappily, he was entirely "lacking in commercial sense," and was consequently bankrupted shortly before the Fabian Society was founded. Thereafter he created a new career for himself as a popular Radical journalist, chiefly on the working-class *Sunday Chronicle,* and, together with his wife, Edith, edited the Socialist magazine *To-day* (1887–89) and wrote the first Fabian roman á clef ("Something Wrong," in *Weekly Dispatch,* summer, 1886). Edith Bland (1858–1924) became a minor poet and successful writer of childrens' stories (under the name E. Nesbit). She also presided over a bizarre ménage a trois that included Hubert's mistress, Alice Hoatson (also an active Fabian), and the children of both women (see sketch of H. Bland in *Sunday Chronicle* [30 Nov. 1890]; Moore, *E. Nesbit*; and H. G. Wells, *Experiment in Autobiography* [New York, 1934], pp. 513 ff; also Lee and Archbold, *Social Democracy*, p. 93.)

The Blands joined the SDF in company with their fellow Fabians J. G. Stapleton, Frederick Keddell, and J. Hunter Watts (the last two being Radical journalists) early in 1885, following the first great schism, but withdrew in protest against the "Tory gold" scandal before the end of that year. Thereafter, Hubert Bland (especially as editor of *To-day*) was an outspoken opponent of the SDF and its rhetorical militancy, although within the Fabian Society he advocated policies of thoroughgoing collectivism and imperialism that strongly resembled those of the SDF. Despite temperamental differences and early disagreements, he became a close ally of the Webbs in the 1890s, chiefly because of their increasingly similar interpretations of collectivism.

Edward Reynolds Pease (1857–1955) came from a wealthy Quaker family in Yorkshire and, before his conversion to Socialism, was a stockbroker in the fashionable West End of London. The naïve socialist idealism that resulted from his conversion was satirized in the Bland's roman á clef, "Something Wrong" (see above), of which he was the hero. From 1885 to 1888 he sought to give expression to his Socialist faith by working as a cabinet maker near Newcastle on Tyne; after 1890 he devoted the remainder of his life to the service of the Fabian Society as its full-time secretary. (For his family connections, see N. Annan, "The Intellectual Aristocracy," in J. H. Plumb, ed., *Essays in Social History* [London, 1955], pp. 265–66; also his obituary in *The Times* [7 Jan. 1955].)

Charlotte M. Wilson, described by Sidney Webb as a "Rosetti young woman with dense hair" and aesthetic clothes (Webb to Shaw, 11 Nov. 1884, BM 50553), was a graduate of Newnham College, Cambridge. Originally a follower of Morris, she was converted to Anarchism by Kropotkin in the mid-eighties and became a leading member of his Freedom Group, editing and publishing its newspaper, *Freedom,* 1886–88. For personal impressions, see Moore, *E. Nesbit,* pp. 78–79; Anne Fremantle, *This Little Band of Prophets* (New York, 1960), pp. 55 ff., and the character "Gemma" in E. Voynich, *The Gadfly* (London, 1897). For her role in English Anarchism see H. Seymour, "Early English Anarchism," in J. Ishill, ed., *Free Vistas,* 2 vols. (Berkeley Hts., N.J., 1933–37), 2:119 ff., and G. Woodcock, *Anarchism* (Harmondsworth, 1962), pp 419–20; also Wilson's letters to Shaw (BM).

Appendix C: Some Disputed Points Regarding Fabian Permeation

Several historians have recently argued that the theory of permeation described in chapter 8 was accepted only by a faction of the Fabian Society and was opposed by such leading Fabians as Bland and Besant, who were, as has been seen, its chief proponents. Among such historians, Paul Thompson has argued that Annie Besant aimed to turn the Fabian Society into a political party, and that when her efforts failed she left it for the SDF.[1] It was shown in chap. 8, however, that Besant was the most outspoken Fabian advocate of a Radical-Socialist political alliance—the crux of the policy of permeation—and was also an active permeator of Radical working-class organizations. There is no evidence that she sought to turn either the London Fabian Society or its provincial branches into a political party; nor did she abandon the Fabian Society for the SDF. Rather, she joined her current male companion, Herbert Burrows, in the latter organization in the fall of 1888—a time of increasing Fabian–SDF rapprochement—without either leaving the Fabian Society or accepting the political methods of the SDF.[2] As for Bland, his Fabian essay indeed contained strong criticism of the policy of permeation, but this neither made him a consistent opponent of that policy nor an active supporter of the SDF, as Eric Hobsbawm has contended.[3] On the contrary, Bland also advocated a Radical–Socialist alliance in most of his writings—even in his Fabian essay he agreed that it was a necessary short-run policy—and he seldom lost an opportunity of attacking the SDF in print. His differences with the majority of his fellow Fabians, therefore, were not so much over the policy of permeation as over his more thoroughgoing advocacy of collectivism, his greater determination to prevent Socialism from becoming watered down with Radicalism, and his less optimistic view of the probable results of cooperation with the Radical Party. These points, however, formed the basis of his opposition not as much to permeation as to

1. Thompson, *Socialists, Liberals, and Labour*, pp. 97, 118, 139.
2. See Nethercot, *First Five Lives*, pp. 277 ff. Rapprochement is indicated by Fabian articles in *Justice* (Nov.–Dec. 1888); Besant's unchanged advocacy of liberal values and of Radical-Socialist political alliance—both anathemas to the SDF—were also proclaimed in *Justice* (see "Socialism and Individuality," 6 Oct. 1888, and "Socialists and Radicals," 13 April 1889. The latter was editorially repudiated.)
3. Hobsbawm, "The Lesser Fabians," in Munby, ed., *The Luddites*, pp. 233–34.

the extreme gradualism of Webb and Wallas, with its implication that Socialism need never arrive in any full-fledged form.[4]

Bland and Besant, moreover, were among the leaders of the first serious attempt to implement the policy of Radical–Socialist alliance: the running of three Fabian candidates with Radical backing in the London School Board elections of November 1888. In support of these candidates they were instrumental in establishing Joint Democratic Committees (made up of "two delegates from each [existing] Democratic Organization") in many electoral divisions. These committees, which were intended to mobilize and unify the left-wing vote, were first proposed by Webb, then promoted by Besant in her magazine, *The Link,* and eventually received support from the influential Radical daily, *The Star,* where Fabians enjoyed a measure of influence in 1888–89.[5] Fabians such as Webb (who became secretary to the Finsbury committee), Wallas, Shaw, Bland, and Besant then actively permeated the committees. Their influence may perhaps be detected in the collectivist measures adopted by many of the committees; their success is more clearly evident in the election of two (of the three) Fabian candidates who ran with the support of the joint committees—Annie Besant and the Reverend Stewart Headlam —whereas all the SDF candidates lost heavily.[6]

These were the first political achievements of Fabian permeation.

4. See Bland "The Socialist Party in Relation to Politics," *Prac. Soc.* (Oct. 1886 and Feb. 1887), and "Editorial Notes," *To-day* (July 1887, Nov. 1887), as well as "The Outlook," in *Fabian Essays,* esp. pp. 214–18. In 1890 Bland finally launched an open attack on "Webbite opportunism." (See Shaw to Olivier, 16 Dec. 1890, BM 50541, in Laurence, ed., *Collected Letters,* pp. 228–29.) It did not last long.

5. See letter from Webb in *Link* (2 June 1888), endorsed by Besant in the lead article. (In contrast, *The Star* only endorsed the Joint Democratic Committees in July 1888.) Besant also presided over the founding of the Central Democratic Committee for the metropolitan area at the *Link* office in Sept. 1888. The question of Fabian permeation of *The Star* is very confused, due to Shaw's exaggerated claims regarding its effectiveness. What is clear, however, is that Fabians were always able to publicize their views through its letter column; that it frequently published material by both Shaw and Webb in 1888–89; and that its assistant editor, H. W. Massingham, was effectively Fabianized long before he joined the Society in 1891. (See Massingham to Shaw, 20 Oct. 1893, PP, II, *4a,* 15, claiming that he had been a "Collectivist" and a "permeator all my days.")

6. E.g., the (very Webbish) draft program of the Finsbury Joint Democratic Committee (Fabian Archive), which included demands for free primary education, public secondary school scholarships and publicly supported technical education, and free school meals. Tower Hamlets adopted a similar program under Besant's leadership. Election results are in *Link* (24 Nov. 1888) and *Justice* 24 Nov. and 1 Dec. 1888). Bland was the unsuccessful Fabian candidate.

They seemed to justify high hopes for the success of that policy in the future, especially as they soon led to an offer of Radical support for Fabian candidates in the forthcoming London County Council (LCC) election.[7] In fact, little came of that offer, and the Fabians played a very small part in that election, only gradually building up their influence in the new "municipal parliament." Yet despite the relatively minor role played by Fabians in the early years of the LCC and in the municipal Progressive Party, which soon came to dominate it, the latter party—an alliance of Liberals, Radicals, and Socialists with a program of advanced social reforms—may almost be regarded as a textbook example of applied permeation. (It was precisely the sort of political alliance demanded by Annie Besant, for example.) Unhappily, most of the effective permeating, at least prior to 1890, was not done by Fabians but by members of other Radical groups with similar reform programs.[8] Consequently, although the Progressive Party and its work closely conformed to what the Fabian theory of permeation prescribed, they were not, to any great extent, the results of Fabian political activities.

This conclusion is important because it illustrates both the way Fabian theory tended to outrun Fabian practice and the fact that it was Fabian theory (not practice) that made the chief contribution to the development of English Socialism. Fabian political tactics were constantly bedeviled by a tendency to permeate the wrong people (John Burns, for example, instead of Keir Hardie) and to bet on the wrong political horses (such as Liberal Imperialism). The record is so bad that it almost justifies the view that the early Fabians were unable to understand the way English politics worked.[9] But with theory it was otherwise. From the beginning Fabian theory looked forward to the establishment of a Labour Party with a Socialist basis, while insisting that before such a party was actually established there must be an adequate constituency for it, created by educational and propaganda campaigns in working-class organizations and by per-

---

7. Massingham to Shaw, 3 Dec. 1888, BM 50543. The offer came from the Grand Panjandrum of E. London Radicalism, Professor James Stuart, who (contrary to Thompson, *Socialists, Liberals and Labour*, p. 99 n.) was greatly admired by the leading Fabians.

8. The most important of these groups was the London Municipal Reform League, whose leader, J. F. B. Firth, died in 1889, creating an opportunity for Sidney Webb to take over much of the work of permeation that Firth had begun. For the definitive account of the Fabians and the LCC, see McBriar, *Fabian Socialism*, chap. 7.

9. See, e.g., E. Hobsbawn, "The Fabians Reconsidered," in *Labouring Men* (London, 1968), pp. 252–53.

meation of the left wing of the Radical Party (which would have to supply most of the personnel for the new party). It also saw that such a party would have to have extensive trade union support.[10] Fabian tactics following 1890 by no means conformed to those principles—the leading Fabians, in practice, proved to be poor judges of when circumstances were ripe for any sort of action (as their reactions to the founding of the Independent Labour Party and the Labour Representation Committee demonstrated)—but Fabian theory held up much better, by specifying pretty nearly the specific conditions under which those organizations and the British Labour Party were actually founded. And that, in the long run, proved to be the great strength of the Fabian theory of permeation, when seen as part of the larger Fabian view of Socialist politics.[11]

10. These conditions were spelled out most clearly in *A Plan of Campaign for Labour*, Fabian Tract No. 49 (London, 1894).

11. This sort of permeation should not be confused with the "permeation" intermittantly practiced by the Webbs in the 1890s and early 1900s, which consisted of persuading prominent politicians to promote collectivist reforms. The latter tactic, of course, had no connection with the goal of establishing a labor party and was only a tangential feature of the more comprehensive Fabian policy of permeation, described in chap. 8 above.

Bibliographical Note

This is essentially a selective and critical guide to the literature on which the present book is based. Complete citations of all manuscripts and published works used in this study will be found in the footnotes and are not repeated here. A more comprehensive bibliography of works on British Socialism and allied movements will be found in Henry Pelling, *Origins of the Labour Party,* 2d ed. (Oxford, 1965), pp. 235–45. The present note is intended primarily to supplement it.

PRIMARY SOURCES

Manuscript Collections

Manuscript sources for British Radicalism and Socialism in the 1880s are exceptionally rich and many of them remained relatively unquarried until quite recently. Among the sources for the history of Fabian Socialism, the most important and extensive are the Passfield Papers (BLPES), containing correspondence, memorabilia, essay and lecture drafts, and diaries of Sidney and Beatrice Webb; and the Shaw Papers (BM 50665–50705), containing, inter alia, drafts of lectures and articles, newspaper clippings, lecture notes, notebooks, and correspondence of Bernard Shaw. Shaw's manuscript diary (longhand transcription by Blanche Patch, BLPES), listing his activities from 1885 onward, should also be mentioned here. Much of Shaw's correspondence (which is scattered among a variety of libraries) has recently been published and some of his early lectures and essays have been printed in collections of his nondramatic writings (see Published Works below). Otherwise the material in these collections remains largely unpublished. Other important Fabian collections include the Graham Wallas Papers (BLPES), containing his letters, memorabilia, essay drafts, and notebooks; the correspondence of William Clarke with his American patron, Henry Demarest Lloyd, in the Lloyd Papers (WSHS); the correspondence of Thomas Davidson with the Founding Fabians and other Socialist worthies, in the Davidson Papers (Yale); the correspondence and lecture drafts of Andreas Scheu (IISH); the archives of the Fabian Society, including its minute books, membership lists, memorabilia, and publications; and the correspondence of its secretary, Edward Pease (Nuffield). Collections of less importance to the present study include the John Burns Papers (BM 46281–46345), William Morris's correspondence and Socialist diary (BM 45298–45335), the Edward Carpenter Papers (Sheffield Central Library), the Alf Mattison Papers (Brotherton Library, Leeds University), and the Socialist League Papers and correspondence of Marx, Engels, and Eleanor Marx Aveling (IISH).

Among the major sources for the history of late Victorian Radicalism are the Mill-Taylor Collection (BLPES), containing the bulk of the correspondence of John Stuart Mill and Helen Taylor; the Dilke Papers (BM 43909–43943), containing correspondence, essay, and lecture drafts of Sir Charles Dilke; the Frederic Harrison Papers (BLPES), containing his correspondence with major literary and political figures; and the Positivist Archive (BM 45228), containing correspondence of other leading Positivists. All throw valuable light on the development of ultra-Radical ideas before the advent of Socialism. Of less importance for this study are the Jevons, Courtney, and Cannan Collections (BLPES), the Joseph Cowen Papers (Newcastle City Library), and the very extensive Howell Collection (Bishopsgate Institute).

Periodical Publications

Cheap printing costs together with the literary ambitions cherished by most of the Socialists and Radicals discussed in this book combined to make the "little magazines" and house organs of Radical and Socialist sects rich primary sources. In addition to such established Radical weeklies as *Reynold's Newspaper* (with the largest working-class readership), the *Weekly Dispatch,* the *Echo,* and the Secularist *National Reformer,* ultra-Radical opinion in the 1880s was represented by three more specialized journals: the *Radical* (1880–82, semi-Socialist), *The Republican* (renamed *The Radical* in 1887; traditional but friendly to Socialism in the late eighties), and *The Democrat* (1884–90, Henry Georgian). Among daily newspapers, the *Pall Mall Gazette* and its weekly digest, the *Pall Mall Budget,* supported parliamentary Radicalism throughout the 1880s, and the *Star* (begun 17 Jan. 1888), with which several Fabians were initially connected, took a more advanced Radical line and achieved unprecedented influence in London Radical politics. In the Midlands this was accomplished by the predominantly working-class (Manchester) *Sunday Chronicle* in the late 1880s.

Socialist opinion was represented by the two weekly house organs of the SDF and Socialist League, *Justice* (begun Jan. 1884; edited by Hyndman until 1886), and *The Commonweal* (ed. William Morris, 1885–89; thereafter quasi-Anarchist). In the late eighties these were supplemented by the nonsectarian *Labour Elector* (Dec. 1888–Feb.

1889, ed. H. H. Champion; then amalgamated with Kier Hardie's *The Miner* under the new name of *Labour Leader*: Feb.–Aug. 1889). More important to the present study were the variety of smaller and more personal monthly journals of a Socialist or semi-Socialist persuasion that flourished in the 1880s: *To-day*, originally a Freethought journal (1883), then edited in the SDF interest by Bax and Joynes (Jan. 1884–Jan. 1887), and in the Fabian interest by Hubert Bland (Feb. 1887–June 1889); the *Practical Socialist* (Jan. 1886–June 1887), virtually a Fabian organ, but privately edited and printed by T. Bolas, who subsequently printed the *Leaflet Newspaper* (Feb.–June 1888) and *The Socialist* (July 1888–Apr. 1889) with a similar Fabian/ Christian Socialist slant; and *Our Corner* (1883–88), Annie Besant's personal magazine, combining Secularism, Malthusianism, and an increasing emphasis on Socialism in the later 1880s.

Christian Socialist opinion was represented by the *Christian Socialist* (1883–91), originally edited by Champion and Joynes, then by Christian Socialist clergymen; and the *Church Reformer* (1882–95), virtually the personal journal of the Rev. S. D. Headlam, a Fabian. The first tended to moralized Marxism in its early years, the latter to Henry Georgism, but both shared a tendency to quote heavily from the works of George and Ruskin. Anarchist opinion was represented by *The Anarchist* (Mar. 1885–Aug. 1888), ed. by the Fabian, Henry Seymour; and *Freedom* (Oct. 1886–1936), ed. until 1894 by the Fabian, Charlotte Wilson. The former expounded individualist Anarchism, the latter Anarchist-Communism inspired by Kropotkin. More ephemeral journals included *Common Sense* (May 1887–Mar. 1888), an early exponent of independent labor politics, edited by H. H. Champion; and *The Link* (Feb.–Dec. 1888), edited by Annie Besant to promote her political projects. Finally, the great liberal reviews—the *Nineteenth Century, Contemporary Review,* and *Fortnightly Review*—devoted much space to Socialism and social problems in the 1880s.

Published Books

The personae of this study were such prolific authors that space limitations forbid a list of all their books. Fortunately recent scholarship has produced definitive editions of the works of the most prolific among them that virtually supercede all earlier editions. Thus, in the case of John Stuart Mill, the University of Toronto Press is currently publishing the *Collected Works of John Stuart Mill* (Toronto and London, 1963–) in meticulously edited critical editions. Volumes already published include *The Earlier Letters, 1812–1848,* ed. F. E.

Mineka, 2 vols. (1963); *The Later Letters, 1849–1873*, ed. F. E. Mineka and D. M. Lindley, 4 vols. (1972); *The Principles of Political Economy*, ed. J. M. Robson, introduction by V. W. Bladen, 2 vols. (1965); *Essays on Economics and Society*, ed. J. M. Robson, 2 vols. (1967); and *Essays on Ethics, Religion, and Society*, ed. J. M. Robson (1969). Other important and authoritative editions include *The Autobiography of John Stuart Mill*, ed. J. J. Coss (New York, 1924), and *The Early Draft of Mill's Autobiography*, ed. J. Stillinger (Urbana, Ill., 1961).

Among leaders of the English Socialist revival, only Morris's and Shaw's works have been collected in similarly authoritative editions. For the former, see *The Collected Works of William Morris*, 24 vols. (London, 1910–15), supplemented by May Morris, ed., *William Morris: Artist, Writer, Socialist* 2 vols. (Oxford, 1936); P. Henderson, ed., *Letters of William Morris* (London, 1950); and E. LeMire, ed., *Unpublished Lectures of William Morris* (Detroit, 1969). Hyndman's numerous works are mentioned in the footnotes to chapter 3; they have not been edited or reprinted.

Most of Shaw's published writings will be found in *The Standard Edition of the Works of Bernard Shaw*, 38 vols. (London, 1930–55), but these will soon be partly superceded by *The Bodley Head Shaw: Collected Plays with Their Prefaces*, ed. D. H. Laurence; and they must be supplemented by the *Collected Letters of Bernard Shaw*, ed. D. H. Laurence, vol. 1, *1874–1897* (New York, 1965), vol. 2, *1897–1910* (New York, 1972), and by several collections of his essays and other nondramatic writings: D. H. Laurence, ed., *Selected Nondramatic Writings of George Bernard Shaw* (New York, 1965); D. H. Laurence, ed., *Platform and Pulpit* (New York, 1962); L. Crompton, ed., *The Road to Equality: Ten Unpublished Lectures and Essays, 1884–1918* (Boston, 1971); and S. Weintraub, ed., *Shaw: An Autobiography, 1856–1898* (New York, 1969).

No other works by early Fabians have been similarly collected and edited, but some have been reprinted and have become almost classic texts. First among those is G. B. Shaw, ed., *Fabian Essays in Socialism* (London, 1889; frequently reprinted, with the most accessible recent edition being the Jubilee Edition, London, 1948). Almost equally important is Edward Pease, *History of the Fabian Society* (London, 1916; 2d ed., 1925; frequently reprinted), an account of the Society's first thirty years containing much documentary material. Other works by Fabians that are important for the 1880s include: Graham Wallas, *Men and Ideas* (London, 1940), collected essays with some reminiscences; Margaret Olivier, ed., *Sydney Olivier: Letters and*

Selected Writings (London, 1948) ; Annie Besant, *Autobiographical Sketches* (London, 1885), and *An Autobiography* (London, 1893) ; H. Burrows and J. A. Hobson, eds., *William Clarke: A Collection of His Writings with a Biographical Sketch* (London, 1908) ; and W. Knight, ed., *Memorials of Thomas Davidson, the Wandering Scholar* (London, 1907). Finally, Beatrice Webb's diaries, edited and richly annotated by herself, *My Apprenticeship* (London, 1938), her life until 1892, and *Our Partnership* (London, 1948), the Webbs' joint life from 1892 to 1912, with a brief background sketch of Sidney, are perhaps the most illuminating of all documents describing the intellectual and cultural milieu from which many of the early Fabians came.

SECONDARY SOURCES

General Works

The most useful historical study of the century preceding the 1880s is Asa Briggs, *The Age of Improvement* (London, 1959) ; its insights into social and intellectual tendencies are unparalleled. R. C. K. Ensor, *England: 1870–1914* (Oxford, 1936), is a sound political history of that period with some useful insights into social movements written by a Fabian of the second generation. Perhaps the most useful among recent socio-economic histories of Victorian England is Eric Hobsbawm, *Industry and Empire: The Making of Modern English Society, 1750 to the Present Day* (New York, 1968) : a brilliantly argumentative work that is heavily tinged with orthodox Leninism. Recent scholarship on nineteenth-century social and religious history is usefully surveyed in G. Kitson Clark, *The Making of Victorian England* (London, 1962), and the same author has continued his reinterpretation of Victorian history in *An Expanding Society: Britain, 1830–1900* (Cambridge, Eng., 1967). A much less successful attempt to deal with social issues of late Victorian England through some of its major personalities is Herman Ausubel, *In Hard Times* (New York, 1961). Finally, the old, sometimes erroneous, but remarkably comprehensive survey of social movements and attitudes in the 1800s, Helen M. Lynd, *England in the Eighteen-eighties* (New York, 1945), remains useful and has not been superceded.

Works on Radicalism, Secularism, and Positivism

The most comprehensive survey of English Radicalism from the 1760s to 1914 is also the weakest: S. Maccoby, *English Radicalism,*

6 vols. (London, 1935–61) consists chiefly of documentary materials interspersed in an extremely dry narrative of parliamentary politics emphasing the role of Radicals. A biographical survey of Radicalism in the same period, J. W. Derry, *The Radical Tradition, Tom Paine to Lloyd George* (London, 1967), is somewhat broader in scope but is still conceptually weak. A more sophisticated study of Liberalism and Radicalism in London is Paul Thompson, *Socialists, Liberals, and Labour: The Struggle for London, 1885–1914* (London, 1967); its chief focus, however, is on the rise of Socialism and Labour politics. The most important study of Radical movements (with much attention to Positivism) in the decades prior to the 1880s is Royden Harrison, *Before the Socialists: Studies in Labour and Politics, 1861–1881* (London, 1965), but John Vincent, *Origins of the British Labour Party* (New York, 1967) also has useful comments on the nature of Radicalism. E. E. Barry, *Nationalism in British Politics* (Stanford, 1965) throws light on Radical collectivism, and H. V. Emy, *Liberals, Radicals, and Social Politics, 1892–1914* (New York, 1973) illuminates the later developments of the "new Radicalism."

Political biographies are also essential to an understanding of the "new Radicalism." Among the most important are the flamboyant *Life of Joseph Chamberlain* by J. L. Garvin, 3 vols. (London, 1932–34), which presents its subject as a hero in history. It should be supplemented by the more prosaic and scholarly but scarcely less uncritical study, P. Fraser, *Joseph Chamberlain: Radicalism and Empire, 1868–1914* (New York, 1967). Also essential are S. Gwyn and G. M. Tuckwell, *Life of the Rt. Hon. Sir Charles Dilke* 2 vols. (London, 1917), an admiring but honest official life, and the more recent and scholarly study, Roy Jenkins, *Sir Charles Dilke: A Victorian Tragedy* (London, 1958). Among recent biographies, perhaps the most useful is S. E. Koss, *Fleet Street Radical: A. G. Gardiner and the* Daily News (Hamden, Conn., 1973).

The most important studies of the Secularist movement are J. E. McGee, *History of the British Secular Movement* (Girard, Kan., 1948), a prosaic narrative; J. Eros, "The Rise of Organised Freethought," *Sociological Review,* 2 n.s. (1954); S. Budd, "The Loss of Faith," *Past and Present* 36 (1967), a study of Secularist biographies; and H. B. Bonner and J. M. Robertson, *Charles Bradlaugh* 2 vols. (London, 1898), an official life of the leading Secularist in the 1880s.

The most important studies of British Positivism are W. M. Simon, *European Positivism in the Nineteenth Century* (Ithaca, 1964), which is definitive, given its overly narrow definition of its subject; W. M. Simon, "Auguste Comte's English Disciples," *Victorian Studies* 8

(1964) ; and R. Harrison, *Before the Socialists* (cited earlier), which is authoritative on Positivist influence in the mid-Victorian labor movement.

Works on John Stuart Mill

The major biography of Mill is Michael Packe, *The Life of John Stuart Mill* (London, 1954). In most respects it must be accounted one of the great biographies of the century, but it takes a narrowly individualist view of Mill and is especially unsatisfactory with regard to his Socialism. The latter deficiency is effectively remedied by J. M. Robson, *The Improvement of Mankind: The Social and Political Thought of John Stuart Mill* (Toronto, 1968), a comprehensive study of Mill's thought that comes close to being definitive. The forthcoming life of Mill by Gertrude Himmelfarb should also contain a very different interpretation of his social thought. Among more specialized studies, Joseph Hamburger, *Intellectuals in Politics: J. S. Mill and the Philosophic Radicals* (New Haven, 1965), and Shirley R. Letwin, *The Pursuit of Certainty: David Hume, Jeremy Bentham, John Stuart Mill, and Beatrice Webb* (Cambridge, Eng., 1965) successfully relate Mill's social thought to his early career. Pedro Schwartz, *The New Political Economy of John Stuart Mill* (Durham, N.C., 1972) is a rather orthodox survey of Mill's economic thought. New literature on Mill, which is voluminous, is listed regularly in the *Mill News Letter* (published by the University of Toronto).

Works on the History of Socialist Thought

The most masterly and comprehensive survey is still G. D. H. Cole, *History of Socialist Thought,* 5 vols. (London, 1953–60), esp. vols. 1–3: *The First International* (1953), *Marxism and Anarchism, 1850–1890* (1954), and *The Second International, Part I* (1956). Despite the vast scale of this project, these are works of remarkable sensitivity and insight. In contrast, the more pedestrian Max Beer, *History of British Socialism,* 2 vols., new ed. (London, 1940) is valuable chiefly on the earlier stages of the movement. More recently, George Lichtheim, *A Short History of Socialism* (London, 1970) has provided a brilliant, analytical reinterpretation of the development of Socialist thought, with special attention to the English Socialist revival. Other recent studies of that revival include the thorough but rather pedestrian *Origins of the Labour Party, 1880–1900,* by Henry Pelling, 2d ed. (Oxford, 1965), and a more innovative study by Stanley Pierson, *Marxism and the Origins of British Socialism: The Struggle for a New Consciousness* (Ithaca, 1973), which concentrates on case studies of leading Socialists and sets its analysis within the broader context of English intellectual history. Older, more flamboyant narratives of the Socialist revival that convey something of the flavor of the events are G. Elton, *England Arise!* (London, 1931), and J. Clayton, *The Rise and Decline of Socialism in Great Britain, 1884–1924* (London, 1926). Recent research on the history of British Socialism is listed in the *Bulletin* of the (British) Society for the Study of Labour History.

Works on the SDF, Hyndman, and Morris

The oldest account of the SDF is H. W. Lee and E. Archbold, *Social-Democracy in Great Britain* (London, 1935), a work of reminiscence by two early members. The most authoritative account is the biography of its founder, *H. M. Hyndman and British Socialism*, by C. Tsuzuki (London, 1961), a work of solid, if uninspired scholarship, which may be supplemented by Hyndman's own memoirs: *The Record of an Adventurous Life* (London, 1911), and *Further Reminiscences* (London, 1912). P. Thompson, *Socialists, Liberals, and Labour* (cited earlier) and E. P. Thompson, *William Morris, Romantic to Revolutionary* (London, 1955) are also very useful on the early SDF. Studies of William Morris are very numerous. The most important are his official biography, J. W. Mackail, *The Life of William Morris* 2 vols. (London, 1899), which is forthright, if unsympathetic in discussing Morris's Socialism, and E. P. Thompson's *Morris,* a work of thorough scholarship and magnificent execution, which is flawed by its misguided attempt to present its subject as an orthodox Marxist. More balanced discussions of Morris's Socialism will be found in J. Hulse, *Revolutionists in London: A Study of Six Unorthodox Socialists* (Oxford, 1970); S. Pierson, *Marxism and British Socialism,* (cited earlier); and in G. D. H. Cole, *History of Socialist Thought* (cited earlier). For recent research on Morris, see the *Journal of the William Morris Society.*

Works on the Fabian Society

Edward Pease, *History of the Fabian Society,* is still the best and fullest account of its early years. More recent histories, such as M. Cole, *The Story of Fabian Socialism* (London, 1961) and A. Fremantle, *This Little Band of Prophets: The Gentle Fabians* (New York, 1959) are chiefly superficial narratives, strongest on anecdotes. (Fremantle's book, however, is so disorganized and full of errors that it is unreliable.) A. McBriar, *Fabian Socialism and English Politics, 1884–1918* (Cambridge, Eng., 1962) is the only serious scholarly study of the

Society in its early years. Although thorough in covering its subject, it was written without using the collections of manuscripts listed in this bibliography so that its usefulness is somewhat limited. It may be supplemented by the useful brief discussions of the Society in Pelling, *Origins of the Labour Party*, and Pierson, *Marxism and British Socialism*, and by Eric Hobsbawm's brilliant attempt to portray the early Fabians as antiliberal and authoritarian: "The Fabians Reconsidered," in *Labouring Men: Studies in the History of Labour* (London, 1964) —a distillation of his still stimulating and controversial Ph.D. thesis, "Fabianism and the Fabians, 1884–1914" (Cambridge, 1950).

Works on Individual Fabians

By far the largest number of such works are studies of Shaw. The most useful and comprehensive biography of Shaw is Archibald Henderson's massive but pedestrian *George Bernard Shaw: Man of the Century* (New York, 1956), although the same author's earlier and more graceful *George Bernard Shaw, Playboy and Prophet* (New York, 1932) is a better book. The first biography to use the Shaw Papers as the basis of a comprehensive reinterpretation of Shaw's early thought and personality is J. Percy Smith, *The Unrepentant Pilgrim* (New York, 1966). H. Pearson, *Bernard Shaw: His Life and Personality*, rev. ed. (London, 1961), and S. Winsten, *Jesting Apostle* (London, 1957) derive special (if questionable) importance from their claims to draw upon undocumented private conversations with Shaw. Unfortunately, the only extensive study of Shaw and Marxism, P. Hummert, *Bernard Shaw's Marxian Romance* (Lincoln, Nebr., 1973) is flawed by a very inadequate understanding of Marxism and by a wholly misguided attempt to portray Shaw as a life-long Marxist. Finally, Allan Chappellow, *Shaw—the "Chucker-Out"* (London, 1969) must be mentioned as a curious combination of (often ill-informed) commentary on Shaw's ideas with a useful anthology of his fugitive pieces from the British Museum. Recent Shaw research is listed and reviewed in *The Shaw Review* (University Park, Pa.) and *The Shavian* (London).

Other Fabians have attracted considerably less scholarly attention. Nevertheless, Annie Besant's varied and bizarre career has been the subject of several biographies, of which the most recent and most thorough on her early years is A. H. Nethercot, *The First Five Lives of Annie Besant* (Chicago, 1960); it is massive in scope but not always accurate in details. The shrewdest interpretation of her personality is still Gertrude M. Williams, *The Passionate Pilgrim* (London, 1931). Sidney Webb has not yet received a biography, although an official life is currently being written by Royden Harrison, but his early years have been briefly chronicled in biographies of his wife: M. Cole, *Beatrice Webb* (London, 1946); Mary A. Hamilton, *Sidney and Beatrice Webb* (London, 1934); and Kitty Muggeridge and Ruth Adam, *Beatrice Webb: A Life* (London, 1968). The last is the most readable and reliable. Much useful information is also contained in M. Cole, ed., *The Webbs and Their Work* (London, 1949). Graham Wallas has recently been the subject of a careful and sensitive study in intellectual history: Martin J. Wiener, *Between Two Worlds: The Political Thought of Graham Wallas* (Oxford, 1971). Though not a biography it contains much valuable biographical information. Finally, Doris L. Moore, *E. Nesbit* (London, 1933), a study of Edith Bland, also contains interesting information on Hubert Bland. No other Fabians have been studied at similar length, but there are brief and not always accurate biographical sketches of Olivier, Wallas, Bland, and Clarke in E. Hobsbawm, "The Lesser Fabians," in L. M. Munby, ed., *The Luddites and Other Essays* (London, 1971).

Acknowledgments

First among the institutions I wish to thank are the libraries where most of the research for this book was done. Preeminent among these are the British Library of Political and Economic Science (at the London School of Economics), where special thanks are due to the manuscript librarian, Mr. Allen, and the British Museum Library. Without their aid and cooperation this book could not have been written. For invaluable aid at other stages of research and writing, I must also thank the University of California libraries at Berkeley and Riverside, the Yale University Library, the University of Michigan Library, the Library of the Wisconsin State Historical Society, the Library of the International Institute of Social History in Amsterdam, the New York Public Library, the University of Chicago Library, and most of all the Newberry Library in Chicago, which has been a home to me in the rewriting of this book. My heartiest thanks to all of them.

For the financial aid that made this book possible, I am deeply indebted to Yale University for fellowships enabling me to undertake the research for the doctoral thesis that became this book; to the London School of Economics, which sponsored me as a Visiting Research Student; and to the National Endowment for the Humanities, whose award of a Junior Fellowship enabled me to undertake further research for this book at a later date.

I must also thank London House, Mecklenburgh Square, for providing congenial surroundings on several summer visits to London, and the University of London's Institute of Historical Research for providing an academic home base on such visits—a debt that I share with two generations of American scholars abroad. Finally, I must thank the Pacific Coast Branch of the American Historical Association for bestowing its annual award for 1968 on an earlier manuscript version of this book.

For permission to publish material that is not in public domain, I wish to thank the Society of Authors, trustee for the Bernard Shaw Estate, for permission to publish quotations from Shaw's published writings; the Passfield Trustees, for permission to publish quotations from the early writings of Sidney Webb; Miss May Wallas for similar permission with regard to her father, Graham Wallas; and Yale University, for permission to quote from the correspondence of Thomas Davidson.

Among the many persons who have read parts of this book and offered advice and encouragement, I am especially grateful to my graduate adviser at Yale, Professor Franklin L. Baumer, whose helpfulness has been unflagging at all stages of research and writing, and to Professors W. H. Dunham and L. P. Curtis. For directing me to some sources I had overlooked and for sharing his copies of rare materials with me, I am also grateful to Hal Draper of the University of California Library, Berkeley; and for comments on later versions of the manuscript, I am grateful to my colleagues, Alex DeGrand, Jane Stedman, Burton Kendle, and Walter Weisskopf. For typing, proofreading, and general encouragement, I wish to thank especially Sandra Noone, Linge Curtis, my sister Maryellen Bieder, Pauline Rose, Joe Russo, and Tony Burrell. Without them the manuscript would never have reached the press. Judy Metro, of Yale University Press, was also exceptionally helpful in editing this book. Finally, for help of a very different sort, I wish to acknowledge the enduring inspiration of my teachers at Davidson College, who gave generously of their own time and resources to sponsor a quite extraordinary honors program in English history and literature. To two of them, now deceased, this book is gratefully dedicated. In a real sense, it began with them. Finally, I must add that for errors and omissions that have remained in this book, despite such excellent advice and counsel, I alone am of course responsible.

Index